Hard Charger!

Hard Charger!

◆

The Story of the USS Biddle (DLG–34)

James A. Treadway

Rear Admiral Thomas F. Marfiak USN (Ret.)

Captain David L. Boslaugh USN (Ret.)

iUniverse, Inc.
New York Lincoln Shanghai

Hard Charger!
The Story of the USS Biddle (DLG–34)

Copyright © 2005 by James A. Treadway

All rights reserved. No part of this book may be used or reproduced by any means, graphic, electronic, or mechanical, including photocopying, recording, taping or by any information storage retrieval system without the written permission of the publisher except in the case of brief quotations embodied in critical articles and reviews.

iUniverse books may be ordered through booksellers or by contacting:

iUniverse
2021 Pine Lake Road, Suite 100
Lincoln, NE 68512
www.iuniverse.com
1-800-Authors (1-800-288-4677)

ISBN-13: 978-0-595-36009-3 (pbk)
ISBN-13: 978-0-595-67313-1 (cloth)
ISBN-13: 978-0-595-80460-3 (ebk)
ISBN-10: 0-595-36009-2 (pbk)
ISBN-10: 0-595-67313-9 (cloth)
ISBN-10: 0-595-80460-8 (ebk)

Printed in the United States of America

To the officers and men of USS *Biddle* (DLG/CG-34)

Contents

Foreword ix
Preface xi
Our Surface Navy in Danger of Extinction? 1
The DLG Class Guided Missile Frigates 22
Missile Cruisers in the Cold War 38
Department Organization Aboard a Guided Missile Cruiser 41
Biddle at Bath 48
Commissioning 55
Shakedown and Never Ending Trials 59
When Computers Went to Sea: Technicians of the Digital Navy 71
Yes, I Was a Biddle DS 96
Ready for Combat 103
The Gulf of Tonkin—1968 115
WESTPAC I 123
WESTPAC II 139
WESTPAC Interlude 149
The Gulf of Tonkin—1972 153
Battle at PIRAZ 162
Biddle—A Young Warrior 182

The Phoenix Rises From the Ashes 207
The Heart of the Ship 209
Seakeeping. 213
Clash With Kadaffi 216
Biddle Middle Age. 224
A Grand Old Lady Gets NTU 233
Decommissioning 259
Biddle's Last Cruise 262
All Hands Reunion 264
This Is the Captain Speaking 267
Commanding Officers USS Biddle (DLG/CG 34) 279
HULL THIRTY-FOUR 281
HULL THIRTY-FOUR II 283
Table of Acronyms and Abbreviations 289
Works Cited 297
Contributors 301

Foreword

Tom Marfiak

Great ships have a way of imprinting themselves indelibly on our hearts and on the pages of history. The guided missile destroyers and cruisers of the Cold War period, representing the apogee of the shipbuilders' art in so many ways, did more. They represented the synthesis of the lessons learned from hard combat in World War II, the advent of the jet age and high-speed data links, and set the stage for the fleet of today. Furthermore, they were the forge on which the spirit and hardiness of sailors was tempered to a fine edge. This book, told by the participants, is the story of one of the greatest of them, the USS *Biddle* (CG-34).

The last of the single ended guided missile frigates, her exploits, the story of the men who sailed into harm's way, begins in a Maine shipyard, and ends, as these things must, in another shipyard years and thousands of sea miles away. The intervening years saw sailors come and go, commanding officers leave their imprint, and a proud tradition established. The adventures, both amusing and sad, are the stuff of seafarers everywhere. What is unique in the story of USS *Biddle* is her presence at the cutting edge of complex fleet operations throughout her career. From an accelerated training cycle after commissioning, to her final series of systems upgrades, her crews never settled for second best. Her excellence in war, in fleet exercises, in applying technology to resolving the problems of multi-platform warfare, was unquestioned throughout her experience. Those of us who were privileged to serve aboard her during those years grew in our personal and professional experience. Our memories, and the memories of those who sailed the great seas in her sister ships, and the doughty guided missile destroyers that sailed alongside, are the stuff of legend. As it is said, "they don't make them like that any more."

Truly they were thoroughbreds. The destroyers that ran the Atlantic convoys, or that pounded their way into the Pacific, displaced about 1800-2100 tons. Their freeboard was measured in inches or a few feet at best—and their combat range was the measure of their five-inch guns. In Vietnam, they were the gun ships, ranging freely along the shoreline, their brass accumulating on deckhouses as a measure of their combat experience. The new frigates, soon to be designated cruisers in an early "truth in advertising" campaign, were another breed entirely. They packed an enormous missile system, several sensors, air, surface and sub-surface, and a powerful communications empire built into their 8,000 ton hulls. The entire ship was driven by an intricate engineering plant that demanded constant vigilance and precision. As a sea keeper, the hull was unparalleled, rising easily to thirty foot swells. When others were driven to a stop, her great bow would continue to leverage apart the seas. In the far oceans of the world, north and south, she kept alive American naval presence.

This first hand account may mark a trend. The experience of generations of seamen and officers who grew to manhood aboard these ships would become the leaders of the next ships of the fleet. They would learn, first hand, the value of time, and training, and responsiveness. And their builders, having sent them to sea with their best, would learn how do even better, so that the future, where we are now, would be as capable as it has proven it can be.

We all treasure those nights when the stars are bright, and the wind and seas are gentler. But we learn so much more when we must overcome great obstacles, restore capability under pressure, and fight our ships in the worst of circumstances. Then we truly find out what we are made of. Then the value of our country's trust in our training and seamanship becomes apparent. This is one of those stories. This then is the story of one Hard Charger, inspired by her first captain, sustained by successive crews, and, until the very end, a valiant contributor to the freedom we enjoy today.

Preface

James Treadway

Thirteen months after commissioning, USS *Biddle* (DLG-34) anchored at Da Nang, South Vietnam, prior to her first of three combat deployments to the Gulf of Tonkin. In a few days, *Biddle* would be on duty as Positive Identification Radar Advisory Zone (PIRAZ) control ship, positioned 30 miles off the coast of North Vietnam. Her primary mission was to serve as the first line of defense against an attack on our carriers 100 miles to the south at Yankee Station.

During a career that lasted almost 27 years, *Biddle* steamed in harm's way and fulfilled her primary mission many times. Each time she was given an assignment, *Biddle* performed at a level that few naval combatants have attained, before or since. She was a proud ship, and as with any warship, there are as many stories to be told as there are men who served aboard her. Many of these stories are compelling, important, and worth saving to remind us that we did a difficult job during difficult times, and we came home when many did not. A few stories rise to the top. *Biddle's* defining moment occurred on a moonless night during her third Gulf of Tonkin deployment when five North Vietnamese MiG aircraft attacked her. The officers and men who were there tell the story on the following pages. Other stories may not be quite so dramatic, but they are undeniably important in their own right because they clearly show the sacrifices we made and the training we endured.

Biddle and the ships in her class occupied a pivotal position in the lineage of modern cruisers. Preceding them were the light and heavy cruisers of the World War II era and the 1950s-era frigates in the *Coontz* and *Leahy* classes. Though all were capable combatants with the latest radars, guns, and missiles, they still lacked the ability to process large numbers of high-speed airborne targets which could rapidly penetrate fleet defenses. Thus, in desperation, the Naval Tactical Data System was born. We explore in substantial detail the reasons why, and how, a new class of ships and the NTDS were developed to counter this new threat. We also discover how *Biddle*, particularly in her early years, contributed to the success of the NTDS as well as how *Biddle's* weapons and combat systems were upgraded during periodic overhauls to keep her strong and vibrant.

The first person narrative format of this book is not conventional and the long quotes and personal accounts are unedited except for spelling and punctuation. I want to tell the history of *Biddle* through the words of the officers and men who served aboard her. Also, parenthetical references to first person accounts from contributors, most of which were e-mails, were omitted to enhance readability.

Our Surface Navy in Danger of Extinction?

David Boslaugh

They were young, they had hardly any training, and they had almost no flying experience so they were easy prey for ship's gunners and new high performance Allied fighters. Furthermore, the Kamikaze's principal weapon, the Zero fighter, was relatively light and often did not penetrate their target ship's structure upon impact. Sometimes in the excitement of the attack the young pilots forgot to pull the lever that armed their 550-pound bomb, so the bomb did not explode when they hit their target ship. Nevertheless, in their simultaneous massed attacks against Allied task forces, from all directions and at all altitudes, the Kamikazes sank or fatally damaged 363 ships and killed 6,600 sailors. A sign of even more potent weapons to come, the Japanese rocket propelled, pilot controlled Ohka standoff bomb had more than one and one half times the impact speed of the Zero which made it much harder to shoot down and gave it more than two and a half times as much energy to penetrate a target ship's structure. An automatically guided Ohka type standoff weapon would be a definite threat to the surface fleet in the years following World War II.

The Allies responded to the Kamikaze threat with new tactics, new fighters, and new fleet dispositions including specially equipped, and specially protected, radar picket destroyers with new height finding search radars placed a long distance from the main formation in the direction of the expected threat to give early warning of an air attack. It was found that the best way to deal with the Ohka standoff bombs, given early radar warning of the approach of the bombers carrying them, was to deploy fighters to shoot down the mother airplanes before they came within weapon release range of the main formation. U.S. naval radar, invented only in the mid 1930s, thus proved itself over and over again in the Pacific conflict. More than one historian noted that the atomic bomb may have ended the war with Japan, but it was radar that won the war. But, even with radar's great contribution, it had its problems.

The shipboard radars in a WW II task force were capable of generating a massive amount of 'data' about air targets on their glowing screens. This flood of rapidly changing radar data called for a large, well trained, smooth functioning team of human radar plotters, voice radio target tellers, fighter director officers, and gunnery coordination officers to effectively use the data. Normally each ship in a formation was assigned a wedge shaped bearing sector to survey and plot the range, bearing and height of every radar target in that sector. Plotters then had to manually calculate the course and speed of each assigned target, determine whether friendly, hostile, or unknown, and make all that data and derived information, along with an identifying track number, available to the target tellers who broadcast all the data on their ship's assigned targets to all the rest of the ships in the formation. Other plotters aboard each ship then built comprehensive summary plots of all radar targets for use by the gunnery coordinators, fighter directors, and command decision makers on each ship. It was a system prone to human error, noisy radio circuits, fatigue, and lapses of short-term memory. There were times in massed Kamikaze attacks when the system became near saturation and began to falter.

Chief of Naval Operations, Admiral Ernest J. King, in an October 1945 letter to the chiefs of the Navy's material bureaus for ordnance, aeronautics, and ships, summarized what he wanted of them with regard to improvements in the ability to effectively use radar. Specifically he called for "A method of presenting radar information automatically, instantaneously, and continuously and in such a manner that the human mind…may receive and act upon the information in the most convenient form; [plus] instantaneous dissemination of information within the ship and force (Bryant 141).

This was a task calling for some form of information automation; there would not be a quick or easy solution.

In July 1944 a new twin jet German Messerschmitt Me 262 attacked an RAF de Havilland Mosquito reconnaissance airplane which escaped its high speed pursuer only by hiding in a cloud bank in the nick of time. Before then, no airplane in the Luftwaffe could catch up with a Mosquito (Boyne 41).

By the end of the conflict both the RAF and the U.S. also had operational military jet aircraft, and on 14 October 1947 Captain Charles E. Yeager, piloting the Bell X-1, removed all doubt that military jets would soon be flying at speeds faster than sound.

In 1948 the Royal Navy conducted practice fleet air defense exercises against multiple high speed jet attackers and found that, thanks to the increased attack speeds, even with the best, most experienced men the air defense radar plotting teams generally fell apart when the number of simultaneous air attacks exceeded twenty. In similar exercises in 1950, the U.S. Navy found that about half of the new high speed jet attackers penetrated the fleet's fighter defense zone unengaged. If they had been real Soviet style massed air attacks, there was concern that the task forces would have been slaughtered (Bailey). To some senior officials the survivability of the U.S. surface Navy was in doubt. New shipboard defensive weapons having far greater engagement ranges than existing AA guns, and new ways of assimilating radar data and managing the deployment of these weapons in concert with friendly high speed interceptor aircraft were urgently needed.

The "Three Ts"

Work on devising a new shipboard long range air defense weapon had actually begun in 1944 as an anti-Kamikaze weapon. It was to be a 65-mile range, ramjet-powered supersonic missile which would be guided by the launching ship to the vicinity of the attacking aircraft which would then set off the missile's high explosive charge by activating the missile's proximity fuse. An elaborate, high precision electro-mechanical analog fire control computer aboard the launching ship would take inputs from the ship's long range air search radar to lock a pencil beam fire control radar onto the target and would then generate intercept guidance orders to the missile.

The Bureau of Ordnance (BUORD) named the missile "Talos", and at war's end the Office of the Chief of Naval Operations (OPNAV) directed BUORD to keep working on the missile as a future defense against hostile jet aircraft (King 288).

The Talos missile was an expensive bird, and one was expended in the each of the numerous test firings needed to test the elaborate, complex system. However, many of the test flights were to evaluate some part of the system other than the expensive missile. The solution to using a Talos missile on each test firing was a much cheaper, shorter range expendable test platform powered by two-stage solid propellant rockets. The less expensive test platform could achieve the needed supersonic speeds and could reach out about 20 miles, far enough to support the test program.

By 1949 BUORD managers noted that the solid rocket test platform was quite reliable, and if given an explosive warhead it could be a potent short range air defense missile. OPNAV authorized turning the test platform into a shorter range missile which could be fielded as a tactical weapon even sooner than Talos, and could be installed in smaller ships than required by Talos, which needed a heavy cruiser sized platform. The new missile was called "Terrier." In a final beneficial management decision, BUORD modified the Terrier missile with an improved sustainer rocket motor, and no launch booster, into a ten-mile range single-stage missile which was small enough to be carried on destroyer sized ships to give them an air defense capability beyond the range of existing guns. The bureau named the smallest missile "Tartar", and the three missile systems together became known as the "Three Ts."

The thirty-foot long Talos missile needed huge shipboard magazines to carry a significant warload of missiles, and cruisers were the only appropriate sized ships to carry that missile system. Therefore, in the late 1950s a number of World War II cruisers were stripped of some, or in some cases all, of their six or eight-inch gun turrets to make room for Talos missile batteries. Three heavy cruisers, Albany, Chicago, and Columbus saw not only their 8-inch turrets removed fore and aft to be replaced by Talos missile systems, but also their three and five-inch gun mounts removed in order to install two Tartar batteries port and starboard (Navy Department 823). The smaller Tartar missile systems were slated for fitting aboard new-construction guided missile destroyers.

The medium range Terrier missile system, however, was too large for conventional destroyers. Some Terrier systems were fitted in former WW II six-inch gun cruisers and a few were slated for aircraft carriers, but finally the supply of suitable WW II veteran cruisers ran out. A new class of air defense ship, having a displacement midway between that of a destroyer and a light cruiser, was needed to carry the Terrier missile system. The first of the new class, the 'guided missile frigate' USS *Coontz* (DLG-9), was so designated as being an offspring of the new, larger destroyer leader (DL) type ship, but with a 'G' added to the type designation to indicate that it carried guided missiles.

The Navy has usually, for good reasons, shunned purely special purpose ships, and so, even though the new guided missile frigates' primary mission was fleet air defense, they were also armed with five-inch guns and anti-submarine weapons backed up with a state of the art sonar system. Each succeeding class of guided missile frigate leading up to USS *Biddle* (DLG-34) gained more in size, displacement and capabilities until many wondered why the U.S. Navy did not call a spade a spade. Or in this case, why were not these cruiser sized and capable ships called cruisers? More about this later.

Still, An AAW Battle Management Problem

The Saddest Words of Tongue or Pen, Are those Words 'It Might Have Been'

During World War II the Royal Canadian Navy (RCN) provided 48% of all Allied escort ships for Atlantic convoys, but in spite of this lion's share' contribution of convoy antisubmarine forces, the RCN got virtually no respect from the Royal Navy or the US Navy who called all the shots regarding how the RCN would use its considerable anti-submarine warfare (ASW) assets Vardalas 66). At war's end the Canadians vowed never again! In any future global conflict they intended to put themselves in a position to be in charge of transatlantic convoy management rather than just a silent junior partner; and what better way than to develop an automated fleet-wide ASW management system.

The Canadians began work in 1948 on such a digital automated shipboard system to have the capability to "capture, extract, display, communicate, and share accurate tactical information in a timely manner." (Vardalas 67) Though primarily oriented to processing sonar data and closely coordinating tactics among convoy escort ships and hunter-killer ASW groups, it was also designed to accept and process radar data. The RCN named their concept the Digital Automated Tracking and Resolving System (DATAR.) In 1948 the U.S. Army's Electronic Numerical Integrator and Computer (ENIAC) was the only existing all-electronic computer in the world, but many academic and business organizations had been inspired by the Army machine to start designing even more capable and more versatile general purpose digital computers, including Feranti Limited of Great Britain. In 1950 the RCN selected Feranti-Canada to build a shipboard version of their vacuum-tube computer with rotating magnetic drum memory to be the computing power behind DATAR.

Three systems complete with the Feranti computers, sonar and radar displays from which targets could be manually entered into the computer, and, perhaps most importantly of all, a digital data link having 80-mile range, were installed in two minesweepers and a shore station. The system could accommodate 64 targets with 40-yard resolution (Friedman 49). The RCN began testing DATAR on Lake Ontario in August 1953, and it worked! It needed improvements and tweaking, but it worked. The RCN was well on its way to being the world leader in automated seaborne combat management systems, and they had good reason to believe they would never again be the junior partner in Atlantic convoy management.

The two shipboard systems filled the entire after half of the two minesweepers, and major overheating, brought on by 3,800 vacuum tubes in tight space confines, was one of the problems to be addressed. Unfortunately fire broke out on one of the test ships and the system was destroyed. Lack of funds to rebuild the system resulted in project termination, and perhaps the only lasting benefit was the knowledge and experience gained by Mr. Stanley F. Knights, chief scientist on DATAR, who would later give invaluable consulting support to the U.S. Navy's Naval Tactical Data System project (E. Swenson, 29 Sept. 1987, Page 5). Even though emphasis of other nations would remain on using more familiar analog computing technology to solve the AAW battle management problem, the Canadians were truly bold and prophetic in the selection of one of the world's earliest digital computers for their system. In the end digital technology would prove to be the correct route.

Analogs: Too Heavy, Too Complex, Too Unreliable, and Too Little Capability

By the late 1950s the U.S. Navy was hard at work fitting the Three T missile systems into a variety of existing and new-construction ships. Also, new supersonic carrier-based fleet air defense interceptors were coming on line. Furthermore, radar, the means of long range warning and precision tracking of air attackers, was already there and improving every day. But there was still a missing ingredient in the mixture. It was being repeatedly demonstrated that WW II style manual radar plotting teams, voice radio target telling among ships in a task force, and human fighter direction and gunnery coordination, no matter how expert and well trained, was not up to the volume, speed, and precision demands of managing individual target selection and deployment of task force missile batteries, guns, and fighters in the face of a saturation air attack by new high-speed aircraft. Some form of information automation was still the obvious answer; but how?

Analog computers were the conventional approach to information automation, and they had served the fleet well since before WW II, primarily in the form of electromechanical fire control computers wherein the turn of a shaft might represent target speed and mechanical component resolvers could represent target location. Although the mechanical computers were accurate and reliable, they could process only one target at a time, whereas WW II massed Kamikaze saturation attacks had involved as many as 900 attackers coming from all directions and altitudes.

Nevertheless, most initial attempts to automate AAW battle management, other than the Canadians, relied on analog computing methods. In 1951 the Royal Navy, facing the same problems as the U.S. Navy, began work on their Comprehensive Display System (CDS) which featured 96 target tracking channels fed by operators moving cursors to pick radar targets from search radars and enter them into target tracking channels. Each target tracking channel was the electromechanical equivalent of a rudimentary analog fire control computer, and operators could also set switches indicating track number, estimated altitude, friendly, hostile or unknown, whether assigned to weapons, as well as other target parameters. The information stored in the tracking channels was then written as a synthetic air situation picture back on top of the operator's radar scopes.

Evaluation of CDS aboard the British aircraft carrier HMS *Victorious* showed that, when the system worked, it was a great step forward from manual plotting teams. CDS showed enough promise to warrant installation aboard another R.N. aircraft carrier and four guided missile destroyers (Howse 264). It also piqued the interest of the U.S. Navy who tasked the Naval Research Laboratory (NRL) at Washington, D.C. to acquire one CDS system and evaluate it for USN use. NRL concluded that CDS was indeed a great improvement over WW II style AAW battle manage methods; however the Lab also found the system unreliable due to the large number of mechanical components, bulky, suffering in accuracy due to effects of temperature changes on the many components, and expensive. They did not propose the system for USN use, but rather proposed an improved electronic version, still in analog computer form, however (Gebhart 381).

The Naval Research Lab named their all-electronic system the Electronic Data System (EDS), and began design work in 1953. EDS featured 24 electronic target tracking channels which not only stored and displayed the same target parameters as the British CDS, but also, by virtue of its electronic circuitry, was able to compute target velocities. This feature not only aided fighter interceptor controllers, but also moved the artificial target symbols on the operator's radar scopes which enabled a single EDS operator to simultaneously manually update eight target tracks as compared to the two-tracks-per-operator in the Royal Navy CDS. Furthermore, in a significant step forward, a teletype data link automatically broadcast the stored information on each target to other similarly equipped ships in a task force. On board the receiving ships the teletype data was changed back to electrical voltages to show the remotely transmitted track information on the receiving ship's radar scopes.

Evaluation of the Naval Research Laboratory system at sea in 1955 aboard four destroyers showed that the system's reliability and usefulness warranted installation of 16 more systems aboard selected major combatant ships—primarily guided missile cruisers. Even though a great improvement, EDS needed more track storage capability, greater accuracy, and the capability to store and display even more information about each target to fully resolve the fleet anti-air battle management problem. More improvement was needed, and no more than the twenty systems were acquired (Gebhart 384) (Graf III-2).

A shipboard missile system had to be more than just a magazine full of missiles, a launcher, a fire control computers, search radars and fire control radars. A central control station was needed to direct all the other elements, and to feed selected high-threat air targets from the air search radars to the fire control computers, which would slew the pencil-beam fire control radars into position to search for and lock on to the target. The control station was termed a 'weapons direction system.' or WDS. The WDS needed to have an inventory of high threat air targets ready to feed to the fire control computers, and so were equipped with a limited number of target tracking channels, usually eight, in the Talos, Terrier, and Tartar systems. They were, in effect, small versions of the Electronic Data System, but without a data link that could have integrated their combat picture with that of other task force ships.

The weapons control officers were thus forced to make their own value judgments as to which targets on a manually grease penciled transparent vertical summary radar plotting board should be manually selected on the search radar screen to be fed to the tracking channels, and with no knowledge, other than inter-task force voice radio, of whether a selected target might already be engaged by another gun or missile system or perhaps by an interceptor. EDS was installed in a few missile cruisers to serve as the weapons direction system and so partially solved the problem with its data link. But there was still a serious problem in fleetwide AAW battle management in making best use of the potent new shipboard missile systems and high-speed carrier launched interceptors.

SAGE, The US Air Force's Answer

In March 1950 the US Air Force had begun work on a digital automated system that addressed virtually the same air battle management problem, on a nationwide scope, with which the Navy was struggling. They called it the Semi-Automatic Ground Environment, or SAGE for short. In some ways the Air Force challenge was simpler than the navy problem because SAGE would be located in fixed ground sites (27 total) sites situated around the country. These sites would not move, whereas Navy ships attempting to data link the positions of tactical air targets to other units must know not only where the target is with respect to the ship, but also precisely where the constantly moving ship is, or the target coordinates will be in error. The second Air Force advantage was large four-story warehouse sized air defense centers, each having the room to house two of the physically largest computers ever built—IBM AN/FSQ-7 computers each having 25,000 vacuum tubes, and occupying 40,000 square feet (Watson 231-233).

By a strange twist of fate the initial inspiration for the prototype of these massive computers had also come from the Army's ENIAC computer, and had started in life in 1946 as a Navy project called WHIRLWIND, the purpose of which was to be the heart of a sophisticated aircraft flight simulator for the Navy's Bureau of Aeronautics. Just when the Bureau had become terminally frustrated with the WHIRLWIND computer's growing costs, the Air Force recognized it as exactly what they needed for their SAGE system. By 1953 the SAGE project had progressed far enough for the Navy to take a close look at it as a possible solution to the task force AAW battle management problem. The Navy study postulated a new special type of ship—a combined radar site, floating computer center, and command ship.

Each of the command ships would be fitted with massive vacuum-tube computers similar to the SAGE machines, but hardened to survive the shock, vibration, and corrosion rigor's of shipboard life. Two computers would be required on each ship, as at the SAGE sites, so that one could always be in maintenance having its ever-failing vacuum tubes methodically replaced, or in hot standby ready to replace the operating machine whenever it failed. The special ships would have to be cruiser-sized at least, and one would operate with each task force, building a fleet-wide air battle picture and transmitting it over a digital data link to all air defense ships. Navy planners finally rejected the concept because the task forces could be vulnerable to a single-point failure because destruction of that single ship would leave the task force blind. Furthermore Navy ships must often act alone, and it was decreed that each air defense ship, from guided missile frigate on up, should have similar self contained automated capabilities (Graf III-2).

The Navy Solution

In 1954 Rear Admiral Rawson Bennett, Chief of Naval Research, temporarily detached Lieutenant Commander Irvin L. McNally from the Navy Electronics Laboratory at San Diego, California, to take another, closer, longer look at SAGE and to report back to him possible on ways to extend the SAGE concept to sea. McNally was to spend six months on a tri-service study team, called Project Lamplight, at the Massachusetts Institute of Technology, who was managing SAGE development. He would be in company with approximately 100 other civilian engineers, Air Force and Army officers working on ways to improve continental air defense. McNally and civilian engineer Everett E. McCown were to be the only Navy representation, and to help increase his clout with the many senior officers from the other services, McNally was spot promoted from Lieutenant Commander to Commander (Graf III-3).

This was not McNally's first spot promotion, for almost all his promotions had been thus because he had been continuously put into new jobs above his pay grade. Entering the Navy in 1932 as a way of riding out the Great Depression until he could get a civilian job where he could use his degree in electrical engineering, he had started as an enlisted radioman, and by 1936 he had risen to Radioman First Class. By late 1937 he was a Warrant Radio Electrician, and in 1940 he was assigned to the Naval Research Laboratory in Washington, D.C. to attend the first US Navy course in radar—taught by the Laboratory's inventors of U.S. naval radar.

Later, in 1941, McNally was assigned to be one of the instructors in the first course in radar taught to American naval officers. Prophetically, one of his students was a young ensign, Edward C. Svendsen, about whom more will be said in this narrative. By early December 1941, McNally was living aboard USS *Pennsylvania* lodged in Drydock 1 at Pearl Harbor Naval Shipyard. His mission at Pearl Harbor, to set up and run a radar maintenance school for Pacific Fleet sailors, was almost prematurely terminated when a Japanese bomb destroyed the ship's medical aid station where he had volunteered to assist on the morning of 7 December. He was spared only because the doctor in charge had asked him to go below for a supply of gas masks and battle helmets. When he returned, all were dead.

By June 1942, the radar maintenance school was in operation, and McNally had been spot promoted to Lieutenant (Junior Grade) to help match his responsibilities in operating the school. A year later, after McNally had been spot promoted to full Lieutenant, he happened to show Vice Admiral Lockwood, Commander of the Pacific Fleet Submarine Force, a rudimentary, but working, radar antenna which could be fitted to a submarine periscope. Lockwood was flabbergasted, and the next day McNally found himself aboard a Pan American clipper bound for San Francisco with orders to proceed to the Radar Design Branch in the Bureau of Ships in Washington, D.C. Here his first priority was to get his periscope antenna into production. McNally was soon spot promoted to Lieutenant Commander, and eventually took charge of the Bureau's shipboard radar design group, which he headed until 1949 when he was posted the Navy Electronics Laboratory in San Diego to be radar program manager.

While working on Project Lamplight, McNally had, perhaps, one advantageous piece of knowledge that none of the 100 other technical participants possessed. While in charge of the Bureau of Ships shipboard radar design group, he had done considerable work with engineers of the Bell Telephone Laboratories where the new technology of transistors had been invented. One of the Bell Labs engineers had even given McNally one of their infant transistors and he had tried it in a number of kinds of circuits in place of a vacuum tube. By virtue of his experiments, he likely knew more about transistors than any other person on the study team, regardless of their level of academic degree or rank.

He was convinced that a digital computer having the computing power of the SAGE computers could be built of transistors which would not only allow the computer to be packaged into a small shipboard compartment, but also would run on only a few thousand watts of electrical power as compared to the one and one half million watts of power needed by one SAGE computer—mainly to heat incandescent vacuum-tube filaments. The SAGE managers considered transistors to be an immature, unreliable laboratory curiosity that would soon pass, but nevertheless said they would be willing to endorse McNally's system concept back to the Chief of Naval Research with some reservations.

McNally conceived of a computer-based seaborne battle management system wherein every combatant ship from guided missile frigate on up would be equipped with the system, and all participants would have similar capabilities including the ability to assume task force command functions in an emergency. The primary difference between smaller ships and major combatants would be more computer processing power and more operator positions on the larger ships. In remembrance of WW II saturation Kamikaze raids he called for larger ships to be able to process as many as 1000 targets at one time. (This would later have to be cut back). A key component of the system would be a fleetwide automatic digital data link that would allow all participating units to share in the task force target tracking load, and allow all to see the same composite air battle picture including 'pairing' lines that would show which ship or interceptor was engaging what target.

As in SAGE, the operator positions would be special radar consoles that had the ability to show not only the raw radar picture from search radars, but also computer-generated symbols indicating each target, whether it was friendly, hostile or unidentified, whether it was an aircraft, surface ship or submarine, its computed speed and heading, whether it was experiencing emergency conditions, whether it was assigned to a defensive weapon, and, if so, what kind of weapon, and on what ship, and if it was assigned to fighter interceptors, which interceptor, and which ship was controlling that interceptor.

The system would also assess all hostile targets and compute which targets seemed to be most threatening, which should be assigned to weapons first, and to which weapon. If assigned to airborne interceptors, the system would compute heading, speed and altitude orders for the interceptor, and might even automatically steer the interceptor into firing position with a ship-to-air data link. He also called for new shipboard radars designed specifically to interface with the new digital system, and for airborne early warning radar aircraft that worked as equal participants with the ships on the data link.

McNally condensed his concept to 15 typewritten pages, and sent it off to the Chief of Naval Research. Rear Admiral Bennett forwarded the paper on to the Office of the Chief of Naval Operations (OPNAV) without change, with the recommendation that the Navy start work on this at once. OPNAV summarily passed the paper on to the Chief of the Bureau of Ships with the direction to expand the paper in more technical and operational capabilities detail with special emphasis on assessing the state of the new technologies, especially transistors and computers, which would be essential to making this system a reality. (McNally, CDR Irvin L., Interview with D. L. Boslaugh, 20 April 1993.)

McNally was detailed to report to the head of the Electronics Design and Development Division, Captain W. F. Cassidy, in the Bureau of Ships where he was given the task of fleshing out his concept. McNally knew the capabilities and future potential of radar like the back of his hand, but he had been only lightly exposed to digital computers. He told Cassidy he desperately needed technical help from someone well versed in digital computers, especially transistorized computers, which he feared was an impossible request to fulfill. Amazingly, Cassidy told him he would have help there that same day. To McNally's further amazement his new collaborator was no other than the former young ensign, Edward Svendsen—now a commander, to whom he had taught the fundamentals of radar in 1941, some 14 years previously.

Svendsen was not allowed to tell McNally how he had become an expert in computers, but he was probably as well steeped in the cutting edge of digital computer state of the art as any person alive. He was allowed to tell McNally, to his added astonishment, that he was at that very time directing the development of an experimental large scale transistorized computer.

After Svendsen had completed McNally's radar course at NRL he returned to the battleship *Mississippi* where he became radar officer, and then with the advent of shipboard combat information centers (CIC) during the course of the Pacific conflict, he became the ship's CIC officer, wherein he and his men largely built and equipped their new CIC themselves. He therefore knew the technology of radar almost as well as McNally, and CIC functions perhaps even better. He grasped intuitively how digital computers could help automate the laborious manually and intellectually intensive CIC battle management processes, and he was excited at the prospect.

Svendsen had remained aboard Mississippi until the fall of 1944 when he was ordered to the U.S. Naval Postgraduate School at Annapolis to get a masters degree in electrical engineering. Upon graduation he entered a strange and arcane new world. He was assigned to the Naval Computing Machine Laboratory, at St. Paul, Minnesota, as technical officer. In this case 'computing machine' was a euphemism for 'electronic code breaking device', and Svendsen found himself in charge of developing electronic code breaking aids for the Navy's cryptologists at the Naval Security Group Command.

The Computing Machine Lab was physically collocated with a small company named Engineering Research Associates (ERA) who had been secretly helped into being by the Navy's code breaking community to be their material support arm. They were beginning a transition from special purpose code breaking machinery, such as the World War II electromechanical devices they used to break back the German Submarine Force Enigma code, to new general purpose digital computers which they adjudged would be even better at codebreaking. Here again, the inspiration had been the Army's ENIAC computer. ERA would eventually become the Univac Division of Sperry Rand Corporation.

Svendsen had been technically in charge of building the Navy's first two large scale vacuum-tube codebreaking computers, named Atlas I and II, and which were located at the Naval Security Station in Northwest Washington, D.C. He had subsequently been transferred to the Bureau of Ships where in 1955 he was in charge of the 'Special Applications Branch', which included the secret Computer Design Section, physically located at the Naval Security Station. At the time they were hard at work developing a transistorized version of the Atlas II, which was intended to be a desk sized full scale computer that could fit directly in the workspace of a Navy cryptologist for his personal use. A personal computer! (Svendsen, CAPT Edward C., Interview with D. L. Boslaugh, 3 Feb. 1995)

Captain Cassidy assigned the two commanders a small room in the Main Navy building from which he even ripped out the telephone to enable complete privacy. They specified a system built of standardized 'building block' equipment units whereby large or small ship systems could be assembled with multiples of the standard computers, operator displays, and data link equipment. Furthermore, the system on any ship could be expanded at any time by simply plugging in more computers or 'multiple function' operator consoles.

The system would be hard to kill. They would minimize susceptibility to 'single point' system failure by having at least two of every critical equipment type so that if one failed the system could continue to run at a reduced capability with the remaining unit. For example, even the smallest system, as installed on a guided missile frigate, would have two computers and two of most other essential components. Graceful degradation in the face of component failure, rather than outright stoppage would be a hallmark of system design. Even if a system lost both computers, the operator consoles would continue to function as standard radar repeaters so that the ship would be no worse off than a ship not equipped with the system.

Svendsen specified that, rather than using existing rotating magnetic drum memories, or mercury delay lines, or memories that used charged spots on the face of a cathode ray tube, the system's general purpose, stored program computers would have magnetic core memories. These new 'core' memories were just coming into experimental use, and Svendsen was already using them in his new transistorized cryptographer's 'personal computer.' The two commanders researched, calculated, and wrote for about a month during which they expanded McNally's original 15 page concept paper to a fifty page document having not only more technical and operational detail, but also convincing rationale that the system could be built (Svendsen Interview 3 Feb 1995).

In late August 1955 the Bureau of Ships sent McNally's and Svendsen's Technical and Operational Requirements document for a 'Navy Tactical Data System' off to the Chief of Naval Research who positively endorsed it to OPNAV, stating that system development should start immediately. OPNAV responded by finding project start-up funds and tasking the Bureau of Ships to establish a project office to build the new system in the shortest possible time.

The two commanders had convinced the Navy to start building a major, AAW battle management system that would form the automated anti-air battle management aid of every ship in the Navy from guided missile frigates on up—based on two new technologies: digital computing and transistors, that barely even existed; and furthermore, on new equipment types that existed only in their minds. In reality, because the new system was going to depend on new, very large, and extremely complex, computer programs, it was also going to depend on a third new technology, that of large scale computer programming, which was so new that no one even recognized it as either an art, science, or technology in its own right. This third unseen technical challenge would almost become the project's undoing.

A Fourteen-Year Task Compressed to Five

The Chief of the Bureau of Ships assigned Commander McNally as manager of the new project and Svendsen as assistant. The office was set up with a technical staff that would never exceed six naval officers and civilian engineers, supported by the equivalent of three full time engineering specialists in the Bureau's radar, communications, and computer design offices. OPNAV realized that the new command and control system, which had an undeniable flavor of command decision making by a giant electronic brain, was probably going to be highly controversial among naval officers. In recognition of the urgency of system development, its criticality to the fleet, and probable controversial nature, OPNAV also set up a small project office in the Pentagon composed of four officers headed by a Captain. Among many other jobs, prime missions of the OPNAV office would be justifying and defending project funding, setting up the needed operator and maintenance training schools, setting up two fleet computer programming centers on the East and West coasts, and selling the new system to a highly skeptical user community.

The normal paradigm for managing a project for a new, highly complex Navy weapon system called for selecting a prime contractor having the needed expertise in all technical areas to be the primary system designer and integrator. The prime contractor would then obtain subcontractors to design and build the needed new equipment in their areas of competence. There were many who said that Bell Laboratories was the only institution in the nation that could possibly pull off such a complex project. McNally and Svendsen, however, thought differently. They reasoned that the Navy, by virtue of its codebreaking computer design experience, its background as the inventor of U.S. Naval radar, and established expertise in radio communications, should be its own prime contractor and system integrator.

The two commanders set up a plan whereby Navy laboratories and engineering activities under task to the project office would develop detailed technical specifications for the many new needed equipment types, and they would monitor and guide selected contractors in designing and building prototype equipment. The prototype equipment would be assembled into an engineering test system at the Navy Electronics Laboratory where engineers and technicians would integrate the system and wring it out in a realistic ship simulation environment. They realized that trying to assemble and test the complex new system for the first time aboard an active Navy ship would be a predictable disaster.

The small company in St. Paul, Minnesota, that had just changed its name from Engineering Research Associates to Univac Division of Sperry Rand Corporation, and who was building the Navy codebreaking computers, was selected to design the new transistorized shipboard digital computers. Univac selected as their project leader a young engineer, Seymour Cray, having a growing reputation as a genius in the use of transistors. Univac was also contracted to develop the prototype computer programs for later turn-over to the new Fleet Computer Programming Centers, and Cray would also be in charge of computer program development. Cray would go on to gain a reputation as a world leader in supercomputer design and manufacturing.

To provide the system's data link equipment the project office picked Collins Radio who not only had the reputation as a leader in high frequency single sideband communications, but had also invented a very capable high frequency digital data link technology. Hughes Aircraft Co. was working on operator displays for the Army's Nike missile system that seemed to have applicability to the Navy system, and they were contracted to design and provide the new half analog/half digital radar display consoles (E. Swenson, 3 May 1988, Pages 53-60).

In the mid 1950s the Navy was accustomed to a schedule of about 14 years from authorization of development of a new electronics system project to installing service test units in the first receiving ships. Much of this time was to accommodate the many needed tests, qualifications, and project reviews by higher authorities inside and outside of the Navy. McNally and Svendsen agreed to a seemingly impossible five-year schedule with the proviso that disruptive reviews and interference in project management by higher authority had to be minimized. They worked out an agreement that, "If we need help we will ask for it, but otherwise just trust our judgment and let us keep going." It was agreed that the OPNAV project office would not require the usual plethora of formal project reviews and status briefings from BUSHIPS, but instead would stay abreast of progress, and problems, by their day-to-day involvement in the project. Chief of Naval Operations Arleigh A. Burke issued an edict that attempts by any senior official to 'micromanage' the project would not be tolerated. He further stated that all project officers in BUSHIPS and OPNAV would be assigned for the duration of the project and would be moved out of the project only with his approval (Svendsen, CAPT Edward C., Interview with D. L. Boslaugh, 3 Feb. 1995).

It seems that the first thing traditionally done when the armed forces starts a new project is to give it a name, preferably something that will form a snappy acronym. In this case, however, for some reason the new project did not have an official name or even a popular name. Maybe they were too busy to stop and think about it. McNally had called it the Navy Tactical Data System in his concept paper, but other project officers called it such things as the Consolidated Electronic Display System, the Fleet Data System, or sometimes the Naval Tactical Data System. Project secretary Frances Bartolomew pointed out to the project officers their inconsistencies in naming the new system in their correspondence, and stated she was becoming embarrassed that nobody seemed to know what the name of the project was. She did not ask them what name they were going to use, but instead declared that she liked "Naval Tactical Data System" and no matter what they wrote in their correspondence that was what she was going to type. The name stuck.

Irvin McNally had risen to commander rank by a series of spot promotions during his 24-year Navy career; however his permanent commissioned rank was only that of lieutenant. In a 1956 letter to the Bureau of Naval Personnel he inquired whether his position on the lineal list of officers could be advanced so that he could compete for captain rank with his contemporary commanders. The Bureau's response indicated that he would not have a chance to compete for promotion to captain during the remaining six years of a normal 30-year Navy career, convincing him that his best option was resignation from active duty.

Just prior to his retirement in June 1956, McNally wrote two more technical specification documents that would have long lasting impact on future shipboard combat systems. They described two new shipboard search radars that would be designed specifically to work with NTDS. One would be a three-dimensional search radar of unusual range and accuracy for air intercept control and designating targets to missile systems, the second would be a two-dimensional search radar for detecting air targets at long ranges and passing them to the three-dimensional radar for precision tracking. The two new radars would eventually become realities designated respectively AN/SPS-48 and AN/SPS-49, and *Biddle* would be in the first group of ships to receive the combination of the Naval Tactical Data System and the new SPS-48 three-dimensional search radar. McNally's final contribution would be, as the head of Raytheon Corporation's Search Radar Laboratory, to design and build the AN/SPS-49 search radar, which would be acknowledged the most capable U.S. Navy long range two-dimensional radar for over three decades (McNally Interview 20 April 1993).

The Sea—The Monster That Ate Science

Naval ship commanders are of necessity highly conservative when it comes to accepting new weapon systems because the consequences of failure are so severe in the seagoing environment. Failure of a new weapon system, or sub standard performance, can mean the death of comrades in battle and loss of ships or aircraft. They understandably want to stick with familiar weapons and techniques that they know from experience will work. As this narrative will point out, the sea, even in peacetime, can be a dangerous place. When news started circulating that traditional shipboard combat information centers were going to be replaced with an automated system built from two immature technologies of which even most of the nation's academic, scientific, and engineering communities knew virtually nothing, it was too much for most seagoing officers.

What made it worse was the reality that the new system was going to be interposed in the direct route of their AAW battle decision making. Some future commanders of the ships to be so equipped even visited the NTDS project office in the Bureau of Ships to tell the project officers face-to-face that even if the system was installed in their ship, they would refuse to turn it on. They declared that no damned computer was going to tell them what to do. An informal survey taken by the OPNAV NTDS project office revealed that naval officers opposed the system by a ratio of twenty to one (Graf IV-23).

Reliability experts, adding fuel to the future user's arguments, calculated that, based on the high count of transistors in NTDS, it could run, at best, for a few hours before failure set in. Even many officers and engineers in the Bureau of Ships shunned the NTDS project because they were convinced of the project's eventual failure, and they did not want to be caught in the undertow when the project sank.

The conviction that Navy electronic technicians would not be able to cope with the new exotic computer technology was another favorite argument of system critics. In Commander Svendsen's mind, however, there was no doubt that sailors could handle the new equipment because he had seen the communications technicians of the Naval Security Group Command readily master their code-breaking computers. The only doubt on Svendsen's part was whether the equipment responsibilities of Navy electronic technicians should be expanded to include new digital devices, or would that give them too many equipment types on which to train and care for. He convinced OPNAV and the Bureau of Naval Personnel to create a new enlisted equipment maintenance rating, the Data Systems Technician, to care for NTDS. The outstanding performance of this new breed of sailor during the crucial years of selling the system to its future users would prove to be most effective in silencing the critics (E. Swenson, May 1988, 59)

By April 1959 all of the prototype NTDS equipment had been delivered and installed at the Navy Electronics Lab land based test site. Furthermore, most of the new, hand picked, data system technicians (DSs) who would be assigned to the service test ships were at the Laboratory where they took classes from the NRL engineers and helped the engineers exercise and test the system during the day, while other shifts of DSs trained on the test system at night (Bureau of Ships, Technical Development Plan for the Naval Tactical Data System (NTDS)—SS 191, 1 Apr. 1964. Page 4-6). Much was learned. Many problems were found and corrected.

Most significantly, it was found that the freezer-chest sized prototype NTDS computers with their 11,000 point-contact transistors per computer were of just marginal reliability and performance for a seagoing system. In October 1959 Svendsen and his assistant project officers made the gut wrenching decision to design and build a new computer regardless of the project's tight schedule. The year before, Fairchild Instrument Corporation had invented the planar transistor, which offered better reliability and higher computer speed, and the project decided to fashion a new computer with the new transistor technology.

The new computer would retain Seymour Cray's architecture, instruction set, and input/output conventions, but every circuit would be of new design to best use the new technology. In nine months Univac designed, built, and tested the new machine, and in tests it vindicated the project officers decision. Reliability was an order of magnitude improved, and it ran twice as fast as the prototype machine (Lundstrom 55-57). Two of the new computers, resembling upright refrigerators, had the same processing power as one 20,000 square foot vacuum-tube SAGE computer.

System testing continued at the Navy Electronics Laboratory until November 1961, but as early as April 1959 the fast moving pace of the project had called for starting the three equipment contractors on production runs to build equipment for three service test ships. To achieve the fast paced five-year project schedule, Collins Radio, Hughes Aircraft, and Univac engineers were forced to design the service test equipment following a moving target as test results were fed into their design process.

At the end of September 1961, San Francisco and Puget Sound Naval Shipyards completed installing the prototype equipment in three service test ships including two new-construction guided missile frigates USS *King* (DLG-10) and USS *Mahan* (DLG-11). The third ship, an attack carrier, had been the subject of great controversy in the Navy because most senior naval officers were aghast at the idea of turning over one of their newest attack carriers to a six-month service testing project. The issue had been settled, however, by a chance meeting between Vice Admiral H. G. Hopwood, Commander-in-Chief of the Pacific Fleet and assistant NTDS project officer Erick N. Swenson in the fall of 1959 following a wedding reception. The enthusiastic young lieutenant described the capabilities of the new system in such a convincing manner that the admiral returned to his headquarters and dispatched a message offering up the attack carrier USS *Oriskany* (CVA-34) to NTDS service test (A. Swenson. Interview 17 April 1993).

By October 1961 the new data system technicians for the three service test ships had been in training for two years at contractor plants and at the NEL test site, and they were now clearly the experts when it came to taking care of NTDS equipment. Even though navy practice was to provide contractor engineers to maintain new equipment during at-sea service testing in order to give the new equipment a fair chance, Svendsen, now a Captain, decided that only navy data system technicians would maintain the new systems during the at-sea evaluation. No one else would be allowed to work on the equipment (Graf IV-23).

Service test task force operations began off San Diego in late October 1961, and the project officers learned a new reality about large, complex digital systems. The prototype NTDS computer programs had been well debugged at the land based test site, and the project managers expected them to function well when installed in the ship systems. Therefore, hardly any time had been scheduled to test the programs in their new seagoing environment. To the project officers' horror the programs failed over and over again. They found that when a computer program is shifted to a new environment, no matter how realistic the shore-based system might have been, the programs must be extensively tested and verified as if they were brand new computer programs.

The six-month at-sea operational evaluation by the Operational Test and Evaluation Force (OPTEVFOR) was a continuing nightmare. It was as much a computer program debug evolution as it was a system test. The testers did find that, when the programs worked, NTDS was far more effective in task force defense than existing manual AAW battle management procedures. Furthermore, the new NTDS equipment under the care of the data system technicians performed flawlessly. The operational evaluation was completed on 1 April 1962, and Rear Admiral Charles K. Bergin, the commander of OPTEVFOR concluded in his report that if the NTDS equipment had performed as poorly as the computer programs he would have had no choice but to give the project a thumbs down (Swallow Letter 16 Nov 1994).

As it was, OPNAV issued a provisional approval for service use for the Naval Tactical Data System. The proviso was that the computer programs had to be debugged and stabilized. A year later a team of testers, engineers, and computer programmers from OPTEVFOR, Univac, and the Fleet Computer Programming Center, San Diego, who sailed aboard the three service test ships for six more months, had the computer programs as solid as the equipment. In March 1963 the Chief of Naval Operations issued final approval for service use for the Naval Tactical Data System (Buships 12-1).

In the meantime, there was no time to lose. In March 1962, a full year before service approval, OPNAV, taking a calculated risk, had directed the NTDS project to begin production of NTDS equipment to outfit seventeen existing and new construction ships. One of those equipment suites was destined for the new guided missile frigate *Biddle* (DLG-34) that would be laid down on the building ways at Bath Iron Works, Bath, Maine, on 9 December 1963.

The DLG Class Guided Missile Frigates

David Boslaugh

The AN/SPS-48 Radar and Weapons Direction System Mark 11

Of the nine guided missile frigates of the DLG-26 Class, four of *Biddle's* sister ships, *Belknap* (DLG-26), *Josephus Daniels* (DLG-27), *Wainwright* (DLG-28), and *William H. Standley* (DLG-32) would also be built at Bath Iron Works. It was always a wonder how the tiny, postage stamp sized shipyard could turn out so many fighting ships so fast. The DLG-26 Class was not the first class of guided missile frigate. Before *Belknap* had come ten of the *Coontz* (DLG-9) Class, nine of the *Leahy* (DLG-16) Class, and the nuclear powered guided missile frigate *Bainbridge* (DLGN-25). Each succeeding class was heavier than the last and looked less and less like a big destroyer and more like a cruiser.

The DLG-26 Class was to be the first group of new-construction ships to have production NTDS equipment installed during construction. Before the NTDS installation in *Belknap*, six other ships had received the new digital command and control system: the three service test ships: *Oriskany*, *King*, and *Mahan*, the nuclear powered carrier *Enterprise*, the nuclear powered cruiser *Long Beach* (both of which had received installations of service test equipment by direct order of Admiral Arleigh Burke), and the heavy guided missile cruiser *Chicago*, which received the first suite of production equipment.

In those ships having missile systems, NTDS was connected to the weapon systems by way of a refrigerator sized electronic box called an Interconnecting Digital to Analog Converter, or IDAC for short. IDAC fed coordinates of selected high-threat air targets from NTDS to the missile system's analog weapons direction systems (WDS), which could usually hold eight tracks, maximum, in their analog tracking channels. The weapons control officer could opt to use the targets from NTDS or he could have his own WDS operators feed targets to the tracking channels from their own search radar consoles. This was an arrangement that was not to last very long.

Crossing the Boundary Line—Origin of Weapons Direction System Mark 11

In the eyes of assistant NTDS project officer Lieutenant Commander Joseph Stoutenburgh, having two sets of search radar tracking consoles on the missile ships was a wasteful redundancy. He questioned why the Naval Tactical Data System could not take on the weapons direction task, and possibly eliminate the need for a significant amount of equipment, as well as a few operators who seemed to be doing about the same job in two different systems. One immediate argument against such an arrangement came from old hands in the Bureau of Naval Weapons who pointed out that NTDS was still a radical, unproved system and they would be putting all their eggs in one fragile basket. Furthermore, they pointed out there were functions in the WDS, such as many firing safety checks and complex missile system engagement logic that NTDS didn't do. They also knew that NTDS computer memory in the missile ships was already loaded to the maximum with almost no reserve to take on any new functions. They were pretty sure they had put this wild idea to bed.

Stoutenburgh persisted. In early 1960 he asked Lieutenant Joseph L. Randolph, newly assigned to the project office, to spend a few months working out the details. Randolph visited numerous missile system support activities and contractors, digested mountains of missile system manuals, studied, and calculated. He concluded that it could be done, that the missile system functions could be worked into the NTDS computer programs, and there could be considerable savings in equipment and operator positions in the combat information centers and weapon control spaces. He showed that he could eliminate six large WDS equipment cabinets, five WDS operator consoles, and the IDAC; in return for three more NTDS consoles a Weapons Control Panel, from which the missile system would be controlled, and a new Fire Control Data Converter that would pass target coordinates and signals in both directions between the weapons and NTDS. It is said that when one old timer in the Bureau of Ordnance learned that the Bureau of Ships had crossed so far over the boundary line of BUORD territory that the missile firing key was going to be on a piece of BUSHIPS' equipment, the Weapons Control Panel, he submitted his retirement papers.

In the new concept, NTDS would automatically analyze each new hostile and unidentified target with its threat evaluation and weapons assignment logic and identify the most threatening targets which should be passed directly via the Fire

Control Data Converter to the missile or gun fire control computers. There was also the promise that target processing time from detection of a hostile target by search radar to assignment to a missile or gun system could be reduced by many critical seconds because of the steps eliminated (Bureau of Ships point paper 1967).

In May 1960 the OPNAV Ship's Characteristic Board approved the Bureau of Ship's proposal on the basis that it eliminated two general quarters personnel, and 7,000 pounds of equipment occupying 300 cubic feet of space. OPNAV designated the new arrangement Weapons Direction System Mark 11 and directed that it would be first installed in the last six ships of the *Belknap* Class, beginning with DLG-29. The decision paper also emphatically stated that it was understood that the new WDS computer programs would be incorporated into existing memory of the two NTDS computers slated for the guided missile frigates, and under no circumstances would more computers be added to the systems. Skeptical and resentful BUWEPS officers still did not think the feat could be pulled off and they demanded that Randolph put in official correspondence that he would accomplish the job or resign his commission. He signed the joint letter to the Chiefs of BUSHIPS and BUWEPS, and many years later retired from the Navy as full Captain with no resignation ever necessary (Mahinske Letter 19 July 1944). It would be a tough and stimulating challenge however.

A moderate sized color photograph displayed on the screen of a personal computer of today requires about 14 million binary bits of information. We think nothing of storing dozens of such photos in our computer's memory, and it puts no strain whatsoever on our computer. It was not always so.

In 1962 when this writer was assigned to the Bureau of Ships Technical Representative office, the successor to the Naval Computing Machine Laboratory at the St. Paul Univac plant, we had an accident one day. A box of ferrite memory cores intended for one of our new NTDS computers had been shipped to us, and we had left the paper bag holding the box sitting on a desk when we went to lunch. When we came back, the bag was gone, and we assumed a Univac engineer had come by for it, but next day when comparing notes we found he did not have the memory cores. Some detective work revealed that the bag had been accidentally knocked into a wastebasket and by then had gone through the plant's incinerator. The ashes were immediately raked out of the incinerator and spread out on a concrete floor. One NTDS computer had 32,768 thirty-bit 'words' in its memory, and sure enough the ashes were full of roughly one million tiny ferrite 'donuts' about one sixteenth of an inch in diameter. Each core made up one memory 'bit.'

Fortunately, ferrite memory cores are the product of a firing process and thus their trip through the incinerator could not have hurt them. We conjectured maybe it even made them better. Each core was worth about ten cents, meaning that about $100,000 worth of cores were there mixed up in the ashes. We and a number of Univac volunteers spent a mirth-filled day picking cores from the ashes with long needles, and it was well worth the effort. Today the 983,040 bits of memory we rescued from the ashes would probably be barely adequate for a child's toy or a wrist watch, but at that time that amount of memory represented a large scale mainframe computer.

Memory was thus precious in more ways than one. To get the extra WDS Mk 11 weapons direction functions into a program that could be contained in the two NTDS computers in a guided missile frigate required Lieutenant Randolph and his contractor engineers to write the needed program additions in the most efficient memory using fashion possible. For example, whenever there was a function that involved calculations, they programmed the solution both in the form of a mathematical algorithm and as a table look-up scheme to find which took less memory. The least memory approach always won out. Even the earliest NTDS computers always seemed to have adequate processing speed reserves, primarily thanks to Seymour Cray's fantastic design capability, and many times Randolph found ways to trade off processing speed in favor of less memory consumption. He quantified a moderately small amount of memory needed to accommodate the WDS Mk 11 functions, and the Fleet Computer Programming Center, Pacific, made a commitment to make exactly that amount of memory, and no more, available in the DLG-29 computer program. In the end Randolph pulled the project off, and his only regret was that he had not placed a large wager with the skeptical BUWEPS officers.

The AN/SPS-48 Radar

The reader will recall that just before Commander Irvin McNally left the Bureau of Ships in 1956 he wrote a specification for a new three dimensional air search radar to work in particular with the Naval Tactical Data System. The document did not tell how to build the radar, it was rather a performance 'spec' for a three dimensional radar like none that had ever existed before, and it was a tough requirement. Three dimensional radars had always been a problem because they had to fill roughly a hemisphere of the sky overhead full of closely spaced radar beams as the radar rotated in order to measure not only range and bearing of a target but also elevation angle. In comparison, a two-dimensional radar had only to transmit only one beam, narrow in azimuth and shaped like a broad fan in elevation, at a given bearing angle.

A two-dimensional radar could thus easily scan at a rate of one revolution every four or eight seconds while sending out beams and receiving target echoes at maximum ranges out to more than 250 miles. Existing three-dimensional air search radars, on the other hand had to either rotate much slower in order to generate the needed number of beams to get accurate elevation measurements, or they had to have their range severely restricted in order to generate all the needed beams at higher scan rates. McNally, however, called for the new radar to simultaneously have a 230 mile range coverage, and the same rotation rates as contemporary 2-D air search radars!

The seemingly impossible challenge was handed to a young civilian engineer, Donald C. Bailey, in the Bureau of Ships small 3-D Radar Development group in early 1960. By May, Bailey had converted the specification into a detailed request for proposals and issued it to the radar industry. Of the twelve companies responding, one, Gilfillan Corporation, a small Los Angeles based company that specialized in ground-controlled approach radars for airports, had a most ingenious solution. They had found a new very high powered radar transmitting tube that had the capability to rapidly change its transmitting frequency.

It was possible, using antenna design techniques that had already been perfected, to cause a radar beam to leave a flat antenna at different elevation angles by changing the transmitting frequency. Gilfillan's ingenuity lay in their idea to 'chirp' the transmitting frequency in many small frequency steps as a beam was being pulsed out from the antenna. The result was a transmitted beam that covered a number of degrees of elevation in one outgoing pulse, and from which the elevation of a target echo could be accurately measured. This 'stacked beam' feature would allow the radar to get the needed elevation coverage with a reasonably small number of pulses, and would, in theory, enable the required range coverage at eight-second antenna rotation scans.

Gilfillan Corp. won the contract for the new AN/SPS-48 3-D air search radar in June 1960. OPNAV directed that the new radar, after it was developed, tested, and qualified, would be first installed in the last six guided missile frigates of the DLG-26 class, beginning with DLG-29, in company with the Naval Tactical Data System and Weapons Direction System Mark 11 (Bailey Interview 22 Oct 1994).

Trouble in the Missile Systems

Each shipboard installation of the Terrier, Tartar, and Talos missile systems was built of tens of thousands of electromechanical components and was incredibly complex. With so many moving mechanical parts, reliability problems were rampant and small reliability or accuracy problems in one component seemed to have a way of being magnified in the complex interactions of the system environment. When the systems worked they very effectively brought down air targets, but they were difficult to maintain, tune, align, and keep in operation.

To make matters worse, the various major components of the systems, such as the missiles, launchers, magazines, fire control computers, weapons direction systems, and fire control radars were the development responsibility of different managers in the Bureau of Naval Weapons. Each manager then supplied his product to a shipbuilder who had the responsibility of installing and integrating the components aboard a ship. Too many things fell through the cracks, and there seemed to be no one authority in the bureau, other than the BUWEPS Chief himself, to set things right.

In 1962 the Secretary of the Navy directed that an overall systems approach, under the direction of a single flag-level project manager, had to be set up to manage the three missile systems. The Director of the Surface Missile Systems Project Office would have a captain level project manager in charge of each system, and they would have technical direction, funding control, and management authority over all of the sub projects that contributed components to the missile systems. Rear Admiral Eli T. Reich was assigned as project director, and Captain Robert P. (Zeke) Foreman became head of the Terrier System Project Office, the office with which the NTDS and SPS-48 radar project managers would interface in building the DLG-26 Class guided missile frigates (Foreman Interview 8 Sept. 1994).

In the fall of 1962 Don Bailey, manager of the SPS-48 radar project, got a call from his boss. Bailey was to go over to Rear Admiral Eli Reich's office and review with the admiral the many problems he had run into with the at-sea evaluations of the SPS-48 radar. Bailey proceeded warily, prepared to do battle with yet another '6,000 pound gorilla' who was out to kill Baileys project so he could get the SPS-48 project money reprogrammed into some other project. It was a way of life with Bailey. He spent as much time defending his project against predatory money reprogrammers as he did in useful management activity.

The admiral grilled Bailey in detail on each of the reported operational evaluation deficiencies. But then, to Bailey's surprise, Reich asked how much money and how much time did Bailey need to fix each of the problems? He asked what other help Bailey needed to get the SPS-48 ready for deployment. Then the 64 dollar question. Was it in any way possible to take eleven month's off the project schedule so that the SPS-48 could be first installed in the DLG-28 instead of waiting for the DLG-29? Reich wanted desperately to get the new search radar into his missile ships as soon as possible. The two hammered out a new schedule, and the help Bailey would need from the Surface Missile Systems Project to accomplish the accelerated schedule. Bailey left the meeting pleasantly surprised.

Next, Rear Admiral Reich asked the Chief of the Bureau of Ships to Send Lieutenant Commander Joe Randolph over to his office. He emphasized that he did not want any other people there cluttering up their conversation. He wanted to talk only to Randolph. The result was another new schedule, this time to get Weapons Direction System Mark 11 installed first in DLG-28 instead of waiting for DLG-29. He also needed to know exactly what support Randolph needed to do that. Armed with this information, Reich convinced the Office of the Chief of Naval Operations to move first installation of both AN/SPS-48 radar and WDS Mk 11 to USS *Wainwright* (DLG-28).

Commander Wayne Meyer and His Amazing Fire Control Radars

A New SORT of Tests

Upon being assigned to the NTDS project in 1962 after graduating from the U.S. Naval Postgraduate School, I sat down with Commander Joe Stoutenburgh, who had replaced Captain Svendsen to discuss my future assignments in the project office. He outlined the history whereby the NTDS computer itself had been used as a test instrument to verify the operability of other equipment at the NTDS test site at the Navy Electronics Lab at San Diego. He said he wanted to explore the possibility of using the computers aboard ship with special testing programs to perform equipment maintenance testing and then system level tests such as radar calibration and alignment, and even overall system operability and readiness tests. I readily agreed to the job, and we established that the assignment would make up about a quarter of my work.

Another quarter of my time was to be spent helping Lieutenant Commander Joe Randolph on Weapons Direction System Mark 11, a quarter on general office activities such as establishing a planned maintenance system and a ship's installation configuration management system for NTDS, and a quarter on setting up a more formalized and detailed program evaluation and review system, known then as Program Evaluation and Review Technique (PERT), for the

NTDS project. Stoutenburgh emphasized that none of us in the small project office could afford to get involved in great detail in any aspect of our assignments. Instead we were supposed to get our work done through other engineers and offices in the Bureau, through contractors, and Navy engineering activities. We were supposed to get ideas and task other organizations to carry them out and institutionalize them. We were supposed to identify problems, get them solved and keep the project moving. He emphasized that, as a lieutenant, I would be doing work far above my pay grade, but "Don't let it bother you." I found that the NTDS project would be a most exciting and stimulating place to work.

When the engineers and technicians assembled the prototype NTDS engineering test system at the Navy Electronics Laboratory they progressively tested each newly added piece of equipment as it was connected to the NTDS computers. For this testing they loaded the computers with special testing programs that were sort of nonsense routines. The programs did not make the equipment perform in an operational manner but rather repeatedly sequenced each piece of equipment through every possible operational feature, condition, and state to verify that the device was performing according to specification. The specialized programs were called programmed operational functional appraisals, or POFAs for short. The POFAs either printed out a report indicating the equipment was functioning OK, or they listed equipment discrepancies found by the program. It did not take too much stretch of the imagination to realize that these programs could be further improved and formalized as maintenance testing aids for delivery to fleet ships as part of the NTDS package.

My first technical task in the project office was to start formalizing the POFAs into complete documented maintenance testing packages for the NTDS installations on each ship class. Then we planned to extend the same concepts as far out from NTDS into the other ship systems as we could push them. The job was to include developing and managing the installation of the required physical changes in the ships' systems to accommodate such system level testing. We would have to make changes to ships cabling, wiring and switchboards in order to send out testing signals from the NTDS computer and receive back test responses, measurements and reference signals. We also realized we would have to develop new analog/digital conversion devices to allow the NTDS computer to talk more fluently with other non-NTDS shipboard systems.

William C. 'Billy' O'Sullivan, the NTDS ship installation engineer, was assigned as project partner in developing the testing package because he would have to be involved in bringing about the required ship system changes. We set up a contract with Univac to work out engineering details, develop the necessary computer programs, verify the computer programs and provide technical support to ship's companies and the activities who would do ship's system acceptance testing.

We laid out a sequential approach to building the test package. First, a method of quickly measuring and correcting radar alignment errors was urgently needed to help eliminate the endemic problem of generating multiple NTDS tracks on a single target, and to ensure quickest possible fire control radar lock-on when a track was passed from NTDS to the missile or gun systems. Therefore after the POFAs would come a series of automated tests to measure alignment errors among shipboard search radars, fire control radars and other sensor systems. These we named System Calibration and Alignment Tests, or SCATs. Following that would be a package of tests to measure and assess the man/machine performance of a number of NTDS functions such as surface navigation, surface and air tracking, weapons direction operations, and air intercept control. This series was named ship systems operational readiness tests (SSORT). The entire package of all the various test types also had to have a name. It became ship's operational readiness tests, or SORT.

One Pass Around Mare Island is All You Get

Belknap (DLG-26), the first new construction ship to receive NTDS, was the first target of the SORT package. *Belknap* was on the building ways at Bath Iron Works, and the builder was scheduled to start NTDS installation in late 1963. This gave us about sixteen months to have the first part of the package ready. Our goal was to complete the entire package including the SSORT tests for the DLG-26.

The mechanically pointed, pencil beam, AN/SPG-55B fire control radar directors of the Terrier missile system were incredibly accurate. In our concept they were to be the primary instrumentation radars for the ship system test packages. Search radar inputs to the automated radar alignment tests were to be entered into the NTDS computer in the normal manner as manually tracked air targets, but there was a problem getting the fire control radar pointing angles and range fed into the NTDS computer. What we needed for our alignment tests were the same very accurate signals that the missile system radar directors sent to the analog fire control computers, but we needed them routed to the NTDS keyset central's analog-to-digital converters.

The missile fire control radars would also be the key reference instruments for the SSORT tests that measured the combined performance of the ship's system and the ship's operators. In the air and surface tracking tests, the fire control radars would be locked onto the same targets that were being manually tracked at NTDS consoles to get a good measure of NTDS tracking accuracy. In the air intercept control tests, we would lock one fire control radar onto the intended air target and one onto the interceptor. The resultant fire control radar measurements, when fed back to the NTDS computer, allowed accurate automated reconstruction of the intercept and assessment of the probability of a kill.

The weapons direction function tests would exercise one missile system in a normal missile shoot while the test conductors locked the other missile fire control radar onto the fired missile soon after launch so that the testing program could record the missile's track and plot how close it came to the target. These radar measurements, in company with recording all operator actions and system events, allowed accurate reconstruction of the engagement sequence, the target and missile tracks, and assessment of probability of missile kill.

O'Sullivan and I visited Commander Wayne Meyer, the Terrier fire control systems manager in the Surface Missile Systems Project Office to get his help in bringing the fire control radar signals back to NTDS. Commander Meyer really did not need an engineering duty lieutenant and a young civilian engineer from BUSHIPS trying to make changes in his fire control systems. His plate of work was already overflowing and, furthermore, Lieutenant Commander Joe Randolph's Weapons Direction System Mark 11 project had already raised the discomfort level in BUWEPS enough.

Meyer listened impatiently and gruffly asked pointed technical questions, but after some discussion, he seemed to sense that, if it worked, perhaps the digital system testing capability could be of some use to Terrier system operability testing. He was a strong advocate of daily system operability testing. Radar alignment in particular was a time consuming evolution requiring test ranges or portable radar targets, hours to conduct and many technical man hours of data reduction, analysis, and plotting.

Meyer agreed to help us run signal cables from the Terrier and Tartar fire control radar directors down the hill to the WDS Mk 11 test site at the Mare Island Naval Schools Command at Vallejo, CA. If we showed that the NTDS computer could calculate the statistics on alignment errors among the test site fire control and search radars while tracking a single aircraft in one pass around the site, he would support making the requisite changes in the DLG-26 Class ships.

In a couple of weeks the cabling had been connected between the systems and we went out to the test site to watch the Univac engineers try out their new radar alignment test programs with live air targets. They worked!, and we brought the test print outs back to Commander Meyer who kept his end of the bargain and endorsed our efforts to get the ship's cabling and switchboard changes in the DLG-26 Class ship's plans. The shipbuilding specifications for the nine ships of the class were already written and embodied in shipbuilding contracts and naval shipyard shipbuilding orders. Billy O'Sullivan and I were thus scheduled to appear before the BUSHIPS Change Review Board (CRB) to try to convince them that we should be allowed to make the system changes.

The CRB was a body of highly critical senior naval officers and civil servants who had to be convinced of the value of each proposed change, that it was feasible, that it could be done without disrupting shipbuilding schedules, and that there was a source of funding for the change. I had hardly opened my mouth at the start of our hearing when the admiral in charge of the board asked, "What in hell is a digital computer?" Fortunately there was a blackboard in the room and I drew and explained a block diagram of a rudimentary digital computer, and it seemed that the board members were staying with it. Next, however, when I stated that sailors would load a special computer program into the computer to run the alignment tests, it seemed to blow their minds. The next question was, "Now what in the hell is a computer program?"

The board members, like most of the rest of humanity in the early 1960s, were accustomed to devices and equipment that did only one thing, and trying to guide them through the concept of a device that could be made to do just about any function that involved handling information by virtue of loading a different program in it was beginning to stretch their credibility. O'Sullivan and I were beginning to despair of getting our system change orders approved when the admiral abruptly brought the meeting to a halt by saying, "I think you can see that we don't know what the hell you two guys are talking about. But, you seem to know what you are doing, and you seem to be honest and sincere. Also, we note that the Terrier project office is supporting your wild ideas." They approved the changes with the strong injunction that if our project ever even showed a hint of shipbuilding schedule delay or disruption claims, it would be immediately terminated. We agreed that was a fair trade and quickly retreated from the hearing room while we were still ahead. O'Sullivan and I would be back before the board many more times as the project progressed.

Development and test of the DLG-26 Class SORT package progressed well, and the computer programs and system changes were verified at the Mare Island test site. The final testing stages at Mare Island provided some exciting times as we graduated from using passing airliners as test targets of opportunity, and arrangement were made for Navy F-4H Phantom fighters and professional air intercept controllers to wring out the tests in a live air environment. The next step was final verification of the computer programs, their documentation, and the ship system changes aboard *Belknap*, which by the fall of 1963 was floating alongside a construction pier at Bath Iron Works. The Sedgewick Hotel at Bath, Maine, would become my home-away-from-home for many months.

You're Doing Research and Development on My Ship!

The Navy Supervisor of Shipbuilding and the management at Bath Iron Works (BIW) had warily agreed to give our Univac engineers evening and weekend use of *Belknap's* NTDS installation—in return for the unproved promise that the automated tests would shorten system checkout time not only in *Belknap*, but also in the four following ships of the class that BIW was building. The individual NTDS equipment test programs, the POFAs, were already in daily use and working well. The next stage, however, the automated system calibration and alignment tests using the missile fire control radars was totally new, and a certain amount of shipbuilder apprehension was building up. The apprehension was somewhat relieved when we first tried the SCATs while the ship was lying dockside with the fire control and search radars tracking a passing airliner. Things went quietly until one of the BUWEPS contractor engineers looked at an NTDS console and realized that the NTDS computer was writing the running averages of the radar alignment errors on the radar scope as the airplane passed by the ship. "I'll be damned!", he excitedly exclaimed, "It's reducing the data right now! Dammit, will you look at this!" Digital technology gained a few converts that day.

The next phase, in the fall of 1964, was testing the test programs while the ship was underway on builder's trials. This brought live roll, pitch and heading inputs from the ship's gyrocompass into the system. The Terrier Project Office also took advantage of the ship's motion inputs to perform further verification testing of the newly installed Mk 76 Terrier missile fire control systems, and a number of BUWEPS contractor technical representatives were riding *Belknap* for this purpose.

Although I had become good friends with the contractor engineers, and they had given us considerable technical support in verifying the workings of the NTDS-to-weapon system interfaces, they were still skeptical of the new digital technology. They, in company with many other weapons engineers, could not grasp how digital computers that executed only one instruction at a time could possibly keep up with the continuum of parallel multiple happenings in an analog world. They also had grave reservations about the reliability of the NTDS computers. They did not see how they could possibly run for more than a couple of hours, at most, before component failures shut them down.

Belknap's data system technicians loaded and ran the ship's NTDS operational computer program, and ship's company operators tracked air targets of opportunity as the ship steamed down the Kennebec River toward Casco Bay on the Atlantic Ocean. Once in Casco Bay the ship was to rendezvous with a Navy airplane, which would be our test target for the day. As the ship entered the bay, our target aircraft called in, and the chief petty officer at the system monitoring panel called over to me, "I'll stop the op program and load your SCAT program now." I nodded OK, and the Chief began typing the commands to stop the computers and load the SCAT program from the magnetic tape unit.

The space layout in *Belknap* had the NTDS computers and peripheral equipment located in a small compartment, called the unattended equipment area, immediately below the combat information center. We did not realize it at the time but, one deck below us, one of the BUWEPS contractor engineers had been occupying himself watching the blinking lights on the computer maintenance panels. Suddenly we heard rapid footsteps coming up the ladder from the unattended equipment area, and the engineer burst into the CIC. "I knew they couldn't last!," he shouted. Like a halfback spiking the ball after an 80 yard touchdown run, he exulted, "NTDS is down! The computers just stopped!" Without even looking up, the Chief murmured, "Go look again." By the time the engineer got back down to the computers, the magnetic tape reels were spinning and the lights on the computer maintenance panels were blinking again. This time he emerged very slowly at the top of the ladder with a most puzzled and downcast expression. He retired to a dark corner of the CIC to think over what he had just seen.

As *Belknap's* construction and testing proceeded toward commissioning as a U.S. Navy ship, a new factor entered our equation, Captain John T. Law. Captain Law, first Commanding Officer of *Belknap*, had just come from a tour in Washington, D.C., in the Office of the Chief of Naval Operations. Unfortunately for us, as one of his last acts in OPNAV, he had written the new OPNAV instruction on the formal procedure required when arranging to get ships and aircraft services to support research and development projects. Captain Law took a great interest in NTDS and he made it a point to attend many of our working meetings with the shipbuilder and members of his crew who were participating in systems checkout. He also visited the NTDS Project Office from time-to-time, and we filled him in on our planned activities.

After every meeting Captain Law would usually exclaim, "It sure looks like you're doing research and development on my ship." Whereupon he would hand me a copy of the OPNAV instruction on use of fleet assets for research and development support. I would protest that the test proofing was just part of the normal shipbuilding process for the first ship in a new class, and I would remind him of all the extra training and project office assistance his crew was getting by participating in the tests.

In truth, we were learning that the first ship of a class with a new NTDS system did need time reservations during shipbuilding and sea trials to check out the automated test package computer programs as well as the new NTDS operational computer programs. To alleviate the problem in the future, we worked the required time reservations, funding and support requirements into the general BUSHIPS shipbuilding specifications for future first ships of a class, but that didn't help us much in dealing with Captain Law on *Belknap*.

USS *Belknap* became a commissioned U.S. Navy ship on 7 November 1964, and after two months of fitting out at Boston Naval Shipyard, the ship left for her assigned home port at Mayport, Florida. The next phase in the ship's life was to be two and a half months of Ship's Qualification Trials where the ship's company would be coached by a Ship Qualification Assist Team (SQAT) in shaking down and learning the operation of the new weapon systems. The bulk of the SQAT team was made up of BUWEPS field activity and contractor missile system specialists, and we arranged to add a handful of our own contractor and Navy technical specialists to the team They were to teach ship's company how to run the programs and interpret the test results; and, on *Belknap*, to verify that the SSORT computer programs worked properly in live air intercept and missile firing operations. The qualification trials still had an undeniable flavor of research and development.

I rode the ship with the team during the first week of trials, and compared notes with Captain Law at week's end. His summary was, "Boslaugh, you're still doing research and development on my ship, and I'm thinking of kicking your team off." After some negotiation he agreed that the team could continue for another week, after which he would call me in Washington to discuss the fate of the testing program for the following week. For the next two months, except for every third week when I rode the ship, Captain Law called me at the NTDS Project Office every Friday night. He would fill me in on test and training progress, exclaim that I was still running an R&D project on his ship, and formally evict my team from the ship. We would then negotiate the conditions for continued test conduct, and by Monday morning the team would somehow be back aboard *Belknap*.

Toward the end of *Belknap's* Ships Qualification Trials during a visit to the Terrier System Project Office I described the travails of SSORT testing on *Belknap*. Wayne Meyer, now a captain, grinned and said that he would be the last person to rejoice in someone else's misfortune, but that he was usually engaged in the same sort of informal shipboard research and development and received the same kind of feedback from some skippers. He noted that his team had tested a number of new Terrier system features aboard *Belknap* during the qualification trials and had drawn an unusually small amount of flack. He laughed and said, "Now I know who was drawing the fire."

The SPS-48 Radar and WDS Mk 11 Go to Sea

Wainwright (DLG-28) was laid down on the Bath Iron Works building ways on 2 July 1962 and launched on 25 April 1964. It was to be the first ship to receive the combination of the new AN/SPS-48 radar and Weapons Direction System Mark 11 incorporated into the Naval Tactical Data System. By September 1964 all combat system equipment was installed and ready for checkout with computer programs. The moment of truth had arrived for Lieutenant Commander Joe Randolph's Weapons Direction System Mk 11 equipment and new computer program.

We were overjoyed when we learned that Captain 'Zeke' Foreman, head of the Terrier missile system project had been assigned as prospective commanding officer of *Wainwright*. He had lived and breathed the Terrier system and WDS Mk 11 for the past few years, and we knew that he had but one goal—to make the new system work. The Bureau of Naval Personnel had also done something else uncommonly intelligent. The Bureau had also assigned two of *Wainwright's* future key personnel, prospective CIC Officer Lieutenant Clifford L. Laning and Chief Data Systems Technician Michael Snodgrass, to the Weapons Direction System Mark 11 test site at Mare Island during the preceding year. There they had participated extensively in evaluating the SPS-48 radar, WDS Mk 11, and the Fleet Computer Programming Center's new NTDS operational program for DLG-28 and the rest of her class.

Laning and Snodgrass had not only done testing at Mare Island, they had made suggestions for system improvement, many of which were now embodied in the new equipment and computer programs. They were part of the crime. They went so far as to set up and give classes on the new system not only to their own ship's company but to Bath Iron Works engineers and technicians, and following ship's companies. They were now the experts and they sparked the team that tested and verified the new combat system installation. When the time came for personnel from the Fleet Computer Programming Center, Pacific, in San Diego to install and test the new NTDS operational computer program containing the WDS Mk 11 functionality aboard *Wainwright*, the team of ship's company, BIW, and Programming Center personnel had the program debugged and up and running in the incredibly short time of three days of round the clock work (Laning Letter 21 Jan. 1995). It could have taken weeks. The new combat system was ready to go to sea.

Thus it would come to pass that when USS *Biddle* (DLG-34) became a commissioned ship of the line on 21 January 1967 she would be one of seven new ships having the tightest integration of sensors, men, and weapons as well as the shortest reaction time from detection of a hostile target to taking that target under fire of any ship in the U.S. Navy

Missile Cruisers in the Cold War

Tom Marfiak

To understand the USS *Biddle* in the context of her distinguished record of service, we must first understand the role these cruisers played in the Cold War. They were the natural extension of the destroyers that served with such gallantry throughout the Second World War, Korea and Vietnam. They were armed to the teeth, and had the advantage of sensor and combat systems that far exceeded anything their predecessors had enjoyed. And, like any great lady, they were maintenance intensive. Their crews, proud to serve, took extreme care to ensure that their topsides were spotless, their weapons systems ready, and their engineering plants ready to sustain combat operations at the heart of the far ranging carrier battle groups.

The searing experience of the Kamikaze attacks in the Pacific campaign gave birth to a series of programs to ensure that the fleet would never again be so vulnerable. Missile systems were developed, capable of striking a target at ranges in excess of thirty miles. Search and fire control radars were perfected that enabled tracks to be identified well beyond that. All of these systems and more had to be manned by numbers of talented operators, maintained by technicians who knew missiles, computers, and electronics intimately, and provided a constant source of reliable electricity and cooling from their complex engineering plants. All of this had to go forward while the great ship leapt through all sea conditions and kept pace with the fast moving carrier. From the confines of the bridge, to CIC, and to the ever-busy spaces of the engineering department, teamwork was the key. Each center of excellence depended on the other to do its job perfectly, without delay, to ensure the optimum performance of the mission.

By the mid to late seventies, these ships were reaching their peak. The fleet was modernizing around them. The long, sleek destroyers of WWII vintage had been replaced with the *Knox* class frigates, with their single screws and large sonars, testimony to the Soviet submarine threat. The densely packed combat systems of the *Adams* Class guided missile destroyers, also propelled by 1200 psi steam systems, added significant punch to the battle group, and substantial close-in defense to the carrier. Their position in plane guard, or close to the ever trailing Soviet tell-tale *Krivak*, was part of the normal scene at sea.

Yet the top of the line remained the guided missile cruisers. To serve aboard was considered an honor. To fight her alongside the enormous bulk of the carrier, in all the world's oceans, was considered the highest mark of professional excellence. Power, grace, elegance, sea keeping—these ships had it all. Packed into their eight thousand tons was a veritable city of striking power, over four hundred men, working seamlessly to keep their ship at the finest degree of readiness, whatever the conditions, however long the hours or days, or however high the seas.

Many will remember the debate over the merits of the double and single ended cruisers. The former were armed at both ends with a Terrier missile system. They were purely anti air warfare machines. The latter, of which USS *Biddle* was a member, were single ended, carrying a massive Standard missile and antisubmarine, or ASROC, launcher system forward, and a single five-inch gun aft. They were nuclear capable. In addition, substantial secondary armament, first three-inch guns and then Vulcan Phalanx systems, afforded close-in protection. They were the equal of their peers, the nuclear powered cruisers and the remaining gun cruisers still at sea, the flag ships like USS *Albany* and the others. The talent on the bridge made it all mesh, whether operating with the carrier or in solo operations against the Soviet fleet. That talent was amplified by the resources of CIC, assembling operational information in real time, and giving the bridge team the benefit of it all. Teamwork, then and now, made the difference. USS *Biddle* was always in the front rank, testimony to the sustained excellence of successive generations of crews and a distinguished line of captains.

These men, the leaders who had come to their commands from the trials of World War II, the Korean War, and Vietnam, who had mounted the ladder of command through the demands of their profession, were the ideal to which we all aspired. They each had their own style of leadership, from the lofty and distant, inspiring through example and the well chosen word, to the personal and unique, about whom stories are still told in Happy Hours and reunions. Yet, they all achieved the union of mission and crew and ship to sustain the United States at sea when the security of the world, and the maintenance of the peace, depended on it.

This book is about one ship, one series of brave crews and their commanders. It would be difficult, even with audio and visual support, to convey the environment in which they operated, yet the astute reader will know that between the lines is the story of dedication and sacrifice, the entire ship leaning forward as a whole, into the night and the blowing spray, ready, always ready, for the next challenge. Take yourself to the bridge, where the only light is the dim sweep of the radar consoles, and voices are subdued as the great ship races through the fleet to a new station. Imagine yourself in combat, surrounded by glowing screens and the clamor of multiple communications circuits as the complex ballet of air, surface and subsurface forces is brought to perfect coordination. All of this is sustained by four giant boilers, two engine sets, and innumerable pumps driving two great shafts propelling the cruiser to whatever speed might be required, and then some.

They are now gone, these wonderful ships, and their crews are aging. But we remember them.

Their successors are the AEGIS cruisers and destroyers of today, driven by gas turbines, carrying enormous missile loads and destined to carve out a new mission in long range anti-missile defense against inter-continental threats—a long reach from their brothers of the Second World War and the gun line off the coast of Vietnam. If you are patient, you may still find them in the inactive ship maintenance facilities, their paint fading, their masts long since stripped of their purposefully rotating antennas, their decks strangely absent of human form. But we remember them rather as they were—alive and humming with activity, the energy of steam stretching throughout their limbs, ready to unleash incredible power at the nod of the head, or the utterance of a quiet word of command.

Where men stand to the watch today or tomorrow, in the dark of night, or in the gray mists of early dawn, off some far hostile shore or in the midst of ships assembled to execute the needs of the United States and her allies, these stories have great relevance. There is a common tie amongst all of those who go to sea in the great waters of the world, locked in the embrace of such ships as these. Let us remember, and be glad.

Department Organization Aboard a Guided Missile Cruiser

Tom Marfiak

The steam powered cruisers of the Cold War shared many of the cultural characteristics of their predecessors, the big eight inch gun cruisers, with only a third of the crew. Their commanders, senior captains of significant professional attainment, mirrored that heritage. They were characters in their own right. Some were colorful, while others took refuge in the aerie of command. In any event, it was a special privilege to serve under their leadership, to learn lessons of seamanship and command under their aegis. The organization that extended beneath them involved four principal departments—Weapons, Operations, Engineering and Supply, with Navigation serving under the Captain and Executive Officer to assure the safety of the ship in all circumstances. Department heads were Lieutenant Commanders, while the Executive Officer, a full Commander, would serve the senior Navy Captain in command. How were they organized? What responsibilities did they perform? The following paragraphs will attempt to give you, the reader, some idea of how they came together to create the true essence of the ship, its combat effectiveness.

The Role of the Commanding Officer

During this period, Commanding Officers came in many different forms. Some had been schooled in the Navy of the great gun cruisers, and tended to continue that tradition. Others understood the new systems much better, and worked to gain the most from them. All were adept at making their ships highly capable units of the fleet. Working through the Executive Officer and department heads, they imprinted their standards on the crew and on the operations of the ship itself. Even today, years later, their names are part of our memory. Some of them, Commanding Officers of USS *Biddle*, have spoken here. Their recollections could be mirrored by those of other captains during the same period, or those of captains of our AEGIS cruisers today. The tasks are the same, and the environment, intolerant of neglect or inaction, is unchanged.

Standing on the bridge or in the midst of CIC, the chatter of the watch ongoing, the Commanding Officer represented the ship and all who sailed in her. His alone was the responsibility, according to Navy regulations, for her safety and operational effectiveness. The actions of the department heads, or the keenness of the Executive Officer, could assist him, but they could not take his place, or be an adequate excuse for inadequate performance. He alone had to integrate all aspects of the command, consider the timing of each operation, and plan each operation in his head, balancing intelligence and real time knowledge.

The Role of the Executive Officer

"XO," is a cherished position within the Navy. Second in command, next to the Commanding Officer, confidant, war fighter, organizational wizard, he is adept at thinking on his feet, adapting to every circumstance, no matter how fast events might move, to keep the ship at peak efficiency. He is the arbiter for the majority of issues between the departments, and the chief planner for the evolutions that each ship must accomplish on a daily basis. His department, the Yeomen of the ship's office, is responsible for the all-important Plan of the Day governing the activities of all departments. In port, his duties include the handling of all correspondence, the preparation of all disciplinary matters and the interaction between embarked staff and the ship's company. At sea, he is everywhere. There is no better school for command than Executive Officer of a cruiser.

Navigation Department

The Navigator reported to the Commanding Officer, but in the matter of course worked most closely with the Executive Officer. Generally a senior Lieutenant, the Navigator was an experienced lad of upward pretensions. His department was composed of Quartermasters, an enlisted rating with particular responsibility for charts and navigation techniques. It was their job to keep the ship going in the right direction, on the premise that "A collision at sea can ruin your whole day." In the days before electronic navigation, they maintained the paper charts, plotted the courses, kept the logs and timekeeping pieces, and generally managed the entire bridge. Since celestial navigation was still practiced, they were instrumental in keeping the sextants ready, training the junior officers in that fine art and plotting the results of the sights taken. When entering a foreign port, particularly one not often visited, they were key and essential, researching the available resources, laying down the courses to be followed and competently plotting the approach.

It is important to note that this navigation expertise was not unique to the Navigation Department. The Operation Department also kept a close track on the ship's navigation and the teamwork between the two departments kept the ship in safe water at all times. Many groundings might have been avoided had that teamwork not broken down, or had the commander not neglected to heed the warnings of one source or the other.

Weapons Department

The Terrier Missile system, the nuclear weapons and the guns and torpedoes of the ships armament all came under the management of the Weapons Department. Gunners Mates administered to the readiness of the five inch mount and the three inch gun mounts (to be replaced by Harpoon launchers in later iterations). Missile Gunners Mates cared for the magazines and launchers. Fire Control Technicians watched over the fire control directors vital to the effective operation of the missile firing system. Together, they formed the heart of the Weapons Department.

The Weapons Department also included the deck division, headed by the First Lieutenant. He had a very difficult job—leading the First Division, generally composed of the least talented and educated on board, to assure the smartness of the ship's outward appearance, including the boats and boat handling, and multiple ship's evolutions, such as refueling at sea, where technical knowledge and deck seamanship both came into play. It was the mark of a smart ship that such evolutions, no matter how complex, could be carried off with smoothness and precision.

Since these ships also carried nuclear weapons, there was an entire level of security and administration that was added to the standard tasks. Administration and security were carried to extraordinarily high levels. Periodic examinations, conducted by gimlet-eyed inspectors from the shore establishment, were designed to insure that no comma was neglected. All of it added to the aura of a cruiser sailor—high professionalism, higher standards, no errors permitted.

Below the water was an entirely different story. Equipped with a large hull-mounted sonar, an ASROC missile capability and torpedo tubes, the cold war cruiser could be a formidable anti-submarine warfare opponent. Sonar Technicians, schooled in the vagaries of underwater acoustics, watched over the sonar and ASW-related weapons systems. In concerted ASW operations, they manned consoles in CIC to talk with airborne sensors, both helicopters and maritime patrol aircraft, to prosecute Soviet submarines in proximity to the battle group.

Needless to say, the care and preening of their systems occupied a majority of their time.

Operations Department

The Operations Department would be superseded in later cruisers by the Combat Systems Department, a combination of the Weapons and Operations Departments of these days. However, in the sixties and seventies, the Operations Department was the natural development of the weapons/operations synthesis that had begun during World War II. Arleigh Burke would have loved to have this capability. The Operations Officer and his department manned CIC, the nerve center of the ship. The Operations Specialists inhabited CIC, manning the radars and plotting stations as well as the communications and providing the backbone of the combat organization. They were augmented by the communications gang, the Radiomen who handled Radio Central and the Signalmen who handled all the visual communications, including flashing light and flag hoists. Seventy years after Jutland, we were still reliant on visual means for close-in maneuvering. In addition, the Electronics Technicians and Radarmen were responsible for the care and feeding of the sensor systems, the surface and air search radars, perpetually turning above the masts, to provide input to the crew in CIC and to alert the weapons operators when the missile systems were called on.

Once underway, whether for three weeks or six months, they went on the watch twenty four hours a day, as did the rest of the crew. One did not have to ask who was on watch, or wonder who would answer the net. Unless there had been a dire event, the same voice would answer, the same steady professional would be there. Nelson's lines of frigates off the coast of France must have had the same steadiness on watch.

Engineering Department

These cruisers were built about an engineering plant that filled fully half the hull and extended into every nook and cranny. The centerpiece of the array was a steam plant with twelve hundred pounds per square inch of pressure. World War II destroyers operated a steam plant with six hundred pounds per square inch of pressure. With the added displacement of the modern cruiser, only the massively increased energy of the 1200 psi system could provide the propulsive energy to move the ship in excess of thirty knots. But, as anyone will tell you who served aboard these ships, it came at quite a cost. First, mistakes could be fatal; a steam leak could cut off an arm. A fire could gut an engineering space. Standards had to be very high. Second, before the days of strict examinations, qualifications varied widely. No matter how smart a ship looked from the outside, danger always lurked within. The best cruisers operated seamlessly, making the difficult look easy.

The master of this domain was the Engineering Officer, alias "CHENG." To be called by that name was not a term of Chinese endearment, but a note of respect, for the Engineer and his department provided the energy that was the life of the ship. All the services, from production of water and light to propulsion and operation of boats, that made her live and made possible every other task on board, was the responsibility of the Engineering Department. Assisted by several junior officers, the Engineering Officer administered to an empire that included all the propulsion systems, the boilers, steam turbines, and electrical generation plant, the evaporators that supplied the purest water for the boilers and crew and the myriad of auxiliaries that provided the special power needed by the combat systems, the boats and davits, the gun systems and sonars and radars, the galleys and laundries and the damage control preparations that would determine the ship's survivability in the event of damage or attack.

Propulsion systems were the domain of the Boiler Technicians, the Machinist Mates and the Electricians Mates. Each was a very different group. The BT's were rough and ready, tattooed and hardworking, surrounded by their boilers, fuel rigs and pumps. If you had their allegiance, there wasn't much you couldn't do. The MM's ran the plant, with its gleaming deck plates, boards full of gauges and engine rooms crammed full of machinery, including the all-important evaporators that produced the water upon which the life of the ship depended. The EM's ran the electrical plant, and with their brethren, the Interior Communications Technicians, provided the types of electricity, from 60 cycles to 400 cycles, that drove the vast array of systems on board. There were, of course, union differences, but woe betide the unfortunate member of the Weapons or Operations departments who might cast an unfortunate remark in their direction. On shore and at sea, they were one team, one fight.

Beyond the propulsion spaces, the Auxiliary Officer held sway. His division had responsibility for all the systems that supported the ship outside the propulsion box. Ice cube maker not working? Air conditioning awry? No problem—a call to Damage Control Central would soon result in a capable response.

The Damage Control Assistant, another key adjunct to the CHENG, had responsibility for working with all the departments to assure the proper status of every door, hatch or closure within the ship, as well as all the emergency pumps and damage control lockers throughout the ship. Memories of the Okinawa campaigns were still strong within the Navy then. From shoring to fire fighting apparatus, readiness of each component of the DCA's empire was expected at any moment. As the events of the USS *Belknap* collision emphasized, the moment might come when the ship's survival depended on them.

They cared for the boats, the gig, the whaleboat and utility boat (a large personnel carrier). They took care of the helicopter refueling and lighting and the extensive water wash down system, designed to cleanse the ship of nuclear fallout, in the event of such an engagement. They handled everything from the ice cream machine to the movie projectors.

One key component of the Engineering Department was the Machinery Repair Shop. They could fix or repair just about anything on board. With their lathes and welding equipment, they could make parts for washing machines or gun systems, boat steering systems or valve stems. Some of them were unconventional human beings, with earrings and tattoos, but they were wizards on their task, and kept us going notwithstanding the circumstances.

Supply Department

The Supply Officer and the Supply Department provided all those things that make life livable, from pay to clean laundry, from repair parts to paying foreign vendors for fresh vegetables. Their labors were unceasing. The galley worked around the clock to prepare top quality meals. Many a mid watch was made more enjoyable by a shipment of fresh rolls from the early baking cycle. The Pay Clerks and Supply Clerks kept the records up to date and, no matter how intense the operations, ensured that pay records were kept accurately and questions answered with dispatch. No task was too small or too unimportant.

Foremost among those tasks was the need to feed the crew. The gleaming kettles in the galley were never empty for long. The ovens turned forth a constant stream of meals, from pizza to roast beef. In the wardroom and the chief's mess, special meals might be concocted, served on Navy china and accompanied by such things as spices and A-1 sauce not available in the general mess. The wardroom, in the finest Navy tradition, dined on starched white tablecloths, with china and sterling silver cutlery. The Executive Officer, as president of the mess, presided. The Steward's Mates presided over all with pride and efficiency. The Supply Department ran it all.

Far below the main decks, the laundry provided clean clothes, starched khaki uniforms and carefully packaged underwear on a regular basis. There were certainly irregularities, as when one's favorite shirt returned reduced to one third of its original size, but they were few and far between, and contributed immensely to the merriment of wardroom conversation when they did happen.

The true measure of the Supply Officer would come into play when there was a major casualty to a key system, or when a call on a foreign port required the utmost in collaboration with foreign vendors. The best supply officers excelled on those occasions, conjuring up parts from nowhere, and making deals for foodstuffs and tours for sailors that kept up morale.

Department Coordination

Obviously, the work of all the departments had to be coordinated closely to ensure the proper working of the ship. Every morning the XO would call his leaders together for Officers' Call. Notes would be exchanged and the day's activities reviewed. One had the chance to observe the relative health and energy levels of one's peers. Then, throughout the day, cooperation between and amongst those key department leaders would resolve one problem after another, just as it does today. Again, in the evening, Eight O'clock Reports, generally conducted at 1930, before the evening watch or movie call (depending on one's circumstances), would provide yet another opportunity to assess the readiness of the command to conduct the next series of operations. Each meeting might be followed by a series of communications to key department command centers. The Engineering Officer, for example, would provide his "Night Orders" to the department, detailing tasks to be performed overnight, information on what to prepare for the next day, and the alignment of the plant during the next several hours. Similar orders would be prepared for the other departments. The Captain's "Night Orders" would give overall direction to the bridge and watch teams. It was always understood that he could be called in an instant if circumstances so indicated. It would be the brave watch officer, in CIC or on the bridge, who did so. In any event, it was seldom required—if operations were intense, the Captain would already be on the bridge or in CIC. One did not have to ask.

Biddle at Bath

James Treadway

Authorized by Congress on 17 September 1961 and ordered by the Navy on 16 January 1962, *Biddle's* keel was laid on 9 December 1963, the three hundred forty seventh keel laid at Bath Iron Works (BIW), Bath, Maine. *Biddle* was the last of nine *Belknap* Class guided missile frigates and the eighth built by BIW of the *Leahy* and *Belknap* Classes. The fact that she was the last of her class to be built is significant—*Biddle* was the recipient of the accumulated knowledge and experience from building seventeen similar, if not identical, ships. *Biddle* was christened by her sponsor, Mrs. William H. Bates of Salem, Massachusetts, and launched on 2 July 1965.

With *Biddle's* completion still nine months away, members of the nucleus crew began arriving in early 1966. *Biddle's* first NTDS Officer, Lieutenant Robert Gerity, was the first officer to report aboard when he arrived in February. Fresh from duty as instructor and division head at NTDS School at Mare Island, California, and, before that, CIC Officer at Dam Neck, Virginia, Lieutenant Gerity assumed duties as Acting Prospective Commanding Officer (PCO) and NTDS Officer. He remembers that "she was frozen in ice and had puddles of ice in interior compartments that were opened to the outside. The superstructure was unpainted and cables were strung everywhere. I was fortunate to have a good friend in DLG-32 (*Standley*, tied next to *Biddle*) who was able to help me get oriented."

Lieutenant Gerity had served in one other new construction ship less than six years before and was well prepared to tackle the problems encountered at BIW. The administrative workload was heavy. Lieutenant Gerity continues: "The nucleus crew had to learn a lot about Builder's Trials (BT) and Preliminary Acceptance Trials (PAT), the trial card system (a list of deficiencies), who does what at Naval Ship Systems Command (NAVSHIPS) and the Type Commanders staff. There is only the school of hard knocks for that. I was very fortunate to have some talented people to help me during this period, such as DSC Dave Johnson, whom I had the foresight to Shanghai when I got my orders to *Biddle*. I was especially pleased by the high quality technicians we got ordered in, both ET's and DS's."

When I reported aboard a few weeks later, Lieutenant Gerity exclaimed, "Congratulations, Petty Officer Treadway, you are the first enlisted man to report aboard." Well, it turns out, maybe not. Thirty four years later, at *Biddle's* first "All Hands" reunion, DC Chief George Rochefort claimed that when he reported aboard, no one was at the nucleus crew headquarters at BIW, so he took some time off to locate housing. Meanwhile, I had reported aboard and submitted my orders, thus becoming the first enlisted man to "officially" report aboard even though George may have arrived first. Soon, the trickle became a steady downpour and the pool of sailors swelled to fill the billets.

Biddle's first commanding officer, Captain Maylon Truxtun Scott, a descendant of Revolutionary War naval officer Thomas Truxtun, reported aboard as PCO in June 1966. A 1943 graduate of the U.S. Naval Academy and a World War II combat veteran, Captain Scott had previously commanded the USS *Otterstetter* (DER-244) and USS *Mitscher* (DL-2). Captain Scott, a destroyer man for his entire career, was well suited for the formidable task before him—transform a lifeless steel and aluminum vessel brimming with the latest weapons and computers into a high tech fighting machine and then take that vessel into combat in a very short period of time. Even before receiving his orders to *Biddle* he was working to form the team that would be the nucleus crew. By the time he reported aboard he had chosen "Hard Charger" as *Biddle's* call sign, forgoing the opportunity to choose "Great Scott." Soon after his arrival at BIW, Captain Scott's "Can do" attitude was firmly embedded in the ship's structure which resulted in *Biddle* being able to complete a rigorous shakedown training in record time and then depart for combat operations in the Gulf of Tonkin (GOT) one year and one day after commissioning.

Under Captain Scott's direction, *Biddle's* nucleus crew established a solid foundation for future crews—a foundation based on attention to detail, preparation, teamwork, and technical prowess. *Biddle's* exemplary 27-year career was constructed on that foundation. One officer remembered that Captain Scott "knew more about people and how to effectively manage and motivate them than any other commanding officer I ever knew. That was a quality that no one else could have provided and probably the single, essential key to most of *Biddle's* success. He is, and remains, an amazing, contradictory, odd, corny, sophisticated, marvelously successful officer. That's another book." The same officer went on to say "There were some unusual (compared to other ships I served in) dynamics among this crew as, for a period of the entire year following commissioning, no one left [the ship.] In retrospect, some very astute personnel management techniques were employed to take advantage of this situation and permit the full sweep of the considerable talent among us to focus on tasks up the track. This approach made all the difference."

Lieutenant Commander Fred Howe, *Biddle's* first Weapons Officer, captured the spirit of the time:

> The first recollection I have of *Biddle* was seeing her from the Kennebec River Bridge at Bath. It was my first trip over to Bath from Brunswick where I had checked into the BOQ earlier in the afternoon and I was not familiar with the exit for the Iron Works. By the time I realized my error I was past the point of no return and on the bridge. I shot a quick glance down to my right; there she was, with the huge numerals "34" on her bow. My heart must have skipped a beat—it was just breathtaking.
>
> When I got down to yard level later, the impression was even more overpowering. My previous ships were *Gearing* class destroyers and a minesweeper. *Biddle* was about four times the size of the destroyers and, because the ship was essentially empty then, without fuel, water, ammunition, stores or crew, she was floating well above designed waterline. Lying alongside the pier at the northern end of the yard, the ship simply dominated the skyline in that part of Maine. It was almost surreal: how could this apparently tiny collection of shops and buildings have created such an enormous, magnificent ship? I was in awe.
>
> Those of us who were members of the nucleus crew would discover over the next several months that the modest building facility known as the Bath Iron Works was home to the world's finest shipbuilders. When one of our sister ships was grounded in Boston that fall the BIW workers were livid that someone had damaged "their" ship. It was an example of the pride that we saw displayed continually, right through the day they delivered the ship to us in Boston, sweeping and swabbing every deck and carrying ashore with them every scrap of trash that had accumulated on the ride down from Bath. BIW had delivered us a clean ship and it was clear to each of us that they expected it to stay that way.

Ensign Peter Trump, *Biddle's* first Sonar Officer, remembers another officer who made many positive contributions to *Biddle*: "Another advantage for *Biddle* was the inclusion of Lieutenant Bob Carr in ship's company. Bob was assigned to the Superintendent of Shipbuilding, Bath, and had overseen the installation of combat systems in several of the ships of the class. Due for re-assignment, he decided to leave with *Biddle* as the Missile Systems Officer so he had added incentive to make sure everything was done right! After leaving *Biddle,* Bob went on to create the first Naval Shipyard Combat Systems Office at Philadelphia Naval Shipyard."

By June, most electronic equipment had been installed and was being methodically tested even though not all spaces had electrical power. Shore-powered droplights were common throughout the ship. Occasionally, the blinding light and poisonous smoke generated by a welder making last minute changes filled a space. Many deck plates that covered false decks in spaces such as Combat Information Center (CIC) were removed, exposing both the arteries that pumped life-giving electric power to lifeless electronic equipment and the synaptic connections that allowed the ship's brains to see, hear, comprehend, and respond.

Biddle still belonged to BIW. Consequently, the nucleus crew was not allowed to touch equipment that would soon be their responsibility. We were allowed to observe and ask questions, however. This opportunity was not wasted—I personally visited all of *Biddle's* spaces, including weapons and communications spaces that would soon be off limits to general traffic. As a result, I learned how the ship was built, where things were, how cables were routed, and how equipment was secured. This knowledge would soon become important when, under the pressure of combat operations, malfunctioning equipment had to be quickly repaired under difficult conditions. Lieutenant Gerity recalled that

> All of the nucleus crew officers had the responsibility to keep track of their equipment and spaces, what BIW was doing, and prepare proposed trial cards for the Board of Inspection and Survey. If a problem went undetected, it would become *your* problem later. I don't recall that in the electronics area we had many problems.
>
> Captain Scott was in charge all the way from Newport, even before he had orders. We would let him know of any kind of problem such as a tech needing a change of orders, or some perceived construction problem and he would fire out priority messages from Newport. Those often annoyed the recipient since MTS (Captain Scott) would send them Friday afternoon and they would have to be acted on Saturday.

A shipyard is an interesting place to visit—especially a shipyard with a strong reputation for quality such as BIW. Scattered over the BIW complex of piers, dry docks, and cavernous buildings, were several ships in various stages of construction. They ranged from almost completed ships such as *Biddle* and *Standley* to skeletons with little more than a keel in dry-dock. *Standley* was commissioned on 9 July 1966.

Occasionally I wandered around BIW on errands or to learn more about shipbuilding. In one long, skinny building, I found machinists turning long, skinny stainless steel propeller shafts on giant lathes. A lathe operator confided that it takes many months to turn a propeller shaft from stock material. If the machinist who is turning a propeller shaft dies, the shaft is scrapped and a new one is started. Only that machinist knows all the peculiarities and imperfections of a particular shaft and a shaft must be perfectly balanced. The story sounds credible...

The workforce and effort required to build as many as six ships at one time, piece by piece, is incredible. Michael Sanders, in *The Yard*, described BIW employees building the USS *Donald Cook* (DDG-75) as "To the more than five thousand electricians, pipefitters, welders, braziers, tinknockers, riggers, anglesmiths, straighteners, blasters, and shipfitters who labored out on the deckplate to put it together piece by piece, and to the legions of naval architects, draftsmen, and marine engineers who designed its parts and supervised its construction, it is Hull 463, the four hundred and sixty third to slide down the ways of Bath Iron Works since the yard's founding in 1884 by an ambitious local named Thomas Worcester Hyde, a Civil War general and Medal of Honor winner." (Sanders x)

Sanders described the physical plant from the Carlton Bridge over the Kennebec River as, "Viewed this way, from end to end, the yard resembles a child's erector set, a toy city left out in a jumble on the playroom floor at bedtime, all odd angles and thrusting fingers of steel, on the ground barely discernable everyday objects—a stake-bed truck, 55-gallon drums, a pile of steel pipe, wooden beams lying in a tangled heap. Closer in, there is an order to this chaos. BIW runs from the foot of the bridge down the waterfront about a mile and a half out towards the edge of town, but penetrates back from the shore only narrowly, with two-story houses and storefronts of Washington Street butting right up against its back." (viiii)

The Bath-Brunswick area of Maine provided many opportunities for a young sailor to see the sights. (After all, that's one of the reasons we joined the Navy, isn't it?) In the fall, when the autumn leaves were at their most colorful, I went flying in a small plane with shipmate DS2 Matt Lewis. Mesquite leaves and prickly pear don't change their color in West Texas, so the fall change of colors was spectacular to me. When I learned that the scoutmaster from my Boy Scout troop in San Angelo, Texas, was living in Rockland, Maine, I took a Greyhound bus for a weekend visit. I was rewarded with an impressive aurora borealis at night, authentic Maine lobster, and a day of sailing in Rockport Harbor in a two-masted schooner built by hand from timber cut from a nearby island.

By the fall of 1966, my brother, BT fireman Ray Treadway, received orders to report to *Biddle*. Ray had been serving in the rusty WWII repair ship USS *Jason* (AR-8) in San Diego and was very happy to get orders to a brand new guided missile frigate. The congressman from our district, who was a member of the House Armed Services Committee, had pulled some strings to get Ray assigned to *Biddle*, much to the disgust of *Jason's* commanding officer.

I eventually moved off base from Brunswick NAS to a room in Bath that was conveniently located one block from BIW. One night I was playing poker with an old Maine Indian named Paul who also rented a room in the house. A hand was dealt; Paul picked up his cards, looked at them, let a loud fart, and died of a heart attack on the spot. We never did look at his hand—it may have been a good one—or maybe a really bad one. Even though it happened very late at night, there was a statement for the ambulance service in his mailbox early the next morning.

Ensign Trump recalls the housing situation for some of the nucleus crew officers: "Several of the officers found housing in neighboring Brunswick, Maine near the Naval Air Station. Bob Gerity, Wes Boer and I were there and were soon joined by Fred Howe. At the time I drove a Volvo P1800 coupe, essentially a two-seater. In the spirit of the times, we car-pooled often. When it was my turn to drive, it was amazing to see Fred Howe, a big man, fold himself into the cramped rear "seat" of the Volvo!"

As *Biddle* neared completion in the fall of 1966, preparations began for Builder's Trials. The nucleus crew was invited, but only as observers. Due to the tides, *Biddle's* first cruise down the Kennebec River to the open waters of Casco Bay required us to be aboard well before daylight—4 or 5 AM, as I remember. At the appointed time, tugs nudged *Biddle* from the outfitting pier and she began the cautious journey down the twisting Kennebec River. This was my first cruise ever, so I had no idea what to expect. BIW employees masquerading as Navy cooks served breakfast on the mess deck—the meal was outstanding. Lieutenant Gerity fondly recalled, "I will always remember heading down the Kennebec for the first time, hoping everything would work OK, and marveling at all the old civilian farts running things."

The cruise was uneventful, as we had hoped. Preliminary Acceptance Trials, which allow Navy representatives to check out the final product, followed in a few weeks. After acceptance, the Balance Crew joined the Nucleus Crew then the ship entered a short Fitting Out Availability period, the last major hurdle before commissioning.

BIW delivered *Biddle* to the Navy at the Boston Naval Shipyard on 10 January 1967. The Portland Press Herald reported that "The six-hour cruise from Bath to Boston was a frigid, but smooth trip, attended by colorful (nautical) costumes, business meetings, guided tours, submarine sightings, and curiosity" (Langley 1). The submarine, according to the article, was the USS *Jack* (SSN-605) on her first sea trials. *Jack* was on her way back to Kittery Shipyard with Vice Admiral Hyman G. Rickover on board. The article also reported that 50 BIW women employees, who represented approximately 50% of all women employees at BIW at the time, made the trip. Allegedly, one of the women briefly took the wheel.

Ensign Trump recalled that *Biddle* had some work done on the sonar dome about that time:

> Somewhere in that sequence, the ship sailed to Boston for a brief dry-docking in the South Yard of Boston Naval Shipyard to groom the sonar dome. *Biddle's* dome was a rigid stainless steel dome, not the rubber dome of later designs. It could be pumped out and entered from a trunk without maintaining a positive internal pressure. The sonar array consisted of eight stacked rings of seventy-two elements each or 576 elements in all. The array hung from the forward end of the keel. Together with the dome, it drastically increased the draft of the ship. The access trunk contained a vertical ladder several decks tall. At the base, a small watertight hatch provided access to the dome. It was not ventilated and in most climates the condensation formed a rain forest effect. Effective preservation was impossible; rust was rife from the beginning.

Commissioning

James Treadway

Biddle's commissioning took place on a bitterly cold, clear New England morning. The ceremony began with an invocation, welcoming remarks, and introductions. The commissioning directive was read, which was followed by the national anthem and the raising of the U.S. flag, the Union Jack, and the commission pennant. The highlight of the event occurred at the exact moment the ship was commissioned. As the ensign was raised and then unfurled, the apparently vacant ship exploded to life as 386 members of the crew, hidden below decks, raced to their stations along the rails on the port side. Missiles were loaded on the launcher, radars rotated, and the 3-inch and 5-inch guns were manned and turned to position. Called "Ship Alive," it was a remarkable sight and the well-rehearsed production drew an appreciative round of applause from the audience. *Biddle* had come to life!

Captain Scott read his orders and then assumed command of the United States Ship *Biddle* (DLG-34). He then directed the Executive Officer Commander Robert L. Brown, to set the first watch. The personal flag of the Commander in Chief, U.S. Atlantic Fleet was broken with ruffles and flourishes, the Admiral's March, and a 17-gun salute. Captain Scott's remarks followed, after which he introduced the principal Speaker, Admiral Thomas H. Moorer, Commander in Chief, U.S. Atlantic Fleet. The benediction concluded the formal ceremony, which made me very happy because I was very, very cold having stood at attention or at ease for what seemed like hours. Nevertheless, it was very impressive ceremony and I was very proud to be a crewmember of the newest ship in the United States Navy, USS *Biddle* (DLG-34). I still am.

Other dignitaries who attended *Biddle's* commissioning were two descendants of *Biddle's* namesake: Brigadier General Nicholas Biddle, U.S. Army (Retired), and Mrs. Anthony J. Drexel Biddle; and 13 admirals including Admiral Thomas Moorer. The Boston Sunday Advertiser reported a lighthearted moment when Admiral Moorer stepped to the podium to deliver his speech. "As he launched into his address, a tug maneuvered a big tanker into a berth close by. Four times he opened his mouth. Four times the tug whistle gave out with: [a loud blast.] With the historic event about to be reduced to shambles, the Navy's top ranking admiral in the eastern hemisphere 'sank' the tugboat by telling the audience: *I didn't think that Captain Scott was going to give me this kind of competition!"* (Hickey)

Things went well for Admiral Moorer soon after attending *Biddle's* commissioning. He was promoted to Chief of Naval Operations (CNO) on 3 June 1967 and to Chairman, Joint Chiefs of Staff on 2 July 1970. His association with *Biddle* continued for many years. In 2001, well into his 90s, he accepted an invitation to be principal speaker at *Biddle's* first "All Hands" reunion. Unfortunately, he had to cancel at the last moment.

Officer of the Deck Lieutenant (junior grade) Harper and Petty Officer of the Watch (POW) FTM1 Belanger assumed the first forward quarterdeck watch, while Ensign Trump and RDCS Graham assumed the first aft quarterdeck watch.

After the formalities subsided, I learned it was my duty to give tours of the ship to visitors and, since I was the first enlisted man to report aboard *Biddle*, to cut the commissioning cake.

The commissioning of a Navy ship is saturated with tradition. Some traditions were explained in *Biddle's* commissioning brochure:

> The commissioning ceremony marks the acceptance of a ship as a unit of the operating forces of the United States Navy. At the moment of breaking the commissioning pennant, USS BIDDLE (DLG-34) becomes the responsibility of the Commanding Officer, who together with the ship's officers and men, has the duty of making and keeping her ready for any service required by our nation in peace or war.
>
> The commission pennant is believed to date from the 17th century, when the Dutch were at war with the English. The Dutch admiral TROMP hoisted a broom at his masthead to indicate his intention to sweep the English from the sea. This gesture was answered by the English admiral who hoisted a horsewhip, indicating his intention to subdue the Dutch. The English were victorious, and ever since, the narrow "coachwhip" pennant has been adopted by all nations as the distinctive mark of a ship of war.
>
> The modern U.S. Navy commission pennant is blue at the hoist with a Union of seven white stars, and a horizontal red and white stripe at the fly. In lieu of a commission pennant, flagships fly commodores' or admirals' personal flags, hence the term flagship.

Another interesting tradition that dates back to wooden ships is that crewmembers present at commissioning are entitled to a plank from the deck of the decommissioned ship. Thus, we are known as plankowners.

The commissioning brochure also had a brief biography of *Biddle's* namesake, Captain Nicholas Biddle, Continental Navy. The following excerpt explains why four U.S. Navy ships have been named *Biddle*:

> On 7 March 1778, (Captain) Biddle in RANDOLPH, 32 guns, engaged HMS YARMOUTH, 64 guns. Despite this disadvantage of firepower and a severe wound received early in the action, Captain Biddle directed the fire of his ship. British Captain Nicholas Vincent later reported that Biddle fired three deadly accurate broadsides to his opponent's one. After twenty minutes, fire apparently penetrated the powder magazines of RANDOLPH and the ship exploded, sinking instantly. Captain Biddle and his 315 man crew perished leaving only four survivors.
>
> Thus ended the illustrious career of Captain Nicholas Biddle, Continental Navy. His life may have ended short of its twenty-eighth year, but his spirit lives on; in this Nation, this Navy, and this ship, which bore his name.

Biddle (DLG-34) was not the first ship to bear his name—three Navy ships preceded her. According to the commissioning booklet, the first *Biddle* (PT 26), a torpedo boat, was also built by Bath Iron Works as hull number 30. She was launched 18 May 1901, displaced 196 tons, had a length of 175 feet, and a beam of 17 feet. She carried a crew of only three officers and 23 enlisted men.

The second *Biddle*, a destroyer that saw action in World Wars I and II, was launched on 3 October 1918 and commissioned on 22 April 1919. Considerably larger than her predecessor, DD-151 displaced 1,154 tons, had a length of 314 feet, and a beam of 31 feet. Her armament consisted of four 4-inch .50 caliber guns, two 3-inch .23 caliber guns, two .30 caliber guns, and twelve 21-inch torpedo tubes in triple mounts. DD-151 had a crew of six officers and 95 enlisted men.

The third *Biddle*, DDG-5 (formerly DD-955), was commissioned five years before DLG-34 on 5 May 1962. A gorgeous ship with a length of 437 feet and a beam of 47 feet, she displaced 4,500 tons—slightly less than one half of DLG-34's displacement at her decommissioning. DDG-5's vital statistics also include a main armament of Tartar missiles, Anti-Submarine Rocket (ASROC), and two 5-inch/54 guns. Her crew consisted of 17 officers and 305 enlisted men. Renamed *Claude V. Ricketts* in 1964, she was manned by an international crew as part of the NATO Multilateral Force.

Beyond the Ceremony

The commissioning of a ship has implications far beyond the ceremony. Lieutenant Commander Howe's account defines the spirit of the first crew:

> At some level early in every sailor's life he realizes that going to sea, into the deep water and out of sight of land, is a leap of faith. Unconsciously he expresses this faith every time he sets sail that his vessel, large or small, will withstand the elements and bring him home. More to the point, a sailor casts his lot with his shipmates on each of these occasions; a common, unspoken pledge to each other. For man-of-war's men the pledge must perforce include the conviction that his shipmate is committed to stand beside him no matter what.
>
> At the time of her commissioning *Biddle* represented the state of the art in naval shipbuilding. Her combat system was the most technologically advanced and integrated sea control capability in the world. Those of us who sailed her knew intimately her power, but I don't think we appreciated fully at the time what that first crew meant. We were too close to the situation in those days and much too busy to step back and see the big picture. Only many years and many ships and many crews later do we now realize what we were part of then.
>
> Every rated crewmember ordered to *Biddle* "in connection with commissioning and fitting out" and every one of the two dozen officers who made up the first wardroom was a product of the best and most complete training the service could provide. Each was also a proven performer in the specific job he would have in this new ship. A few arrivals were determined to be unlikely candidates and were gone very early in the pre-com period.
>
> As a consequence of these factors, the shipmates that we went to sea with following commissioning comprised one of the finest, most professionally skilled and motivated teams ever assembled. We had no superstars but what we did have was far more important to the moment; a spirit of common purpose was among us, and a palpable determination to be the best. By creating this atmosphere *Biddle's* plankowners fulfilled their most critical responsibility in establishing a tradition of superior performance that would serve the ship throughout her life.
>
> No one who has spent long at sea would dispute the fact that every ship has its own personality and that, at bottom, "the ship" is really the crew. Nothing could provide stronger evidence of this than the fact that among those of us who served in that first crew, *Biddle* lives in our memory and in the faces of our shipmates long after the ship itself belongs to the ages.

Shakedown and Never Ending Trials

James Treadway

Warships undergo a demanding series of trials after commissioning collectively known as shakedown before they join the fleet. *Biddle's* outstanding performance during shakedown and post-shakedown was no accident.

Shakedown, which under normal conditions is exceptionally demanding on a ship and its crew, took on new meaning when we learned that the combat arena known as the Gulf of Tonkin would be our first deployment. The Nucleus Crew, those who had joined the ship in the builder's yard, and the Balance Crew, those who had assembled in Norfolk under the Executive Officer, combined shortly before commissioning to fully man the ship. The crew that had recently commissioned *Biddle* was now focused on proving the ship's equipment, learning the skills required to pass all tests required of a man-o-war, then immediately put those skills to use in a combat environment.

To help *Biddle* prepare for the GOT combat environment, a group of officers and one enlisted man from the Operations Department were flown to the USS *Fox* (DLG-33) on Positive Identification Radar Advisory Zone (PIRAZ) station in the Gulf of Tonkin. PIRAZ control ships maintained continuous positive identification of all aircraft within the radar advisory zone. Wes Boer remembered that

> Mostly, all Ops folks went to schools before reporting aboard—or during the months of fitting-out. That was essentially true for the whole crew. I personally came from a school where I was on the faculty teaching Anti-Submarine Warfare (ASW) (WWII-type tactics rather than standoff engagements, however) and other Ops related stuff.
>
> As teams, we went to various schools to practice on simulators. But, one of the main reasons Baker, Gerity and I flew over to the Tonkin Gulf was to observe PIRAZ on-scene action in CIC, etc. and to collect computer tapes of the action (with actual voice-overs as I remember) which we could run for

training drills in-port or underway. That was pretty good stuff. We could run the tapes without the voice-overs showing air and surface action as occurring with our own guys passing info between team members, locking-on, simulating launch sequences, etc.

All that training paid off when we finally relieved Red Crown (USS *Chicago*, a "real" cruiser) on PIRAZ station. As I remember, we achieved a fairly seamless transition.

Biddle Wardroom Dances with Disaster

The plan was to have the men fly from the east coast to Subic Bay, Philippines, where they would catch a C-2 Carrier On-board Delivery (COD) to the USS *Forrestal* (CVA-59) at Yankee Station. The final leg would be a short helicopter ride from *Forrestal* to the waiting *Fox* at PIRAZ. After leaving the *Fox*, they were to visit the Air Force facility and Marine Tactical Data System (MTDS) installation at Monkey Mountain near Da Nang and then return home. All objectives would be met, but not without a dangerous diversion along the way.

A group consisting of Operations Officer Bob Baker, NTDS Officer Bob Gerity, CIC Officer Wes Boer, Communications Officer Jim Checkett, and Senior Chief Radarman R.R. Graham arrived without incident at Cubi Point, Subic Bay. While waiting for the COD to deliver them to the *Forrestal*, *Biddle's* best young officers, in the finest traditions of the U.S. Navy, found a beer machine by the pool at the BOQ that dispensed San Miguel beer for a quarter. We can assume Chief Graham found similar facilities at the Chief's Club. The COD was 20 minutes late getting airborne which may have saved the lives of everyone on the plane. Lieutenant (junior grade) Checkett recalled that

> On July 29th of that year we were running about 20 minutes late on a COD flight from Subic to the USS *Forrestal* in the Gulf of Tonkin. We were in the landing pattern when a Zuni cooked off on a F-4 Phantom parked on the starboard side of the ship just aft of the Island. It went flying across the flight deck and hit the belly fuel tank of an A-4 setting off that entire horrific tragedy. Years later I found out that the pilot of that A-4 was John McCain, and I have since seen actual footage of him scrambling out of the cockpit before it blew up.
>
> Of course, the COD being late might have saved our lives, otherwise we would have been on deck at around 1030 hours, and from what we could see of what went on from up there, that would have been the epitome of "being at the wrong place at the wrong time." Next thing we know, rather than landing, we got bingoed to the marine base at Chu Lai and then Da Nang where we were thrown off the plane and they started ripping all the seats out to fly back

to pick up wounded, etc. They were doing the same things to every other aircraft in the area.

Wes Boer also remembered the tragic incident very well: "Yes, I was there and will never forget our near miss. We were actually on a long approach path to *Forrestal's* flight deck when we pulled up and away. I'd estimate we were 30 seconds from tail hook time—and possible disaster. Eventually, when we landed first at Chu Lai and Da Nang and the hatch was opened, we were greeted by jungle heat, humidity, and smoking mortar holes in the immediate vicinity. The bad guys had shot up the place about 90 minutes earlier. I found that a bit unsettling."

Bob Gerity recalled that

> First, we were diverted to Chu Lai, a Marine air base where we sat around for a bit. We used some old rocket canisters set in the sand as urinals, then went off to Da Nang where all of *Forrestal's* aircraft had arrived. There were several other officers from *Forrestal* and the Carrier Task Force (CTF) 77 staff on our plane who were anxious to get back out to their ship. After an hour or so, we took off and flew out to *Oriskany*, which had her own fire some time before. Smoke was still spewing from *Forrestal*. I was concerned too since I had a neighbor in Norfolk who was serving in her. He was ok it turned out.
>
> We spent at least one night on board *Oriskany*. There was a fire alarm that night and the guy I was rooming with was especially jumpy since he had been on board when the earlier fire occurred. He insisted that we get out to the hangar deck until the fire, if any, was out. It turned out to be a false alarm.

Wes Boer confirms the fake fire...

> Indeed there was a fire alarm on *Oriskany* later that night. I had just laid my head down and closed my eyes when I heard a southern voice on the 1MC say "Far. Far. Fire in compartment" umpty-ump. I did the math in my head and realized I was lying only about two frames forward of the fire site.
>
> As aircraft carrier compartmentation can be befuddling, I had mentally gone over the two or three escape-option routes available: As I was well forward (in Boys' Town) the most dramatic escape route was to dash forward a few compartments to a gun tub on the starboard side, jump overboard, and hail the next plane guard destroyer about a 1,000 yards in our wake. (It now occurs to me that someone had to yell "Man Overboard!" for that to succeed as envisioned because we were steaming in the dark.) Anyway, with hat and shoes in hand, I chose the direct route and dashed up the passageway just outside my compartment, and ran aft toward the wardroom—one of the few places on board which I had navigated to more than once.

> Enroute, I passed a small working party surrounding a mop locker or some such compartment. I continued the dash aft and said to myself "Whoops...could they be...?" I turned around and strolled back to the working party and confirmed that they were at the site of the false alarm.

Anxious to find a ship in the Tonkin Gulf that was not on fire or about to be on fire, our party eventually made their way to the *Fox* without Chief Graham who had separated from the group in Chu Lai and never caught up with them. The group enjoyed *Fox* hospitality (without 25 cent beer) and got a good look at the Gulf of Tonkin combat scene. Six days later, our explorers reversed their course and headed home. Communications Officer Checkett continues the story...

> I remember later in that trip we went to Da Nang as part of our scheduled indoctrination. We visited the Air Force and Marine facilities at the top of Monkey Mountain that we eventually would link our NTDS system up with in the GOT when we relieved as PIRAZ. When we were in Da Nang I felt a high sense of semi-fear, anxiety and vulnerability. As soon as we got to the top of Monkey Mountain and realized there were 25,000 U.S. Marines camped out at the bottom, I never felt safer in my life! Plus, as an added attraction, the facility was completely air-conditioned! Not only was the facility air conditioned, which was an ungodly relief from the stifling heat and humidity down below, but I also have a distinct memory of lots of marble floors in a place which was kind of awesome.

History of the Ship—1967

The following paragraphs, which are excerpts from *Biddle*'s *History Of The Ship* (1967), summarize her pre-shakedown, shakedown, and post-shakedown activities. The number of trials *Biddle* underwent in one year was incredible—35, maybe more.

> BIDDLE first put to sea on Builders Trials 30 November—1 December 1966 and one week later successfully performed Preliminary Acceptance Trials (9-11 December). One month later, on 10 January 1967, the builders delivered BIDDLE to Boston Naval Shipyard, Boston, Massachusetts, where the ship was accepted on behalf of the Navy by Rear Admiral Means Johnston, Commandant, First Naval District.
> One day later the Balance Crew joined the Nucleus Crew on board and began functioning as a team to commence Fitting Out Availability at Boston Naval Shipyard.

Shakedown and Never Ending Trials   63

On 21 January 1967 BIDDLE was placed "In Commission, Special." On that [day], Captain Maylon T. Scott, USN, assumed command and reported to Commander, Cruiser-Destroyer Force, U.S. Atlantic Fleet for operational control. The principal speaker at the commissioning ceremonies was Admiral Thomas H. Moorer, then Commander in Chief U.S. Atlantic Fleet and subsequently appointed Chief of Naval Operations.

A short 45 days later, during which a two day FAST cruise along side the pier (20-21 February 1967) and a two day Consolidated Operability Test at sea (22-23 February 1967) were conducted, Fitting Out was completed and BIDDLE put to sea the very next day—in a fully "in commission" status.

Also on this day, 24 February 1967, BIDDLE was administratively assigned to Destroyer Squadron Twenty-Six in Cruiser—Destroyer Flotilla Eight.

Covered with ice, BIDDLE made her first port of call in Newport, Rhode Island for a quick series of degaussing checks. [*A ship's disturbance of the magnetic field is detectable by other ships, submarines, and aircraft. Degaussing or deperming makes a ship safe against the action of magnetic mines.*] Leaving Newport a few hours later, the ship set course for Yorktown, Virginia to load ammunition and missiles. On 28 February, BIDDLE proceeded to Hampton Roads and the Virginia Capes operating area and remained three days to conduct sonar calibration trials and aircraft tracking drills.

Arriving in Mayport on the 4th of March, BIDDLE began an intensive three weeks of Missile Qualification Trials with over 40 hours devoted to air tracking/missile designation exercises alone. Independent ships exercises were also conducted during the three week period, including gunnery practice, replenishment at sea, NTDS Link 11 data exchange, and ECM drills. Submarine tracking was also scheduled but was cancelled when the servicing submarine suffered a propulsion casualty.

Having been operational for exactly one month, BIDDLE departed the Jacksonville Operating Area for the Atlantic Fleet Weapons Range in Puerto Rico ready to conduct the crucial ships qualification trials (SQT) missile firings on 29 March 1967.

On the missile range, BIDDLE'S outstanding team of professional missilemen scored SIX hits with SIX missiles.

[Tom Marfiak note: This is significant—it defies the odds! Scenarios are challenging—new systems and people—yet *Biddle* achieved the highest performance possible. Augured well for the future.]

Following a brief period in San Juan, BIDDLE continued shakedown training with Ant-Submarine Warfare Ship Qualification Trial (1-14 April) followed by six weeks of Shakedown Training under Commander Fleet Training Group at Guantanamo Bay, Cuba (18 April—26 May 1967.) From 29 April to 3 May 1967 BIDDLE also conducted Final Acceptance Trials and made a weekend visit to Montego Bay, Jamaica.

BIDDLE earned an overall grade of EXCELLENT for Shakedown Training, the highest Shakedown/Refresher Training mark ever made at Guantanamo for a ship of her type. This is especially significant considering the foreshortened period of training. The official record states:

> Time available to the ship compared to prescribed time for type: Ready for sea; independent exercises enroute: Accomplished in 5 days with 21 days prescribed.
>
> Shakedown Training at Guantanamo: Accomplished in 32 days with 70 days prescribed
>
> From Guantanamo Bay, BIDDLE headed home for Boston via the missile range where another successful firing operation was conducted, and via Yorktown, Virginia, again, to off-load missiles and ammunition prior to entering the Shipyard.

BIDDLE arrived in Boston 2 June 1967 to begin a brief but well deserved liberty period prior to beginning Post Shakedown Availability (PSA) at the Boston Naval Shipyard commencing 7 June 1967.

Originally scheduled for three months, the PSA was extended six more weeks to end on 30 October 1967. This extension allowed for the installation of additional equipment, certain modifications and routine Post-shakedown adjustments. Among some of the new features added were an additional NTDS computer, greatly expanded communications capability and special equipment for improving BIDDLE'S already formidable air detection and tracking systems in preparation for future extended special deployments overseas.

On 29 September 1967 BIDDLE successfully achieved an outstanding milestone in the career of a major combatant. On that day, BIDDLE successfully passed the Special Weapons (nuclear) Acceptance Inspection, seven weeks ahead of schedule. Only two other CRUDESLANT units have achieved that distinction. The successful NWAI meant that BIDDLE was certified capable of handling special weapons should the need arise.

On 31 October 1967, BIDDLE left her temporary homeport of Boston and proceeded to her new homeport, Norfolk, Virginia, once again going by way of Yorktown to rearm. On 3 November 1967 BIDDLE arrived home—NORFOLK!

BIDDLE took only four days to get acquainted with Norfolk, Destroyer Squadron Twenty Six and Cruiser-Destroyer Flotilla Eight before deploying again on 7 November for a two-week training cruise. The list of accomplishments on this cruise is also formidable: helicopter land/launch qualification; underway replenishment qualifications from a fleet oiler (AO) and ammunition ship (AE); ASW training including ASROC and tube-launched torpedo attacks on the submarine *Amberjack*; Extensive drill in surface and air gunnery; air intercept controller qualifications; damage control, engineering casualty control and ECM drills. Special CNO project test and evaluations were conducted concurrently in conjunction with these events. During this busy period, BIDDLE took a full day to collect antenna radiation pattern data off Charleston, South Carolina.

After returning to Norfolk on 17 November 1967, BIDDLE was active in preparing for and executing a special weapons demonstration as well as inspection by the Squadron Commander, Commander Destroyer Squadron Twenty-Six, Captain Thomas E. Bass III, U.S. Navy.

During the 17-30 November in-port period, Vice Admiral Charles K. Duncan, USN, Commander Second Fleet, informally inspected BIDDLE and sent the following message:

"It was a great pleasure for me to visit BIDDLE yesterday. I was most impressed with the obviously high state of morale of the officers and bluejackets of your command, and with the cleanliness of the ship. The high standards of military smartness, neatness and appearance displayed in BIDDLE are commendable. I am confident the ship will carry out her vital forthcoming tasks with skill and competence."

Underway again on 1 December 1967 for a training cruise in the Caribbean, BIDDLE continued Special CNO project tests and evaluations. A detachment from VC-8 was also aboard to provide drone target services for surface and anti-air gunnery. In engineering, a number of damage control and casualty control exercises were conducted plus a 25-knot economy run and a full power run.

During a two day stop in San Juan, Puerto Rico, Rear Admiral Vincent P. Healey, USN, Commander Cruiser-Destroyer Flotilla Six, broke his Flag in BIDDLE on 7 December 1967. On the following day, BIDDLE, departed for sea and continued training. After observing four successful firings of Terrier missiles by BIDDLE, Rear Admiral Healey hauled down his Flag. This was the first time a Flag Officer's Flag had been flown in BIDDLE at sea.

At Culebra Island on 10 December 1967, BIDDLE qualified in Naval Gunfire Support without the benefit of any prior rehearsal firings. Later that same day, a jet-powered drone was "vaporized" (direct hit) by BIDDLE during a Terrier missile firing exercise. BIDDLE engineers then made a high-speed endurance test run from the Culebra Island area to the Chesapeake Light Ship in about 30 hours slowing only for gunnery exercises with drone aircraft. Once again BIDDLE stopped by Yorktown, Virginia, this time to restock ammunition, missiles and torpedoes after many periods of extensive gunnery firings.

On 13 December 1967 BIDDLE arrived in Norfolk to begin a combined Christmas leave and upkeep period and extensive Preparation for Overseas Movement (POM).

On 18 December 1967 Rear Admiral James F. Calvert, USN, Commander Cruiser-Destroyer Flotilla Eight made his first inspection of BIDDLE, the latest and newest unit to join his Flotilla.

On 21 January 1968 BIDDLE celebrated her first year in commission as a full-fledged unit of the fleet.

31 December 1967

Biddle was very busy for an entire year—loading missiles and ammunition, pre-shakedown operations, missile qualifications, ASW training, shakedown training, final acceptance, even more training cruises and even more training after that. We spent a lot of time in the Roosevelt Roads area of Puerto Rico testing our missiles, guns, radar, fire control systems, and the NTDS. Shooting a Terrier missile or Anti-Submarine Rocket (ASROC) was loud and fun but I think I enjoyed the 5-inch and 3-inch guns more. Shooting the 5-inch/54 in fully automatic mode was very impressive.

Occasionally something would happen to remind us that even training could be very serious business. Ensign Trump explains:

> We once managed to get submarine services for an Anti-Submarine Warfare Exercise (ASWEX) during the pre-deployment training period. I launched an exercise ASROC on the target sub and the MK 43 or MK 44 torpedo actually worked as advertised. It searched, acquired and set a collision course—it only forgot to veer away and surface. Instead it actually ran into the sub to their great consternation! They conducted an emergency surface but found only a dent in a ballast tank. The torpedo was never seen again. Official logs would be needed to pinpoint the time and location. Also, during what we now call the—Combat System Qualification Test (CSSQT)—on the Atlantic Fleet Weapons Integration Test Facility off Roosevelt Roads, PR, we had a Terrier go ballistic. This is still spoken of in hushed tones, but it can't have any security or PR implications any longer.

Lieutenant Commander Howe explains how to make a Terrier missile go ballistic:

> The authorized firing areas within the Atlantic Fleet Weapons Range (AFWR) are generally associated with geographic positions that ships exercising on the range will occupy. From these positions ships are restricted to shooting within certain bearings that protect nearby land areas and other traffic. The restrictions are naturally constructed with ample safety factors but it is nonetheless understood that all firing must take place within the authorized sectors.

Biddle was firing on the north range of AFWR on this occasion, which meant that firing was restricted to a generally easterly direction. For some reason our earlier targets on this day had all been presented to us south of the positions we expected them and, as a result, we were continually watching the target bearing to ensure that we were inside of the southernmost firing boundary, which generally protected the islands of Culebra and the northeastern corner of Puerto Rico. The earlier shots had been BTs (beam-riders) and all taken well inside of the authorized area.

The last shot in our predeployment firing plan in December '67 was scheduled to be an HT (homing) warhead (as opposed to an inert, telemetry package) fired against a high altitude, high speed target. It was standard practice to propose firing profiles (all had to be approved in advance) that, if successful, would result in intercepts along at the boundaries of the expected maximum performance for the missile fired. Pushing the performance envelope in this manner was standard practice.

The target for this shot was an AN/AQM-37A, a very small, high speed, rocket-propelled, single use target usually launched by an A-4 aircraft. The A-4 was tracked easily by the SPS-48 and the fire control radars but the target was considerably more of a challenge. When the pilot launching the target called "separation" and broke away sharply, everyone had to be absolutely certain that the fire control solution was being computed on the target and not on the A-4. Added to this challenge was that fact that the target was viable for only a very brief period (a couple of minutes) as it sped through the range area. These constraints created a very tense period and everyone had to be on his toes.

Bob Carr was engaged in a nonstop conversation with the SPG-55B fire control radar operators to verify that they were on the target and decide which system had the best track as we would need to decide before firing which radar would control the intercept. Jack Sutton and I were glued to the target bearing because the elevation was substantial and the range was short so the bearing was changing rapidly. We wanted to make sure that we could get the shot off before we hit the safe firing boundary.

Finally the decisions were concluded; we had a solid track on the target, a radar was chosen, the target bearing was within limits, and it was "Bird Away."

By the time the firing occurred the target was nearly overhead and, for whatever reason, the missile never guided. This probably happened because "front-lock" with the controlling radar was never achieved due to the target's extraordinarily high angular velocity. At any rate, the controlling radar was shut down according to doctrine a brief time (10-15 seconds) after intercept had been calculated to occur. This should have caused the missile to self-destruct but bridge personnel reported seeing no evidence of warhead detonation. The shot was evaluated as a failure by AFWR. It was our first failure in the life of the ship.

Two days later, en route to Norfolk we were advised that a farmer walking his fields south of El Yunke (Sierra de Luquillo, the rain forest on the east end of Puerto Rico) had discovered the remains of our missile. Calculating the fall of our shot revealed that the missile had flown close to 100 miles and evidently not destructed until impact. It got so much farther west than we expected by virtue of our failure to recognize that the solution for this very high, very fast target built into the launcher orders for the homer a huge lead angle that caused the missile to be fired well beyond the authorized bearing. We had simply been watching the wrong indicator. It was a lesson we never forgot.

It was a long, tough year, but it was not without some good times and some good liberty. San Juan, particularly Old San Juan, was excellent. I will never forget sipping dark Lowenbrau at Lum's on the waterfront in Old San Juan.

St. Thomas, Virgin Islands, was an exceptional liberty port as well. My most memorable recollection of St. Thomas was the cheesecake at the Hilton hotel on the top of the hill. To this day *that* cheesecake is the standard for all cheesecakes. Liberty in Montego Bay, Jamaica was good, but the beer was bad. Red Stripe, I think. The water in the eastern Caribbean was the clearest water I have ever seen. I hope it still is. Guantanamo Bay, known by *all* servicemen as Gitmo, was like prison—no liberty, no fun. But, I remember standing on the fantail late one afternoon and looked down to see a hammerhead shark that was, and this is no shit, 15 feet long. The only good time we had at at Gitmo was when we left. Countless sailors must feel the same way.

I can barely recall a rather funny scene when we were in the Gitmo area. A ship from a foreign navy, possibly Turkish, was having General Quarter drills while anchored not far from *Biddle*. A large, simulated hole on the main deck was marked with chalk which required traffic on that side to find an alternate route. Instead of using the other side of the ship or going up a ladder to the next level, most sailors chose to hang over the side directly over the water and make their way along the side of the ship hand over hand. It was quite a scene.

Biddle made a high speed run one morning when the seas were as smooth as glass. When I walked back to the fantail during the run I saw that *Biddle* was kicking up a rooster tail much higher than the fantail. Later I learned that *Biddle* had achieved a record 37-1/2 knots on peacetime screws. This record may still stand—it is often recalled at reunions and happy hours whenever *Biddle* men get together. In addition to the high-speed run, it is said that *Biddle* came to a full stop on that run within the length of the ship.

When I asked Captain Scott about the high-speed run and emergency stop, he commented, "I did not spend much time on the fantail when we were at full power with all boilers on the line, and if I remember correctly, it was more than 37 1/2 knots. Yes, many times that rooster tail was BIG. But, what you really missed, and I did too, was to stand there on the fan tail when we were at full power and then went ALL BACK EMERGENCY FULL...WOW!!! However, I think we only did that several times, and for special reasons..."official." What were you doing back there anyway? Ho, Ho." Sorry, Captain, the statute of limitations applies—no Captain's Mast for me!

When *Biddle* was in Gitmo, a rather funny incident (now) occurred to young Ensign Trump. He explains:

> Let me recount one sea story from the early days. When we were in GITMO for refresher training, one of the many things we had to do to earn a passing score was to prove we had all the publications on the official list. Of course, we were short a couple of SECRET pubs in the ASW world. It was suggested to me, as I was but an Ensign, after all, that I should go seek out my counterpart on another ship and borrow the needed pubs so they could be shown to the trainers. This seemed reasonable, so off I went to see what I could do.
>
> Sure enough, I found a sympathetic officer on another ship who handed me his copies of the documents on my assurance that I would return them soon. By the time I got back to the pier where *Biddle* was moored, she was not there! She was steaming out of the harbor on a simulated emergency sortie!
>
> Looking back now, I can't think why I didn't just go back and return the pubs to my generous, if incautious, new friend, but I didn't. Instead, I went to the BOQ and slept uneasily with the contraband pubs under my pillow. The next morning, the ship came back and I went aboard to show the pubs. I don't think I had the opportunity to get back off and return the pubs for several hours. My new friend was on the point of nervous prostration when I returned! He figured that he had been had by some security team scam and was on the point of going to his Weapons Officer to confess. He was very grateful to get the pubs back; but I don't think he was unhappy to see me go away! Maylon and Fred (Lieutenant Commander Fred Howe, Weapons Officer) thought it was a grand joke.

The incident did not affect Ensign Trump's ability to get promoted. He left Norfolk in January 1968 as Lieutenant (jg) and returned in September as a Lieutenant. Lieutenant Trump clarifies how it happened: "In those days, promotion from Ensign to Lieutenant (junior grade) was pretty much automatic after some period of time—perhaps 24 months. I was definitely still an Ensign for the commissioning in January '67. Sometime that year I advanced to Lieutenant (junior grade). Subsequently, when Lieutenant Bob Harper (ASW Officer) left us, I "fleeted up" to ASW Officer and WO2 Bob Friedell joined us as Sonar Officer. During the deployment, I was given an early promotion to Lieutenant by virtue of filling a Lieutenant billet in the War Zone (and Captain Scott's recommendation, of course.) if memory serves me correctly."

[*BACKGROUND: The Naval Tactical Data System was a remarkably successful project at the beginning of the shipboard digital revolution. Today, the AEGIS Combat System and its successors embody the latest in technology and complex computer programs. In the case of NTDS as installed on Biddle, a handful of naval leaders had the foresight to conceive a new way to manage large numbers of much faster hostile targets that could threaten the fleet. Next, their new concept was brilliantly designed then implemented in the form of the Naval Tactical Data System, which incorporated a large group of disparate weapons, sensors, computers, and technologies into an integrated package. Finally, in order to remain an effective combat system, NTDS had to improve through both the introduction of new technologies and by correcting problems found in the fleet. This chapter tells how Biddle was at a vanguard position in the latter effort.*]

When Computers Went to Sea: Technicians of the Digital Navy

David Johnson

The digital revolution that produced NTDS was more than the introduction of new technology and computer programs into U.S. Navy ships. It was also supported and enhanced on ships at sea by technicians of all ratings from within the combat system. These technicians had to deal with all the things not foreseen by the engineers who developed NTDS, many examples of which are provided later in the chapter.

Many of the original NTDS technicians had experience with systems from the WW II and Korean eras, complete with vacuum tubes and limited logistics or maintenance support. The digital revolution required new thinking to adapt to new technology, maintenance, and operating methods. In more recent years, what was the latest technology for *Biddle*-era ships is now old, outmoded, and replaced by electronic innovations such as high-capacity computers embedded in major equipment to wide-band fiber-optic networks. These, too, are being mastered by the technicians of the day just as the complexities of the initial digital revolution were mastered by the pioneer technicians of that long-ago time.

The full story of how NTDS began and was developed and deployed is well told in David L. Boslaugh's book, *When Computers Went to Sea*. However, NTDS technicians were at the center of the process because NTDS was the major digital component introducing the new technology. This chapter is derived from *Biddle's* early years, including pre-commissioning and shakedown, told from the perspective of the Data System Technicians. It is, however, intended to typify the experiences of technicians on sister ships all the follow-on crews that sailed on these great ships of the *Belknap* Class.

It should be recognized that the digital revolution did not just start with *Biddle* and her sister ships. Indeed, there were already a number of ships equipped with NTDS at sea. There were also special-purpose ships such as ocean-going survey ships with various digital systems, albeit generally older technology such as rotating drums for storage of data. Some shore stations also existed that used this digital technology for intelligence, logistics, and Command functions.

When NTDS was declared a real program, the call went out for NTDS technician candidates to man the first three service-test ships. This was several years before the Mare Island Combat System Maintenance Training Center (CSMTC) was opened and the Data System Technician rating and its training formally established. Fortunately, many of the technicians who responded had some level of digital experience, however limited, which made them valuable assets in the initial phases of the NTDS technical-support task. Before Mare Island, these first NTDS technicians, keeping their existing rating badges, were selected from throughout the Fleet. These ratings included virtually every technical and some operational ratings, and were cycled through factory schools to learn maintenance and operation of computers and peripheral devices, display consoles and associated units, data transmission systems, and even NTDS computer program fundamentals.

When the NTDS school was established at Mare Island in 1962, before the full-blown CSMTC was commissioned, many of these technicians formed the nucleus of the original staff. They were augmented by other senior technicians recruited from all Navy activities, who were experienced and well-trained at various advanced technical or "B" schools. They were sent to Computer Basics at Great Lakes, and then to the famous basic computer programming school at San Diego fondly called "Sink U" after Captain Robert Sink, who was in charge. This writer was fortunate to be in the latter group of NTDS recruits as an Electronics Technician. However, the whole prospective staff spent several months together at the old Naval Electronics Laboratory Center (NELC), San Diego before transiting to Mare Island and creation of the NTDS school. This assemblage of technical experts had also been to the excellent Navy Instructor Training School. Under the leadership of the officers who were responsible for fulfilling Navy training requirements, they set about creating a training environment that stressed both classroom fundamentals and hands-on equipment maintenance unique to the digital world.

An important adjunct to the usual technician training approach was an NTDS Systems Technician course. This was intended to support the new technician category that augmented the three basic NTDS technician ratings: Computer, Display, and Data Transmission. The Systems Technician course was unique in that it covered all the NTDS equipment, selected NTDS computer programs, interfaces with other subsystems, and basic shipboard operations. In addition, it also stressed a key part of the NTDS maintenance philosophy, computerized system testing and alignment. This led to a system-level manning and training approach that was to be significant for the new *Belknap* class of DLGs then being built.

These ships introduced the revolutionary NTDS with WDS MK 11, which brought the Missile and Gun systems directly into electrical integration with NTDS. By way of the NTDS computer programs, the tactical application of these weapon systems was also controlled by decision-makers and other operators connected by the digital environment. And, of initial concern to some traditionalist at the Command level, the NTDS data links connected all ships into a larger operational environment that made system maintenance even more demanding. These developments are discussed later on to show how important they were to *Biddle's* success (and the success of sister ships) in shaking out the bugs from the new systems, interfacing devices, and computer programs.

The Bureau of Ships (BUSHIPS), later the Naval Ships Command (NAVSHIPS), that created NTDS had no way of knowing in advance just what would be required at sea to handle the myriad of possible failures, deficiencies, and new requirements that would emerge. That's why Headquarters had the foresight to create technicians and Maintenance Officers who could deal with the unexpected and turn Service Test ships into mature and reliable deploying assets.

Of significant importance to ships at sea, especially in combat situations, is the role of electrical power, cooling water, heating and air conditioning, Electronics Casualty Control, and standard Damage Control. Most of these considerations were not completely modeled and evaluated during NTDS development, since they were not part of the engineering process at the time. These became the focus of much of *Biddle's* operational and technical work, starting with the realization during Refresher Training at Guantanamo Bay that NTDS was not just another suite of electronics equipment. It took a while for the trainers to realize that damage control and electronics casualty-control procedures and training should be modified to really challenge these ships. *Biddle* and other ships worked hard to refine these important survival tools. The lasting effect of *Biddle's* experiences on the Navy's improvement in these areas from the OPNAV and NAVSHIPS perspective will be described.

To fully appreciate the experiences documented herein you have to envision not only just NTDS and its computers, but also the then-emerging Combat System entity as the collection of subsystems is now generally defined. That definition represents transition from basically stand-alone systems to the federation of these systems into a functional entity with enhanced mission capability and survivability as driving concern. With federation and integration achieved by a variety of interface techniques, the combat system for a number of years was not a well-identified composite entity with well-integrated subsystems for a number of years.

Most subsystems, some of which were analog and mechanical, were still independent entities for maintenance and some operations. Interfaces were often limited in their information-transfer capability, such as single-wire circuits carrying non-digital single-function signals. Computers at sea, capable of communicating with each other and many other equipments, made possible extensive and rapid changes in definitions and relationships between systems. However, many effective non-digital interfaces from legacy systems were retained by adapting them to the digital systems via converters of various types.

The evolution of interfaces is a major component of the full realization of advantages provided by digital systems and their designed-in electrical and functional relationships. Part of the challenge during these early years of the digital revolution for the technicians of all ratings was to keep those interfaces working correctly. This included recognizing failures and misalignments, and even on occasion identification of technical deficiencies in equipment and computer programs that sometimes could be corrected on board by experienced personnel.

Fortunately, there were dedicated technical and computer-program support activities established ashore to provide direct support to ships as problems and suggested improvements were reported via the several feed-back systems.

Lessons learned during those early years of NTDS/WDS maturation soon found their way into ship-class improvements and design requirements for new ships. These applied lessons also included documentation, training, and logistics, all things of great interest to shipboard technicians.

The following examples of somewhat anecdotal (but well-documented at the time) shipboard technician experiences are provided to show the range of accomplishments of the outstanding technicians who kept systems operating. These stories represent a small subset of those experienced on all ships, including *Biddle*, over the life span of these great ships. It is hoped that any Navy technician can relate to most of these situations in one way or another, and that the technicians who participated in these events may remember the details with pride.

Fundamentals of Success

NTDS training at Mare Island combined the knowledge and experience of staff and factory training, and was not class-specific except as needed to use available training documentation. The curriculum stressed integration with other systems and working across interfaces, and was one of the fundamental aspects of why NTDS technicians succeeded. Eventually, the new NTDS/WDS equipment suite and computer programs were being tested at the Mare Island Test Site whose facilities were also part of the Schools Command facility. As staff and students became available, especially those headed for one of the new DLG-28 Class ships, they were used to support test and evaluation work being done. This was a great advantage to the core DS staff and future ship's technicians, since they were involved in various aspects of NTDS systems and training development that increased their individual knowledge and skills.

The practice of staff involvement in NTDS engineering work started before Mare Island was in business, as the staff gathered at NELC, San Diego for training in basic computer programming, and hands-on experience with NTDS equipment. Most of this select group immediately got into the flow of NTDS development and evaluation that was still being done at NELC. This gave them a broad perspective about NTDS and its relationships with other ship systems. It was because of this perspective that on *Biddle*, as on most NTDS ships at the time, we viewed NTDS as the center of the ship universe, with all else sort of peripheral to it. This was done to assure that the forward-looking concept of this radical digital world was somewhat isolated from the traditional systems and concepts that were still in place around the ship.

NTDS was the new and unproven component of the combat system. Its newly-developed WDS MK 11 replaced a lot of analog fire-control equipment (and moved the firing key to BUSHIPS, per David Boslaugh). NTDS technicians knew that they had a big job to prove their competence and NTDS reliability. A Planned Maintenance System (PMS) package and its integrated maintenance approach existed, and provided a good foundation for refinement of digital-system maintenance as a function of lessons learned in the real world at sea. In addition, we were closely associated with all other technicians, with whom we developed common interests because of the close coupling created by digital and analog interfaces that bound our systems together. Automated system maintenance and alignment testing was already a proven concept, was part of the PMS packages for NTDS and some weapon systems, and continued to be refined and expanded as experience allowed. Automated system maintenance and alignment testing, already a proven concept, was part of the PMS package and continued to be refined and expanded.

As key NTDS technicians reported aboard, *Biddle's* expressed maintenance philosophy was informally defined to allow most problems being experienced by other systems and not yet resolved to be provisionally attributed to NTDS. This decreased to a large extent the uncertainty about cause versus effect, since little about NTDS was known by other ratings. The DSs would then set about isolating the problem source and, if not an NTDS problem, help others in the Combat System and Hull, Mechanical and Electrical (HM&E) organizations to find and fix it. Sometimes it was an operator's problem due to lack of experience with specific console or ancillary-equipment particulars.

This philosophy minimized finger-pointing, centralized problem reporting and tracking, and made the DSs into the experts on which NTDS reliability (and thus mission integrity) often relied. In addition, the basic rule for DSs was that if an operator says there is a problem, assume there is a problem and stand at his side until we got a good understanding of the situation. This sometimes resulted in additional training for operators, some of whom were still in the initial stages of mastering the NTDS and WDS MK 11 console modes and the associated operational requirements.

There were some awkward situations early on because, understandably, some ship's engineering-plant personnel had limited understanding of the unfamiliar demands NTDS was placing on ship services. Electrical and cooling services had seldom been challenged before by the requirements of such sophisticated (and sensitive) equipment. However, other systems such as the AN/SPS-48 Radar and the high-power AN/SQS-26 Sonar were also beginning to place demands similar to those of NTDS, adding to the complexity of supporting this new confederation of high-tech systems.

The underlying doctrine of the NTDS leadership was dynamic support of Command requirements, the operators, the interfaced or federated systems, and thus the ship's missions. To assure seamless and consistent support to all users of NTDS/WDS facilities, the DSs were the designated experts for computer program loading and system reconfiguration for operation, testing, or training. This approach also sharpened the abilities of the DS team for rapid fault recognition and isolation, working in conjunction with the experts on the other side of the interfaces or in the functional operator organization. Constant practice at computer reloading and system reconfiguration under operational constraints proved to be invaluable in the demanding Tonkin Gulf environment.

The centralized maintenance approach (actually, centralized technical operations in support of tactical operations) was also practiced to some extent on many of the other NTDS/WDS MK 11 ships due to the training established at Mare Island for Missile Fire Control and NTDS system technicians. That in itself is a story, not much remembered by most. However, the concept of centralized casualty reporting and response coordination is now a basic part of ships operations under current Navy maintenance and readiness-management guidelines, and will be discussed below.

Biddle experiences, as well as those of the other ships of the class, provided guidance for work done in all phases of ship systems development and crew training. Many of those experiences were experiments permitted by Command and NTDS officers to see if they improved readiness-management concepts and practices as combat-system definitions and management began to evolve.

Preparing For NTDS/WDS System-Level Integrated Maintenance

Weapon systems have always had rigorous daily operability testing as a PMS requirement to assure operational readiness and to detect any degradation of performance. NTDS/WDS MK 11 provided the computers to run the Daily System Operability Test (DSOT) in digital form (DDSOT). A key test device was the Dynamic Synchro Data Source (DSDS) as described in David Boslaugh's book, Chapter 8. The DSDS was developed to convert digital target designation data from NTDS computers running the DDSOT program to synchro signals for designation of test targets to the fire control systems. Repeat-back sampling of synchro signal was provided by the NTDS Keyset Central converter. These tests complemented many other automated tests provided as part of the Ship Operational Readiness Test (SORT) package.

As a couple of the DLG-28-class ships were nearing completion, it was determined at Mare Island that the only training for crew members in the new WDS MK 11 and automated testing was being done at Bath by *Wainwright* experts such as DSC Michael Snodgrass. The NTDS/WDS training plan was modified to have a Terrier Missile System chief and an NTDS System chief cross-trained at Mare Island in concepts of each other's systems. This was followed by time together in the Test Site running the various tests to provide in-depth knowledge of the capabilities and use of the SORT package. It also covered the new digital test system hardware and software, and how to properly interpret dynamic indications and printouts of results. Setup of systems and switchboards was critical, and restoration after testing to a normal configuration quickly and correctly was a necessity in the at-sea environment. By running these tests in a laboratory environment at Mare Island, many of which were new and complex, and responding to a range of problem situations, the objective of training a well-functioning team for each ship was met.

So, in consultation with *Wainwright* experts and others, the NTDS Systems Technician staff developed a 7-week course. Four weeks were spent cross-training selected system FTs and DSs in fundamentals of each other's system. Three weeks were devoted to joint laboratory system testing and familiarization with integrated maintenance practices. Most ships eventually got their teams, including *Biddle*. The concept worked fine, and contributed to the success of the WDS MK 11 and to the value of well managed interface testing and maintenance.

An interesting sidelight to the DDSOT computer program was its documentation. Developed by one of the Navy laboratories specializing in weapon systems, the DDSOT computer program itself was developed by an engineer who combined system knowledge with programming skill. However, the primary documentation at delivery time was just hard copy listing of the program's instructions and data design, but a flow chart was also required. So, a staff DSC knowledgeable about both the DDSOT and computer program documentation was assigned to assist its programmer with developing the flow charts. This was done expeditiously by the two sitting at a table, and as the programmer read the listing and described the implemented functions, the DSC drew the equivalent flow charts. The Navy learned to better define computer program deliverables, and the DSC learned much useful information that he took to his ship.

Biddle played a major role at Bath Iron Works during final construction in supporting completion of the first NTDS System Manual, another story worth repeating. As NTDS with WDS MK 11 gained visibility and its tight integration with the gun and missile systems were noted, there was concern that NTDS documentation was not as complete at the system level as was that for weapon systems. Accordingly, several staff instructors from the NTDS System course at Mare Island were called in one Saturday for a meeting with Lieutenant Commander Joe Randolph from NTDS headquarters at BUSHIPS. The result was assignment of these instructors on a collateral-duty basis to develop a comprehensive NTDS system manual covering a wide range of subjects about hardware, software, interfaces, operation, testing, routine maintenance, performance monitoring, fault isolation, and impact assessment of faults, however detected. After months of intensive work, a draft manual was completed. Since *Biddle's* System DS was on the development team, it was decided that shipboard assessment and completion of certain subject areas could be done upon arrival in Bath. This was done on an after-hours basis, and the initial manual was completed with a proper shipboard orientation. It proved to be a suitable complement to other shipboard documentation of the time, such as the Weapon System OPs and the Ship's Information Book. Over time, the manual was redesigned to accommodate additional ship classes and differences within each class and turned over to contractors for production.

The Bureau of Ships provided as part of the SORT package a modified tactical program with extensive data extraction capabilities to allow capture of critical data during missile shoots and other exercises, or for use in training. Data reduction programs were run off-line to provide technical and operational time-line and statistical details and thus an evaluation of total system performance. These techniques have for some time been incorporated into combat system design for on-line use and real-time system evaluation.

Technician Networking for Mutual Support

Since the digital revolution at sea was just gathering momentum during *Biddle's* early years, much of the work required by the DSs had few precedents to use as guidance. However, there was at the time a close relationship between many of the original DSs (who were converted from a number of other technical ratings) and their Weapon System counterparts from Mare Island. These were personnel who had gone to the DLG-28-class ships with WDS MK 11 prior to DLG-26 and 27 being retrofit. This created a network of experienced technicians that was frequently used to exchange opinions and recommendations from sister ships on problems, ideas, and lessons learned.

Dealing with the Unexpected

The at-sea success of NTDS/WDS MK 11 and related systems was not always the result of designed-in features. As will be related below, making complex things work together on a ship, along with all the other things happening on a ship at sea, often became the job of on-scene technicians, operators, and leaders. A respected NAVSEA engineer officer with responsibility for combat system design was heard to remark that systems are frequently procured and bolted down on ships and left up to the crews to refine maintenance and operation in the at-sea environment. *Biddle* and others worked hard at identifying and fixing those things not otherwise accounted for. Over time, this provided lessons learned for future ship projects so as to assure consideration of as many things as possible during design, construction, and testing.

WDS MK 11 was as revolutionary within the analog missile and gun community as was NTDS itself within the traditional Operations community. Commander Joe Randolph of BUSHIPS was way ahead of most of us with the digital WDS concept and its implementation (see David Boslaugh's book, Chapter 8). *Biddle*, among other ships, helped smooth the transition process and provided solid evidence that the digital approach to weapon control was effectively supported by the DS rating.

The initial evidence was developed during *Biddle's* PSA period in Boston in 1967. Concern within the Weapons community in Washington surfaced about how effective would be maintenance of the WDS MK 11 equipment if assigned to the DS rating. Equipment included two standard NTDS consoles used by WDS operators and associated WDS hardware such as the Fire Control Data Converter (FCDC) and the Weapon Control Panel (WCP). Switchboards were also involved, as was another NTDS console devoted to precision target tracking using the SPS-48 radar. One of the two NTDS Height/Size consoles was also part of the precision tracking ensemble.

It was thus recommended by the Weapons office that separate parts lists and PMS actions should be developed for those devices within the Weapons ratings. *Biddle's* NTDS Officer and his System DS were assigned to the job. What resulted was a report that established clearly the commonality of consoles with other NTDS consoles, availability of trained and capable DSs with supporting documentation, and spare parts already within the NTDS logistics system. Accordingly, the decision was taken to leave WDS MK 11 within the NTDS area of responsibility. We quickly learned to work effectively with our counterparts in the Weapons systems, and on most ships this approach was satisfactory.

A very difficult problem involved the ship's 400 Hz 100KW generators that persisted through shakedown. The SPS-48 radar and NTDS were routinely set up by the Electrical Officer to run off the same generator so that there would always be a stand-by generator available. Unfortunately, from time to time the NTDS consoles would startle operators by having the symbol displays just fly apart for a second, and then return to normal. We eventually found, after many hours of observation, that the radar transmitter would occasionally trip off-line (cross bar), which created an uncontained power surge at the generator felt by NTDS and its sensitive equipment. Voltage regulators of the time were not able to respond fast enough to prevent the surge from reaching consoles. After some negotiation, NTDS and the SPS-48 radar were put on separate generators and problems did not recur. This characteristic of the display equipment, among other power-related weaknesses, was eventually designed out of future versions of NTDS equipment. Also, solid-state converters have now replaced generators and provide built-in voltage regulation.

Some serious lessons were learned about how use of the wrong materials could result in major problems in the high-humidity environment of the Tonkin Gulf. As radar video distribution requirements increased during installation of new systems, several high-power video amplifiers were installed during the first PSA to improve signals to all video users. Lots of radar switchboard video cable connections were either remade or newly-made, using standard soldering techniques. Early in the 1968 deployment, the Display techs found recurring problems with some of the connectors, resulting in video failure out of the switchboards. Coincidentally, they also found that the video amplifiers seemed to be cooking the plastic-covered leads from the small amplifier vacuum tubes, which were soldered, to the associated circuit boards. The leads would then short, requiring a new amplifier tube to be soldered in. These problems confounded our collective wisdom until one of the Display techs concluded that acid-core solder was used during PSA when radar switchboards were reconnected to the video amplifiers and other users. After redoing all such known connections, that problem was resolved.

However, the video amps continued to cook leads. We then noticed that these problems occurred mostly when humidity got high in the unmanned but air-conditioned equipment room, not unusual at that time and was the same situation which had apparently also surfaced the switchboard connector problem. Some of the failed vacuum tubes with their charred plastic-covered leads were shipped to Naval Ship Engineering Center, Norfolk Division (NAVSECNORDIV), the BUSHIPS equipment technical support activity. A reply was shortly received: the manufacturer had failed to use inert tubing on the leads. In the occasional humid environment the reaction of plastic out-gassing and moisture formed a corrosive acid sufficient to eventually eat away the insulating plastic coating which allowed the wire leads to short out. Replacement tubes with properly insulated leads were received and another small but critical problem solved. The humidity problem was subsequently reduced when the Display techs began to check the external heat exchanger that cooled the space and notified the responsible "A" (Auxiliary machinery repair) gang, which supported equipment outside of the propulsion plant, of any problem, however slight.

During the early months of *Biddle's* active life, Terrier Standard Missiles in the Surface mode on WDS MK 11 ships were noted for missing their targets. After analysis by a team of Missile engineers, the team arrived on *Biddle* one Friday afternoon to test for a suspected possible cause. This test required services of *Biddle's* programmer and system technician, because it was thought that the problem was due to a capability of the NTDS/WDS MK 11 computer software to actually change the mode of a missile on the launcher rail. This was thought to happen on orders from the NTDS computer after the Surface mode was set up by the Fire Control Computer in control of the launcher and its missile. However, due to the in-depth knowledge of *Biddle's* personnel about how the NTDS program worked, and with the capability to demonstrate that remote mode changes were locked out on assignment of the launcher to the FCS computer, we got a clean bill of health. The problem was later found to be in the missile itself. This turned out to be a useful exercise for *Biddle*, because she gained another level of credibility in the WDS community.

Computers, Peripherals, and Related Systems

The Computer Room technicians were responsible for the very key elements of the digital system. They also had a tough job because the computers themselves were so reliable that little need for repairs existed. This was good for the system, but provided limited practice for these experts. However, they were kept busy monitoring operations around the clock and doing required PMS checks. Emphasis was placed on over-maintaining the Magnetic Tape Unit (MTU), however, which was the only mass data storage and retrieval device available to NTDS at the time. This meant assuring detailed attention to the performance of the servo units that drove the heavy magnetic tape reels, and maintaining read/write head condition and alignment to tight tolerances.

Occasionally a challenging problem would occur that gave the computer technicians a challenge. For example, NTDS had two 5KW 400Hz generators for computer primary power to assure more close regulation of this critical service that was available from ship's 400 Hz power. One day in the Tonkin Gulf one of the generators developed a fairly severe vibration. This unit had always had a slight tremor, but experts had not found sufficient reason to remove it. Unfortunately, *Biddle* was on her own this time, and a major effort was undertaken to remove the rotor and muscle it down to the machine shop. After being trued up on a lathe by a skilled machinist, it was muscled back and reinstalled. After testing, the generator worked properly, but retained a slight vibration for the duration of the deployment. Fortunately, modern power technology prevents that sort of burden on the digital maintainers.

While the FCDC was a marvel of electronic design and contained complex control and converter circuitry, the interfaces with Missile and Gun computers tended to be unstable and difficult to align. Long transmission cables contributed, requiring precise signal phase measurements and feedback adjustments. However, thanks to the technician network, DSC Snodgrass on *Wainwright* had solved the problem in conjunction with Fire Control technicians, and word got around before the resulting ORDALT was distributed. With permission of Command, *Biddle's* DSs and FTs installed a set of precise input amplifiers in the MK 119 fire-control computer to accept and stabilize FCFDC analog output signals. FCDC alignment procedures were modified as required. The same fix was applied to the FCDC'sGun System computer channel, too. This emphasized the need for (and suggested the advantages of) "digitizing at the source" as was eventually possible when digital designation and repeat-back capabilities were provided by digital fire-control computers.

The FCDC was another equipment lacking well-done parts listings. The Computer Room techs decided to take on the task of producing improved listings while spending long hours on watch in WESTPAC. Every FCDC part was evaluated, using the technical manual, and all available logistics information verified. The resulting parts list was neatly typed and submitted to NAVSECNORDIV for reproduction and distribution to the other seven ships with the FCDC. However, documentation rules dictated that such material must be produced in sufficient quantity for copies to each possible interested activity. The required quantities exceeded funds available to do the job. However, technician persistence eventually saw most ships provided with a copy informally.

This interest in complete parts lists was created by an incident involving the new CP-1218 digital computer installed with the Beacon Video Processor at PSA. Spare parts were not loaded out at the time of computer installation, for some reason now forgotten. At the time, parts in the computers were marked only with proprietary codes from the manufacturer, so it was difficult to identify components such as transistors by standard electronics designators. As luck would have it, a transistor failed in the CP-1218 computer, and could not be typed or cross-referenced with available information. The computer tech used a storage-trace-storage oscilloscope to map out the performance curves of another transistor removed from the computer, and then found a transistor in Supply that closely matched those parameters. Fortunately, spare parts and a parts listing soon showed up. Technicians like that are assets, indeed.

The wisdom of over-maintaining the MTU was proven when *Biddle* and other ships were provided with a new NTDS computer program. To offset the limited computer memory, and since there was not yet available a way to expand memory, the Fleet Computer Programming Center at Dam Neck had developed a way to provide the additional tactical functions needed in the changing threat environment of the Tonkin Gulf. This method, called Dynamic Modular Replacement, required the program tape with the dynamic modules to reside on the MTU all the time, with the MTU always ready to respond to load commands. When a particular tactical function not already in memory was required by CIC, an operator entered the specified code which the computer used to make room in memory for the new function (or sometimes multiple functions) to be read in from the MTU. The required function on tape was read in and activated. There was no room for error by either an operator or equipment, and response time was critical for such functions as engagement. After several months of use, and to *Biddle's* relief, this capability was replaced by standard programs. The Computer Room technicians never failed to assure a full-up MTU all the time. Today, of course, huge memories and high-tech mass storage devices provide sufficient capability to perform all required tasks without resorting to the DMR method.

Because of its good working relationship with the NAVSECNORDIV engineers, *Biddle* was often the test bed for field changes and other system improvements. One change installed just before deploying to WESTPAC was a capability to run both NTDS tactical computers from a single Real Time Clock (RTC). Since each computer had an RTC, switches were provided to allow selection of one or the other for both computers. This was installed as a reliability backup capability, but it resulted in a long-term improvement to CIC operations. It was a common situation in the early days of Tonkin Gulf operations for ships to report that displayed tracks would sometimes backup some small distance, and then continue normal movement. This was shown to be caused by the track updates done by one computer to be out of time correspondence with another computer receiving the tracks for display. This didn't happen on *Biddle* because the computer RTCs were always in correspondence when a single clock was selected. The RTC field change was expedited to all ships, and the programs also modified to exchange time across the intercomputer interface. Today's combat systems use a central time base, distributed to all computers and other users of a Real Time Clock.

The Computer techs met their match one day when an intermittent memory problem began to occur in one CP-642 computer. After standard trouble-shooting over several days had failed, unconventional tests of memory were tried. Again, no problems found. In desperation, a senior technician took a flashlight and inspected every connector and attachment such as fuse holders feeding the computer. A very slight discoloration around the fuse holder of one phase of the 3-phase 400 Hz input from the 5KW generator was found. It was a shot in the dark, but experience had shown that this was not a normal condition. The fuse holder was replaced and the intermittent memory problem never recurred. Good technicians always look for the indications everyone else has missed. That, plus good luck, another technician tool.

The WDS MK ll unit that controlled the launcher, showed computer loading and firing recommendations, and contained the firing key was the Weapon Control Panel (WCP). It was very reliable, containing both digital and analog electronics, since it talked to the NTDS/WDS computer and also to the launcher and the fire-control computer. It also contained dozens of small indicators containing low-wattage grain-of-wheat bulbs. When the WCP was on and in the operate mode, all indicators were on, they would flash or change brightness as an engagement was in progress. Unfortunately, the WCP was required to be activated for long periods of time when in the combat zone, and ran through the small bulbs in great quantity. *Biddle* technicians developed a simple field change that provided a front-panel switch that reduced illumination to a standby level without affecting the tactical state of the unit. When action was expected, the switch was operated to bring the illumination level back to normal. This change reduced the usage of bulbs down to a few per month. This is another example of how engineering did not consider the full scope of the operational environment, and how the sailors fixed it.

The Ship's Programmer

During the early years of DLG operations with NTDS, each ship had a Ship's Programmer billet that was to be filled by a qualified programmer, officer or enlisted. This was already customary on larger ships such as CGs and CVs. On *Biddle*, the NTDS System Chief was assigned to that billet as a collateral duty. Close cooperation with the Computer Room technicians and CIC personnel were key components of analyzing and possibly fixing program problems, using any available time slice to poke and peak at the offending program code. Having both equipment and program responsibilities made it possible for the Chief to better integrate all phases of NTDS maintenance and problem definition. It also required close coordination with Command and the NTDS Maintenance Officer to assure no impact on rules, regulations, and mission requirements. During those days, NTDS computer programs were not always completely debugged when delivered. This lack caused many system problems to be difficult to trace to the actual source, hardware or software or, in some cases, operator mistakes. It also meant that, as is sometimes now the case, the ship became the Beta tester for the programming activity. Much has been written about this situation, but *Biddle* managed it fairly well.

Ships in general provided a steady stream of trouble reports to the Fleet Programming Centers. As did some other ships, *Biddle* also usually provided with her reports a program fix, tested and often installed. We were always careful to fully document each shipboard change made, and over time had a local patch library that was used to update new programs as delivered on station. *Biddle's* programs were controlled to avoid unnecessary bit-fiddling, with the result that more than once sister ships asked for copies of our tactical programs because they were solid and mostly debugged. For some reason, even though all our software fixes were Command approved, documented, tested, and submitted to FCPC for formal incorporation as approved, programs continued to be delivered while containing some of the same problems that had been previously reported.

Biddle was a regular contributor to the NTDS Newsletter produced by the Fleet Computer Programming Center, Dam Neck. The Newsletter allowed the sharing of *Biddle* experiences in hardware and software corrections and maintenance with other NTDS ships. Other ships did the same, which benefited all ships, the programming centers, and schools. The newsletter became part of the de facto technician network. *Biddle* also provided regular reports on improved maintenance checks worked out by NTDS technicians to complement standard PMS feedbacks.

Biddle's objective in WESTPAC was to assure continuous combat system availability around the clock. It had been observed that the war usually stopped about 2400 to allow maintenance and other non-tactical tasks to be performed. Someone observed that some day the war might not stop so conveniently. So, it was decided that *Biddle's* programmer would develop some simple test functions embedded in the tactical programs to support on-line use by operator function code entry. This very simple, end-around test software verified alignment of the WDS MK 11 designation/repeat-back circuits and control/status circuits when unable to run DDSOT. This concept was expanded over time to cover some other systems and equipment. In addition, the limited built-NTDS in program monitoring and fault detection logic was expanded to provide new status information as the system operated. As new computers and additional memory have become available, this concept has expanded to cover virtually all ship systems, including the engineering plant.

Data Link Operations and Maintenance

The initial NTDS configurations included a huge amount of data communications equipment that constituted the data links. Link 11 included computer program functions, a terminal set (the AN/SSQ-29 modem), a communications system (the AN/SRC-16), and three dedicated topside antennas. This was a not only a complex subsystem, but the radio system was integrated with standard ship's communications via patch panels in Radio Central and couplers and tuners in the main Transmitter Room. The history of this system is interesting, well outside NTDS interests, and the technical requirements for its maintenance and operation were almost overwhelming. Accordingly, the Data Link technicians worked closely with RDs, ETs and RMs to assure correct setup of communication plans and minimize inter-frequency interference. *Biddle's* link techs were truly the best, as demonstrated by the years of success in Link operations and communications support.

And, yes, there was also another radio, antennas, and terminal for the aircraft-control link, Link 4A. This link was not activated in the Fleet until the early 1970's due to technical problems, and was in a layup state on *Biddle* during this time.

Biddle's data-link success got started during her first predeployment workup at Roosevelt Roads. The first four-participant Link in the Atlantic Fleet was established and maintained while *Biddle* served as the Net Control Ship (NCS). Each participant in Link 11, whether a ship, aircraft, or shore site, is called a Participating Unit (PU). This level of successful operation for such a new ship was a pleasant surprise, especially on the East Coast, but not unexpected because of the time already spent grooming the Link system. This included radios, data terminal, antennas, and operator procedures. Bravo Zulu messages from COMNAVLANTFLT were received, and Hard Charger was a proud ship. This led to continued successes on deployment, where *Biddle* was required by CTF 77 to be NCS when in the Tonkin Gulf op area.

Adding to the complex data communications operation in the Tonkin Gulf was the Marine Air Control Squadron (MACS) at Da Nang. Equipped with the Marine Tactical Data System (MTDS), which also included radars and missile batteries, they were the only shore-site PU and participated like all other PUs. However, the MACS also served as the gateway for Air Force non-real-time tracks (called Iron Horse tracks at the time). Such tracks were collected around the North end of Vietnam by various detection methods unique to the Air Force. The Air Force Tactical Data System (TDS), code named Buick, processed all such sensor reports and was located near the MTDS site on Monkey Mountain. The two sites were connected by a data line.

Prior to the first WESTPAC deployment in 1968, *Biddle* dispatched the NTDS System Chief to Cherry Point to spend some time with the MACS that was to deploy to Da Nang. *Biddle's* Ops Officer and NTDS Officer had learned that this MACS would be the unit at Da Nang with which joint operations would be conducted. It was deemed wise to establish technical contact since both units were new and would need lots of coordination on station to be successful. This proved to be a useful contact, since early on ships close to Da Nang could not maintain reliable Link operations with the Marines, while ships at some distance could. After many discussions about the problem, *Biddle* made a trip to Da Nang and sent a party to visit both the Marines and the Air Force. Eventually, it appeared that the MTDS antenna farm on Monkey Mountain did not have a good ground plane. This resulted in only long-distance communication via the generated sky waves, and no shorter-range communications because no ground wave was generated. By moving their antenna farm, the problem was fixed and the U.S. Navy was off the hook. *Biddle's* Link technicians were pleased, because they could find no technical reason for the problem in their equipment. This situation also initiated a maintenance regimen for *Biddle's* link equipment that emphasized keeping receivers as hot as possible and noise to a minimum. One of the four SRC-16 radio channels was groomed each day, another case of over-maintaining, perhaps. However, the enhanced maintenance standards worked out by the Link techs became PMS and factory standards. That's another reason why *Biddle's* Link 11 was one of the best.

USS *Chicago*, a guided-missile cruiser, spent much time in the Tonkin Gulf wrestling with an age-old problem called third-order harmonic interference. This was the result of running Link 11 at low frequencies and high power, often needed to assure good Link operations or for long-distance normal communications. The offending antenna was the 4-section long-wire fan antenna, the biggest communications antenna on ships at the time.

Third-order harmonics tended to interfere with other communication frequencies at or near the harmonic frequency, which is a multiple of the basic transmitter frequency. Such harmonics usually result from faulty antennas and nearby structural components of dissimilar metals that have weathered to form electrical diodes, called the "rusty bolt" effect. This combination reradiates harmonic frequencies and the more power in the fundamental frequency the more in the harmonics.

Chicago's experts redesigned the long-wire antenna to use more advanced antenna wire with a PVC coating, and also inspected the ship to find many cases of the so-called "rusty bolt effect" in the form of dissimilar metallic junctions, loose fittings, and effects of rust and corrosion. *Chicago* submitted a Field Change Proposal (FCP) and sent *Biddle* a copy.

Biddle was beginning to have severe harmonic problems during the 1968 deployment. So, the DSs were given permission to rebuild the antenna using *Chicago's* FCP. Antenna wire and special fittings were procured with TYCOM desk help. The Philadelphia Naval Shipyard provided newly-designed wire mounts made from a fiberglass material. Norfolk Naval Shipyard provided strain insulators with a newly-designed safety link. The new antenna was assembled with great effort, and extensive grounding and weather-proofing added around the masts. An inspection of over 800 groundstraps between the aluminum superstructure and the steel deck, plus topside ladders on the ship, found several hundred points of deterioration, which the deck force and technicians fixed. The result was almost full elimination of the harmonic problem, even at maximum power settings on the SRC-16. This configuration was used on the 1969 deployment, and was most effective for all modes of communication using the long wire antenna. This was the most ambitious undertaking by *Biddle* DSs of all the projects undertaken. BZ, all of you who worked on this modification.

Biddle's SRC-16 techs also used built-in SRC-16 frequency standards and signal analysis equipment to evaluate the performance of other ships in the net. These techs could determine if a radio was off frequency, and by how much. They also could determine, via some skillful interpretation and computations, if the frequency standard used to time-base the Link radios and modems was out of calibration. These were tools used by *Biddle* as NCS to fine-tune Link operations, PU by PU.

The SRC-16 radio contained electronic switches called cross-point relays, whose function was to set up configurations of radio channels, tuners, couplers, and antennas as selected at a control unit. Early version of these relays, such as installed on *Biddle* during construction, were temperamental and internal contacts would often stick. In the way of experienced technicians, the Link techs would remove a stuck relay and slam it on the rubber deck mat. They almost always worked after that repair. This widespread problem was corrected when the manufacturer issued new relays that worked correctly.

One impressive use of ingenuity by the Link techs resulted from a failure in the Link 11 address panel and control unit of the SSQ-29 modem, located in CIC. After a momentary withdrawal from the Link 11 net, and turn-over of NCS to another PU, the technicians opened the unit, determined the failure magnitude, disconnected the offending circuitry and used some clip leads to restore a limited PU capability. *Biddle* rejoined the net, and continued Link operations in this unofficial casualty configuration until repairs were made. Upon completion of the work, *Biddle* again took NCS and continued operations.

The Ship's Programmer teamed up with the Link technicians and CIC Track Supervisor to determine why a CV with a new NTDS program had started to send abnormally long transmissions. The team estimated what the transmit cycle should approximate, give the track load at the time. A Link data-extraction function was activated, which was a *Biddle* assignment by CTF 77, using a modified computer program. The extracted data was reduced with a special program that decoded messages and printed out results. What was found was the result of a failure to completely test and debug the new carrier program. There was an operator-requested function on the CV that required transmission of a single message type seven times. This was intended to be one time in seven consecutive transmit cycles. A programming error had each cycle sending the message 7 times, then 6, down to 1 time for each operator action. *Biddle* sent out an advisory message to the carrier, and the problem was fixed.

A one-time unusual event occurred in the Tonkin Gulf during Link 11 operations involving at least eight Participating Units (PU) and several E-2C Hawkeye airborne early-warning aircraft. This was prior to activation of the secure (encrypted) link. As Net Control Ship (NCS), *Biddle* was monitoring operations and noticed that what appeared to be a net PU had started into a constant transmit mode. Simultaneously, confusing tracks began to appear on ship NTDS consoles around the operational area. NCS quickly stopped interrogation of PUs to stop the cascading of bad track data, but the offending transmitter continued to offend. It was suspected that the North Viet Nam countermeasures folks had recorded and then played back on the same frequency several minutes of Link operations. *Biddle's* SUPRAD intelligence team was alerted to analyze the emitter, but it stopped before they could respond. Needless to say, that example of effective jamming of Link ll gave CTF 77 concern, but it was not a surprise. Precautions were taken to carefully monitor the net for any more anomalies, but none were noted. The encrypted secure link capability was activated not too long afterwards. *Biddle* technicians later assisted an NSA representative in Subic Bay with checkout of the crypto system on several ships.

Reliable Link 11 operations became a *Biddle* characteristic, due to the technicians with mastery of the equipment and our capability to find, fix, and report Link-related computer program glitches originating on other ships. The accumulated experience also resulted in a couple of extra days at sea when in Norfolk to help the Fleet Computer Programming Center at Dam Neck check out some Link changes and problems.

Display and Beacon Video Processing Systems

The *Biddle's* display system was of the AN/SYA-4(V) family. While a distinct upgrade from the initial SYA-1 series, it remained a challenge for technicians and sometimes new operators. As on most ships, constant work on the display system was required to catch all the problems, small or large, that could occur in this very complex equipment. It was also operated around the clock, and suffered from the normal wear-and-tear of any units with human operators. Some interesting maintenance actions and equipment modifications were developed by *Biddle's* Display Technicians to handle unplanned problems.

Among many improvements to SYA-4 display equipments, *Biddle* technicians developed a field change to keep missile range circles at the correct ranges as console range scales were changed. This helped quiet complaints from ship's operators and embarked staff, since each range setting would see the circles have a different diameter, and improved confidence in the accuracy of displayed information.

One continuing problem was that the track-ball units, used to move the cursor around, would become rough in operation. Each unit contained a set of costly and small ball bearings, and replacement would require considerable work. The simple fix was provided by toothpaste, any brand. After removal from the console, the unit was opened enough to allow a small quantify of toothpaste to be forced into each bearing. After a few minutes of bearing rotation, the roughness was usually gone, if only temporarily.

Operators also caused problems that later became fixes. During a WESTPAC deployment, there would be alerts at the System Monitor Panel (SMP) resulting from an illegal switch closure at an NTDS console. A Display Tech would usually respond, and never located a problem. However, it was noted that this alert occurred usually when a specific operator was on watch. Close inspection one night found that he had created a constant track-ball enable state, abnormal at the time for his console, by sticking a knife blade into the switch opening to keep it closed. This saved him a sore thumb, he said, since the button didn't have to be pushed each time the track ball was needed and the console worked OK. Since this also placed a heavier processing load on the program for that console, he was instructed to case his knife.

A critical event at Gitmo during Refresher Training set the tone of casualty recovery on *Biddle*. While steaming out for the final battle problem there was an unplanned electrical power loss to CIC. Using the preplanned casualty-control procedures worked out during precomm, *Biddle* technicians quickly secured power to affected equipment in preparation for restoration of power by the engineers. This was done to minimize failures in the sensitive display consoles of the time. Upon power restoration and console reenergizing, seven consoles were found to have power-supply failures. Display techs started repairs at once, and by the time GQ sounded for the battle problem six consoles were up. The seventh was repaired shortly thereafter. That experience was proof that intensive practice and in-depth understanding of how to respond to problems was key to controlling and restoring casualties throughout the combat system.

Maintaining a uniform level of video display on all consoles was a constant problem. Cathode Ray Tube (CRT) degradation occurred gradually, and would cause operators to turn up video gain and burn holes in the phosphor which showed both radar video and symbols. This was not tactically appropriate, since it degraded the display of video and thus reduced operator effectiveness. Other conditions could occur, such as reduced output from a video amplifier. *Biddle* Display techs developed a video-distribution maintenance method and diagrams that used a total path analysis from sensor to CRTs, with Minimum Discernible Signal (MDS) factors to achieve a fairly standard of video display quality. This process was used to determine when to change the CRTs or identify video chain problems. It was simple, but effective in setting maintenance standards. This package was largely incorporated by NAVSECNORDIV into a formal video maintenance manual that was developed for PMS use.

While the DLG 28-class NTDS suite was the best of its day, engineering continued at the manufacturers to refine equipment capabilities and correct deficiencies in design. The Display Techs were always busy installing field changes, some of which were many hours per console. With a dozen or more consoles, days and nights begin to run together. However, the work was done, and done well.

Biddle received one of the earliest Beacon Video Processor (BVP) installations, considered as part of the Display system for maintenance. The BVP was a very complex digitized signal processor that operated under control of a computer program in the CP-1218. The BVP was also required on the input side to operate with old-technology IFF and defruiter systems. A defruiter was an electronic filter that assured that no random pulses, called False Replies Uncorrelated In Time, or

FRUIT, got into the BVP signal processing section. Unstable BVP operation was immediately noticed, characterized by frequent inability to detect and decode valid IFF returns. *Biddle's* BVP technician analyzed the likely cause as unstable and out-of-BVP-spec pulse pairs from the IFF system. These pulse pairs, or mode tags, were used by the BVP to synchronize its internal processing of each IFF mode as generated by the IFF system. With cooperation of the ETs, who owned the IFF system, the problem was traced to old-technology delay lines that created the mode tags. We opened up the sealed delay-line unit and carefully moved soldered taps on the delay line until outputs were within the range of BVP requirements. To the satisfaction of the BVP and IFF techs, proper operation was restored. The "modified" delay line served perfectly for the remaining months of deployment.

Sometimes doing things correctly gets a technician in trouble. *Biddle* was in the middle of an Operational Readiness Inspection with visiting experts on board, when during a tracking exercise using the BVP had a major failure. The BVP technician was dispatched, quickly isolated the problem and effected a repair. He reported the system back up in a short time, and the inspectors were impressed with how well the casualty was handled and corrected. Unfortunately, one of the ship's officers was not pleased, and later called the DSC to his cabin to explain why the failure occurred if we had done all the PMS. Sometimes good technical explanations fail, but we were pleased that the inspectors were pleased.

Strange problems not covered in school or technical manuals were not unusual in the Display suite. One such problem resulted in a sweep jump at consoles selecting a specific radar. Radar sweep is generated in each console using sine/cosine pulses produced in a Radar Azimuth Converter (RAC). Each RAC gets radar antenna bearing information from its connected radar. The RAC outputs pulses as the antenna rotates, and the consoles generate sweeps from those pulses. This is all high-speed signal generation, and pulses must be within tight tolerances for proper display of the radar position as a smoothly rotating sweep on a console. The assigned Display tech spent hours checking circuits and pulse trains, all of which were apparently normal. Finally, he was able to set up a precision oscilloscope in such a way that he detected an extra pulse being produced by the Radar/RAC chain. It was very narrow, but got into the pulse trains and was sensed by the sweep circuits in the consoles so as to create the jumping effect. This was a sweet victory against technical odds that only technicians can appreciate.

Other Technical Challenges and Contributions

In relating incidents such as attempted herein, it is difficult to pick a few from the hundreds that could be of interest and that demonstrate the nature and capabilities of the sailors entrusted with making complex systems work. *Biddle* sailors of each crew, and sailors of all other ships, have always shown a level of competence and mastery of complex machines that set standards which assure that tomorrow's ships will also be well served. Following are some examples of the larger scope of technician involvement in ship systems that show how lasting effects are achieved by the actions taken by the guys on the deckplates on each watch.

The SPS-48 radar was another integral part of the WDS MK 11 equipment suite. The original radar system did not have a Moving Target Indicator (MTI) capability, needed to see targets in clutter and weather. *Biddle* deployed in 1968 with the first MTI unit (brassboard model) and two engineers from the manufacturer. The radar operated with MTI all day, and the engineers made improvements and repairs at night. The result was an MTI capability that soon was installed on all ships. In addition, *Biddle* continued with SPS-48 support as the test platform for Operational Evaluation to determine radar characteristics in the at-sea environment. Such factors as blind speed, target glint and scintillation characteristics, burn-thru, and others were evaluated by Navy experts from Operational Test and Evaluation Force (OPTEVFOR). Lessons learned were incorporated into radar doctrine for all ships with this radar suite, updated with MTI to the SPS-48A, and used by *Biddle* on the next deployment.

Electronic warfare systems were very elementary during *Biddle's* early years, while threats from the Soviet bloc were constantly increasing and proliferating. The Navy used *Biddle* as the test bed for an experimental passive and active EW system, named Shortstop. In late 1969 a Navy survey team was on *Biddle* to begin the process of designing the Shortstop installation, due for installation at the next overhaul. We assisted with determining equipment locations and made recommendations for improving existing installation problems. *Biddle* and Shortstop deployed in 1972, and demonstrated the full range of active and passive capabilities, including extensive Electronic Intelligence (ELINT) data recording and analysis. Today's SLQ-32 EW system and later variants are derived from *Biddle's* Shortstop installation and lessons learned from extensive operations.

Biddle NTDS technicians were required to become knowledgeable in the ship systems that provide power, water, air, HVAC, and Damage Control resources. They also practiced a version of Electronic Casualty Control (ECC) that was an NTDS-oriented extension of standard Repair 8 ECC operations. Repair 8 was one of the numbered repair parties used in a GQ situation or as required to provide manpower and equipment to control battle damage such as fires, flooding, plus equipment and personnel casualties. During Repair 8 ECC and all other operations, the NTDS technicians learned to work with all other technicians, operators, and the Engineering Department personnel to solve NTDS and other problems as the need arose. In turn, progress was made on *Biddle* in formulating organizational concepts that require such cooperation across all ship's administrative boundaries of departments and divisions. This attitude goes back to the days of DLG 28-class NTDS/WDS training at Mare Island, where the system technicians were trained to think broadly and work with everybody to solve problems. All these are facets of the modern readiness-management concepts used throughout the Fleet today. These concepts support centralized and coordinated actions, standardized communications, rapid response to mission requirements with effective technical operations, and cooperation among all shipboard personnel.

We didn't realize it at the time, but one of the most significant and continuing contributions of DLG 28-class Readiness Management fundamentals is found in an OPNAV-required system now found throughout the Fleet. It is called the Combat System Operational Sequencing System (CSOSS), and was created by the AEGIS cruiser USS *Yorktown* (CG-48) to support the comprehensive shock trials and survivability assessment in which the crew was required to respond to all casualties and damage from each blast. Only limited tools for total combat system casualty-control training and support was provided, *Yorktown's* C.O. determined, so from the deck plates came the requirement for CSOSS. CSOSS optimizes the built-in features of the AEGIS Combat System as a highly-automated and monitored system with extensive fault-detection and reconfiguration features. CSOSS provides the tools such as procedures, diagrams, and status boards to support the sailor's role in readiness management. As part of a Navy/Government/Contractor team, some former *Biddle* sailors contributed to development and institutionalization of CSOSS at the shipboard and NAVSEA levels, incorporating lessons-learned as appropriate.

CSOSS is a functional companion to the HM&E world's Engineering Operational Sequencing System (EOSS), and is also modeled after EOSS. On *Biddle*, the concept of central coordination of combat system problems was done in vestigial form. However, the integration of systems and the central location for monitoring readiness and managing configurations is close to how CSOSS supports the integrated combat system on almost all surface-ship classes today.

Yes, I Was a Biddle DS

James Treadway

The phrase "May you live in interesting times" unquestionably applied when *Biddle's* keel was laid in December 1963. The shock and horror of President Kennedy's assassination two weeks before had stunned the world and drove this nation into deep mourning. The Cold War was raging; hardly a day passed without another reminder that nuclear war not only possible, but also likely. The Bay of Pigs invasion in April 1961 and Cuban missile crisis in October 1962 pointed to Cuba as a trigger that could start World War III. At the same time on the other side of the world, the smoldering fire in Vietnam that France could not extinguish was a few months from flashpoint. Elements of the Seventh Fleet were already in the Gulf of Tonkin and U.S. advisors were on the ground in South Vietnam. These events are ancient history now, which my students at the technical college where I teach like to remind me. Perhaps they are, but they occurred at the zenith of the Cold War and define the time that created a Cold War cruiser, the USS *Biddle*.

At that time I was a freshman architecture major at a small junior college in San Angelo, Texas. The U.S. Congressman from our district had tried to get me an appointment to the U.S. Naval Academy, but my grades were not strong enough. So, with more bad grades than good ones on my transcript and the hot breath of the draft on my neck, I decided to follow the advice of my uncle and join the Navy. Uncle Pete, a Navy officer who served in USS *Salamonie* (AO-26) at the Battle of Leyte Gulf, was a positive influence for me 40 years ago and remains so today at the age of 86. After a few farewells and one last round of partying, I boarded the bus on 21 July 1964 that would take me to San Antonio to be sworn in. I turned to wave to my mom and dad—she was crying and he was smiling. Early in the morning on the next day, San Diego boot camp welcomed its latest batch of raw recruits—I was in the United States Navy!

Soon after arriving at boot camp, an event occurred that would change the lives of millions of Americans and divide this nation as few events have. On 2 August and again on 4 August 1964, the USS *Maddox* (DD-731) and USS

Turner Joy (DD-951), while on patrol in international waters in the Gulf of Tonkin, were allegedly attacked by North Vietnamese naval craft. In retaliation, President Johnson ordered attacks against North Vietnamese naval forces and shore positions. The Vietnam War had begun. *Biddle's* hull was less than half complete.

Boot camp recruits couldn't watch the evening news, but we did get letters from home—we heard rumors that something had happened in a place called Vietnam. Where the hell is Vietnam, anyway? We knew immediately that something important had happened because waves of military aircraft could be seen heading west over the Pacific almost daily. Many wondered if we would actually go to Vietnam.

After scoring high on the battery of tests given to determine job aptitude and then completing boot camp, the Navy sent me to Radarman "A" school at Treasure Island, San Francisco. The first phase of the school was basic electronics—DC and AC circuits, vacuum tubes, and basic radar theory. Deciding that knowledge of electronics was something that I could use as a civilian, I studied hard and tried to stay out of trouble. The hard work paid off when the Navy offered to send me to Electronics Technician "A" school, also at Treasure Island. Again, I studied hard and applied myself and, again, the Navy made an offer I couldn't refuse—extend my enlistment for two years and attend Data Systems Technician "A" and "C" schools at Mare Island, just up the road at Vallejo, California.

When I started Data Systems Technician "A" school in the summer of 1965, *Biddle* had recently launched; her hull and superstructure were virtually complete. Meanwhile, on the opposite coast, I had discovered that the learning environment at Naval School Command, Mare Island, was outstanding. The structured classroom environment, excellent instructors, and fascinating subject matter combined to create an atmosphere that not only piqued my interest, but it also allowed me to achieve levels of learning that far exceeded any previous effort. One instructor, Data Systems Chief (DSC) Eggers I believe, seemed particularly interested that I perform well at school. His encouragement helped to keep me focused on the difficult task of learning about difficult subjects. The result was obvious—I consistently was number one or two in each class.

The basement lab, which was filled with equipment that we had learned about in the classroom, was my home away from home. It was the crucible of the course. After instruction about a particular piece of equipment in the morning, the class would get "hands on" experience on the same equipment in the afternoon. That evening, I would supplement the classroom instruction with many more hours alone in the lab studying schematics, taking measurements, sharpening my troubleshooting skills, and becoming even more familiar with the equipment.

The Univac Digital Trainer (UDT) was one piece of equipment that attracted my attention. A functional, transistorized 15-bit digital computer with memory, arithmetic logic unit, and a Friden Flexowriter for input and output, the UDT was an excellent training device and a crude precursor of today's personal computer. Many hours were spent writing simple programs, storing them on paper tape, and then reading them back later. Like its much bigger brother the Univac CP-642 computer, the UDT had front panel lights and switches that allowed a programmer to enter a "bootstrap" program which, when executed, allowed more complex programs such as operating systems, to be loaded. We didn't call them operating systems back then, they were "Executive Routines," I believe.

The lab was populated with most of the equipment I would see aboard ship—the display consoles and readouts, central pulse amplifier, symbol generator, and radar azimuth converters. I had the most fun was when one of the radars on the roof was turned on and I could chase signals from the input of the radar azimuth converter, through the radar signal distribution switchboard, to a console's display.

The basement lab also served as a test bed for new equipment. Bob Gerity, while an instructor/division head at DS School, recalled that "Down in the basement some serious testing was taking place on the first generation of a direct digital-to-digital fire control system. Having served in an analog Talos cruiser, I had seen the problems trying to get target data from the radars in CIC to the fire control system. This new system, to be installed in the DLG-28 Class frigates, promised nearly instantaneous transfer of target coordinates from CIC to the Fire Control System."

Digital logic circuits—simple building blocks connected to perform complex functions—fascinated me. No less fascinating was learning that there were numbering systems other than base ten. The binary and octal systems, which use only the digits zero and one and zero through seven respectively, seemed to be a natural way to count. Today, the hexadecimal system (base 16), which uses zero through nine and the characters A through F to represent numbers, is the most common way to count and address physical memory in the personal computer world. Adding hexadecimal numbers such as BADF00D (yes, BADF00D is a legitimate number) and 4520FF3 in my head and converting some numbers from decimal to hexadecimal is not difficult at all—thanks to my Navy training and almost 40 years in the business.

Life as a student at Mare Island had a limited, lighter side. Other than a data processing course I took at Vallejo Junior College at night, little time was spent off base. Mare Island Shipyard, where nuclear submarines were built, was a large part of the base. I recall strolling by the USS *Vallejo* (SSBN-658) on the day she was launched. After a tour that included the missile room, I took the opportunity to watch the launching ceremonies with the crowd directly in front of the brand new boat. When the submarine finally and reluctantly slid down the ways, a group of officers stood at attention on both planes and saluted forward, in the direction of the crowd. Just as the boat hit the water, most of the officers lost their balance. Some were precariously hanging on a rope fence, their feet directly over the water. At that moment, a formation of Navy jets that were on the deck, in the middle of the channel, pulled vertical in full afterburner—BAM! BAM! BAM!—directly over the sub and much to the delight of the crowd. It was quite a sight—almost like something out of McHale's Navy.

At the conclusion of data systems school in the spring of 1966, I had received a first class education courtesy of the United States Navy. I knew as much about electronics, computers, radars, and equipment in the Data Display Group of the Naval Tactical Data System as a young man could. The education not only prepared me for the job to be done aboard ship, but it also became the genesis from which subsequent educational pursuits began, including graduating summa cum laude from college with a degree in computer science. Equally important, my two-year Navy technical education and four years of practical experience aboard *Biddle* implanted a deep and inextinguishable desire to learn, explore, and excel.

NTDS Data Display Equipment Maintenance

Of the three NTDS hardware groups, the data display group represented the largest group of equipment, which included the display and readout consoles in CIC; auxiliary equipment in equipment rooms below CIC; the Identification Friend or Foe/Selective Identification Feature (IFF/SIF) systems associated with the two air-search radars; and radar signal distribution equipment connected to all search radars including Airborne Early Warning (AEW). IFF/SIF equipment seemed to be the most reliable with an "up-time" approaching 100%. Their dependability was not a surprise considering the liberal use of integrated circuits and the absence of mechanical parts in the primary components of the IFF/SIF system, the BVP (Beacon Video Processor) and digital defruiters.

Interface equipment such as the CPA (Central Pulse Amplifier), RSDS (Radar Signal Distribution Switchboard), and RAC (Radar Azimuth Converter) also enjoyed a respectable MTBF (Mean Time Between Failures). Surprisingly, the

RSDS with two motors and mechanical parts that switched radar signals enjoyed a low failure rate—probably due to internal heaters that kept the cabinet's internal humidity low. The RSDS low failure rate was confirmed in Boslaugh's *When Computers Went to Sea*. RACs, with the exception of the all-digital SPS-48 48 RAC, were susceptible to problems with the electromechanical module that converted the analog voltage indicating the radar's azimuth to digital signals required by NTDS.

Display consoles in CIC required regular attention, however. The electromechanical track ball that radarmen used to position the screen's cursor required frequent cleaning due to cigarette smoke contaminants (smoking was permitted in most parts of the ship, including CIC in those days), spilled drinks (soda and coffee) and dirt contamination. High-voltage components in the focus and astigmatism programmer and the high voltage power supplies failed regularly and required periodic adjustment. Fluctuations in the ship's 400 cycle generators occasionally blew out the less-than-robust power supplies in display consoles.

AN/SYA-4 consoles were strange beasts—half analog and half digital. The high voltage components that drove the CRT with video, sweep, and symbols could knock a technician across the room if he were not careful. I vividly (and painfully) recall when that happened to me while troubleshooting a Focus and Astigmatism Programmer during heavy seas. Luckily, the 5,000 volts of direct current went only through a fingertip to ground. The spark sounded like a rifle shot, tripped several circuit breakers, and left a pin-sized hole in my right index finger. The consoles opened with a hand crank and would open up like huge jaws for the technician to gain access. We often joked that we would use an RD (later the rate was changed to OS) for our shorting probe before touching anything on the inside to troubleshoot.

The display console's digital logic boards were housed in two slide-out drawers in the bottom of the unit. Each drawer had two rows of identical logic cards, which were populated with an array of NOR gates. The NOR gates were simple resistors and discreet transistors epoxy-encapsulated in a carrier that was soldered to the printed circuit board. Back panel wiring connected NOR gates together to form flip-flops, counters, and other logic functions.

The height-size console, which allowed operators to determine the altitude of a target and estimate the size of a group of aircraft, was a difficult piece of equipment to maintain. Radarmen did not like them because they were difficult to use, while technicians did not like them because they were difficult to adjust and troubleshoot. It was rumored that height-size consoles on some ships were so unreliable that they were turned off and left off. That was not the case on *Biddle*.

Michael Daugherty, a fellow data systems technician who was onboard *Biddle* from 1985 to 1989 and participated in the installation of the New Threat Upgrade (NTU), remembered the height-size console: "We had the height-size console from 1985 until 1987. It was removed as part of the NTU. I cannot recollect ever seeing it turned on during the final two years of AN/SYA-4 displays existence. The radarmen used to hang their gas mask all over it and it made for a great bookshelf."

Biddle was equipped with a top-secret black box, now declassified, called Seesaw. Seesaw was MiG IFF, which enabled *Biddle* to positively identify a target as a MiG—if the MiG's transponder was on and working. During "tight" situations when MiGs were in a threatening posture or mixing it up with friendlies, a halfsecond interrogation would help sort out the good guys from the bad guys in the crowded skies over North Vietnam. Seesaw was installed just before *Biddle's* first WESTPAC deployment without the benefit of factory training on the device. Nevertheless, my instructions were to "Keep it working, no matter what." I cannot recall one Seesaw failure during *Biddle's* first two deployments. Seesaw would be an important asset during *Biddle's* third Gulf deployment.

The majority of the work performed as a Display technician was on equipment within the Display group itself. Occasionally, it was necessary to work directly with technicians in other groups to pinpoint the source of a problem in a tightly integrated electronic environment. A problem with the intermittent drop in quantity of IFF/SIF returns, which was described in the previous chapter, is a good example.

Solving the problem required the combined talents of both a Data Systems technician and a radar specialist in the Electronics Technician rating—an ETR. Difficult to diagnose problems with the all-digital AN/SPS-48 radar often required talking technical with a 48 radar Fire Control Technician or one of the on-board Gilfillan engineers. Missile Fire Control Technicians (FTMs) were called when there was a problem with the NTDS/Weapons interface. Power fluctuations, voltage spikes, and "losing the load" were problems resolved by working closely with the Engineering Department. (A close working relationship with the Engineering Department persisted until *Biddle's* last years. Michael Daughety remembered that "Engineering was also very good about maintaining our chilled water systems by keeping the filters changes and the pumps operating. About once a month we would have to lug 5 gallon cans of distilled water from #1 Engine Room to the 05 level, which is where the expansion tank was located to replace any lost water.") It was clear from the top of the *Biddle* organization down to my level that we were a professional team and highly competent in our respective areas. It was a great working environment.

Ready for Combat

James Treadway

Biddle was a handsome man-o-war. Long, lean and muscular, she was a true greyhound—always ready to race tens of thousands of miles to her next assignment, ready for combat. Her Terrier missile launcher forward, 5-inch gun aft, and 3-inch guns port and starboard, punctuated her offensive capabilities. The multitudes of antennas mounted on almost any available surface were her eyes and ears to a hostile world. Internally, her engineering plant generated 85,000 horsepower which propelled her well beyond her published speed yet provided comfortable living conditions for her crew and electric power for her equipment.

Her primary mission was to provide Anti-Air Warfare (AAW) and Anti-Surface Warfare (ASUW) defense for a fast carrier task force. *Biddle's* secondary mission was to provide defense against other surface ships, Anti-Submarine Warfare (ASW), and to conduct Naval Gunfire Support (NGFS) in support of amphibious operations. What kind of ship did the Navy get in 1967 for $70,000,000 that could meet mission requirements?

Biddle displaced 6,570 tons (standard) and 7,930 tons (full load) and had a length of 547 feet, a beam of 55 feet, and a navigational draft of 28 feet 10 inches. *Biddle* had approximately the same displacement as a World War II light cruiser, yet could accelerate and maneuver like a destroyer. Four Babcock and Wilcox boilers generated 1,200-psi steam that turned two geared turbines, two shafts, and twin six-bladed screws with 85,000 horsepower. Advertised top speed was 32 knots—but we knew we were much faster. The engineering plant generated 6,800 KW of electrical power and 24,000 gallons of fresh water daily.

Terrier Missile System

Biddle's main AAW armament was a deck-mounted missile launcher that could load and launch two supersonic Terrier missiles every 30 seconds. Since the missile weighed 1.5 tons, launch and internal handling systems were highly automated and completely mechanized. Missiles were fed on launcher feeder rails through blast doors to the launcher from the strikedown area where technicians had "winged and finned" the birds. A massive hydraulic system assured the load sequence would elapse in less than a second. The strikedown area received missiles from two large, rotating port and starboard rings from the magazine, directly below the strikedown area. The two rings were tangentially connected to a third ring on the ship's centerline below the top two rings. The mechanism resembled the old style coke machines and was commonly called a 'coke machine' for that reason. One problem with the design was that the rings took up an enormous amount of room. It was the best mechanism we had at the time, however. Later, engineers figured out how to launch missiles from an array of vertical tubes at main deck level.

Each ring held 20 missiles for a total capacity of 60 missiles. Most DLGs carried two training missiles known as TSAMs and one Anti-Submarine Rocket (ASROC) trainer, which reduced the capacity to 57 war rounds. After loading two missiles, the launcher could slew to firing position in eight tenths of a second. Once missiles were launched (usually two were fired almost simultaneously at the lead target) the launcher automatically returned to position to load two more. The SPG-55 missile fire control radar pointed to the target with a pencil-thin beam of radio frequency energy, which the missile (minus the booster) would intercept then follow to the target. The missile warhead would detonate just before impact, bringing down the target. The system worked amazingly well—*Biddle* had scored many direct hits on both low-speed and high-speed targets during target practice. Amazingly, *Biddle's* sister ship *Sterett* splashed a MiG in the Tonkin Gulf at a range of 9,500 yards when the entire missile, including booster that had not separated, made skin-to-skin contact with the MiG. The MiG was inside the minimum range—close enough to have his picture taken with a hand held camera.

During shakedown missile firings, I occasionally walked a few steps to the bridge from my station in CIC to watch a launch. To describe the event as impressive is an understatement. The tremendous roar from the solid propellant booster was deafening in itself. Add to that the fact that the missile quickly exceeded the speed of sound and the blinding flash of light, and the smoke it generated—I would have paid to see it.

The behind-the-scenes technical details of how to get a 3,000-pound missile to travel at Mach 2 then hit an incoming object traveling at near Mach 1 is fascinating reading. *Biddle's* Weapons Officer, Lieutenant Commander Fred Howe, explains how it's done:

The AN/SPG-55B radars were the sensors for the MK76 Missile Fire Control System (MFCS) and were greatly improved versions of their predecessors, the 55As. All of the missiles we carried were either BTs (Beamrider, Tail control) or HTs (Homing, Tail control). These missiles were likewise vast improvements over the earlier BW (Beamrider, Wing control.) missile. Tactically we employed only the BTs as vehicles for the special weapon warhead.

The 55Bs broadcast four separate streams of intelligence: capture, guidance, tracking, rear reference. The broad "capture" beam into which the BT was launched, captured and steered the missile into the "guidance" beam. The "guidance" beam was collimated to a separate "tracking" beam that was locked on to the target. The BT essentially flew up the guidance beam until it came into the proximity of the target. The special weapon version of the BT carried a beacon that permitted the MFCS to calculate the separation between the range of the target and range of the missile (R-Rm). When that difference reached a preset value the warhead was triggered. This process placed the warhead under positive control, not allowing the warhead to detonate absent the signal from the controlling radar.

The principal conventional tactical missile was the HT. The HT was designed to perform a lead-collision intercept, and essentially fired as if you were shooting at a duck and you aimed at where you expected the duck to be at intercept. In addition to the beams described above, the 55B also emitted a rear reference signal coded in order to permit the HT, after launch, to identify the radar it was to guide on. The HT continued to receive this rear reference signal throughout flight as well as the target return signal from the guidance beam and continuously solved the resulting geometry to fly an intercept to the target. When it arrived in the proximity of the target the onboard Target Detecting Device would automatically trigger the warhead. Needless to say the HT had much greater range and altitude capability as it continually corrected for target maneuvers.

The HT also had some surface-to-surface capability as long as the 55B could "see" the target and the sea state was not too high to provide an unambiguous target return.

5-inch/54 and 3-inch/50 Guns

A dual-purpose rapid fire 5-inch/54 aft and two 3-inch/50 Mk 34 guns amidships gave *Biddle* AAW and NGFS capabilities. Designed during World War II, the 3-inch/50 fired a 13-pound projectile six miles with several fuse options. The 3-inch/50 was optical sighting only. To hit a target, you did it just like shooting squirrels—get the target in your sight, lead a little, squeeze the trigger. Weapons Officer Lieutenant Commander Fred Howe provided more details bout the 3-inch 50: "The 3-inch/50 gun's primary control was provided by independent DLOS (disturbed line of sight) (lead-computing) gunsights. The accuracy and usefulness of these directors was very dependent on operator experience. At some point we "discovered" an SH1 who had experience and he was able to string together impressive air bursts on a number of sleeves during Shakedown. (We quietly moved him from port to starboard without fanfare.) No one else ever got a single burst that I remember. The secondary control for the 3-inch was provided by the MK68 GFCS (with AN/SPG-53A radar), which was the primary control for the 5-inch gun. The 3-inch projectiles were point detonating (PD), armor piercing (AP) or proximity."

Biddle's 5-inch/54 gun was manned by a crew of 14 and had a rate of fire of 20 rounds per minute at the maximum automatic rate. With a muzzle velocity of 2,650 feet/sec, the 70-pound projectile gave the gun a maximum range of 25,900 yards (5-in/54 Mk 42). The SPG-53 radar/director tracked the target and pointed the gun in the right direction. Both the 3-inch/50 and 5-inch/54 were called into action during *Biddle's* 1972 MiG engagement and both performed extremely well.

ASW Components

Biddle's ASW components consisted of the most sophisticated sonar equipment available at the time. The SQS-26 (BX) bow-mounted sonar provided passive and active capabilities and provided target information to a MK-114 semi-automatic underwater fire control system. The bulbous stainless steel sonar dome contained 576 transducer elements in a cylindrical array, eight rings stacked atop one another of 72 elements each. ASW weapons included the long range ASROC that was fired from the forward missile launcher; torpedoes launched from port and starboard triple-tube launchers; and Drone Anti-Submarine Helicopter (DASH), a radio controlled pilotless helicopter armed with a torpedo. [*Eventually, with the retirement of the DASH system, a manned aircraft—the SH-2 Seasprite would be embarked…aviators in the wardroom!* (Marfiak)]

Combat Information Center

Combat Information Center, which was located immediately aft of the bridge on the 03 level, was the heart and soul of the ship. The physical layout of CIC was modular, with each module serving a particular function such as air control, sonar, weapons control, electronic warfare, underwater battery control, and surface operations. Most modules were composed of one or more multi-function NTDS display consoles such as Track Supervisor, Weapons, Height/Size, and Flag officer. The elevated and enclosed Flag area and Weapons area, which included the missile launch console, were conveniently located forward in CIC, allowing the captain to step from the bridge to CIC in a few seconds.

CIC was quiet, air conditioned, and dark except for the amber glow of radar sweeps and the illumination provided by countless tiny incandescent lamps and status boards that made information available to the officers and men at their stations. Conversations between console operators and their unseen counterparts were muted, professional, and couched in the appropriate military jargon. When the ship was underway and CIC was manned, equipment maintenance was accomplished without the benefit of adequate lighting, which required an expert knowledge of the equipment being repaired.

The Naval Tactical Data System

If CIC was the heart and soul of the ship, then the NTDS was the brains. NTDS hardware and maintenance responsibilities within the Data System Technician rating, was functionally divided into the Computer, Display, and Communication groups. On *Biddle*, two Data Systems Chiefs had their hands full attempting to control a dozen or so technicians who actually did the work. Overseeing the entire group was an NTDS Officer who really had his hands full.

David L. Boslaugh, author of *When Computers Went to Sea—The Digitization of the United States Navy*, stated in an e-mail:

> The *Belknap* Class of guided missile frigates, of which *Biddle* was the ninth ship of the class, were the first ships to have the Naval Tactical Data System installed during ship construction. Before *Belknap*, only six other existing ships had received the new digital system—as a backfit. *Biddle* was also the seventh ship to have a radical new concept in its weapons direction system, through which targets were relayed from sensors to the missile and gun fire control systems. These ships were the first to have the weapons direction function incorporated directly into NTDS, which brought about not only a savings in previously redundant CIC personnel and equipment, but also, and far more importantly, greatly reduced reaction time between sensing a new hostile target and taking it under fire.

Two Univac CP-642A solid-state digital computers were the central components of the Computer Group. The CP-642A descended from the AN/USQ-17 unit computer, which was designed at Univac in the mid-1950s by NTDS program managers and supercomputer guru Seymour Cray. Cray, in turn, had based the design of the pioneering transistorized USQ-17 computer on his experience designing room-filling vacuum-tube super secret code breaking computers, some of the first general purpose computers in the history of computing, for the U.S. Navy's code breakers."

Even though the USQ-17 boasted numerous technological advances such as direct memory-to-memory high-speed data communications between two computers, a one instruction block data I/O controller, a large number of input-output channels, and a novel external interrupt scheme, it eventually ran out of processing steam (Boslaugh 159, 162, 163). The 642's memory contained 32,768 30-bit words of ferrite core memory. A 32-bit word length was preferred, but transistors at that time did not have sufficient power to drive the load. The refrigerator-size cabinet contained approximately 3,800 printed circuit cards plugged into a dozen slide-out racks. To "boot" the 642, the first instructions were punched in by hand into front panel registers. This small program read a paper-tape bootstrap program into memory, which allowed the executive routine (today called the operating system) to be loaded from the magnetic tape unit. The Computer group hardware list also included a keyset central, paper tape punch and reader, magnetic tape, teletypes, and a data signal distribution switchboard.

Biddle's NTDS computer configuration would probably be recognizable to most old plankowner DS's as late as the NTU installation in 1986. Michael Daugherty describes Hard Charger's configuration at that time: "We also had the SMP, which was the remote control for the 642B computers. It seems to me that *Biddle* was upgraded from 642A computers to the B models at some point in time. You could control the master slave configuration, and perform other functions with the SMP. It was located in CIC. I am not sure if it was part of the original configuration. When I reported for duty, we had three 642B computers, two 1218 Computers and the ECMU. The ECMU was the external core memory unit to give the (operating system) more memory resources. The thing never broke. Being a computer tech, I spent a lot of time in front of the 642B computers making voltage adjustments to the memory arrays drawers. Once they were tweaked just right, they ran nicely."

Primary components of the Display group were the Plan Position Indicator (PPI) consoles, height-size consoles and auxiliary readouts in CIC; radar azimuth converters for the SPS-10, SPS-40, SPS-48, and Airborne Early Warning (AEW) radars; radar signal distribution switchboard; central pulse amplifier; symbol generator; and video signal simulator.

The Identification Friend Foe/Selective Identification Feature (IFF/SIF) components, which included the Beacon Video Processor (BVP, defruiters, and Seesaw, were a functional subgroup of the Display group. Hughes Aircraft had developed the BVP to automatically track the IFF beacons of friendly targets in a rich target environment such as the Tonkin Gulf, allowing controllers to concentrate on other tasks such as detecting hostile targets. Defruiters significantly reduced the amount of spurious IFF responses called "FRUIT" that were triggered by IFF/SIF interrogators aboard other ships and aircraft. FRUIT was an acronym for False Replies Uncorrelated In Time, hence the term, "defruiter."

Amid considerable secrecy, a small, top-secret box named Seesaw was installed in CIC just before departing for the Gulf. Seesaw was a MiG IFF interrogator that we did not want the North Vietnamese military, or anyone else, to know that we had. *Biddle* used Seesaw to help controllers separate the good guys from the bad guys in the crowded skies over North Vietnam. Unlike "friendly" IFF interrogators that operated continuously, Seesaw was normally turned off, and then manually switched on momentarily as the antenna's azimuth approached a target. Leaving Seesaw on continuously would have given away our secret and our position. Factory training and spare parts were not available. This was not a problem during the first two deployments, as the device did not fail.

Biddle's Crew, Ready for Combat

The skill and dedication of the officers and men who served in *Biddle* for almost 27 years are the reasons why *Biddle*, without exaggeration, was always ready for the fight. Indeed, the complex mechanical and electrical components described above, when properly installed, maintained, and operated, allowed *Biddle* to perform her primary and secondary missions. But it was the hundreds of thousands of hours of hard work during yard periods and during each cruise that made *Biddle* work as designed. Furthermore, the operational structure of the ship and how she operated during peacetime and war was intelligent and flexible yet allowed the ship to immediately respond to any threats at any time. *Biddle's* officers, under the captain's direction, carried out that policy. Lieutenant Commander Fred Howe describes how *Biddle's* sailors prepared for combat:

> One of the most rewarding events that career members experience is that of sailing into harm's way with U. S. Navy sailors. Normally a uniformly carefree lot, sailors moving toward expected hostilities take on an entirely new attitude about their responsibilities, both personal and professional.
>
> From the first day out of Norfolk headed for the Pacific, the ship's principal focus was to prepare itself for whatever threat we were to meet. As a result of the experiences of those who had visited our predecessors on station in the Gulf, we knew that in a departure from the classic battle scenario, the ship would be required to maintain a high degree of readiness around the clock

when on station. Trouble would likely come when it was least expected and we have to be prepared to defend our ship from a standing start while cruising (Condition III) without the luxury of falling back on full General Quarters (Condition I) manning. The daily exercise of every Condition III watch was the corporate signal that this was for real.

The response from the crew was immediate. We very quickly discovered that it was almost totally unnecessary to instruct anyone in the purpose of his duties. Planned Maintenance System (PMS) and Daily Systems Operability Tests (DSOT) began early without any coaching or reminders and their stringent requirements were closely scrutinized by every participant. Watchstanders developed their own techniques to assure themselves that they and their mates had explored every useful approach to readiness. We learned to live for long periods with partially set material conditions that buttoned down most hatches and forced traffic through scuttles that could be rapidly closed. Any other time, under any other conditions, such inconvenience would not have been countenanced. Now, everyone understood.

Condition III cruising watches, which, in theory, had always had the responsibility for the full operation of the combat systems suddenly confronted that reality. Junior members were thrust into the position of actually loading and firing their weapons. Suddenly no one could know enough about how his equipment operated and all of the myriad casualty procedures. Suddenly every member of the crew became visibly concerned about his responsibilities to his shipmates and whether he was personally ready. For most of us this was our first experience in preparing for the real thing. For all of us, our shipmates' reaction to the coming unknown gave us renewed confidence in them and in our ship.

Biddle's Organizational Structure

Biddle's organizational structure in 1968 consisted of a commanding officer, an executive officer, and five departments whose names reflected their broad responsibilities: Weapons, Operations, Engineering, Supply, and Navigation. Each department was further divided into divisions, with each division composed of men of one or two ratings that defined their specialty—cook, machinist mate, gunners mate, signalmen, boiler technician, and corpsman are a few of the ratings required to keep a large, complex, and powerful sea going vessel underway for extended periods. The organizational structure changed over the years to reflect changing operational goals and strategies—but not to such a degree that transplanted plankowners and decommission crew members would not feel at home. Ratings have come and gone as well. My Data Systems Technician rating dissolved into two different ratings. Some DSs became Electronic Technicians (ET) and others became Fire Controlmen (FC). But there are still cooks, machinist mates, gunners mates, signalmen, boiler technicians, corpsmen, and other ratings that may never change. For the benefit of the unlearned landlubber, a quick tour of *Biddle's* organization as she stood out for her first deployment is given the chapter, "Department Organization Aboard a Guided Missile Cruiser."

Cold War Cruisers vs. WW II Cruisers

While Cold War cruisers of the *Belknap* Class represented the state of the art in shipbuilding, weapons, radar, and computers, they were not the only game in town. World War II light and heavy cruisers had been converted to carry Terrier and Talos missiles since 1955 and a few heavy cruisers had both missiles and the NTDS installed. The first World War II heavy cruiser to install Terrier missiles was the *Boston* (CAG-1), formerly CA-69. *Boston's* sister ship *Canberra* (CAG-2), underwent a similar conversion in 1956. By 1960, the light cruisers *Galveston* (CLG-3) and sister ships *Little Rock* (CLG-4) and *Oklahoma City* (CLG-5) had installed Talos missile launchers aft while retaining 6-inch guns forward. Light cruisers *Providence* (CLG-6), *Springfield* (CLG-7), and *Topeka* (CG-8) were hybrid combatants as well, with Terrier launchers aft and 6-in guns forward. Finally, three heavy cruisers, *Albany* (CG-10), *Chicago* (CG-11), and *Columbus* (CG-12) had their 8-inch guns removed and Talos launchers installed in their place (Boslaugh 59).

The first and only World War II heavy cruisers to receive NTDS were the double-ended cruisers *Albany* and *Chicago* (302). David Boslaugh remembers that *Columbus* was scheduled for NTDS but the installation was cancelled, possibly due to a carrier fire that destroyed much of the carrier's NTDS equipment. He also recalled that "*Chicago* became the first to receive production NTDS equipment. At one time, *Galveston*, *Little Rock*, and *Oklahoma City*, all WW II cruisers converted to missile ships, were considered for NTDS, but never got it. No other WW II cruisers got NTDS, although a few WW II carriers got the system. There was some thought of putting NTDS on the *Iowa* Class battleships when they were taken out of moth balls, but it was never done. We even did studies of replacing the battleship fire control computers with digital computers, but concluded if it aint broke, don't fix it."

When asked what WWII cruisers with missiles brought to the game, Boslaugh remarked that "*Chicago*, *Albany*, and *Columbus* ended up without any guns at all. Their 8-inch turrets were removed and they got Talos missile batteries fore and aft with two Tartar missile systems amidships. They were strictly heavily armored fleet air defense ships. What they brought to the game was their large size, which could accommodate the huge magazines required by the Talos missile system.

Their big missile load is what drove OPNAV's desire to install NTDS on the ships."

During *Biddle's* first two Gulf deployments, it was an unusual occurrence if *Biddle*, *Long Beach*, or *Biddle's* older and heavier (18,000 ton) sister ship *Chicago*, was not on PIRAZ station. Muscular *Chicago*, with her unusually tall superstructure, twin Talos launchers fore and aft and twin Tartar launchers port and starboard, was an impressive sight. My most vivid recollection of *Chicago* was when she relived us one foggy morning at PIRAZ. I had stepped out of CIC on the starboard side near the signal bridge to look in the direction that the SPS-10 surface search radar indicated *Chicago* was—a few thousand yards off the starboard beam. It was deathly quiet—calm water does not to make a sound on a ship dead in the water. Invisible at first, *Chicago* gradually became a dark area in the fog, then a shadow of a ship, and finally a ghostly silhouette. Even after she had closed within a few hundred yards, the upper third of her superstructure was still obscured by fog. *Chicago* eventually closed to a point where her true size was apparent—she seemed to be as large and as powerful as her namesake city. A short time later, after pleasantries and hard data had exchanged, *Chicago* relieved *Biddle* of her duties and we slowly slipped south into the fog. I wonder if, as *Biddle* steamed away, a sailor aboard *Chicago* thought, "That *Biddle* sure is a fine looking ship."

The above scene, in which one magnificent man-o-war quietly relieves another a few miles off the coast of North Vietnam, would be repeated many times by four combat tested cruisers—*Biddle, Chicago, Long Beach*, and *Sterett*. All ships had in common their immense fighting power, NTDS, and their MiG kills, yet they pointed in two different directions. *Chicago* pointed back to World War II, when long range big guns and heavy armor defined state of the art. Nuclear powered *Long Beach*, an early recipient of NTDS and a revolutionary new steered-array radar, the SPS-32/33, was an ancestor of today's AEGIS combat system. *Belknap* Class representatives *Biddle* and *Sterett* also pointed to the future, but without a nuclear propulsion system. Nevertheless, the contributions they all made were instrumental in building the AEGIS combat system.

Cold War Cruisers vs. AEGIS Class Cruisers and Destroyers

It is interesting to compare *Biddle's* physical attributes with her descendants, the Arleigh Burke destroyers and *Ticonderoga* cruisers. Displacements are comparable between all three classes. At decommissioning, *Biddle* displaced 8,800 tons, while modern DDGs displace between 8,315 and 9,200 tons, with the heavier displacement belonging to hulls 79 and above. *Ticonderoga* cruisers are slightly heavier at

9,600 tons. *Biddle's* 55-foot beam exactly matches *Ticonderoga* cruisers but is somewhat slimmer than *Arleigh Burke* destroyer's 59-foot girth. *Biddle's* 547-foot length was considerably longer than modern day *Burke* destroyers at 505 feet for Flights I and II, and 509-1/2 feet for Flight IIA. *Ticonderoga* cruisers, at 567 feet, are long and tall.

Superstructure differences between Cold War and modern day cruisers and destroyers are significant and obvious. Technical people are quick to observe that rotating radar antennas are gone on modern combatants, having been replaced by the stationary AN/SPY-1 radar. The SPY-1 not only replaced rotating air-search radar antennas, but also the missile fire control directors. Macks, which combined the functions of antenna masts and smoke stacks, are history. *Burke* destroyers have a very clean single antenna mast protruding from the deckhouse. Stacks, now called funnels, on *Burke* destroyers are noticeably shorter than *Biddle's* macks since the exhaust from their General Electric LM 2500 gas turbine engines is much cleaner than the nasty exhaust generated from burning fuel oil. Stacks resemble jet exhausts, which is exactly what they are. Superstructure components such as the deckhouse are faceted, much like the stealth fighter.

As an interesting side note related to the AEGIS Combat System on *Ticonderoga* Class cruisers, co-author Tom Marfiak added that "During Operation Iraqi Freedom in the spring of 2003, several scud missiles were fired in the direction of allied forces in Kuwait. Patriot batteries were able to engage them all, I'm told. In 12 of 13 engagements, they were cued onto the launch event by the AEGIS platforms operating in the northern gulf. It was an impressive display of joint capability, and a significant technical accomplishment. We could not accomplish the same degree of integration in 1991."

Biddle's antiquated missile launching system was replaced by the much simpler Vertical Launching System (VLS), which further enhanced the new, clean image of new DDGs. [One disadvantage of the VLS that I can think of is that you can't run a couple of birds out on the rail anymore to "show off.] The 5-inch 54 Mk 42 gun gave way to the 5-inch 54 Mk 45 lightweight gun and the worn out 3-inch 50 was finally relieved by the far more capable Vulcan Phalanx close-in-weapons system (CIWS).

All of the deck improvements listed above, coupled with what appears to be a concentrated effort to remove small items from the upper decks, resulted in a much cleaner appearance. Not readily noticeable is the fact that AEGIS cruisers and destroyers have an all steel superstructure instead of the aluminum superstructure found in the *Belknap* Class. The only remaining non-steel components above decks on *Burke* destroyers are parts of the funnels and antenna mast. Seventy tons of Kevlar in some above deck spaces provide further protection. Apparently, lessons were learned from losing 20 men on HMS *Sheffield* during the Falklands War, 37 men on USS *Stark* during the Persian Gulf War, and seven men from the USS *Belknap* and USS *John F. Kennedy* collision in 1975. The damage *Belknap* incurred was truly horrible.

The modest, uncluttered decks of AEGIS ships belie their combat capabilities—they exceed by a magnitude, maybe more, *Biddle's* capabilities in 1968. The AEGIS Combat System integrates the state-of-the-art AN/SPY-1 phased-array radar, which has both air search and missile guidance capabilities, with the computer-based command and decision element, and the medium to long range Standard missile. This level of integration was only a dream when *Biddle* deployed to WESTPAC in 1968. The AEGIS system can automatically detect and track more than 100 targets simultaneously. If warranted, the system can simultaneously concentrate beams of radar energy on emerging targets 250 miles distant on the port side while directing multiple Standard missiles toward their hostile targets 100 miles distant on the starboard side. The Standard missile has demonstrated a Theater Ballistic Missile Defense (TBMD) capability. Low flyers of any kind stand little chance of penetrating this AEGIS, which means, "shield." If a hostile aircraft or missile manages to do so, it still must break through 3,000 rounds per minute of 20 mm cannon fire from a Vulcan CIWS and the 5-inch/54. Representing the very last line of defense, the Vulcan's obscene burping sound alone is enough to deter most attackers.

Biddle is Ready for Combat

By today's standards, *Biddle* would be inadequate in a combat environment. Such is progress. But in 1968, as *Biddle* deployed for the first time, she was a brand new multi-mission ship loaded with the most advanced sea-going combat system in the world. Her crew, from the Captain to the lowest Seaman, was trained to perform at level that would enable her to perform her mission in a combat environment and return safely. *Biddle* was ready for combat.

The Gulf of Tonkin—1968

James Treadway

The war in Vietnam, though not militarily successful, must have been a complete success as far as the architects of the *Leahy* and *Belknap* classes of guided missile cruisers were concerned. In *When Computers Went to Sea*, Boslaugh states, "Off Vietnam, the Naval Tactical Data System was called on to perform, at some time, every tactical function envisioned by its designers, such as air intercept control, and gun and missile weapons direction, however, it was mainly pressed into new services. The heaviest load on the system was composed more of air traffic control functions than tactical battle functions, and the system was augmented with features such as the beacon video processor to give it more of such capability."

Not only was the Gulf of Tonkin environment a proving ground the digital fleet, the Vietnam experience also served to eliminate fleet officer's apprehension about sharing command with a sinister electronic brain, and removed all doubts about the utility of the new system.

While the early parts of the Vietnam war proved that NTDS could handle non-tactical assignments, *Sterett's* and *Biddle's* successful MiG engagements in the latter years of the war confirmed that *Belknap* Class frigates were capable of fulfilling their primary mission of defending battle group carriers and defending themselves. Flush with these successes and armed with a constant stream of improvements from the fleet by ships such as *Biddle*, engineers continued to improve the performance of NTDS with system upgrades while other engineers were designing the next generation platform—the AEGIS combat system. Thus, from the WWII era fleet to today's AEGIS based platforms, the CG-16/26 classes were the transition—from sailors, training, manning, operational techniques, and link management—it all was preparation for today's fleet. This is the story of one ship, one tradition, emblematic of an era.

The remaining pages and chapters do not provide an exhaustive, historical analysis of this small part of the Vietnam War. Instead, they tell the stories of the officers and men who played deadly games with MiGs in the Gulf of Tonkin. They tell the story of a young lieutenant in CIC who made a split second decision that would either save lives aboard his ship or get him court-martialed—he "bets his bars." In another story, a MiG is so close to *Sterett* that the ship's Terrier missile booster did not have time to separate—the entire missile actually made skin-to-skin contact with the MiG. We will answer probing questions: What happened in CIC when 500 knot MiGs are detected on the deck at a range less than 20 miles? What do Gunner's Mates think when firing 3-inch proximity shells at night at a low flying invisible target?

These compelling stories demonstrate how ships were attacked and how they reacted. Granted, this little known part of the war was fought from the relative comfort of an air-conditioned CIC. From CIC, using the latest digital computers and long-range radar, well-trained sailors and officers controlled and directed the various types of weapons and countermeasures brought to bear. Fortunately, these systems and their operators succeeded because the Navy had the wisdom and foresight to envision and then design and implement the Naval Tactical Data System and integrate NTDS with shipboard sensors, communications, and weapons systems. A major contribution to at-sea success of these new systems that were based on digital computers and computer programs was due to the Navy decision to entrust these systems to a new breed of sailor who understood integrated systems, digital electronics, and computer programs.

The foundation of all ship operations in maintaining required levels of readiness prior to combat operations and in responding to problems during intense operations was then, and remains, specialized analysis tools and the sailors skilled in their use. During the era of early NTDS, which included Vietnam, this fundamental and vital component of weapon system success was being evolved and expanded by a combination of sailors, engineers, and computer programmers. While outside the scope of this book, some examples are provided to show the complexity of shipboard systems and the real-world environment in which men and machines must effectively function and interact to survive. In addition, the nature of early digital technology as it existed during this time required sailors to be innovative in detecting and correcting problems for which there were no precedents, often in the rigorous conditions of combat and round-the-clock operations. Today's Navy ships are beneficiaries of the lessons learned and skills sharpened on those first ships of the digital revolution.

In the aftermath of the 1968 TET offensive, *Biddle* would begin Seventh Fleet operations in the Gulf of Tonkin after relieving the cruiser *Chicago* as PIRAZ control ship on 6 March. Considering the complexities of the mission, it might seem unusual that PIRAZ was *Biddle's* first combat assignment. *Biddle* would be well prepared for the task, however. Immediately after commissioning, *all* tasks were subordinate to successful shakedown completion and preparation for PIRAZ.

An advanced team of *Biddle* officers visited PIRAZ in July of 1967, six months before departing for the Gulf of Tonkin. As a result of the visit, extensive changes in communications, Electronic Counter Measure (ECM), and additional crew berthing for the augmented PIRAZ crew were made. Additionally, Captain Scott developed a "new readiness posture that allowed continuous high level operational commitment with a minimum of disruption of shipboard day to day routine." This posture allowed any combination of missile quarters, gun quarters, general quarters, and readiness condition Zebra to be set, which enabled *Biddle* to respond to any threat quickly and completely. Furthermore, *Biddle* had the ability to electronically simulate the Gulf of Tonkin airspace environment in CIC during the months prior to her arrival in the Gulf and heavy emphasis was placed on all tenets of Anti-Air Warfare. *Biddle* was as ready for PIRAZ and combat as a new warship could possibly be.

Missile Ship Duties in the Gulf of Tonkin

The role of the U.S. Navy during the Vietnam War had many facets. Brown water operations such as Market Time, Game Warden, and Southeast Asia Lake, Ocean, River and Delta (SEALORDS) are well documented in print and in film; Blue water operations at Yankee and Dixie Stations received considerable media attention as well. One lesser-known aspect of the Navy's involvement in Vietnam is that ships equipped with Talos, Tartar, or Terrier missiles systems and the Naval Tactical Data System protected US Navy carrier groups to the south and engaged the North Vietnamese along the coast of North Vietnam and in the skies over the Gulf of Tonkin. These ships occupied PIRAZ and North or South Search and Rescue (SAR) stations. Often these ships operated within sight of the shores of North Vietnam and were escorted by a "shotgun"—an older gun-type destroyer that placed itself between the beach and the PIRAZ or SAR ship in case of attack from shore. PIRAZ operations were coordinated by NTDS ships designated as call sign "Red Crown," stationed between Yankee Station and the northern Tonkin Gulf.

PIRAZ

PIRAZ missions in 1968 involved multiple roles—the positive identification of all aircraft in the zone, advisory and positive control of aircraft, early warnings of hostile aircraft, warnings of impending border violations, and the identification and destruction of hostile aircraft. Other PIRAZ functions included locating and assisting stricken aircraft and emergency search and rescue. The volume of aircraft in the advisory zone often exceeded 100 and sometimes several hundred. Most radar contacts were U.S. Navy, Marine and Air Force aircraft on missions but there were South Vietnamese Air Force aircraft and commercial traffic as well. To further complicate matters, Red China was not far to the north and Hainan Island was just over the horizon to the east. PIRAZ was a demanding, dangerous environment.

NTDS equipped ships were the only surface combatants capable of performing all the tasks, and they were scarce. NTDS ships included large missile cruisers such as *Chicago* and the nuclear-powered *Long Beach,* and DLGs in the *Belknap* (including nuclear-powered *Truxtun*) and *Leahy* Class. *Biddle's* contribution to this complex, constantly changing environment was urgently needed—hence the accelerated shakedown training. The hours were long and the rewards, beyond professional pride in accomplishing the missions, were few, but *Biddle* would quickly meet the challenge with three extended deployments in five years "on line" in the Gulf of Tonkin from her homeport of Norfolk.

Red Crown was located approximately 100 miles north of the widely known Yankee Station from which Navy carriers launched attacks on targets in North Vietnam. From this location, assigned ships performed PIRAZ missions. *Biddle* would monitor the entire northern war scene with her long-range air search radars, the SPS-40 and SPS-48. With North Vietnam 30 miles to the west and Yankee Station 100 miles to the south, the PIRAZ station was an ideal location from which shipboard air traffic controllers could identify and control friendly aircraft going to and coming from North Vietnam. Additionally, using NTDS tactical computer programs with large track capacity, ships did flight-following during ingress and egress. This was particularly important when raids were made up of many dozens of aircraft, both to keep track of the aircraft and to make sure that no hostile aircraft infiltrated formations of returning friendly aircraft. The sorting-out function was known as Tomcat.

Red Crown was also an excellent location to monitor enemy activity from the DMZ north to the border with China, often with the help of embarked intelligence systems and personnel known as "Spooks." PIRAZ with other ships at NSAR and SSAR provided the first line of defense should North Vietnam decide to launch an attack against carriers at Yankee Station. *Biddle* would assume other duties in the Gulf of Tonkin, but none would be more critical to the conduct of the air war in the Gulf than as PIRAZ control ship.

The MiG Threat

PIRAZ was located approximately 30 miles southeast of Haiphong, North Vietnam's largest port city. Sprinkled west from Haiphong to Hanoi and south to Vinh were numerous airfields from which MiGs launched sorties to the south toward the Demilitarized Zone (DMZ), and east or southeast to the Gulf of Tonkin. Occasionally, MiGS would go "feet wet" at very high speed in the direction of naval forces only to break off the attack at the last moment. They would also fly below hilltops when "feet dry" to make it more difficult to track them by radar. In either case, any MiG activity anywhere in North Vietnam got instant attention from the US Navy in the Gulf.

NTDS equipped ships with long-range air search radars and missiles were an ideal platform to engage MiGs and great sport was made of it. One of the first ships to receive NTDS, the nuclear-powered *Long Beach*, fired Talos missiles at seven MiGs during 1967 and 1968 (Boslaugh 354). She made history on 23 May 1968 when she destroyed a MiG at a range of 65 miles with a Talos missile after engaging a target that was first tracked and reported by other ships with long-range radar using NTDS consoles, computers, and digital data links (354). (There is now an automated system for ships and aircraft known as Cooperative Engagement Capability or CEC. The concept has been extended so the unit performing the engagement can be separate from the unit launching the weapon. This concept was central to the aborted Arsenal Ship.) The event was the first time that an enemy aircraft was shot down by a ship-launched surface-to-air missile. *Long Beach* shot down her second MiG in June 1968, again at a range of 65 miles (354). By war's end in 1975, only three other naval combatants would successfully engage MiGs with missiles or gunfire, though there were other missile firings that did not intercept. There is not an official count of how many MIGs were shot down by Navy missiles or guns. However, *Warship International* credits only *Long Beach*, *Chicago*, and guided missile frigates *Sterett*, and *Biddle* with five confirmed kills and two probable kills (Gibbs 319). Indeed, warships that shot down a MiG are a select group. In contrast, USN and USMC air-to-air combat MiGs kills were predictably more plentiful with 122 enemy aircraft shot down and 16 known USN/USMC aircraft lost to MiGs, a 7.6 to 1 exchange rate (Nichols 167).

Playing games with hostile MiGs was not easy. The minimum requirements to play the game successfully were a highly trained crew and perfectly functioning equipment. If either element was lacking, a fortunate MiG pilot would live to fly another day or a warship took a hit with a 250-pound bomb. Hostile MiGs were not the only threat to Navy ships fortunate enough to pull duty in the Gulf of Tonkin. North Vietnamese patrol boats, some equipped with anti-ship missiles, were a threat from the DMZ north along the coastline to the border with China. North Vietnamese gun emplacements occasionally shelled ships that operated inside the range of their guns. Sadly, another threat to naval forces in the Gulf of Tonkin—friendly fire—took its toll as well.

Engaging MiGs with guns and missiles was not the only option available to NTDS equipped ships—a more successful tactic was to use air intercept controllers to direct Navy or Air Force fighters to hostile targets on the controller's screen. In *When Computers Went to Sea*, Boslaugh states that *Biddle* conducted 168 fighter intercepts during her three deployments to Vietnam and that on her third deployment, *Biddle* controllers were responsible for directing 13 MiG kills (355). Shipboard intercept controllers chalked up their earliest kills in 1967 when *Fox* (DLG-33) intercept controllers downed a MiG 17 and MiG 21 (354). Shortly before *Sterett's* Dong Hoi engagement in April 1972, her intercept controllers directed Air Force fighters in a MiG-21 splash in February then two more MiGs in March. Senior Chief Radarman Larry Nowell directed Air Force and Navy fighters to 12 MiG kills in 1972 from his NTDS console aboard *Chicago*, winning the Distinguished Service Cross in the process (355). Finally, *Truxtun* was credited with 11 MiG intercept kills during her 1972-73 Gulf deployment (355).

North and South Search and Rescue

The Navy's efforts during the early phases of the war to retrieve downed pilots from North Vietnam and adjacent waters were successful an average of only one in six attempts (Nichols 119). Furthermore, by 1967 the Navy had lost at least seven helos to the enemy during SAR missions (120). Without a dedicated organization trained specifically for combat SAR, the poor performance would have continued. Soon after Helicopter Combat Support Squadron Seven (HC-7) was formed, losses dropped to zero (120).

Ships bound for SAR or PIRAZ duty took aboard a permanent helo detachment consisting of a Landing Signal Officer (LSO), damage controlmen, fueling personnel, and chock men. Ships such as *Biddle* also had limited capabilities for helicopter maintenance. The general procedure was to position modified Sikorsky SH-3A "Big Mother" helos aboard ships at North SAR and South SAR as close to the egress point as possible. During major strikes, SAR helos would become airborne and orbit offshore to reduce even further the time required to reach and rescue a downed pilot.

The nature of the job entailed considerable risk. *On Yankee Station* described two SAR missions that illustrate the point. The first story, while not a Navy SAR mission, reveals the extreme risks that were sometimes taken. The mission involved an Aerospace Rescue and Recovery Service (ARRS) attempt to rescue a Navy Crusader pilot southwest of Dodge (Hanoi.) The HH-3 crew had located the downed pilot and was hovering inches above the triple canopy jungle. The jungle penetrator cable was lowered to its limits but was too short and NVA soldiers were putting bullet holes in the fuselage. Rather than add power and "Get the hell out of Dodge," the pilot lowered the HH-3 into the trees enough that the F-8 pilot was finally able to grab the sling. Unfortunately, the rotor blades were "cutting timber" and losing rotor blade tips. Now severely damaged and almost uncontrollable, the HH-3 pilot made it to a nearby clearing where a Jolly Green picked up survivors and the damaged HH-3 was lifted out later that night. The F-8 driver was rescued but several HH-3 crewmen were injured and one was killed.

The other story involved a backseater who ejected out of a RA-5C Vigilante near the coast during a reconnaissance mission. The pilot was killed and locals had surrounded the backseater, who was carrying a standard issue .38 pistol with the first two chambers empty and a .22 automatic. He had waded into the water where a local militia took his .38 and pointed it at the flyer while another North Vietnamese civilian covered him with a rifle. At that time the aviator could see the SAR helo approaching from the east and an A1 and F8 strafing the beach. The RESCAP pilots could see the predicament the flyer was in so they continued to distract the Vietnamese with low-level strafing. The distraction provided the young aviator with enough time to extract and load his .22 pistol. The rifleman caught a bullet in the head, which caused the other Vietnamese to reflexively pull the trigger of the .38 pistol. Since the first two chambers were empty, the flyer had enough time load and fire again. With the last militiaman floating in the surf, the backseater started swimming at flank speed toward the SAR helo and rescue.

Often *Biddle* pulled SAR duty and was either directly or indirectly involved in rescuing downed pilots. On 16 June 1968, *Biddle* assumed NSAR responsibilities while retaining the PIRAZ function. At first light, *Biddle* closed *Jouett*, received the "Clementine Two" helo and detachment, and then proceeded to NSAR while *Jouett* headed south. Three days later, Lieutenant (junior grade) Trump remembers, "I recall staying up far beyond the end of my watch one evening listening to the radio chatter as a SAR helicopter made a daring rescue in the DMZ and barely made it back to South SAR—the pilot was subsequently awarded the Congressional Medal of Honor." The following citation from the web site www.medalofhonor.com describes the action:

> Citation: For conspicuous gallantry and intrepidity at the risk of his life above and beyond the call of duty as pilot and aircraft commander of a search and rescue helicopter, attached to Helicopter Support Squadron 7, during operations against enemy forces in North Vietnam. Launched shortly after midnight to attempt the rescue of 2 downed aviators, Lt. (then Lt. (J.G.)) Lassen skillfully piloted his aircraft over unknown and hostile terrain to a steep, tree-covered hill on which the survivors had been located. Although enemy fire was being directed at the helicopter, he initially landed in a clear area near the base of the hill, but, due to the dense undergrowth, the survivors could not reach the helicopter. With the aid of flare illumination, Lt. Lassen successfully accomplished a hover between 2 trees at the survivors' position Illumination was abruptly lost as the last of the flares were expended, and the helicopter collided with a tree, commencing a sharp descent. Expertly righting his aircraft and maneuvering clear, Lt. Lassen remained in the area, determined to make another rescue attempt, and encouraged the downed aviators while awaiting resumption of flare illumination. After another unsuccessful, illuminated rescue attempt, and with his fuel dangerously low and his aircraft significantly damaged, he launched again and commenced another approach in the face of the continuing enemy opposition. When flare illumination was again lost, Lt. Lassen, fully aware of the dangers in clearly revealing his position to the enemy, turned on his landing lights and completed the landing. On this attempt, the survivors were able to make their way to the helicopter. En route to the coast he encountered and successfully evaded additional hostile antiaircraft fire and, with fuel for only 5 minutes of flight remaining, landed safely aboard U.S.S. *Jouett* (DLG-29).

On Saturday, 21 April 2001, the Department of the Navy commissioned the Arleigh Burke Class guided-missile destroyer USS *Lassen* (DDG-82).

WESTPAC I

James Treadway

On 9 January 1968, as *Biddle's* first birthday approached, her leave and upkeep status was terminated and pre-overseas movement preparations began. One significant problem remained, however. *Biddle* had received the first installation of the AN/SPS-48 Moving Target Indicator (MTI), an important component of *Biddle's* air search capability since it helped separate moving targets from the clutter. After a 10 day underway period in November to solve the problems proved fruitless, ITT-Gilfillan engineers J.E. Dinsmore, J.G. Tyrell, and L.A. Denkers made preparations to get underway. At least two of the gentlemen remained aboard *Biddle* for most of *Biddle's* deployment and were considered to be part of the crew. Mr. Tyrell had been in *Biddle* since early 1966.

On *Biddle's* first birthday, 21 January 1968, the completion of the 50-item checklist in the Procedure for Getting Underway was begun in preparation for getting underway the next day for the Gulf of Tonkin. A birthday message from Captain Scott focused on our accomplishments since commissioning and announced that *Biddle* was "cited by CINCLANTFLT as the top destroyer type in the Atlantic Fleet to complete shakedown training during 1967."

With all items on the Procedure for Getting Underway completed at 1430 on 22 January, USS *Biddle* (DLG-34) got underway on her first deployment. As Norfolk and a year of training disappeared behind her, new opportunities soon appeared on the forward horizon. An eight-month around the world cruise in a new guided missile frigate was dead ahead. Actually, what was ahead was more training. The Plan Of the Day (POD) for 23 January, our first full day underway, listed the following training items: flight following training, sinuous course/casualty steering training, PIRAZ lecture, PIRAZ Team training, ECM training, Helo team training, general quarters, missile/gun firing exercise, ULQ6/Chaff drill, and damage control training. The PODs for the next week weren't much different. Going to war is serious business.

On 27 January *Biddle* passed 60 ships waiting to enter the Panama Canal at Colon, at the Atlantic entrance. Nine hours later we had transited the Canal, made a fuel stop at the U.S. Naval Base, Rodman, Canal Zone, and were enjoying our first liberty call in the city of Balboa. I was surprised to learn that the Pacific side is further east than the Caribbean side. (Look it up on the map.)

The next morning *Biddle* set sail across the mighty Pacific at 27 knots. At this speed the vibrations, heat and the crushing cacophony of sounds in the engine and boiler rooms were unbearable to the uninitiated but tolerated by the men—all unsung heroes—who worked there. The boiler rooms, as wide as the ship itself, were bursting with the pipes, gauges and pumps required to produce 1200 pound steam that propelled the 16,000,000 pound *Biddle* toward her destination. Large diameter air conditioning ducts forced chilled air into these spaces to offer some relief from the heat. If asked, boiler technicians and enginemen might respond, "You get used to it."

Training did not stop during the transit—any drill could be expected at any moment. Guns were fired almost daily and the klaxon announcing general quarters was common as well. It was a surprise then, when on a lazy Sunday afternoon we heard, "This is *not* a drill. General quarters, man your battle stations!

"The North Koreans had recently captured the spy ship, USS *Pueblo*, and tensions were rising all over the world. Everyone was expecting the North Koreans, Red Chinese, or Russians to try something. Our sonar had picked up a submerged target that we were not able to identify. Not taking any chances, general quarters was sounded, which probably scared the hell out of the fish and fishing boats that were masquerading as Russian subs. "Secure from general quarters." On to Pearl....

Training continued during our high-speed transit to Hawaii. *Biddle's* Command History for 1968 states "Throughout the transit, intensive training was in progress which developed a team from a conglomeration of highly trained individuals. Utilizing training tapes in the NTDS and Communications gear, a realistic environment was created in the Combat Information Center which made for smooth assumption of PIRAZ duties once on station in the Tonkin Gulf."

Honolulu was *Biddle's* next port of call. We anchored a few miles outside of the entrance to Pearl Harbor to clean up the ship before continuing. A small amount of fuel oil was accidentally pumped over the side and BT3 Treadway, whether he was responsible for the act or not, had the duty of cleaning the side of the ship.

Biddle, now sparkling, entered Pearl with topside personnel lining the sides in silent respect as she passed the sunken USS *Arizona*. I tried to imagine the destruction that occurred at Pearl Harbor on 7 December 1941. Six days later,

Biddle stood out for Guam, pausing to fire two Terrier missiles at the Barking Sands Range.

Biddle stopped at Guam for fuel, and then departed for Subic Bay, Luzon, in the Philippine Islands. Soon after Guam disappeared in our wake, we spotted a Russian intelligence trawler that had been missing for several weeks. We reported the trawler's position for the benefit of our submarines in the Guam area.

Biddle anchored in Subic Bay on 24 February to replace the ammunition and missiles expended in transit. The remainder of the week was spent dockside for repairs, modifications, and loading stores. A U.S. Naval Security Group detachment of electronics eavesdroppers embarked and *Biddle* took aboard two 50-caliber machine guns and an 81 mm mortar.

Before relieving *Chicago* (CG-11) at PIRAZ, *Biddle* dropped anchor on 5 March in Da Nang harbor for briefings with the Air Force and Army. An advance party from *Biddle* was also aboard *Chicago* and *Kitty Hawk* (CVA-63) for more briefings from our task force commander's staff and other Naval Air Attack Carrier Striking Force personnel.

When asked what he remembered about Da Nang, Bob Gerity replied, "Some memories of Da Nang come to mind. While we were anchored there in that big harbor, there was cannon fire in the hills to the north but guys on R & R were water skiing around the ship! Once when Bob Baker and I flew in there from a carrier (*Kitty Hawk?*) in a C-1, we received some bullets in the wing, which were discovered after landing. Another time Baker, Wes, and I arrived at Da Nang and all the aircraft from *Forrestal* were there due to that huge fire they suffered. This was after we had flown out from Cubi Point and had to make a stop at the Marine base at Chu Lai where the urinal consisted of some rocket tubes stuck in the sand. War is a bitch!"

War was indeed a bitch at that point in the Vietnam War. The 1968 Tet Offensive had just begun on 31 January, the first day of the celebration of the lunar New Year. Over 100 cities in South Vietnam were under attack, including the capital of Saigon. Eight enemy battalions had attacked the former imperial capital of Hue, which was defended by three U.S. Marine Corps, three U.S. Army, and eleven South Vietnamese battalions. The outpost of Khe Sahn was under relentless attack and would remain so until April. With over 37,000 Vietcong and 2,500 Americans killed, the offensive was not a military success. It was, however, a political and psychological victory for the communists by contradicting U.S. government claims that the war had been won.

Good Morning Vietnam

Biddle relieved *Chicago* as PIRAZ control ship on 6 March. An actual buoy north of Yankee Station, PIRAZ was the northernmost point of naval activity in the Gulf except for North Search and Rescue (NSAR.). While operating as PIRAZ control ship, *Biddle* maintained a position within five miles of the PIRAZ buoy, steaming under ten knots except when recovering helos. From the PIRAZ vantage point *Biddle* could see most of the northern part of the war with her SPS-40 and SPS-48 long-range air search radars. With a range of about 240 miles we could pick up aircraft as far south as the DMZ, west into the interior of North Vietnam, north to China, and east to Hainan Island.

Hostile aircraft often feigned an attack from North Vietnam, but we were vigilant in detecting, tracking, loading missiles on the launchers, and then illuminating threatening targets with missile-guidance radar as part of the final firing sequence. Lieutenant (junior grade) Peter Trump, *Biddle's* Sonar Officer, remembered that "During the first period, the enemy sent an aircraft out to fly around us. Before we could get permission to engage he flew away home. Often MiGs would test *Biddle* by launching an attack, then turn back when the Terrier missile illuminators activated, but before missiles could be fired and then fly out to the intercept point. The capability to illuminate a target without actually firing is recognized as a self-defense countermeasure option that can be useful, and is included on even the newest AEGIS ships of today."

Biddle's first on-line period at PIRAZ and Southwest Anti-Air Picket Station was punctuated by heavy Navy strike activity in the Hanoi and Haiphong area, frequent harassment from MiGs who seemed to enjoy testing *Biddle's* defenses, and long hours keeping *Biddle's* equipment in tip-top shape. We were ready for some *real* liberty.

Kaohshiung, Taiwan, and Hong Kong

With the first of three periods on-station under her belt, *Biddle* headed east to our first port of call, Kaohshiung, Taiwan. Taiwan's emergence as a major economic factor in the Far East was evident when *Biddle* arrived on 2 April 1968. Biddlegram #3, a periodic update of *Biddle's* activities mailed to the families and friends of Biddlemen by Captain Scott, described Kaohshiung as "A mixture of old and new with clear evidence of progressiveness and building a viable country was reflected everywhere. As an indication of this teeming progress, the small efficient harbor was jammed with 125 large merchant ships. We enjoyed our brief respite, but we kept our eye on our next port of call, the recreation and free port Mecca of Asia Pacific—Hong Kong!!"

Kaohshiung had plenty to offer as a liberty port, but it paled in comparison to Hong Kong. The sights, sounds, and smells of Hong Kong were the highlight of the cruise as far as this sailor is concerned. Biddlegram #3 described Hong Kong as: "All they say about it is true—progress, beauty, massive population, mixed cultures, picturesque, land of bargains, and the best cuisine."

Victoria Peak, which faces north looking over the top of Hong Kong, the harbor, and Kowloon toward the New Territories and China, provided a breathtaking view from which I could appreciate where I just came from, or pick a place to go. The restaurant food was indescribably good, and I didn't have to return my tray to the scullery when finished. Bargains abounded in every area—jewelry, clothing, antiques and electronics were a few. The stereo equipment I bought there is gone, as is the tailored suit, but I still have the hand made leather briefcase that I bought in the Wan Chai district. I took a ride on a junk from Junk City across the harbor on the last night we were in port. Junk City, a floating city of several thousand junks, was eventually eliminated by city officials because it was considered to be an eyesore. That was unfortunate—Junk City was one of the things that made Hong Kong unique.

Relaxed after a two week "vacation," *Biddle* returned to the Gulf of Tonkin on 16 April to relieve *Chicago* at PIRAZ. The hectic pace continued. In Biddlegram #4, Captain Scott claimed that, "During the last PIRAZ period it was not uncommon to simultaneously: land or launch helos from our flight deck; control our Navy's interceptor aircraft; lock-on and track ready to fire our Terrier missiles; and stand ready to use our guns in self-defense. To quote our departing Seventh Fleet Commander:"

> My appreciation to you who have served and fought so well. Combat is the most demanding taskmaster of all endeavors; each of you may take justifiable pride in your many accomplishments. The outstanding record compiled...has been noted by all echelons of command. There is no greater or demanding task than to carry the standards of your country into battle, and no greater reward than having done so well. Each of you deserves a full measure or your nation's praise. RADM Sheldon Kinney

The Gulf of Tonkin presented different problems to different groups at different times. I asked Sonar Officer Lieutenant Peter Trump to elaborate the problems the sonar group encountered in the Gulf.

I do not recall any special preparations for operations in the Gulf, which is comparatively shallow water and the AN/SQS-26B(X) was designed for deep water. It was comparatively low frequency sonar. In the active mode, reverberations made it largely useless in the Gulf. So we maintained a sonar watch in the passive mode, for the most part. Sometimes ducting would result in a noise spoke from South SAR, or some such, but we seldom heard anything that attracted much interest. It was difficult to keep the Sonarmen alert with an ineffective system in a comparatively low ASW threat environment.

More interesting was simply keeping the system operating and aligned. By today's standards, the equipment was pretty challenging. It was all analog, of course, and sensitive to change in almost every respect. The displays, in particular, were unstable. Long-term integration was accomplished in a "scan converter"—a double-ended CRT with a screen in the middle. The gun in one end would "write" data on a charged screen at sonar rates while the gun in the other end would "read" the data from the screen at television rates.

Another challenge was the LAPS—Louis Allis power supply—a pair of large (1,000 lb rotor) motor generator sets, which provided the transmitter power (3,000 amps @ 80vdc). Strange critters, indeed, for sonarmen to take care of. Very good for vaporizing screwdrivers, however. These things were located on the keel just aft of the sonar dome. In any kind of a sea, the motion was accentuated; in a quartering sea such as we experienced on the endless transit across the Indian Ocean to Madagascar, it was hazardous to your lunch.

Half the Sonarmen were frustrated and annoyed for the entire War Zone experience. There were two small berthing compartments amidships which each accommodated 12, as I recall. They were both assigned to 4th Division, initially. However, the starboard compartment was turned over to the spooks—Security Group personnel—while they were aboard and the sonarmen relocated forward with 1st and/or 2nd Division. I don't remember the rationale for that move, but I do remember objecting to it ineffectively at the time and the bitterness it caused.

We had the sonar T/R (transmit/receive) switch overhauled in Yokosuka. This was a 512-pole double throw solenoid actuated switch the size of a two-drawer file cabinet. It was filling up with metal particles as the contacts wore away. No one had ever seen such a critter there before, but those clever people did the job.

Yard Work at Yokosuka, the Black Ship Festival

Biddle was relieved of her second tour of duty at PIRAZ by *Long Beach*, at which time we steamed north to Yokosuka, Japan, for yard work, then to Shimoda, where *Biddle* was to represent the United States at the annual Black Ship Festival. Immediately after we docked at Yokosuka, hundreds of Japanese shipyard workers stormed the ship, eager to get started. Their work ethic and enthusiasm were clearly evident—a nice surprise to me considering the likelihood that some of them had fought against us during WW II. I saw no evidence of resentment.

I did not pass up an opportunity to visit Tokyo since it was so close. As the tour bus headed north along Tokyo Bay, I remembered that Japan surrendered aboard the battleship *Missouri* in Tokyo Bay just a few weeks before I was born.

On the morning of 16 May the U.S. Ambassador to Japan, along with 25 other officials, embarked in *Biddle* for the 70 mile cruise to Shimoda for the annual Black Ship Festival. The festival commemorates Commodore Perry's opening of Japan in 1853 to U.S. ships which ended centuries of Japan's self isolation. Unsuccessful in his first attempt, Perry returned in the spring of 1854 with a squadron of nine war ships called "black ships" (kurofune) and signed a treaty that opened the ports of Shimoda and Hakodate to American ships. The festival has become Shimoda's major tourist attraction. Accompanying *Biddle* was the destroyer *J.C. Owens* (DD-776). Upon arrival, *Biddle* fired an 11-gun salute, which was returned by the Shimoda battery. According to *Biddle* Press Release dated 6 May 1968, Commodore Perry also fired a salute to the Shogun upon entering the port in 1854. Many townspeople, "expected destruction rather than diplomacy" fled the island at the sound of the guns.

The press release listed other similarities between Commodore Perry's visit and *Biddle's*. Commodore Perry "once lived in Newport, now the sister city to Shimoda." Captain Scott is also of Norfolk and Newport. "On 24 November 1852, Commodore Perry sailed from Norfolk, Va. on the first leg of his Far East mission. USS BIDDLE also departed from Norfolk—on January 22nd—to join the Seventh Fleet in the Far East." The Press Release also described Shimoda being much the same as it was when Commodore Perry visited:

> Shimoda is on the southern coast of Honshu, 70 miles southeast of the modern U.S. Naval base at Yokosuka. It was near Yokosuka in July 1853, that Perry began negotiations for the opening of Shimoda and Hakodate (on the southern coast of Hokkaido). Originally, these two ports were coaling and provisioning stations for American ships.
>
> The negotiations eventually led to the Japan-American Treaty of Trade and Amity in 1860 and sparked the development of Yokohama as a major trading port.
>
> Today, the original treaty ports no longer figure in world commerce. Shimoda is much like Commodore Perry found it—unhurried, charming—and the townspeople are now only curious at the sound of guns in the harbor and sailors marching in the streets.

I concur that Shimoda was unhurried and charming, especially when compared to Yokosuka and Tokyo. An equivalent comparison might be New York City and Martha's Vineyard. The townspeople were friendly and approachable, much the same as rural America.

After returning the embarked visitors to Yokosuka, *Biddle* returned to the Gulf of Tonkin for duty at Southwest Anti-Air Warfare Picket station for four days and then to relieve *Long Beach* (CGN-9) at PIRAZ. *Biddle's* third appearance in the Gulf would be her last for the deployment and her longest. *Biddle's* 1968 Command History describes the situation in the northern Gulf during her third appearance:

> The bombing halt in April north of 19° had not decreased the number of missions overall, restricting operations to south of 19°, MiG activity to the north actually caused an added burden to the PIRAZ function. The LONG BEACH had shot down a MiG with [a] long range Talos missile [while] BIDDLE was in Japan, so the defensive posture of the Gulf ships was heightened—the JOUETT, formerly on a Southern Search and Rescue Station, had moved closer to the beach to enhance the possibility of getting off a shot. Meanwhile, BIDDLE moved north, and, keeping the PIRAZ functions, added those of the Northern SAR by relieving PREBLE (DLG-15).
>
> This was a period of change in the various functions of the ships in most northerly posts. For nearly a month BIDDLE and LONG BEACH exchanged the PIRAZ responsibilities and shifted locations in hopes of luring a MiG within range, but despite several near misses by the JOUETT, no such luck occurred. Finally on the 14th of July, BIDDLE was relieved by LONG BEACH.

Helicopter activity aboard *Biddle* was constant when on station. *Biddle* had a SH3 Sea King (nicknamed "Big Mother") detachment for SAR purposes, while CH46 Sea Knights from Yankee Station carriers provided Vertical Replenishment (VERTREP) services. Occasionally, a UH1 Huey would land too. Landing a helicopter, even a small Huey, on a 50 foot landing pad in heavy seas was problematic, to say the least. Again, training was the key to conducting any exercise where some element of risk is involved. Some training is conducted "on the job," however. Lieutenant Boer explains:

> I remember when we started doing a lot of helicopter landings and launches. On the first day, first helicopter, I tuned into the air control circuit. A green seaman was on the flight deck phones and I could hear all the action. The flight deck OIC was an Ensign (Bishko? Seate?). I had a "schoolbook" understanding of what goes on so I would occasionally offer brief heads-up type tips

on the this-and-that of bringing-in a helo at sea. I did it sparingly so as not-to-distract; after all, I was sitting in a darkened room with dim lights. But I considered it my duty to tune-in and sort of act as a safety advisor. But I had more pressing duties at my own Combat console, so I hadn't monitored our air ops for a few days. I remember saying to myself that I'd better get back to my self-imposed "counseling" duties. I tuned-in and was rendered speechless: I heard this confident-voiced seaman speaking with clipped expertise going back and forth with an equally proficient Ensign bringing helicopters onto our rolling postage stamp of a helo pad.

Sometimes the Enemy is Us

A friendly fire incident occurred on *Biddle's* 1968 WESTPAC deployment that involved *Biddle*, *Boston* (CAG-1), one other US Navy ship, and the Australian DDG *Hobart*. When I attempted to recall some of the details of the incident with DSC David Johnson, he corrected my account with the following story:

> It was a four-plane section of Air Force Phantoms that independently diverted from an in-country mission to a feet-wet operation to which they had not been invited. This all started when a Marine forward observer near the North Vietnam border saw at near dusk what he reported as four helos headed south. There was a ground operation in progress just south of the border (it was a big deal at the time, but I can't recall the details) that made such an incursion sound reasonable. In fact, *Biddle* was just off the beach to block any MiGs that might try to provide air support to the NVA.
>
> We did figure-eights for hours on end to make it difficult for known FROG batteries on the beach to track us. We even loaded our EW program with limited air tracking capability to maintain surveillance of the truck-mounted radars. (FROG means Free Rocket Over Ground, which used two radar trucks for triangulation and a launcher truck. FROGs were bad business, even though it was primarily ballistic in flight. Still don't know why a strike on the FROG units was not conducted.)
>
> After a couple of days, the Australian guided missile destroyer *Hobart* relieved us and we were a couple of hours up the coast back to NSAR, I believe. It was just after dark when the Phantoms heard reports about the four helos, and decided to come out to the op area and check them out. I was monitoring voice communication circuits in CIC just to make sure your console equipment worked, and heard these guys get busy. They came up the coast from the south, and each one reported contacts on their radars, and they apparently concluded that they had jumped four low-flying helos. It all seemed to make sense to the Air Force.

I was in CIC working on a NTDS display console when the formation flew directly over *Biddle* on the deck at high speed—BLAM! BLAM! BLAM! BLAM! the ship shook as they headed toward their targets. Chief Johnson's description of the events continues:

> Without checking in with Red Crown, they started an attack, each Phantom taking one of the four bogies with missiles. The truth is, they had run across four ships in the area *Biddle* had recently left: the *Hobart*, a 75-foot Swift boat in the surf on a clandestine mission, the cruiser *Boston*, and *Boston's* shotgun (a gun-type DD whose name I forget; years later I had an employee who was a junior officer on the DD and gave me his perspective.)
>
> One F-4 reported tracking a helo at 1,500 feet, fired (Sparrow, I think), and reported that the helo had crashed on the beach and was burning. That was the Swift boat, with several casualties and a couple of fatalities.
>
> Another F-4 attacked *Hobart* and sent a Sparrow through the superstructure from aft to the pilothouse, with seven or nine dead Aussies and a bunch of injured. We tied up next to *Hobart* in Subic after she was repaired, and I talked to a chief who said he was on the way to his GQ station and saw the sailor in front of him get almost decapitated when the missile exploded.
>
> Another F-4 attacked *Boston* and did some damage. Pieces of the missile were found on deck, including the serial number.
>
> The last F-4 made two runs on the DD, but missed. Before it could try another run, the ship was at GQ and was starting to shoot, as I recall. By then, Maydays and other traffic in English were filling the circuits, and the brave Air Force dudes broke off and went home. There was a big investigation, and the Air Force finally agreed to play on a more integrated basis with the Navy.
>
> The next night there was another interesting development with *Boston*. She transmitted a Mayday, said she was under air attack again, and asked for air support. Turns out that she saw some AA tracers from an island nearby that the NVA controlled, and some lookout took no chances.

The website at www.gunplot.net devotes a page to the F-4 attack. The site claims that *Hobart* was tracking inbound aircraft they had designated 'friendly' when one of the 'friendlies' launched a missile which struck the starboard side, wounding two and killing one crewmember. Thirty seconds later, *Hobart* took another hit from two missiles. Luckily, one missile's warhead did not explode. The third missile killed a Chief Electrician and wounded two sailors. *Hobart* did manage to fire five rounds from her 5-inch gun at the target. *Hobart* retreated to join *Boston* and *Blandy* (DD-943) as a screen for the carrier *Enterprise* (CVAN-65). Later, as *Hobart* steamed for Subic for repairs, close inspection of missile fragments revealed that the missile was made in the U.S.

The web page also states that on the previous night of 16 June, U.S. Air Force jets sunk USS PCF-19, a patrol craft, killing five, and that *Boston*, *Edson*, USCGC *Point Dume*, and USS PCF 12 were attacked on the night of June 17.

Biddle tied next to *Boston* in Subic Bay a few weeks after this incident took place and I concur that the *Boston* was hit and damaged. Her wooden planks covering the main deck had been reduced to splinters and she had several holes in the superstructure from 2.75-inch rockets.

Playing Games

There were numerous instances when missile-equipped ships in the northern Gulf did not wait for MiGs to fake an attack—navy forces cooked up elaborate schemes to get a MiG close enough to launch a missile. One such incident involved *Biddle*, the guided missile frigate *Jouett*, and cruiser *Long Beach*, trying to "sucker punch" unsuspecting MiG pilots with a long range Talos missile. DSC David Johnson recalls what happened:

> The action took place in the vicinity of Vinh during *Biddle's* 1968 tour. MiGs had begun a series of intrusions into the south of North Vietnam, leading to the conclusion that they were preparing some attacks. Vinh was a North Vietnamese Army (NVA) staging area, and got a lot of attention from strike packages. It was also a hot recovery area for downed aircraft, and so CTF 77 (Carrier Task Force) decided to take action to interdict MiG flights and send a message: stay home.
>
> The plan had *Jouett*, then DLG-29, sit off the coast about 12 to 15 miles and do lots of tracking, and in general, make her presence known. *Long Beach* took position a couple of miles seaward from *Jouett* in total electronic silence, with the NTDS Link 11 in Receive Mode and Talos fire control transmitters in Standby but ready to radiate when ordered. Her presence was masked by *Jouett's* activity, as was planned.
>
> *Biddle* was positioned off Haiphong as North SAR, and her radars could see up the Red River valley to Hanoi. She was also the test platform for the first SPS-48 radar Moving Target Indicator that allowed moving aircraft to be detected among clutter caused by radar returns from clouds, nearby terrain, and waves on the sea surface. That capability was vital for seeing aircraft in all weather and in many jamming situations. Using our search radars and some magic devices (Seesaw—MiG IFF), we were able to detect MiG activity at the various airfields around Hanoi and create firm tracks as they flew south. As MiGs got into *Jouett's* SPS-48 radar detection range, she took tracking and Link 11 reporting responsibility. *Long Beach* was monitoring the Link picture in Receive Only, and would designate the remotely reported MiGs to Talos tracking channels, with fire control transmitters still in Standby.

The Op Order said that when a suitable MiG target was in the area (engageable by Talos but generally outside of Terrier range), CTF 77 would pass the weapons-free command to *Long Beach* over radio as the plain-language phrase "Blaze Away." At that command, track transmitters were activated, and the Talos engagement process commenced. The result: birds were away very quickly, even though the MiGs had probably detected track and illuminate RF activity and were heading for the hills. Engagements were successful at about maximum Talos range.

This process operated successfully at least twice before the NVA figured out that *Long Beach* was present. The result was that few MiGs ventured into that area for a long time.

Long Beach steamed around for a while with her missile houses black from the booster blast, probably as a badge of honor. Bravo Zulu, *Long Beach*!

Biddle was relieved at PIRAZ station by her old friend *Long Beach* (CGN-9) on 14 July after 50 long days at sea and 42 straight days on the line. *Biddle's* first tour in the Gulf included three extended periods that totaled 70 days of on line duty. She had conducted approximately 260 helo takeoffs and landings on her first deployment, a record that would be easily surpassed during her second deployment.

Soon after departing the Gulf it was my honor to receive a Letter of Commendation from Captain Scott and a Citation from Commander Seventh Fleet Vice Admiral W.F. Bringle. The letter stated that I had "demonstrated exceptional initiative, outstanding professional and technical ability, skill and knowledge in effectively maintaining in a continuous high state of reliability and combat readiness the ship's computer data display systems and the vital and sensitive beacon video processing system upon which the ship's mission was fully and absolutely dependent." The Citation added that my "skill and judgment contributed significantly and directly to the successful accomplishment of the ship's mission and to the United States' effort in Vietnam."

What the Hell Was That?

Enemies, both real and perceived, presented themselves in many ways on *Biddle's* maiden cruise. MiGs in the Tonkin Gulf were a known commodity, reasonably predictable, and easily tracked. On one occasion while on PIRAZ station, multiple unknown, unpredictable and untrackable targets appeared on *Biddle's* bow. The event was a cause of concern and almost brought *Biddle* to general quarters. Lieutenant (jg) Jim Checkett recalled that

I was the OOD on the mid-watch on an absolutely cloudless night somewhere in CTF 77's domain. I don't remember who my JOOD was, who was CIC Watch Officer, Quartermaster of the Watch (who may or may have not made log entries), or Bos'n Mate of the Watch. All I remember is that the incredibly fast moving "light show" all happened in a sea level-to-stars quadrant from the bow aft to the port beam. The lights grew smaller than bigger at an alarming rate, making moves impossible for human piloted aircraft, and certainly not your garden variety "weather balloons." As I recall there were somewhere in the neighborhood of a half dozen or so lights—all spherical and all bright like stars. At first we thought they were stars until the unusual movements started....pretty much exactly as described in a slue of UFO sighting reports we've all seen over the years. I tried to see if CIC could track them on the SPS-48, but they had no joy on any of them.

It eventually became hairy enough that I called the Captain to the bridge and there was eventually at least enough concern that some consideration was given to going to GQ. I believe in the end, after our little "light show" ended and our "visitors" disappeared.... either over the horizon or up into the stratosphere...most of us thought for sure it warranted a UFO report, but the damn report was so complicated and time consuming (imagine that!) we shit-canned the idea and continued pressing on.

The reason I called the Captain to the bridge was that every once in a while the targets would suddenly double then triple (or more) in size at a steady angle, which indicated the objects were approaching the ship at a high rate of speed. This implied a threat to the ship and I felt obligated to call the Captain to the bridge for that reason of course, but, even more importantly, one particular other reason.

It seems I was the first Lieutenant (jg) to qualify as OOD Fleet Underway on the ship, most of the others being Lieutenant Commanders. Maylon called me into his sea cabin and told me he was entrusting a lot of responsibility with such a junior officer as myself, not to mention his career, and he wanted to make his rule for waking him up at night anytime the ship was underway crystal clear. He simply said, "If the thought crosses your mind....should I wake the Captain?...you've answered the question!!!" That thought crossed my mind so I woke him up. That was a terrific piece of advice by the way, and I have used it with others who have worked for me over the years in many endeavors. Such a simple rule, but a perfect one. A win-win CYA situation for both parties!

Let's Go Home

Biddle stopped briefly in Subic Bay, offloaded her PIRAZ gear and security detachment, then packed her bags and continued her around the world cruise, stopping first at Singapore. Unlike Hong Kong, Singapore was clean—no trash, nothing out of place, and no homeless people. Like Hong Kong, bargains abounded but with less haggling over prices. The Raffles Hotel, a Singapore icon, was, and probably still is, a popular watering hole. Lieutenant Trump clearly recalls "Drinking a Singapore Sling in the Raffles Hotel listening to the faint echoes of the British Empire." He continues: "The Raffles Hotel was a favored Singapore watering hole during the glory days of the British Empire and was mentioned frequently in newspapers and colonial literature of the day. I believe it had fallen into disrepair and closed in the '50s and had been refurbished and reopened within the year before we stopped there. Again, these are hazy memories; you'll need to do some fact checking. I'm not sure who was with me; the best bets are Jim Simon and John Burns. I remember checking out a department store that same day which was stocked with goods from the PRC—it may even have been owned by the PRC. It was a glimpse of the future; now a great many of our consumer goods come from China. Then it was unlawful to buy or possess such goods."

After liberty in Singapore, we sailed through the Straits of Malacca into the Indian Ocean. Due to our westerly track to the port of Lourenco Marques, Mozambique, *Biddle* crossed the equator at latitude 0000 and longitude 87 East on July 27. When we crossed the equator, I, as thousands of sailors across the centuries had done before me, entered the Domain of Imperial Neptune, and was transformed from a lowly Pollywog into a mighty Shellback.

The seas were very rough for a week all the way across the Indian Ocean until we passed south of the Island of Madagascar. From that point to Lourenco Marques the seas were smooth once again.

Not knowing what to expect in Africa, it was pleasing to find that Lourenco Marques was, in many respects, a sophisticated medium sized city, not unlike many in the U.S. or Europe. Some of the local police were not sophisticated, however, as they did not hesitate to use violent force against citizens for no apparent reason. For example, I had shore patrol duty one night with a Portuguese policeman. As we entered a local drinking establishment a black woman made a remark to the policeman in Portuguese. Without saying a word, the policeman hit her as hard as he could across her back with his nightstick and she fell to the floor. Conscious but unable or unwilling to move, she was left on the floor to contemplate her remark. A few minutes later we enjoyed a fine meal with wine in a nice restaurant as if nothing had happened. Later, we returned to the heavily guarded police station where snarling police dogs kept a man, terrified and tattered, cornered in the main room.

Subsequent to leaving Lourenco Marques, *Biddle* rounded the Cape of Good Hope, entered the Atlantic Ocean and steamed north. After a short refueling effort at the Cape Verde Islands, *Biddle* docked at Lisbon, Portugal, for her first ever port call to Europe. Following a delightful three day visit, *Biddle* headed north, then east into the English Channel en route to her last port of the cruise, Copenhagen, Denmark. The channel transit was at night, at 27 knots, and "interesting." Captain Scott stated that the transit was at "27 knots because I wanted to get the crew rest and the ship cleaned up at anchor a day earlier than going into port. I had not sent position reports on purpose so not to send a false report. Then the damn Russian [cruiser] came by and circled us. Had to send a report to CNO. But I knew one part of CNO did not talk to the other, thus they did not know I was not where I should have been."

After the encounter with her Russian counterpart *Biddle* found itself on a collision course with a sailboat. Peter Trump remembered that "A very small intermittent contact was reported, constant bearing, decreasing range. Captain Scott was notified and did come to the bridge, as I recall it. As we made a slight course change to starboard, the sailor illuminated his sail. I suppose he bounced around a bit in our wake." Captain Scott recalled that "I ordered the signalman of the watch to illuminate the sail of the contact. The part about the reporting of the Russian is a fact too."

Leaving Russian cruisers and sailboats in her wake, *Biddle* soon crossed the path the Allied forces took on D-Day. When the outline of the Normandy coast showed on radar, I envisioned the hundreds of Allied ships that were poised at that spot 24 years earlier, ready to invade Europe.

Copenhagen, like Hong Kong, was a world-class city, boasting outstanding food and drink, a liberal atmosphere, Tivoli Gardens, and very friendly people. I probably had more fun in Copenhagen than anywhere else. Two incidents in Copenhagen were indicative of the times, however. First, when we pulled up to the dock, anti-war protesters reminded us that the war *Biddle* had just left was not popular with everyone. Second, in a similar incident, a local citizen spit on me as I walked in uniform through a crowded market.

Our five-day stop in Copenhagen soon ended and *Biddle* began the last leg of her around the world cruise. We entered the North Sea then turned north to enter the Atlantic north of the British Isles. As *Biddle* steamed toward Norfolk, we encountered a nor'easter and the worst seas of the cruise. All activities ceased except critical functions on the bridge, engine rooms, and boiler spaces. I sneaked a peek outside from the 03 level, which is about 60 or 70 feet above the water line, and was looking *up* at the waves. One second we would lean twenty or thirty degrees to port and a few seconds later we would pitch forward then lean twenty or thirty degrees to starboard. But Bath Iron Works builds great ships and *Biddle* just kept on steaming for Norfolk.

Finally, after surviving a terrific North Atlantic storm with 50-foot seas, *Biddle* arrived home. I never thought Norfolk would look good, but I changed my mind as tugs nudged *Biddle* to the D&S (Destroyer and Submarine) piers. [Almost simultaneous with *Biddle's* arrival, the destroyer *O'Hare* celebrated her arrival from her Middle East cruise by cutting a two-foot gouge into a nearby pier.]

Biddle was awarded the Secretary of the Navy Unit Commendation Citation for her performance in the Gulf of Tonkin on her first deployment. The commendation was awarded not only for her performance as PIRAZ ship, but also for effectively applying "advanced electronic resources and techniques which significantly contributed to the United States air combat operations in Southeast Asia." That part of the commendation got my attention because it was an area in which *Biddle* data systems technicians had made a contribution. CNO Admiral Thomas H. Moorer awarded the commendation for the Secretary of the Navy.

WESTPAC II

James Treadway

Captain Alfred R. Olsen, a 1944 Naval Academy graduate and career cruiser-destroyerman, assumed command of *Biddle* on 17 September 1968. *Biddle* was his fifth command at sea, having served in *Biloxi* (CL-80), *Providence* (CL-82), *Allen M. Sumner* (DD-692), and commanded *Ouachita County* (LST-1071), *Lester* (DE-1022), *John Paul Jones* (DDG-32), and *Sierra* (AD-18).

For the remainder of the year, *Biddle* enjoyed a period of tender availability, more inspections, and an intense multi-ship missile exercise off Puerto Rico with *Dewey* (DLG-14), *Claude V. Ricketts* (DDG-5) and *Talbot* (DEG-4). *Biddle* returned to Norfolk on 25 November where she remained on a leave and upkeep status through the holidays and into January.

1969

Returning to Norfolk on 20 January after a family cruise to Yorktown, Virginia, and a five-day port call to Philadelphia, *Biddle* began preparations for the upcoming WESTPAC deployment. During this time, the AN/SPS-48 radar received a Moving Taget Indicator (MTI) upgrade, which was tested during an evaluation cruise to the Caribbean from 28 March to 1 May. During the cruise, with stops in San Juan, Puerto Rico, and Guantanamo Bay, Cuba, *Biddle* fired six missiles and passed an Operational Readiness Inspection (ORI) with a grade of excellent.

After nine months of upkeep at Norfolk, *Biddle* stood out of Norfolk on 26 May 1969 for her second WESTPAC deployment. Forty percent of *Biddle's* crew was making their second cruise to the Gulf of Tonkin in less than a year. The AN/SPS 48 MTI upgrade was tested again off the coast of Virginia, then *Biddle* proceeded to the Panama Canal. Late in the afternoon on 31 May, *Biddle* entered the first series of locks at Colon, Panama Canal. After anchoring briefly in Gatun Lake and giving the ship a fresh-water bath, *Biddle* began a night transit of the Canal. Captain Olsen's Biddlegram #2 describes the passage: "It was a windless, starry night; the temperature was just right; and the ship glided through the ghostly silence, in many areas seemingly just a dozen feet from the bank of the canal. It was what I'd imagine the Garden of Eden would be like—without Eve, of course! As we neared the Pacific end, the channel narrowed and we found the sides of the Canal brightly-lighted with closely-spaced, blue fluorescent lights, just three or four feet high, which made the water glimmer like a mirror."

After refueling at Rodman Naval Base—no liberty in Balboa this time—*Biddle* set sail for Hawaii. With only a day and a half liberty in Honolulu, Hawaii was also little more than a refueling stop. Biddlegram #2 describes the transit from Hawaii to Guam then to the Philippines:

> We arrived in Apra, the principal harbor of Guam on June 20th and stayed only six hours. The most impressive thing about Guam and the other Mariannas Islands is their height. They rise quickly and sheerly out of the water; all are hilly; some are mountainous. They have a physical presence that most islands don't have.
>
> In our 3,300 mile voyage between Oahu and Guam, we encountered only a half dozen ships. This is not a commercially profitable route and very few merchant ships make the run. In spite of the width and breadth of the oceans, it is a fact that those paths that ships use are relatively narrow and heavily traveled. The route between Hawaii and Guam is not one of those.
>
> From Guam to the Philippines, we crossed the Philippine Sea and transited San Bernardino Strait, one scene of two of our Navy's great victories over the Imperial Japanese Navy in World War II. Today these waters are placid, blue and unmarred by the history they have seen. Our port of call in the Philippines was Subic Bay, a snug harbor, protected by rising hills against the wind and sea, and site of a large U.S. Naval Base, which our friends, the Filipinos, permit us to use. [Subsequently, US—Philippine relations changed. We departed our bases at Clark AFB, Subic Bay, and Cubi Point in late 1998 with only occasional official visits since then. (Marfiak)] We had four days here at the end of June to stretch our sea legs and make voyage repairs preparatory to going on-the-line. It was a welcome break in our long voyage.

It was a long voyage indeed—"11,490 miles in 29 days with only two days in port," according to Biddlegram #2. The spectacular weather encountered in transit would be dearly missed when *Biddle* narrowly missed typhoon Viola, then encountered seemingly never ending rolling seas, squalls, and heavy rains. Nevertheless, the short stop in Subic did give the crew an opportunity to get off a ship with 400 sailors and enjoy liberty 10,000 miles from home with 10,000 other sailors.

Subic Bay was an essential component of the Navy's efforts in the Gulf during the Vietnam War. Virtually all Navy ships coming from or going to Vietnam tied up or anchored at Subic Bay for repair, replenishment, rest, and relaxation. *Bid-*

dle's 1968 Command History describes Subic "As a base with considerable breadth of services (if not depth), it is also the place where most ships proceeding to or departing from the Vietnam War Zone gird or ungird their coins appropriately." Most coins were "ungirded" at Olongapo City, which was conveniently located just across the appropriately nicknamed Shit River. Subic's on-base facilities for R and R were minimal; making Olongapo the only place a sailor or marine could go to have a drink and some fun. There weren't many rules in Olongapo—you could get just about anything you wanted, or did not want—including dead. More than one sailor or marine was found floating face down in Shit River the next morning. The drinking was heavy, the music was loud, women were available, and fights were common. At least that is what I've been told.

Collision at Sea

Three weeks before *Biddle* arrived at Subic Bay, the WW II destroyer USS *Frank E. Evans* (DD-754) was cut in half while operating in the South China Sea with the Australian aircraft carrier HMAS *Melbourne*. *Evan's* severed bow section sank in minutes with the loss of 74 lives. The mangled stern stayed afloat and was towed to Subic Bay and placed in dry dock where most of *Biddle's* crew saw it. The sight of a destroyer ripped in half was a sobering sight and a reminder that sometimes things go terribly wrong in this business. The stern section was sunk as targets in Subic Bay October 10, 1969.

Evans had been on the gun line off the coast of Vietnam before participating in Operation Sea Spirit with *Melbourne* and four other U.S., British, and New Zealand destroyers. At 0300 hours, *Melbourne* signaled *Evans* to assume the position of plane guard 1,000 yards astern of *Melbourne*—a task that *Evans* had already performed several times that night. Inexplicably, instead of *Evans* following established procedure by turning away from *Melbourne*, *Evans* turned to port, directly in *Melbourne's* path. After the horrendous collision, *Melbourne* sailors immediately came to the aid of the men aboard *Evans* by first lowering fire hoses over the side for makeshift ladders then securing *Evans* alongside with wire cable.

John Stevenson, *Melbourne's* commanding officer, recalls the effort to save what was left of the *Evans* and the men aboard her: "It was all very quick, very chaotic, but organized as far as the *Melbourne* was concerned. They all knew what they were doing. The stern half of the *Evans* was secured to the ship, and people hopped over the edge to help survivors back onto *Melbourne*. This heroic effort by *Melbourne's* crew saved the remainder of *Evans'* crew." (Smith)

Visions of the broken, lifeless *Evans* would soon be recalled by Hard Chargers when *Biddle* assumed duty as plane guard for the USS *Coral Sea* (CV-43) at Yankee Station and while we participated in numerous underway replenishments with ships much larger than *Biddle*. The vision of the broken *Evans* again materialized when I learned years later that *Biddle's* sister ship *Belknap* had her superstructure removed from the bridge (03 level) and up after striking the USS *John F. Kennedy* (CV-67) in the Ionian Sea on 22 November 1975. *Belknap* was rebuilt at the Philadelphia Shipyard and re-commissioned on 10 May 1980. The cost to repair *Belknap* was $100,000,000, considerably more than it cost to build the ship.

On Station, Gulf of Tonkin

Biddle dropped anchor at Da Nang harbor on 30 June then relieved *Chicago* at South Search and Rescue (SSAR) on 1 July. Little had changed in the Gulf of Tonkin since her last visit. Like slipping into a comfortable pair of shoes, *Biddle* assumed familiar duties—SAR and PIRAZ, plus new responsibilities as AAWC at Yankee Station and plane guard for the carrier *Coral Sea*.

Extended periods on station generally consisted of watches that were 12 hours on and 12 hours off. Sometimes the DS group was so tired after a watch that instead of winding our way a few hundred feet to our berthing space, we slept on thick foam rubber pads conveniently stored behind tall equipment racks in the computer room, directly below CIC. The area was dark and air-conditioned and the chief knew where to find us if we were needed. As an added benefit, in case general quarters was sounded, we could be on station in thirty seconds or less. The hours were long, but *Biddle's* data systems technicians in the Computer, Display, and Communications groups kept their respective equipment in a high state of readiness.

Sometimes the Enemy is not the Enemy

Biddle's Command History stated that on 10 July *Biddle* and Task Force 77 had evaded typhoon Tess by moving south. Later that month, near the end of *Biddle's* first on-line period, typhoon Viola struck the mainland of China near Hong Kong during which *Biddle* endured three days of steady 30-knot winds out of the west and heavy seas. On the fourth day, we found several North Vietnamese fishermen lost at sea in flimsy bamboo rafts. Biddlegram #2 explains:

> …on the fourth morning as the winds began to abate, we came upon a small bamboo raft, 35 to 40 miles at sea, with two North Vietnamese fishermen

wearily trying to row to shore; then another with a man and a boy; still another with only one man; and finally one which was empty.

There is a tradition among those who go to sea that regardless of war or peace, we aid those who are in distress—we always pick up survivors. I believe this tradition stems from the fact that even in war, opposing Navies find that the sea is their common enemy. And so in this instance, BIDDLE and a destroyer, which was in company, went alongside each of the rafts and offered the exhausted fishermen water and food. They indicated they had been driven out to sea by the winds and had been unable to fight their way back. When they asked if they could come aboard, realizing they had small chance of surviving otherwise, we let them do so.

An excerpt from the cruise book continues the story: "During a period of high winds and rough seas, *Biddle's* helicopter spotted several North Vietnamese fishermen blown out to sea by a storm. In incredibly small rafts, these men had spent several days at sea with very little water and food. *Biddle* gave them food and water and her shotgun USS *Meredith*, was instructed to pick them up. A couple of days later, *Biddle* was instructed to bring the rescued fishermen to Da Nang. There the men were turned over to American Forces. Three months later, in an incident which had large press coverage, the men were given a boat and sent on their way home."

Relief at SSAR

Chicago relieved *Biddle* at SSAR on 1 August at which time *Biddle* departed for Da Nang to deliver the North Vietnamese fishermen to safety. Six days upkeep and liberty in Subic Bay and three days liberty in Manila was the extent of our brief relief from duty in the Gulf. Returning to the Gulf on 15 August, *Biddle* spent the next month shuttling between SSAR and PIRAZ responsibilities, as indicated by the ship's log—15 August—relieved *Chicago* as SSAR, 22 August—relieved *Chicago* as PIRAZ, 24 August—relieved *Chicago* as SSAR, 5 September—relieved *Sterett* as PIRAZ, 10 September—relieved by *Jouett*. Undersecretary of the Navy John W. Warner visited the ship on 19 August to present the Meritorious Unit Commendation and pennant in recognition of *Biddle's* performance during her 1968 WESTPAC deployment.

Bad weather in the Gulf continued with the arrival of typhoon Doris on 1 September. As she had done in early July, *Biddle* and Task Force 77 moved to the south and deeper waters to skirt the storm. Back on station on 2 September, *Biddle* continued her hectic pace at SSAR and PIRAZ until 10 September when she departed the Gulf for Subic Bay, passing close enough to launch our helicopter detachment. *Biddle* bid the helo detachment sayonara, then headed north for Yokosuka, Japan, for 12 days upkeep and R and R. Many Hard Chargers took advantage of the close proximity of Tokyo to take guided tours or to find a shopping bargain. Departing Yokosuka on 26 September, then crossing typhoon alley without incident, *Biddle* arrived Subic Bay on 30 September to prepare for her next on-line period.

Hello Haiphong

During *Biddle's* third period on-line she saw duty first in a tactical support role with our carriers operating at Yankee Station, then as SSAR and PIRAZ. The following incident occurred on 13 October and is a reminder how far north in the gulf *Biddle* once was.

On a quiet, calm morning, I stepped outside for some fresh air and noticed that we were dead in the water and surrounded by hundreds of North Vietnamese fishing boats. Generally, we were far enough from shore that spotting a fishing boat was a rare event. So, why was *Biddle* dead in the water and surrounded by so many fishing boats, and where were we? Clearly, we were somewhere we shouldn't have been. I did not get an explanation—I assumed that we snuck up there under the cover of darkness and were gathering intelligence about North Vietnamese activities. I had observed that most electronic equipment was turned off, apparently to not reveal our position. Eventually *Biddle* slowly turned to the south and began to pick up speed. Electronic equipment returned to service, one at a time. As the surface search radar sweep painted the coast of North Vietnam, a clear outline of Haiphong harbor materialized. North Vietnam's largest port city was just over the horizon. The only other U.S. forces that got that far north were pilots, POWs, and maybe a few submarines. Soon, we were making flank speed south and kicking up a fine rooster tail. As we passed a Russian trawler like it was standing still, my binoculars found a bikini-clad woman on the trawler's deck. Perhaps being in the Russian navy has its benefits.

While conducting research for *Hard Charger!* I asked Captain Olsen why *Biddle* was so close to Haiphong:

> I believe it was midway through our third period on PIRAZ station when we received message orders to proceed north with our "shotgun" destroyer under the cover of darkness to patrol off Haiphong, the principal seaport of North Vietnam, during daylight hours the next day, and then return to PIRAZ. The purpose was to accustom the North Vietnamese to U.S. Navy ships moving around the Gulf without hostile intent. It was a tactical maneuver….no intel-

ligence collection was involved. It was a rainy day, no aircraft were airborne and we saw no ships.

Five or six days later, we again received similar message orders, except that we were to patrol off Haiphong for 24 hours. This time we detected 20 or so military aircraft practicing touch-and-go landings during daylight hours. They knew we were there and were careful not to fly out over the Gulf. We encountered one large Soviet merchant ship departing Haiphong. After several challenges by flashing light, she identified herself and said she was en route to Vladivostok. We later learned that the North Vietnamese had received 90 per cent of the military support they needed by sea and from the Soviets.

I do recall the phenomenon of hundreds of fishing boats coming out after dark, possibly from the island of the Hainan, their black hulls silhouetted against the horizon. We kept them at a distance to preclude a torpedo boat or similar high-speed craft threading its way out of the pack and making a run on us. But I'm not sure whether this happened only during our two northern sorties or whether we saw them on other occasions at PIRAZ station.

Later, Captain Olsen explored his personal records with the following results: "I have found my 'Night Order Book.' It confirms that we twice relocated SSAR northward on the evenings of 13 and 20-21 October. The purpose was 'to accustom the North Vietnamese to our peaceful movement in the northern part of the Gulf of Tonkin.' Not to incite them to action. Concerning fishing junks, I found them to be an on-and-off happening. Not every night. I specifically mentioned numerous fishing junks in our vicinity in early September and again when we relocated to the North 20-21 October. They were numerous, dead in the water and making only two-three knots."

A Blackbird's Brief Appearance

One day (or was it night?) while checking one of the display consoles in CIC I noticed a single radar "blip" just north of the DMZ. On the next sweep, about 10 seconds later, the unknown and untagged target had moved almost ten miles north towards Hanoi. At first I thought it was false echoes or multiple targets popping up in different places. It was quickly evident that this was not a normal target—it covered the distance from the DMZ to Hanoi at 3,000 miles an hour. We had heard there was a top-secret plane operating in the area but we didn't know what it was called. Even the super-fast RC-5A Vigilante was not *that* fast. Later we learned it was a SR-71 Blackbird operating out of Kadena air base in Okinawa. When the still unknown blip reached the border with China, it just kept on going, knowing nothing could touch it at 80,000 feet.

SR-71s were tracked several times by *Biddle's* radar. Bob Gerity recalled a similar encounter with a Blackbird: "The SR-71 incident occurred on my watch and was first sighted by RD2 Mullen, I believe, coming down from China. We put an 'unknown' symbol on him and AW (Alpha Whiskey was Task Force 77) quickly told us to drop that track."

Nuclear cruiser *Long Beach* relieved *Biddle* at northern picket stations on 27 October, ending *Biddle's* month-long visit to the Gulf. *Biddle* made the short journey to the British Crown Colony of Hong Kong for six full days of liberty. For those who had enjoyed Hong Kong during *Biddle's* first WESTPAC deployment, this port call was a wonderful opportunity to see new sights, buy more hand-made suits, and try to find that watering hole down that narrow street off the beaten track in the Wan-Chai district. Or was it in Kowloon?

Plane Guard, USS *Coral Sea*

Biddle departed Honk Kong on 4 November for a brief refueling visit in Subic Bay, and then headed back to the Gulf. From 7 November to 13 November, *Biddle* assumed plane guard duty with *Coral Sea*, which required *Biddle* to maintain a position approximately 1,000 yards astern when planes were launched or recovered. After completing their sorties over North Vietnam, landing planes used *Biddle's* position as a marker when turning base leg to final approach. The plane's near ninety degree bank directly over *Biddle* allowed shipboard observers to peek inside the cockpit. When in this position at reduced throttle, a Phantom's intake compressor makes a distinctive, eerie moan that sent shivers down my spine. Occasionally I could see flak damage, fluids leaking from holes in the wing, or smoke escaping from inside the fuselage. When the plane leveled off, the final approach and landing could be followed with large binoculars on the bridge wings. The symphony of thunder and light as the plane slammed into the heaving deck and the violence of the landing was truly remarkable.

Victor Hanson accurately captured a scene few have a chance to experience: "The skill and courage of pilots have transformed the nightmarish—and, frankly, terrifying to watch—ordeal of receiving and launching planes on a rolling deck into a routine, albeit a deadly one. A half-century history of training and the tragic lessons learned from hundreds of deaths in peace and war have all honed pilots' skills to a fine art. These men risk destruction daily—to make less money than a middling college professor. They call "sporty" what we call terrifying. An empty ocean, jet fuel, sparks, heavy metal, and speed, after all, do not exactly combine to make a safe environment."(Hansen)

WESTPAC II—Mission Accomplished

Biddle made four appearances in the Gulf of Tonkin during her second WESTPAC deployment with each appearance punctuated by calls to the ports of Manila, Philippines; to the familiar ports of Yokosuka, Japan, and Hong Kong; and finally to San Francisco. *Biddle* landed 439 helicopters, conducted 168 fighter intercepts, and rescued survivors from 27 downed aircraft (Boslaugh 355.) On 13 November, her last day on-line, *Biddle* logged her 700th helicopter landing, then started the long voyage home.

The weather had ranged from delightful to frightful—which is not unexpected when traveling the world's oceans. Enroute to San Francisco, *Biddle* received "Smooth sailing" wishes from Vice Admiral W. F. Bringle, Commander Seventh Fleet, and Rear Admiral H. H. Anderson, Commander Cruiser-Destroyer Group Seventh Fleet. Referencing the Admiral's wishes, Biddlegram #7 made the following remarks concerning the transit:

> Having spent considerable time in the Pacific, Admiral Bringle and Admiral Anderson knew very well the hazards of crossing this vast ocean in the late Fall and so their wishes for "smooth sailing" were understood and appreciated. As our 14-day voyage to San Francisco developed, we were indeed fortunate. After the first two days out of Guam, the wind moderated and then, veered until it was abaft our beam. After that, we rolled a bit, but never plowed into the seas. We crossed ahead of the high winds that hit Hawaii in early December and so, had much to be thankful for when we picked up the California coast on our radar.
>
> December is a transitional month in San Francisco. The weather is uncertain. A heavy, dense fog often develops in the morning and persists until afternoon. The rainy season is about to begin. Again we were lucky. We were requested to arrive at the Golden Gate Bridge before sunrise to take advantage of favorable tidal conditions in the Bay. As we approached the coast in the dark and were still well to seaward, we could see the lights of the Bridge! There was no fog! We passed underneath at 6 a.m. without difficulty.
>
> As we steamed into the Bay, there was the Island of Alcatraz, its Federal Prison closed and dark, illuminated only by the large lighthouse that marks its location. Stretching out as far as the eye could see was the San Francisco—Oakland Bay Bridge, three and one-half miles long. Finally, we could see the hills of San Francisco rising up from the water's edge and covered with lights.

San Francisco wasn't home, but it was a lot closer than we had been in many months—we were in the right country but the wrong coast. After three days liberty and outstanding fall weather, we were ready to get underway for the final leg of our 55,300-mile cruise. On 8 December, with Christmas rapidly approaching, the light rain we encountered as we carefully negotiated our way out of San Francisco Bay could not dampen our spirits. That would happen a few days later when, while refueling at Rodman Naval Base at Balboa, Panama, *Biddle* was informed that some locks in Gatun were out of commission and our transit would be delayed. Damn!

We started our early evening transit anyway and anchored several hours later at Gatun Lake during yet another heavy rain. Finally, after another fresh water bath late in the afternoon on the next day, *Biddle* entered the first series of locks that would eventually raise her to the same level as the Caribbean. At last, *Biddle* would face no more obstacles, other than time, in getting home.

This WESTPAC deployment we learned that *Biddle* was the recipient of the Surface-to-Air Missile Systems "Excellence Award" for DLGs in the Atlantic Fleet. Also, Admiral Ephraim Holmes, Commander in Chief of the Atlantic Fleet, informed *Biddle* that she was awarded her second Meritorious Unit Commendation. So, after a 209-day cruise during which we were at sea 80% of the time, a proud, but tired, *Biddle* gently nudged D and S piers at Norfolk, on time. As I gazed over the crowd greeting *Biddle* at the pier, I saw my tired, but proud mom who had just driven 1,500 miles from Texas alone to see her two sons arrive home safely.

WESTPAC Interlude

James Treadway

Among the opening remarks in *Biddle's* 1970 Command History was the statement "Since the day she was commissioned, 21 January 1967, BIDDLE logs have recorded an around the world cruise, two deployments to WESTPAC, and two change-of-command ceremonies. When BIDDLE began 1970, she was in very unfamiliar surroundings, her homeport of Norfolk, Virginia." It would be 28 months before she would be deployed to WESTPAC for a third time, this time more powerful and more electronically aware of her surroundings than ever before.

Soon after returning from her second deployment to WESTPAC, *Biddle* was placed on a restricted availability status for the installation of Automatic Target Detection (ATD)/Automatic Clutter Detection (ACD)/Moving Target Indication (MTI) on the SPS-48 height-finding radar in conjunction CNO Project C/S 64 Operations-Evaluation of the AN/SPS-48(V) ATD/ACD/MTI radar. With the installation complete in mid-April, *Biddle* was underway in the VACAPES and San Juan Operating Area on 13 April for a 32 day training and technical evaluation of the SPS-48 modification. The short cruise included calls to the ports of San Juan, St. Thomas, and, of course, Roosevelt Roads. To give the "48" a real test, *Biddle* steamed independently north to the New York Operating Area and returned to Norfolk on 15 May. *Biddle* continued the CNO Project C/S 64 Operations during weekday cruises for a week until 22 May, when Captain Louis J. Collister, USN, relieved Captain Olsen.

A Kansas native, Captain Collister graduated from Case Institute of Technology with a Bachelor of Science Degree in Electrical Engineering. He served in the aircraft carriers USS *Anzio* (CVE-57) and USS *Randolph* (CVA-15), the cruiser USS *Worcester* (CL-144), and the destroyer USS *Jarvis* (DD-799). Captain Collister commanded USS *Leray Wilson* (DE-414), USS *Fessenden* (DER-142), USS *Leonard F. Mason* (DD-852), and the combat stores ship, USS *Concord* (AFS-5).

Under Captain Hollister's command, *Biddle* continued CNO Project C/S 64 Operations during short cruises in the VACAPES area until the project was completed on 5 June. On 13 July, *Biddle* was again placed on restricted availability status, this time for the removal of the ANS/SPS-48(V) ATD/ACD/MTI modifications. Eight days later, CNO Admiral Elmo R. Zumwalt was in the Norfolk area touring installations when he decided to "drop by." Three days after the Admiral's visit, the Florida's-own Miss Citrus Fruit 1970 visited *Biddle*. (I wonder which visit the crew enjoyed most?)

The next major milestone for *Biddle* was a five month regular overhaul and installation of the Shortstop Electronic Warfare System, the AN/SLQ-27 (XN-1). Preparatory to the overhaul, *Biddle* off-loaded ammunition at the Naval Weapons Station, Yorktown, Virginia, and conducted the annual Family Cruise. *Biddle* was placed in dry dock at Norfolk Naval Shipyard on 28 August. In addition to the Shortstop installation, considerable work was done to *Biddle's* exterior. The Command History stated that "BIDDLE'S sides were sandblasted to deck edge, and painted with a new acrylic paint designed for increased resistance to corrosion. The Deck Force took the 01 level down to the bare deck. The anchor chain was removed, tumbled, sandblasted, and checked for weak links before being repainted. There were modifications to the highline stations due to the installation of the Chaffroc [*Chaffroc is a rocket that dispenses chaff to protect against anti-ship missiles before target lock-on*] deck, and to the fantail lifelines, which had to be re-aligned to go around the aft Whip antennas."

1971

Biddle was still in dry dock in January 1971. The 1971 Command History reported "She was continuing a regular overhaul period combined with the installation of the new Shortstop computerized electronic warfare system. Modifications to the superstructure include the addition of two electronic countermeasures equipment compartments on the 04 and 05 levels. Two multi-beam antennas replaced the exterior mounted ECM equipment on the 05 level near the forward mack. An omni-directional antenna was added atop the after mack as part of the Shortstop system."

April was a busy month for *Biddle*—she was underway three times in the VACAPES Op Area for gunnery exercises and underway replenishment. Since *Biddle's* engineering plant had been modified during the overhaul to burn naval distillate fuel, she was underway again on 30 April to offload 500,00 gallons of fuel oil in order to take on naval distillate. With the overhaul and Shortstop installation complete, *Biddle* got underway on 23 March for weapons system alignment trials. On 3 May *Biddle* returned to the Naval Weapons Station, Yorktown, Virginia, to load weapons and conduct an annual Family Cruise on 6 May.

Biddle was underway again on 1 June for Ship's Qualification Trials (SQT), Weapons System Alignment Tests (WSAT), and Refresher Training in the Caribbean. After successfully passing missile SQT and WSAT, *Biddle* enjoyed a long weekend at St. Thomas, Virgin Islands. Refresher Training continued at Guantanamo Bay, where Captain William O. McDaniel relieved Captain Louis J. Collister as *Biddle's* fourth commanding officer.

Captain McDaniel, after receiving his commission through the NROTC Unit at the Rice Institute in June 1946, served in destroyers *Steinaker*, *Haynesworth Dehaven* and the cruiser *Los Angeles*. He commanded the destroyer *Strong* and the guided missile frigate *Macdonough*. Captain McDaniel also served as Commander Destroyer Division 322 in Norfolk.

Under Captain McDaniels command *Biddle* completed her Refresher Training and live Naval Gunfire Support Exercises at Culebra Island, returning to D and S Piers, Norfolk, on 1 August. Technical evaluation of the Shortstop ECM system began on 7 September and continued with numerous underway periods until January 1972. Representing the DLG class, *Biddle* participated in a comprehensive NATO Seapower review from 25 to 28 September. *Biddle's* 1971 Command History stated that "The ships in the review exercised at missile firing, launch and recovery of helicopters, ASW attack, surface gunnery, and underway replenishment as the carrier (USS *John F. Kennedy*) steamed by in column formation. Additionally, training in ASW, communications, and dual/multi-ship maneuvering was conducted during the remainder of the three days." Such is a day in the life of a DLG!

Following a satisfactory grade from a Nuclear Weapons Acceptance Inspection in early October, *Biddle* passed a Technical Standardization Inspection in December with a high evaluation. All areas related to weapons handling, security, and administration were tested.

Biddle continued to test her new Shortstop ECM system in January 1972. A technical evaluation of the system during two underway periods in mid-January was followed by an operational evaluation in the VACAPES Area from late January through mid-February. "Final operational tests were conducted in the Jacksonville (Florida) Operational Area, 22-25 February and 28 February—3 March," according to the 1972 Command History.

DSC Rodney Merrill describes the installation:

> Shortstop was a threat reactive ECM system. On *Biddle*, Shortstop filled three equipment rooms, ECM-1, 2, and 3. ECM-1 took over the berthing space under the Electronics Technician shop and held the digital equipment—com-

puters, mag tape, printers, Teletype, and symbol generator. ECM-2 above Sonar Control was expanded and held the active ECM equipment, antenna controls, and system test equipment. Adding ECM-3 caused *Biddle's* forward mack to be about twenty feet higher than the other ships of the class. On each side of the ship were the antennas that weighed about three tons each. Because this was a test platform and could not take the full size of the antennas, only the X band antenna for the automatic system was put on the ship. Before leaving for WESTPAC another band was added. Shortstop was a full auto system. It could detect, identify and either recommend or take action, depending on system mode: semi-auto, or auto, in seconds.

Soon after *Biddle* completed testing the Shortstop system, she was assigned Restricted Availability for modifications to accept the Navy's Light Airborne Multipurpose System (LAMPS) helicopter. With work completed in early April, *Biddle* prepared for her first Med cruise.

The Gulf of Tonkin—1972

James Treadway

Increasing domestic pressure from opponents of the Vietnam War and the fact that the war was not going well militarily prompted a gradual withdrawal of U.S. forces in Vietnam soon after *Biddle's* first Gulf deployment in 1968. When *Biddle* returned for her second deployment in 1969, negotiations with North Vietnam were underway in Paris, a prohibition against bombing targets in North Vietnam had been in effect since November 1968, and Commander Naval Forces Vietnam (COMNAVFORV) Vice Admiral Elmo R. Zumwalt's operation Southeast Asia Lake, Ocean, River, and Delta Strategy (SEALORDS) was putting heavy pressure on Communist forces in the Mekong Delta. By 1970, as the U.S. withdrawal continued, the Vietnamese Navy had assumed many SEALORDS operational responsibilities, while U.S. Navy blue-water combatants in the Tonkin Gulf carried the war to the enemy in South Vietnam, Laos, and Cambodia, instead of the heart of North Vietnam. Furthermore, the number of attack carriers at Yankee Station had been reduced from three to two and rigorous cost cutting measures limited fuel, aircraft and ammunition. By 1971, the number of ships dedicated to the Naval Gunfire Support Unit was limited and the battleship *New Jersey* (BB-62), with many other large caliber gun ships, had returned to the United States.

The steady decline of the U.S. involvement in Vietnam reversed in the spring of 1972 when North Vietnam launched their 1972 Easter Offensive. The attack, which broke through the DMZ into the Central Highlands toward Saigon, was countered by increased amphibious activity in I Corps in the northernmost provinces of South Vietnam as well as naval gunfire support in I Corps and the southern provinces of North Vietnam. Within weeks after the Communist offensive began, the interdiction that had been in place since November of 1968 was lifted and the war was being carried to North Vietnam from Saigon to the border of China. Many seaports in North Vietnam, including Haiphong, were mined in an attempt to prevent the importation of military equipment. To support the massive effort, the Task Force 77 attack carrier population grew to an all time high of six carriers.

The North Vietnamese countered the U.S. offensive in several areas. U.S. aerial supremacy over North Vietnam was successfully challenged by a massive employment of anti-aircraft weapons, which included both guns and missiles. Their successes were not matched in air-to-air combat, however. The ever-increasing population of Naval Fighter Weapons School (Topgun) graduates in the fleet had reversed an earlier embarrassing exchange rate. The final USN—USMC fighter versus fighter exchange rate of 5.6 to 1 (Nichols 168) was due in large part to Navy pilots such as Lieutenant Randy Cunningham, the Navy's only Vietnam War ace. North Vietnamese coastal batteries offered some resistance to Naval Gunfire Support activities, but were generally ineffective.

In early April, as *Biddle* was preparing for a cruise to the Mediterranean in June, *Sterett* (DLG-31) was involved in an incident in the Gulf of Tonkin that became known as the "Battle Off Dong Hoi." Ten weeks after the Battle Off Dong Hoi, *Biddle* would be engaged in a similar battle for her life—the "Battle at PIRAZ." The similarities between *Biddle's* battle and *Sterett's* struggle as well as the close relationship between the sister ships require that both stories be told.

Sterett Sets the Standard

DS2 Elden Miller, who was aboard *Sterett* in 1972, described in detail the events of the Battle Off Dong Hoi on *Sterett's* web site. Additionally, Elden and I exchanged many e-mails regarding *Sterett's* and *Biddle's* MiG engagements when we were writing a book about the events entitled *MiGs, Missiles, and MTBs*. The book was not completed but helped launch *Hard Charger!* The following paragraphs summarize the Battle Off Dong Hoi.

Sterett was operating in the northern gulf in April 1972 when she received orders to provide anti-air support for a gun-line mission near Dong Hoi with light cruiser *Oklahoma City* (CLG-5), and the destroyers *Higbee* (DD-806) and *Lloyd Thomas* (DD-764).

After a rendezvous north of Dong Hoi on 19 April, the strike group made their first gun run from north to south with *Oklahoma City* in the lead, the destroyers following, and *Sterett* separated from the group to provide AAW support. According to Elden, "The weather that day was clear but with reduced visibility of less than two miles and was described as 'hazy at best.'" *Sterett* had launched her Light Airborne Multi-Purpose System (LAMPS) helicopter, which was to act as an airborne spotter. *Sterett* had already received permission from 7th Fleet to use missiles if required.

On the first run, all three ships received fire from shore batteries in an apparent attempt to bracket the ships. There were no direct hits but *Oklahoma City* reported shrapnel damage from near hits. *Sterett* had detected air targets below hilltops on the run to the south and was ready if a MiG wanted to see some action. Sure enough, a single MiG 17 suddenly went "feet wet" in the direction of the group just as the group finished their run to the north.

Elden recounts that, "The MiG headed for the *Higbee*, passed over the ship amidships and dropped a 250-pound bomb. The bomb tumbled towards *Higbee*, and passed between the aft stack and the ASROC launcher, barely missing the railings and ended up in the water. It was a very near miss with no damage. This was the first time in Navy history that a MiG aircraft had ever attacked a U.S. Navy ship."

Even though the MiG was inside *Sterett's* minimum missile range, *Sterett* attempted to fire a full salvo of missiles at the target. Only one bird left the rail, however, which narrowly missed. The second bird failed to fly due to a faulty primary firing circuit. The MiG circled for another pass and dropped a second 250-pound bomb that hit *Higbee's* fantail near the 5-inch mount. The bomb penetrated the weather deck into the upper ammunition handing room—the resulting explosion destroyed the mount, the sprinkler system, after steering, and ruptured the aft fuel tanks. Now dead in the water and flames engulfing the entire aft section of *Higbee*, the situation had turned from serious to grave.

The MiG, now 9,500 yards from *Sterett* and at an altitude of 300 feet, banked to the west and headed for the mountains. *Sterett's* fire control radar had locked on the target and the missile that had not fired earlier was fired using a secondary firing circuit. Still inside minimum missile range, the missile did not have enough range for the booster to separate. Elden describes the destruction of the MiG, "The missile struck the MiG dead center where the wings join the fuselage, resulting in instant destruction of the aircraft. This strike was more of a mid-air collision, but highly effective, nonetheless. The extreme accuracy of the launch systems and target designation hardware enabled this pure ballistic shot."

A second MiG had entered the fray but didn't stay long. Apparently, after observing the destruction of his comrade, MiG number two sought safety in the mountains. *Sterett's* fire control radars had locked on the fleeing MiG and a second salvo was on its way. Just after the MiG went "feet dry," all telemetry signals indicated that the MiG was destroyed and the target disappeared from radar. Unfortunately, the incident was eventually labeled a "probable" kill in spite of the fact that one of two Air Force F-4s, who were not officially supposed to be in the area, observed the MiG go down.

In addition to the MiG activity, *Sterett* had been tracking suspicious surface craft in the Dong Hoi area. The North Vietnamese did have Motorized Torpedo Boats (MTBs) but the Tonkin Gulf also tended to generate false echoes. One hostile surface track that was being tracked in Continuous Boat Track (CBT) mode provided vertical video separation, which indicated missile launch and an Anti Ship Cruise Missile (ACM) ECM signature. The incoming target was identified as a SS-N-2 Styx missile which has an active homing system and a 2,000 pound warhead. *Sterett's* aluminum superstructure and lightly armored hull would provide little protection. Furthermore, *Sterett's* Anti-Ship Missile Defense (ASMD) system with rocket decoys and radar reflective chaff was not operable.

Elden summarizes the critical situation: "A hit by the Styx would most assuredly be fatal to *Sterett*. This was the first time a Navy ship had ever been attacked by a cruise type guided missile in a combat situation. The early positive lock by the SPG-55 fire control radar allowed *Sterett* to immediately fire a salvo of two Terriers following the Styx launch. If Sterett would have had to acquire the Styx normally with her air search radars, plot the course via several paints (radar sweeps), and then hand it over to the missile fire control radars, she could never have fired missiles in time to intercept the Styx missile. Bridge lookouts reported seeing *Sterett's* Terriers enter a cloudbank and explode. The Styx was never visually spotted. Following the detonation of our Terrier, the missile target disappeared from radar, and the ECM signature signal ceased."

Battle Off Dong Hoi—The North Vietnamese Version

Stories have two sides and the Battle Off Dong Hoi is no exception. In *MiG-17 and MiG-19 Units of the Vietnam War*, Istvan Toperczer described the battle as told by the North Vietnamese pilots who allegedly flew the mission, Le Xuan Di and Nguyen Van Bay of the 923rd Fighter Regiment. MiG pilots Di and Bay were among ten pilots from the 923rd who had been preparing for an attack on shipping since 1971. Six pilots were eventually selected for the assignment.

On the day of the attack, Di and Bay took off from a secret air base at Gat and flew north toward Ly Hoa. Upon receiving orders to attack, the two pilots headed directly for the puffs of smoke in the Gulf. According to Nguyen Van Bay, "Over the sea Le Xuan Di turned to the left towards USS *Higbee* (DD-806) (sic) and increased his speed to 800 km/h while aiming at the ship. At a distance of 750 m he released his bombs and broke to the left. Both 250-kg bombs hit the ship. He reported this to ground control, and at 1618 hrs he landed at Gat airfield. His speed was too great, however, and Li Xuan Di overran the landing strip and ended up in the arrester barrier, but fortunately neither he nor his jet was damaged (Toperczer 53, 54)."

Friendly Fire Incident Brings *Biddle* Back

Three days before *Sterett's* engagement with the MiG, USS *Worden* (DLG-18) was severely damaged while on North SAR. One man was killed and nine wounded by what was thought to be two errant anti-radiation missiles fired by friendly forces. This tragic incident set in motion a chain of events that brought *Biddle* back to the Gulf of Tonkin a third time to make up for the loss of the damaged ship. In a short period of time, *Sterett* had relieved *Worden* and *Biddle's* Med cruise was cancelled. *Biddle* made preparations for an immediate Tonkin Gulf deployment.

Biddle's CIC and NTDS Officer, Lieutenant Ralph Muse, recalled that

> *Biddle* had just completed six months of technical and operational testing of the Shortstop Electronic warfare system. The EW and NTDS systems on board were configured for use on carriers. The system was successful in handling up to 22 simulated missile attacks at the same time in tests (the simulation was done using special radar and electronics on F8s and F4s to simulate Soviet missiles.) The ship was scheduled for a Mediterranean deployment in June 1972. After six months of Monday through Saturday sailing we were looking forward to the deployment. On Saturday 8 April 1972 we were notified that we would be sailing to an undisclosed location WESTPAC on the morning of 12 April. (So much for our Mediterranean cruise.)
>
> The ship was hardly ready—spare parts were in short supply and we were undermanned. We had only twelve radar men on board when a complement of 30 to 50 was normal. The manning level in Engineering Dept. was even worse. On Monday April 11th the CIC Officer (CICO) was reassigned and I was appointed CICO as well as NTDS officer. The only good news was that we could requisition any parts or supplies we needed from any ship in port (thanks, USS *Josephus Daniels*).

Biddle was ordered made ready for immediate deployment to the Gulf of Tonkin on 8 April. She departed Norfolk for the Western Pacific on 12 April with *Mullinnix* (DD-944) and was joined by *Glennon* (DD-840), and *Sarsfield* (DD-839) on 14 April. Enroute to the Gulf, the DS gang discovered that the reliability of the three CP-642B NTDS computers increased considerably with uninterrupted ship's power applied to them, instead of switching to shore power when in port. As a result of this discovery, failures were drastically reduced by the time *Biddle* reached the Gulf. Also, Lieutenant Muse noted that after picking up additional personnel in Panama, Hawaii, Guam, and Subic Bay, *Biddle* arrived on station with thirty-five radar men, a complete Security Group, and a helo detachment.

Biddle Arrives in Gulf of Tonkin

When *Biddle* relieved Sterett at NSAR on 16 May 1972, it is unlikely that *Biddle's* crew knew about *Sterett's* battle off Dong Hoi the month before. At that time, the Navy did not advertise that a ship had splashed a MiG even though it was a great source of pride and accomplishment for the ship's crew. It is likely, however, that news of the MiG splash had been disseminated to the upper ranks and to the commanding officers of ships entering the Gulf of Tonkin Theater.

There was nothing to indicate that *Biddle* and *Sterett* would accomplish a remarkable feat—back to back MiG kills, with each ship claiming one confirmed kill and one probable kill. So, with two previous Gulf deployments and recent weapons, NTDS and ECM upgrade under her belt, *Biddle* entered the Gulf prepared for any action that might come her way. This would be her final deployment to the Tonkin Gulf and one that her crew would not forget.

The recently expanded war effort presented a different picture than *Biddle's* previous GOT deployments. SSAR, NSAR and PIRAZ stations were still there and *Biddle's* responsibilities at those stations would change little. MiG activity would prove to be a different matter, however. A veteran of *Biddle's* 1969 WESTPAC deployment, OS1 Jerry Kronvall, got a quick introduction to the dynamic war scene. He explains:

> I was the ship's NTDS Air Controller Supervisor when *Biddle* assumed duties as North SAR in the Gulf of Tonkin on 18 May 1972. Sitting at the NTDS console as the main Air Controller, I took control of a section of Navy F-4J fighters that were on station between Haiphong, North Vietnam and us. I thought that this would be same type of aircraft control that happened in our 1969 deployment—long control times but no action.
>
> The F-4s were from VF-161, call sign ROCKRIVERS 110 and 105. On the radarscope were two aircraft that were bearing down on the ROCKRIVERS. I didn't have any friendly IFF or any reports of MiGs in the area so I told the ROCKRIVERS the range and bearing of the strangers (unidentified aircraft) and kept reporting the position of the strangers. I turned the F-4s toward the strangers so they could ID the two planes. The section leader of ROCKRIVER came over the radio saying "BANDITS, BANDITS, BANDITS"—they had identified the strangers as two MiG-19s. Captain Carter was standing behind me so I asked permission to engage and arm the F-4's missiles. Captain Carter gave the order "ENGAGE the MiGs." I told the

ROCKRIVERS to engage the MiGs and they were cleared to fire their missiles. The ROCKRIVERS engaged the MiGs and released two Sidewinders. Both MiGs were destroyed. This happened in the first two hours on the first day on the line.

On 23 May the ROCKRIVERS were back—ROCKRIVERS 100 and 112. Two MiG 17s were coming and they were over Kep, North Vietnam. Captain Carter was once again in CIC and once again I asked to engaged the MiGs and received "WEAPONS FREE" from Captain Carter. Both ROCKRIVERS engaged and shot two Sidewinders. Both MiGs were destroyed.

My memory of one engagement is not logged in the Air Controller's log that I kept but it did make the newspapers back in the US. I engaged one MiG, but before the F-4 released his missile, the pilot of the MiG bailed out. Captain Carter argued with the Admiral on the carrier that I should be given credit for downing the MiG. The pilot of the F-4 came up and apologized for not releasing a missile. I still think that I should have been given credit for downing the MiG. If that happened, I would have been an ace on the first line period.

On 7 June I intercepted a MiG using VF-213 at nighttime. The pilots from VF-213 were heloed to *Biddle* and presented the following story to Captain Carter and myself along with other RDs. We were having problems when an aircraft was hit by a missile or "AAA" fire and the aircraft was damaged, the MiG's would come up and shoot our aircraft out of the sky. VF-213 wanted to come up acting as an A-7 that was wounded. So, we made the F-4 look and act like an A-7. Even the voice comms were the exact duplicate of an A-7. Sure enough, the MiG came up and we engaged the F-4. The Aircraft Combat Maneuvers (ACM) lasted 20 minutes or a little longer. We didn't shoot the MiG down but the MiG's stopped engaging our wounded aircraft for quite a while. This engagement was the most stressful engagement that I did.

On 8 June I engaged a MiG-21 50 miles due east of Phucten, North Vietnam. The F-4s were from VF-214 and their callsign was LINFIELD 211 and 212. The F-4s were fighting for about 15 minutes but kept losing missile lock tones. The engagement was broken off and everyone went home alive.

On 10 June I engaged MiG's with VF-214, on 11 June (my birthday) with VF-151, on 12 June with VF-31 and again on 13 June with VF-123. No kills took place but the engagements were from 10 to 30 minutes long as I recall.

When the action was slow and nothing was going on and CIC was doing the normal things you do in a combat zone. Captain Carter actually directed the action from CIC. This was the first time that I ever saw a Captain do that.

This was not the first time that *Biddle's* commanding officer "directed the action from CIC." Captain Scott set the precedent aboard *Biddle*. In an e-mail, Captain Scott stated "I did ALL, repeat, ALL actions and considered CIC my 24 hour a day place to be during any evolution. The bridge was the location for the JO of the deck and I went there only to look at the ocean to relax. As you know, we ran the ship from CIC with total control from there with watch officer there in total control and I had a seat over looking all of CIC. By no means were they the first and maybe even we were not. Check it out with Bob Gerity or Bob Baker or Wes Boer. It was basic doctrine."

Captain Scott is correct that *Biddle* was not the first to control a ship from CIC—perhaps the precedent was set aboard the test service ships Oriskany, Mahan, and King in the early 60's. Captain Garett Lockee, Wainwright's commanding officer from September 1966 to April 1968, reported in the April 1969 U.S. Naval Institute Proceedings that "The ship's commanding officer spends most of his time in this space [CIC], rather than on the bridge. The ship fights from CIC, not from the bridge, as has been the custom of the past."

I asked Captain Scott if it was it official policy or regulation, personal choice, or a blend of the two to run the ship from CIC. He responded that "It was NOT official policy or regulation. Where I ran the ship was my call. I could have run it from after steering below decks if I so desired. CIC was the location for what were doing. However, if we had been in a different type of operation, maybe it would have been on the bridge part or all of the time and the e with CIC. Even from my cabin or the head." (Who said the skipper doesn't have a sense of humor.)

Kronvall continues:

> The Captain and I usually talked about what we were going to do the next day. During our talks I mentioned that MiGs were coming up and flying to a certain location and then disappearing and then reappearing on the radarscope. This was in the first part of June when the MiGs were being observed by the RDs. This was constant during the month of June and the first part of July. Captain Carter and I along with the rest of the Air Tracking Team and the other Air Controllers also watched this action during their watches. Looking back, they were honing their skills for what was to come.
>
> On 18 June we engaged five MiGs with two F-4s from VF-123. I had a very difficult time (keeping track) of who was who during this engagement. All sidewinders from both F-4s and all sparrows were shot (eight Sidewinders, eight Sparrows). The F-4s were also receiving missiles from the MiGs. The F-4s reported two unconfirmed kills (the F-4s were avoiding missiles and did not take pictures of the kills). Only three MiG's were present when the engagement was over.
>
> On 11 July, using F-4s from VF-123 call sign CLUBLEAF 211 and 212, we engaged three or four MiGs. During the engagement CLUBLEAF 212 was shot down. One MiG lost control during the engagement and flew into the ground. The MiG kill was considered an unconfirmed kill. This was a good

day and a bad day for me. Footnote: Both the pilot and RIO was taken prisoner and released in 1973.

On 18 July SNUG 1 from the Air Force 336th Tactical Fighter Squadron shot down a MiG-21. RD1 Nastasi was the Air Controller and I observed the engagement as an Air Controller Supervisor.

OS1 Kronvall's accounts are illuminating but some claims do not appear to be correct. For instance, the MiG engagements on 18 May, 23 May, and 7 June mention Captain Carter's presence in CIC. Captain Carter did not assume command of *Biddle* until 3 July. Also, he could not have been aboard during "the month of June and the first part of July" when "Captain Carter and I along with the rest of the Air Tracking Team and other Air Controllers also watch (sic) this action during their watches." Furthermore, research from multiple sources found that the Air Force MiG kill on 18 July actually occurred on 15 August by Captains Fred Sheffler (Aircraft Commander) and Mark Massen (Weapons System Officer)—(http://www.f-15estrikeeagle.com/facts/units/336fs.htm).

While enjoying a five day break from duty in the Gulf, Captain Edward W. Carter, III assumed command of *Biddle* in Subic Bay on 3 July. The North Carolina native enlisted in the Navy in 1945 for two years prior to entering the U.S Naval Academy. After graduation from the Naval Academy in 1951, he later earned a Master of Science degree from MIT in 1959. Captain Carter served in *Sanborn* (APA-193), LST 528, *R. K. Huntington* (DD-781), *Boston* (CAG-1), *Farragut* (DLG-8), and *Long Beach* (CGN-9). He commanded *Towers* (DDG-9).

With *Biddle's* fifth commanding officer aboard, *Biddle* returned to the Gulf for her second line period. In an interview, FTG2 Jim Parks recalled *Biddle's* arrival in the Gulf: "Once we were on station in Vietnam, we settled into a routine of watches, work, and sleep. *Biddle* was busy directing air strikes over North Vietnam at PIRAZ station, but jokingly we called it the "sitting duck station." *Biddle* was often close enough to Vietnam to see individual trees on the shoreline, and we were steaming "dead slow." I knew the VC didn't really want us there, and I often wondered why they didn't try to do something about it."

Battle at PIRAZ

James Treadway

Eventually the North Vietnamese did try to do something about *Biddle's* presence 30 miles off the coast of North Vietnam. Lieutenant Ralph Muse, senior officer in CIC when the attack started, recalled that on the night prior to the attack, 18 July 1972, there was very little U.S. Navy air activity over North Vietnam due to the bad weather. However, MiG activity was much higher than normal with more than 50 missions and *Biddle* was tracking as many as 15 MiGs at one time. CWO2 Gunner O'Neal, sitting at the Ship's Weapons Coordinator (SWC) console, also noticed the increased MiG activity, particularly in an area that he suspected was a bombing range. Gunner describes the activity:

> On the night before the attack, Ralph and I were on Condition III watch in CIC from 2000 to 2400 hours, Captain Carter was at the movies. Lieutenant Muse, over a period of time, had told me things of a sensitive nature to allow me to do my job as SWC better. So I jokingly told Lieutenant Muse to tell the "spooks" *[Spooks were on-board intelligence personnel who intercepted and translated conversations between the North Vietnamese]* that if I knew there was a bombing range in North Vietnam I would think that they were practicing dive-bombing attacks from about 35,000 feet. He spoke with them and confirmed what I was seeing. After the movie the Captain came to CIC on his way to his cabin and asked Ralph how things were going. Ralph told him OK and went on to tell him about the MiGs. Captain Carter told Lieutenant Muse, "You had better let me know if that ever happens again."

The next night according to Lieutenant Muse "was very quiet. There was no North SAR ship on station, no [air] activity [over North Vietnam] from our side, and no flights by the MiGs....that was, until late on the 20:00 to 24:00 watch." CWO3 Jerry Van Cleave was on watch in CIC as SWC when Gunner relieved him early. Van Cleave recalled that "Lieutenant Commander Ray Witter was my Combat Directions Center (CDC) coordinator and was due to be relieved by Lieutenant Ralph Muse who had the mid watch. I believe Lieutenant Jim Mleziva was on the bridge as OOD. I don't remember where the captain was at the time but that wouldn't have made any difference since we were operating under the CDC concept (new at the time) where the evaluators were delegated the authority to deploy weapons. After being relieved, I transited the wardroom en route to my stateroom. If I recall, the helicopter crew was hanging out there. I may have had a short cup of coffee with them before heading down to my stateroom."

Lieutenant Muse and Gunner were on watch when a single A-6 went feet dry on a bombing run. Two Barrier Combat Air Patrols (BARCAP) were in their normal "feet wet" position in the far northern Gulf. Gunner continues: "Ralph told the Captain [about the A-6] who told him to keep him apprised of the progress. When the A6 came on the radio saying he had been hit and his co-pilot had been hurt, the Captain was notified and came to CIC. We [*Biddle*] were the PIRAZ ship, Harbormaster, and the SAR coordinator for the Gulf, so we were monitoring the situation. Alpha Whiskey (Task Force 77) told one of the BARCAPs to escort the A6 to the *Midway* and the other one to stay on station to the south of PIRAZ. This [also] caused the secure voice relay plane to also go south as there was no protection for it with only one BARCAP."

OS1 Jerry Kronvall was the controller who picked up the wounded A-6's distress call, "An A-6 aircraft was hit by AAA or by a missile and I answered his mayday call. I was controlling him back to his carrier and talking with the carrier's Air Controller Supervisor. When the A-6 was within 30 miles of the carrier the carrier Air Intercept Controllers (AIC) took control of the A-6. [Footnote: Never did find out how the pilot made out.] During this time Captain Carter was called to CIC and he stood behind me observing the A-6 mayday condition."

As Ships Combat Evaluator, Lieutenant Muse asked the duty officer at the 7th Fleet command center aboard the *Kitty Hawk* to launch the ALERT-5 CAP—two F-4s or F-8s ready to launch within five minutes. 7th Fleet denied the request since the next BARCAP was scheduled to launch in less than an hour and besides, "nothing was going on tonight." This decision left *Biddle* and all ships in the northern gulf with substantially reduced defenses if the fleet was attacked by air. Muse also remembered that there was no ship stationed at NSAR at that time.

Approximately five minutes after the BARCAPS had departed, Gunner recalled that "Lieutenant Muse, who was on the phone with the spooks, told me to check the area south of Hanoi. I hit the Seesaw and painted three MiGs. I assigned missiles systems to the target and the radars got a lock on the target." The targets had been designated "hostile" in the NTDS—their symbols on all screens now reflected this fact.

At that moment DS1 Terry Johnstone was the "on-duty" data systems technician in CIC. He recalled that since there were no air strikes at the time he was monitoring the NTDS from an unused console in CIC. His attention was suddenly diverted to the three hostile tracks that suddenly appeared on his screen. Believing that the tracks were mistakenly entered, he turned to inform Lieutenant Muse that someone had incorrectly identified some targets. Johnstone saw that Lieutenant Muse was talking on the phone while hovering over the operator on the Evaluator console. Terry now realized that the tracks were very hostile, very fast, and very close.

RD1 Kronvall stated that "our 'magic' boxes started to sound the alarm that a MiG or MiGs were close to us. This was about 2215 to 2225 (1015/1025 PM). They were close, at 7.5 to 9 miles—our 48 radar picked them up and automatic tracking was taking place."

"Clear The Fo'c'sle…Fire One…Fire Two…General Quarters!"

Ships Weapons Coordinator CWO2 L. L. "Gunner" O'Neil was the first to spot the MiGs. In addition to the radar "skin" paint, Seesaw verified the MiG's presence with its own signal. Gunner remembers that "the Captain had been notified that one of the BARCAPs was escorting a shot up A-6 back to the carrier. Since the movie was in process he told Ralph to keep him apprised of the status of the CAP. Shortly thereafter we had MiGs feet wet and after acquiring them on the missile systems, the launcher was assigned and the Captain was informed and he said to sound GQ."

With the MiGs "feet wet" less than 20 miles away, and knowing that no friendly aircraft were airborne except the BARCAP to the south, Lieutenant Muse immediately passed the word over the 1MC general announcing system to "Clear the fo'c'sle," then gave the order to fire a salvo of two missiles at the lead MiG. Two birds were on their way within seconds. Gunner noted that the "remaining BARCAP reported a downrange explosion which turned out to be a confirmed kill on one of the MiGs." Then, Gunner announced General Quarters while Lieutenant Muse belatedly made the request for permission to fire at the incoming MiGs from 7th Fleet at Yankee Station.

Gunner O'Neal remembered that "while everyone was getting to their stations Ralph ordered to fire the two missiles that had been loaded. The Captain and all of the regular GQ folks showed up to take charge. I firmly believe that the first two missiles were fired at Ralph's order and everything else was at Captain Carter's direction. I will say that Ralph and I were very busy, he was watching what I was doing and talking to the folks in "spookland" and trying to get the

Captain and the OP's boss briefed on what had transpired and was going on. I was assigning Systems and talking on both radio and sound power phones to the rest of our condition III watch team. I feel the team did a great job, more than I had expected, and in fact saved the ship in those first minutes of confusion when the ship was going to GQ."

CWO Van Cleave noted "about fifteen minutes (give or take a few) after being relieved, I heard two Terriers leave the rail and the GQ klaxon sound almost simultaneously. I had just arrived outside my stateroom. Since we were operating under a GQ watch bill, (personnel currently on station, remained on station) I hustled up to, and ducked into Supplemental Radio (SUPRAD). Other CIC personnel were supposed to go to their standby stations."

Gunner remembers "the ship went to general quarters in their usual slow manner since GQ was a common occurrence. When the missiles were launched the crew really came together. The old timers were helping the new comers and the repair parties were in battle dress, ready to do their jobs. Everything seemed to go like clockwork. After the two missiles were fired there was a brief lull. The captain released our shotgun and told them to stay out of our way and defend themselves. The USS *Gray* did so. During this time I was using Seesaw nearly every sweep of the radar trying to find the other MIGs, Ralph had told me there were five of them."

According to Lieutenant Muse, "The launcher was loaded with two more Terrier missiles within 30 seconds and ready to fire. Both missiles were quickly dispatched toward the second MiG. The first MiG had disappeared from the radar screen when the fire control radar range rate went to zero, indicating destruction of the first MiG. Topside personnel verified an explosion on the horizon, and crewmen aboard *Biddle's* shotgun, the USS *Gray*, also confirmed the kill. The second MiG, apparently after observing the destruction of his wingman and knowing that he had been locked on by *Biddle's* fire control radar, turned toward home and managed to evade the missile salvo heading directly at him."

CWO Van Cleave confirmed Muse's account, "Just as I was hustling up the starboard ladder to SUPRAD I heard the second set of Terriers leave the rail. If my memory serves, that was about a minute (maybe less) after the first two. A few minutes after (or during) the second terrier firing the OOD (Jim Mleziva) executed a hard starboard turn and increased to flank speed. I assumed that Jim was initiating a high-speed zigzag.

OS1 Kronvall, contrary to Muse's and Gunner's accounts, recalled a different sequence of events after the hostile targets were detected: "Captain Carter ordered the missile personnel to engage the MiGs. Two SM2's departed the ship when the MiGs were about five to six miles from us. The ship's warning alarms were located in CIC as well as the bridge, and the Quarterdeck. Captain Carter then pushed the button for the general quarters alarm. The alarm sounded about three times and another two missiles left the rail."

While Lieutenant Muse was still trying to get "birds free" from 7th Fleet and talking with the "spooks" in the radio room, Captain Carter arrived in CIC, where, according to Lieutenant Muse, "the next thing I felt was Captain Carter's hand on my back and 'What the hell have you done!' in my ear."

The spooks verified that the second MiG had returned to base. Lieutenant Muse remembers "After what seemed like eternity, the duty officer at 7th Fleet, a Commander I knew personally, laughed and gave us permission to fire—which we had done at least five minutes earlier."

A short time after MiG #2 went feet dry (approximately 15 minutes according to Muse) the second phase of the attack began when *Biddle's surface* search radar detected MiGs at 500 knots on the deck at seven miles range. Seconds later, both air search radars picked up the targets but the fire control radar was unable to lock on and hold the targets. *Biddle's* remaining defense was her port and starboard 3-inch guns and her 5-inch gun. Unfortunately, the 5-inch gun's fire control system was down with an inoperative amplidyne motor, which meant the gun could be trained in Manual mode only. Also, the 3-inch guns were optical (no radar guidance) and intended for daylight only.

Jerry Kronvall's recollection was that

> Shortly after that our guns opened up and I believe that two more missiles left the ship when the guns were firing. No one came on the 1MC to say "General quarters, general quarters, man your battle stations." Usually it took the crew about seven to nine minutes to man GQ stations—that night it took less than five minutes.
>
> The captain directed me to find some fighter aircraft as we gave control of the aircraft to another ship well before the attack. Captain Carter turned his attention back to the MiGs.
>
> I was watching the scope as the MiGs overflew the ship. *[Author's note: All other accounts mention a single MiG passing over the ship.]* I was feeling there was no place to run, no place to hide and here I'm sitting in front of a console that has high voltage and if the scope blew out, I would be history. Not a good feeling.
>
> There was a report from the bridge that two explosion had occurred in the air. I though that a missile got one MIG on their first run at us. The guns got the second MIG on the second run at us. Before the second missiles left the ship I went on the air control circuit and found two fighter aircraft being refueled in the air. I took control of both aircraft and had them call out their fuel

state, one fighter was just coming off the bag and the other fighter had to be refueled. I directed the one fighter aircraft to us and the second fighter to refuel. The first fighter saw and reported explosions near the *Biddle*. Chief Bump took control of the second AIC console and I briefed him to what was going on. He was manning the console as the guns started to fire.

The ship's missile fire control finally locked on sufficiently to fire a salvo of two more missiles. According to Lieutenant Muse, the range rate again went to zero indicating a direct hit and the spooks heard the third MiG report the hit. Meanwhile, the port side 3-inch gun had opened fire using influence fuzes and the 5-inch gun, after manually training to port, had opened fire as well. Lieutenant Muse remembered that "By this time, the last plane was inside the minimum range of the missile system. The spooks were telling me that the pilot had us in his sight and was going to kill us. Captain Carter was giving the bridge orders for evasive maneuvering. The last plane went dead center over the ship. I was waiting for the explosion. It never came. What happened? Why were we not hit? We may never know."

CWO Van Cleave recollects…

> While we were in our first turn, the 5-inch 54 on the stern started firing. We were accustomed to having daily gunnery drills but were never able to get ten rounds out of a barrel without some sort of delay. I'm told that during the engagement of 19 July we fired 54 rounds of 5-inch 54 ordinance—I didn't count them. And, I never heard a pause from the first round to the last. I'm not a weapons type, but I could guess that ye old 5-inch 54 barrel was a wee bit hot. One of the results of the gun crew's performance was that we never held another gunnery drill from that day until the day we departed the Gulf. As for the old 3-inch 50 guns (port and starboard amidships) they started a few seconds behind the 5-inch 54 and just kept rattling. I have no idea how many rounds of 3-inch 50 ammunition we expended. I do know that is was a significant amount.

DS1 Johnstone, now at his battle station one level below CIC, remembers

> We had fired guns and missiles only on the ranges in the Caribbean. I do not remember that I had ever experienced two guns firing while missiles were being launched. We experienced it in those next few minutes. With the 3-inch gun and 5-inch gun firing the ship was bouncing around like a cork on the ocean. Two more missiles flew as we continued to fire the guns.
> Conversation on the battle phone confirmed that we were probably being attacked by five MiGs out of Hanoi. We were told that Hanoi tower was

being monitored and that there was knowledge that the aircraft were launching and that they were coming out to "get us". There was a report that one of the signal men had seen one of the air planes pass very low between the macks and disappear.

That quickly it was over. The shooting stopped and I think "Charge" was played top side. Captain Carter came on the 1MC and told us that we had saved the ship. He told us that we were the first U.S. naval vessel since World War II to use barrage fire as a defense. He said that our "shot gun" reported that we looked like "the Fourth of July" at the height of the battle, with all of the shells exploding and the missiles leaving the rails.

Lieutenant Muse recalls, "I never again had to ask twice for CAP support from 7th Fleet Command. In a day or two, we went south to a safer position and replaced the missiles we fired, and we hosted a small group of Defense Intelligence Agency, National Security Agency, and Navy Department civilian "experts" who could not understand how the North Vietnamese could come that close to sinking one of our ships. The "experts" insisted that the North Vietnamese would never attack at night, and that it would be a high altitude attack. Another interesting thing about this attack was that it did not make the news; no one knew what we had done. We were never officially there—but we were just glad to get back home in one piece."

As the attack unfolded 7th Fleet began to respond to a threat that, if left unchecked, would threaten not only *Biddle*, but elements at Yankee Station as well. OS1 Kronvall recalled that

> In the Gulf of Tonkin that night were three carriers. One was in standdown; two were available to launch aircraft. It seems that the carriers picked up my voice radio transmissions to the fighter aircraft that we were under attack by MiGs.
>
> After the second fighter departed refueling, which took about 10 to 15 minutes; he was directed to his playmate. Chief Bump and I heard that more fighters were up in the air from two carriers. The third carrier (I believe) came out of the 24 hour standdown and had launched their fighters. By this time the attack was over and the remaining MiGs had returned to their home plates. I used the first fighter to try to cut the MiGs off but they [the MiGs] were moving too fast for an intercept so I joined up the two fighters as soon as I could.
>
> As for the carriers that launched their aircraft, we had about 40 to 60 fighters from the carriers. Da Nang Marines launched their fighters and I believe there were about 10 to 12 sections of two fighters per section. Plus we had about 75 tankers to refuel everybody. It was quite busy.

In summary, the North Vietnam planners did some planning. We had no aircraft under our control; their planes were under our radar until they flew into our radar signals. They did not take into account that the *Biddle* crew would be that good. The crew was outstanding.

With the attack over, Gunner recalled "As usually happens in a period of great stress a few 'funny' things happen. As I went to get into battle dress I found that I didn't have a life jacket. One of the other SWC's had taken it. Also while Captain Carter was talking to Alpha Whiskey (AW) on secure voice making arrangements for the rearming, AW asked if there was anything else that we needed. Captain Carter told him to send about 500 pucker strings as ours were pretty well stretched."

While not particularly funny, CWO Van Cleaves remembered that "The launch of the first two terriers caught the bridge crew unaware. I might say that the Gulf of Tonkin can get very hot in July. So the bridge crew had all of the bridge windows open to catch whatever cool breezes possible. When the first two missiles left the rail all of the smoke and other launch debris engulfed the bridge (inside as well as outside). The bridge personnel couldn't get the bridge windows closed fast enough."

Lieutenant Muse's performance during the attack was a classic example of a young, well-trained naval officer "betting his bars" that he made the correct decision when all of the outcomes had serious, if not catastrophic, consequences. If he had decided to launch a missile and the target was friendly, then he would have to explain his decision at his probable court martial. If he followed established procedure, then it likely would have been too late and the MiGs would have been too close. (In an interview, Lieutenant Muse explained that the procedure was "…to call the Captain, ask 7th Fleet for birds free on the track number of the MIG, then wait until both the Captain and 7th Fleet gave permission to fire.") If he stood around idle and made no decision, then he could have been court-martialed for dereliction of duty…assuming he survived the attack.

Topside Action

Hard Charger! would be incomplete without the accounts of the young men who manned *Biddle's* guns that night; for the outcome of the brief battle hinged on the performance of these teenage men as much as on the officers and men in CIC, the bridge, and the missile rooms. On a ship bristling with high tech computers, radars, and missiles, *Biddle* may have survived the attack intact because the performance level of the men operating a pair of WWII style 3-inch guns and a broken 5-inch gun system far exceeded anything achieved in practice.

"This is no shit. We were supposed to make a Med cruise but went to Vietnam instead. We shot down a couple of MiGs." That is how a *Biddle* gunners mate might start a sea story describing the events of July 19. Jokingly, all sea stories begin that way, but the truth may follow; the reader should pay attention.

FTG2 Jim Parks, as Mount 32 Director, had a unique vantage point from which he could observe the action. The mount director's position is one level above, and behind the gun, closer to amidships. Jim described the director as "a large telescope mounted on a pivot, with handlebars for steering. In theory, I was to follow the target with the gun director, and a gyroscope mechanism inside would generate a lead angle for the gun. I received orders from the Weapons Officer over my sound powered telephone (a headset device), and passed the orders to the 3-inch gun mount under my direction. There was a firing key on the gun director that allowed me to shoot the 3-inch gun when it was under my control."

If you have wondered, as I have, what it's like to be topside when missiles are fired at real MiGs, and the ship is lobbing 3-inch and 5-inch projectiles at an approaching enemy, then wonder no more. Jim Parks describes the action from the Mount 32 Director:

> The night of 19 July 1972 had been no different from any other night up until bedtime. We had been in Vietnam almost two months, and the days had become a dull, boring routine. I don't remember exactly, but either I watched the movie on the mess deck, or played spades, or both that night, as was my usual habit. I do remember that I went to bed promptly at 10 PM.
>
> It was about 15 minutes later when the general quarters alarm sounded. Not being quite asleep yet, I jumped up, jammed my legs into my pants, and rushed to my battle station at the Port Gun Director. While I was running through the ship, I heard the first round of missiles being fired topside. I was the first one at the AA station, with Mount 31 Gun Director FTGSN John Potratz, right behind me. We donned our flak jackets, helmets, and sound powered telephones. Suddenly, the forecastle lit up with an explosion of flame and sounds. For a few seconds, I was afraid that we had been hit! Once I saw our Terrier missile streaking away from the ship, I knew that we were under attack because a second round of missiles meant serious business. Watching a missile launch at night is quite spectacular; the smoke and flames from the exhaust temporarily produced an eerie glow around the forecastle.
>
> I switched my sound powered telephone to the proper circuit, so that I could hear orders from the weapons officer in Combat Information Center. The Anti-Aircraft (AA) officers were just arriving at the AA station when I

heard the weapons officer over my headset shouting "Mount 32, commence fire!" I realized instantly that the enemy must be close if they were ordering us to shoot. I switched my phone to the gun circuit, and passed the "commence fire" order to GMG3 Ron Straight, the Mount 32 Gun Captain. The AA officers were getting outfitted with flak jackets, helmets, and phones when I shouted to them that we had been given the "commence fire" order, turned my director, and began shooting portside.

The Vietnamese picked a great night for an attack; it was a moonless night, with a high overcast, absolutely no light whatsoever. I had no idea what I was shooting at, but I shot at the dark as ordered. After firing 20 or so rounds, one of the AA officers gave me the order to "cease fire." I released my firing key, and passed the cease-fire order to Mount 32. For the next few minutes all was calm.

This quietness only gave me time to worry—our MK68 gun director, which had broken down only a few days before, normally controlled our main 5-inch gun. The amplidyne that supplied electrical current to the motor that turned the director had failed, and it would be another week or two before the new amplidyne being shipped from the states could be installed.

CIC and the bridge must have been a busy place that night. *Biddle* began turning sharply, causing me to hold tightly to a rail to keep my balance. Captain Carter had ordered *Biddle* to turn her portside toward the enemy. Over my sound powered telephone, I heard the weapons officer tell the 5-inch gun crew that there were enemy gun boats approaching the ship, and to swing the gun in that general direction. Although the MK68 gun director was broken and could not turn automatically, FTG2 Jim Wilson was underneath turning a small hand crank, causing the MK68 to turn toward the targets in an attempt to get a radar lock. The 5-inch gun had switched to local control, so that it didn't have to depend on the MK68 gun director.

Suddenly, the 5-inch gun erupted into rapid fire. I turned around, expecting to receive instructions from our AA officers, but the officers were gone! I looked at Mount 31 director John Potratz, and he was pointing down to the deck—both AA officers were face down with their hands over their heads! They were terrified! [*The explanation for this scene is explained fully in the next chapter. Apparently, the two officers were actually helicopter pilots who were caught topside during the heavy action and were seeking shelter.*]

After a brief moment of astonishment, I regained my composure, and then switched my sound powered telephone to the weapons circuit. I heard the order "Mount 32, commence fire portside" being shouted, as though they had been trying to get the message to us. I then relayed the commence fire order to the gun captain, and we began shooting. Once again, a pair of Terrier missiles lit up the front end of the ship, and zoomed off toward their target.

Half blinded by the Terrier missile launch, I was quite surprised that I could see through my director sights that the proximity shells that we were firing were exploding—they must have hit a target! I saw four or five puffs of light and smoke as the shells exploded. It didn't dawn on me at the time how close a target must have been to the *Biddle* for a 3" shell to hit. Gun Captain Ron Straight later confirmed the exploding shells that I saw. I was temporarily deafened by the gunfire, but several others that were topside told me that they heard the MiG fly over us. A few crewmembers claimed that they saw the jet exhaust from the MiG as it flew overhead.

With the Terrier missiles forward, the 5-inch gun aft, and our 3-inch gun amidships, all firing at the same time, it was said that the USS *Biddle* was the first ship since WWII to put up a barrage of fire against an enemy.

I later learned that the gunboats approaching the *Biddle* turned and sped away as soon as the 5-inch gun began shooting at them. I also learned that the first round of Terrier missiles downed one MiG, and the second round of Terrier's probably downed a second MiG. It was never confirmed, but the proximity shells that the 3-inch was shooting likely damaged a 3rd MiG. I would like to think that although the 3rd MiG may have been close enough to us to open fire, it was too busy dodging our gunfire to act. The remaining MiGs then tucked tail and flew back to shore. We stayed at general quarters for at least another half-hour and maybe longer.

After we secured from our battle stations, I went below to the mess deck, and poured myself a large glass of chocolate milk. A large number of the crew congregated on the mess deck, unable to go back to sleep; many of us were half expecting another attack and wanted to be ready. After an hour or so, I had calmed down enough that I could go down to my compartment, and sleep peacefully the rest of the night.

In the following weeks, I began to realize the significance of that event. Due to our constant training and drills, the *Biddle* crew had performed flawlessly. The officers and crew in CIC had picked out the threat immediately and reacted swiftly. Captain Carter chose to position our portside toward the enemy to bring maximum firepower to bear against all threats. The engineering department brought the ship from dead slow to maximum speed in record time. The missile gang and the gunners met the oncoming attack with confidence in their skills and equipment. If any single department had failed its job that night, I'm sure the outcome would have been much different. In my opinion, the USS *Biddle* was the finest ship to ever sail, and I owe my life to everyone on board her that night.

Mount 32 Gun Captain Ron Straight substantiates Jim Park's recollection:

The memory that I have is a little rusty from the years passing. Here is a brief synopsis: General Quarters was called around midnight. Ron Tanner and I were the gunners mates in charge of Mount 32. The gun radar that controlled the guns was not working. All hands that were assigned to Mount 32 were present and waiting with anxiety shortly after GQ sounded.

Approximately the time all hands arrived on location, another missile was launched. A short period of time passed, then suddenly, the ship made an abrupt starboard turn. When the ship straightened out, Ron and I were told to commence fire, peppering the sky at a ninety-degree angle. When the cease-fire order was given, Mount 32 had fired approximately 35 rounds without the gun jamming, which was a first. While everyone was still on edge, there were supposedly small boats spotted on the horizon. The story that I received later was that the boats were US Navy PT boats looking for anything that had been shot down.

Ron Straight does not remember the gun jamming but GMG2 Ron "Mad Dog" Tanner clearly remembers a hang fire on the last shell. "Mad Dog" explains:

> We did get off about 28 rounds that night. The gun was designed for 60 rounds per minute but was manually loaded and never came close to that. The previous best before that night was 15-20 rounds to the best of my recollection. The last shell was a "hang-fire," and after attempting everything else we could think of, we elevated the gun straight up, and Buck took the shell and threw it over the side. It was to say the least a pretty tense moment.
>
> I can't really remember if Mount 31, the starboard mount, got off any rounds or not. Most of the action was on the port side and Mount 32 put up the barrage fire. I believe a total of four terrier missiles were fired. After we started firing, I could hear the 5-inch 54 caliber commence firing a few minutes later, and it was a welcome sound. Everyone worked great together that night, and I have always been proud to serve with the crew of DLG-34.

Other Accounts and Conclusions

At *Biddle's* decommissioning on 30 November 1993, *Biddle's* commanding officer during the attack, Rear Admiral Ed Carter U.S. Navy (Retired), described the events:

> On the memorable night of 19 July 1972, *Biddle* went through two air attacks against herself. First, a raid of three [MiGs], which launched from Hanoi Julong (sic) airfield. *Biddle* launched a two-missile salvo and destroyed the lead MiG at a range of seventeen miles, and the other two turned back home to think about it.
>
> Fifteen minutes later, a second raid of two airplanes at very low altitude closed *Biddle* from the west. How low were they? Well, the first radar to pick them up was the surface search radar. Range was inside seven miles when they were picked up. Reconstruction of NTDS indicated their speed was slightly over 500 knots. That doesn't give you much time, and that doesn't give you a whole lot of chance when their altitude was so low that missile radars could not lock on and we could not engage with missiles.

The 5-inch gun fire control radar was CASREP, and the 3-inch guns were optical control systems only. So *Biddle* resorted to an old World War II tactic used against Japanese torpedo planes—we went into barrage fire, zero degrees elevation, influence fuses, so that every round that fired would at least trigger on the water.

And in the midst of this maelstrom, one airplane disappeared. The other one passed overhead of this girl with their (sic) engines screaming followed by a deadly silence that lasted forever while we waited for what we thought would be the bomb that got us, to fall on us, but it did not.

I had the opportunity, and took the opportunity to walk around the ship after we finally secured from general quarters. I found the post attack unity that existed on this ship far exceeded anything that we had previously experienced in a ship where the attitude was already, "One for all and all for one."

The crew in that night engagement had given their best. And I suppose that at least two or three of them thought that they might be called upon to give their all. There was no boasting and no bragging, just a sense of silent pride in having been tested and found not wanting.

Biddle's battle with five hostile MiGs raises a question—why did the MiG that flew directly over *Biddle* not drop a bomb? A mechanical malfunction or battle damage could be the reason, but I wonder if the pilot screwed up. The pilot probably knew that *Biddle* had just blown one, possibly two, of his comrades out of the sky. His MiG is on the deck going like a rat shot in the nuts, and it's as dark as a whore's heart. The only source of light is the flash from *Biddle's* guns and missiles. He had one hand on the stick and the other hand on the ejection seat release. If he had a third hand, it would be scratching his head while wondering how he's going to get out of *this* mess. Fortunately for *Biddle*, the nervous MiG pilot had misjudged the closure rate while dodging exploding 3-inch and 5-inch projectiles. *Biddle's* darkened outline suddenly appeared directly in front of the startled pilot. His fire control was locked on, but as his shaking hand found the lever that would pickle a bomb, *Biddle's* form passed underneath him, his opportunity forever lost.

Biddle narrowly avoided disaster. The Navy's most sophisticated radars and computers and a ferocious barrage of missile salvos and gunfire allowed one MiG to penetrate *Biddle's* defenses to do whatever damage it could. The low altitude, high speed night attack would probably have been an even bigger surprise had it not been for the recently installed Shortstop system. Lieutenant Muse believes that Shortstop allowed *Biddle* an extra two minutes to prepare a defense—two minutes that may have saved the ship.

DSC Rodney Merrill recalls one aspect of the attack that could have been a big problem: "What follows is what I remember that one of the EW's (electronic warfare technician) told me. How true it is I do not know. During the engagement, *Biddle* had the destroyer USS *Gray* (DE-1054) assigned as a shotgun for protection. As soon as the *Biddle* started shooting they (the *Gray*) lit off all their fire control radars trying to find whatever it was we were shooting at. With the *Biddle* being the biggest target out there, they kept locking on to us. One of the *Biddle's* EW's put the Shortstop system in full automatic mode, so that every time the *Gray* locked on to us, the system would go active and break the lock. How true, I do not know."

What happened aboard *Biddle's* shotgun, the USS *Gray*, when *Biddle* started throwing missiles, 3-inch, and 5-inch projectiles all over the sky? *Gray* crewmember ETR2 Tom Bunce was there and recalls what happened:

> Early on the night of the attack, the ET shop requested to take the SPS-40 long range air search radar down for maintenance. We had one of the best SPS-40 techs in the Western Pacific and because of his skills, we had almost non-stop Air Guard responsibilities. The 40 was in need of work if we were to continue the level of Air Guard that had been expected. The Captain requested that *Biddle* pick up the Air Guard and a few other duties while we went into a quick maintenance period, which included the ECM tuners in the room just below the stack.
>
> I was on the phones just as the EW tech and I finished the SPS-40 maintenance. I heard that the *Biddle* had launched two missiles and both ships where to go to General Quarters. The Ops boss told us to stay put—it did not matter much for me since my GQ station was South ASW plot. The ET shop passed the word that the 40 was coming up, but it would be ten minutes before it was ready to transmit.
>
> Two minutes later, the *Gray* leaned heavy to starboard in what was probably ten degrees of turn. CIC passed the word that *Biddle* decided we could not run, since the *Gray* had no aft defenses at all. I was told both ships were going to charge the oncoming MiGs, and we had a lock. The ship then heaved to the port in a ten-degree turn, and I was told that the *Biddle* felt the lock was possibly on them but could not confirm it, so we needed to break the lock. A lot of bad words then came across the phones saying the mount and director were not even pointed toward the *Biddle*. Lock was broken anyway, and the target never reacquired. The word was then passed that the *Biddle* had opened fire with her guns. Within five minutes, the action was over.
>
> I went to CIC and learned that the carrier delay was due to a stand down order, and the carrier had done just that! No BARCAP and no ready deck is what caused a 20 minute delay in getting air support to the PIRAZ position.

Other Accounts

Research found several other accounts of *Biddle's* battle and there are discrepancies between them and those presented here. It is interesting and educational to study a few tense moments from several viewpoints.

Surface Warfare Interview

In an interview on 12 June 1978, Scot MacDonald, *Surface Warfare* magazine editor, talked with Rear Admiral Edward W Carter, *Biddle's* commanding officer during the MiG attack. The interview, which was found in the archives of the Naval Historical Foundation at the Washington Navy Yard, was published in the January 1979 issue of *Surface Warfare*. In the interview Captain Carter stated: "We knew for some time prior to the night of the attack that the North Vietnamese were planning another attack against the fleet. They had bombed USS *Higbee* back in April, at the time of USS *Sterett's* engagement with the MiGs. All of the various sources we had available to us—they were quite good, including our own observations of the North Vietnamese tactical exercises—certainly made it clear to us that they were preparing for another attack on the fleet. Of course, being on the PIRAZ station, we were the closest to the North Vietnamese mainland. We felt kind of vulnerable, so I had taken a number of measures to improve the readiness of the ship."

Captain Carter stated in the interview that he believed "that whenever the attack came, it would come as a result of a decreased readiness in the Combat Air Patrol. And it happened that way." Just before the attack, BARCAP readiness was diminished when one of the two BARCAPs on station in the northern Tonkin Gulf escorted a damaged A-6 Intruder back to Yankee Station, leaving a single BARCAP south of PIRAZ. This, it appears, is what the North Vietnamese were waiting for.

A solo A-6 Intruder on a night bombing mission over North Vietnam during bad weather sounds doubtful to me. Perhaps it was a very important, but easy target, and the Navy was confident that a single A-6 could do the job. Also, it is difficult to believe that on a night preceded the day before with 50 or more MiG flights over North Vietnam, that the Navy left a single, now vulnerable BARCAP, to protect the fleet. The fact that Lieutenant Muse knew that there were absolutely no friendly planes over North Vietnam and that a BARCAP had returned to Yankee Station was what allowed him (Muse) to launch two birds with complete confidence that the approaching targets were hostile MiGs.

Later in the interview, Captain Carter related a story about two "Big Mother" helicopter pilots from a Yankee Station carrier who, immediately after the first missile was fired, checked on their helo that was lashed to *Biddle's* helo deck, located on the aft end of the ship just forward of the 5-inch gun. At this time, *Biddle* was making 27 knots on a heading that took her away from shore. After the two carrier pilots had completed their inspection and were walking forward on the port side near Mount 32, the second attack occurred. The 3-inch gun started firing, which drove the two pilots back toward the 5-inch gun, which started firing too. With nowhere to go, the pilots "spent the next few minutes under the port boat davits, trying to dig a hole into a steel deck. They were absolutely terrified." Carter then described how the next morning the two pilots (now combat veterans if they weren't before) rescued a downed airman in Haiphong harbor.

During the interview, Carter mentioned that four Terrier missiles were fired—two during the first attack, and two more missiles in the second attack. On the other hand, Lieutenant Muse remembers that six missiles were fired—two each at the first two targets in the first attack and two more on the second attack.

Carter also mentioned that the Navy knew, and it was clear to him from his personal observations as well, that the North Vietnamese were preparing an attack against the fleet. Lieutenant Muse does not remember that kind of information was made available to him as CIC/NTDS Officer, and there was not a general feeling that the North Vietnamese were about to attack the fleet.

Scot MacDonald also interviewed Commander Eugene Heckathorn, *Biddle's* executive officer during the attack. One humorous incident on the bridge that Heckathorn recalled was, "I turned around and looked at the helmsman. He was standing there in his skivvies, with his helmet on...." The commander went on to say that the helmsman did not have a chance to put his trousers on until "after the action was over." Also, Heckathorn recalled that right in the middle of all the action, *Biddle's* sonarmen picked up a sonar contact. The contact turned out to be false, and Heckathorn believed the sonar anomaly was caused by a "hard knuckle"—the rudder making hard, rapid movements during maneuvers.

Biddle's 1972 Command History

A now declassified document, USS *Biddle* Confidential Message, Subject: Command History—Summary of Operations, states "*Biddle* was attacked on the night of 19 July by five MiG aircraft in two raids. *Biddle* destroyed one MiG from the first raid with Terrier missiles and possibly one from the second raid with five-inch and three-inch gunfire. The other MiGs were driven off, and *Biddle* received no damage." There was no mention of North Vietnamese torpedo boats participating in the attack.

In addition to the MiG kill on 19 July, the message lists thirteen MiG kills attributed to *Biddle's* intercept controllers during the period 12 April to 26 October. They are as follows: OS1 Kronvall—4 MiG 19s; OSC Bump—2 MiG 17s, 1 MiG 21; OS1 Nastasi—4 MiG 21s; OS1 Anderson—1 MiG 21, and OS2 Stump—1 MiG 21. Furthermore, the message lists the following ammunition expended in combat during 1972: Missiles—4 Standards (confirming Captain Carter's account); ASROC—one; CHAFFROC—none; 3" projectiles—28 rounds; 5" projectiles—30 rounds.

MiG Attack Tonkin Gulf

MiG Attack Tonkin Gulf—July 19, 1972, by JO3 Tom Kelley, is a press account that was also found in the archives of the Naval Historical Foundation at the Washington Navy Yard. The USS *Biddle* website at http://ussbiddle.org/ reprinted Kelley's account. JO3 Kelley is not listed in *Biddle's* 1972 cruise book as a crewmember. The article repeats several of the discrepancies regarding the solitary A-6 over North Vietnam and the lonely BARCAP left to defend the fleet.

In his article, Kelly states that when the first group of MiGs was detected "feet dry" over North Vietnam, "the captain was summoned to CIC, and their presence was neither unusual or cause for exceptional alarm." Later, when the MiGs went "feet wet" the captain "hustled to CIC", determined that the MiGs were a threat, and ordered General Quarters sounded. The events as they unfolded according to Lieutenant Muse, were as follows: 1.) MiGs detected "feet wet" at low altitude and high speed, 2.) The threat was immediately evaluated by crew in CIC and the captain was summoned; 3.) "Clear the fo'c'sle" was passed on 1MC; 4.) Missiles fired; 5.) General Quarters announced; 6.) Captain Carter arrives CIC.

Holding the Line In The Tonkin Gulf

In the August 2000 *Vietnam* magazine article "Holding the Line In the Tonkin Gulf," Don L. Hart, a young signalman aboard *Biddle*, recalled that after hearing general quarters:

> I climbed out of my rack and pulled on some dungarees that I always kept under my mattress for such emergencies. Then I methodically began making my way up to the bridge. When I reached the mess decks, however, I broke

into a run as did other crewmen headed for GQ stations. Over the ships intercom came a warning to stay clear of our Terrier launcher. We all knew what that meant: Missiles were about to be fired against the enemy.

I reached the bridge just in time to see a pair of Terrier missiles roar from our double launcher. As I ran back to the signal bridge on the outside of the ship, I saw a fireball form in the night sky, split in two and crash toward the dark ocean below. One of our missiles had hit a MiG.

Before the night was over, a total of five enemy aircraft in two separate waves attacked *Biddle*. The ship's crew generally believed, although it was never officially confirmed, that we shot down one additional MiG that night either by missiles or by gunfire, which we used when we had trouble locking on to the enemy aircraft with our air search radar. *[Authors note: I believe he meant to say "fire control radar" instead of "air search radar."]* The other MiGs broke off their attacks and returned to their bases. One, however, flew directly over *Biddle* before seeking safety.

Conclusions

Over time, memories weaken, stories become embellished, and facts become twisted. There are three undisputed facts—1.) Five MiGs in two raids attacked *Biddle* on 19 July 1972. 2.) A Terrier missile in the first salvo destroyed a MiG in the first attack. 3.) One MiG pilot bravely flew directly over *Biddle* and either forgot to drop a bomb or could not.

There are numerous parts of the attack that are not resolved and probably never will be. Among them are the composition of the two raids, the exact sequence of events, the number of missiles fired, and possible damage to a second or third MiG, US activity in the air over North Vietnam at the time of the attack, and North Vietnamese gunboat activity.

Some *Biddle* crewmembers recall that North Vietnamese gunboats joined the attack, but were driven back after a pounding from *Biddle's* 5-inch gun. Others heard that the surface targets were actually U.S. Navy torpedo boats looking for a piece of the action. Lieutenant Muse does not recall friendly PT boats in the area, any gunfire directed toward North Vietnamese MTBs, or any conversations in CIC related to gunboats. On *Biddle's* first deployment to the Gulf, Captain Scott remembers that the coast of North Vietnam produced radar ghosts that resembled real targets. These false returns occurred near the area where in 1999 the destroyers *Turner Joy* and *Maddox* fired on phantom targets. It is unlikely that North Vietnamese gunboats attacked *Biddle*.

Lieutenant Muse, who was present in CIC during the entire attack, had a unique perspective of the events as they unfolded. Also, he was the officer selected to debrief investigators immediately after the attack. Accounts from other sailors in CIC and topside, with few exceptions, corroborate Lieutenant Muse's account. Muse is certain that six missiles were fired in three salvos, which OS1 Kronvall's account seems to support, while other crewmembers remember only four Terriers in two salvos. Lieutenant Muse's account elevates the events from a mere "Sea Story" to an account that represents the most accurate description of the events that you will be able to find.

To be fair, I wrote the Vietnam ambassador to the United States asking for contacts at military agencies in Vietnam that could provide information about the attack. The letter was never answered. A thorough search of the Internet was fruitless as well.

The *Biddle* Deck Log

Information regarding "The Attack at PIRAZ" was requested from several government agencies using the Freedom of Information Act (FOIA). First, *Biddle's* deck log for 19 July 1972 was requested from the National Archives and Records Administration (NARA). The agency reported that they "examined the deck logs for USS *Biddle* and found that the logs for July 1972 were missing from the file. It is unclear whether those logs were ever received from the Navy when they transferred them to the National Archives. We have searched for these logs here, but have found nothing." *Biddle* deck logs for June 1972 were found, however. A second FOIA request was made to the NARA for USS *Sterett* deck logs for 19 April 1972, the date of the "Battle Off Dong Hoi." Those deck logs were found. Why would *Sterett's* logs be preserved and *Biddle's* not?

Another FOIA request was sent to the National Security Agency (NSA), which always had a security detachment aboard *Biddle* in the Gulf of Tonkin. The NSA reported "A thorough search of our files was conducted, but no records responsive to your request were located. An appeal was filed which produced identical results.

It is difficult for me to believe that a U.S. Navy combatant did not record in her logs the fact that five North Vietnamese MiGs attacked her, that she went to general quarters to defend herself and the fleet, and that she responded to the attack by firing four missiles and launching a barrage of gunfire. In an e-mail referencing the missing deck log entries, Lieutenant Muse reminded me, "Keep in mind that the 'folks from Washington' who visited us after the attack told us the 'incident' was to be kept secret and should not be discussed or written about. The first public disclosure was made when the ship returned to Norfolk. Would they have changed the deck log?"

Would they? And why? Lieutenant Muse remembers that there was a detachment of NSA "spooks" aboard during the attack and that the NSA debriefed him soon after the attack, even though the different agencies did not always identify themselves. We can assume with some certainty that deck log entries were made during the attack as a matter of procedure, yet the pages related to the attack later mysteriously disappeared. Did they disappear at the request of a government agency, from further up the military chain of command, or from within *Biddle*?

Biddle—A Young Warrior

James Treadway

Soon after the Battle at PIRAZ *Biddle* assumed additional duties as SAR Coordinator for all forces in the Tonkin Gulf. One month later, on 29 August, *Long Beach* relieved *Biddle* at PIRAZ, at which time *Biddle* left for three days liberty in Hong Kong and two days in Subic Bay. With the MiG attack still fresh in their minds, it is possible that there may have been a little extra partying during those days.

Biddle returned to the Gulf to relieve USS *England* at NSAR on 22 August, *Truxtun* relieved *Biddle* at NSAR on 27 August, and *Biddle* relieved *Long Beach* on 29 August at PIRAZ. Typhoon Elsie unleashed her fury in the Gulf of Tonkin on 1 September, forcing Task Force 77 to evacuate the Gulf until 4 September. *Long Beach* relieved *Biddle* at PIRAZ on 17 September, thus ending *Biddle's* last tour of duty in the Gulf of Tonkin.

Biddle offloaded equipment in Subic Bay from 20 to 24 September then got underway for her return voyage to the United States without Captain Carter, who was in Pearl Harbor to brief CINCPAC, CINCPACFLT, and CINCPACAF on Navy and Air Force operation in the Gulf of Tonkin. No doubt, as *Biddle* stood out of Subic Bay with a four week Pacific transit in front of her, most of her crew had time to reflect on recent events. *Biddle's* 1972 Command History summarized the events:

> During its three line periods in the Gulf of Tonkin, totaling 105 days in the combat zone, BIDDLE directed 102 Navy and 56 Air Force strikes over North Vietnam. BIDDLE'S air intercept controllers directed the destruction of 13 enemy MiG's, 7 by U.S. Navy Fighters and 6 by U.S.A.F. fighters. One additional MiG was destroyed by ship's missiles. BIDDLE directed and/or conducted Combat Search and Rescue Operations which were responsible for the rescue of 5 Navy, 8 Air Force and 4 Marine pilots downed on combat missions. The ship's LAMPS Detachment (HSL-30 Det 4 from NAS Lakehurst, N.J.) flew a total of 711.6 flight hours on ESM/ASMD patrols and CSAR missions during the deployment. During these flights the LAMPS helo con-

ducted extensive electronic surveillance of the North Vietnamese coast, and made the first combat SAR rescue by an SH-2 LAMPS helo on the night of September 11.

Biddle departed Pearl Harbor on 6 October with Captain Carter aboard. After a short Shortstop test for the benefit of embarked Rear Admiral J.E. Rice, COMNAVELEX, *Biddle* continued her passage eastward to San Diego, and then transited the Panama Canal, finally arriving in Norfolk on 26 October. The crew and ship enjoyed a three week standdown, which was followed by a successful completion of a Naval Technical Proficiency Inspection in December.

1973

Biddle greeted the New Year in a leave and upkeep status. After successfully completing a Material Readiness Inspection (MRI) in early February, *Biddle* was underway in the Jacksonville Operating Area with the USS *John F. Kennedy* as *Kennedy* prepared for deployment. *Biddle* and aircraft from *Kennedy* collectively dispatched EX DD-602 *Meade* to the deep in a SINKEX firing. Captain Al Olsen explained that "SINKEX is an acronym for 'sinking exercise.' It is an alternative to selling a ship for scrap and usually limited to 12 ships a year. The ship is thoroughly cleaned so that it doesn't present any environmental risk, towed out to sea where the depth of water is several thousand feet, and serves as target for other ships or aircraft. Besides giving the ships and aircraft practice, a SINKEX is a way to test ship and aircraft weapon performance. I think I'd rather have my ship scrapped than sunk."

In late March *Biddle* participated in the joint exercise Exotic Dancer VI (EXDAN VI), a joint U.S. military exercise involving an amphibious landing force and blockade of a foreign coast. In this case, the "foreign coast" was Cape Hatteras. During the exercise, multi-purpose *Biddle* provided AAW protection during the landing, was task group Electronic Welfare Coordinator, and assumed blockade duty. In mid-April *Biddle* completed her annual ORI in the Virginia Capes OPAREA.

Biddle's next assignment was to serve as host ship for a group of four French warships. Following four days of visiting, all ships got underway for the VACAPES OPAREA for four days of joint exercises. After returning to Norfolk, *Biddle's* crew was awarded five Bronze Stars, 14 Navy Commendations, 19 Navy Achievement Medals, and 46 letters of commendation related to her performance in the Gulf of Tonkin. Vice Admiral D.W. Cooper, Commander of Task Force 77 during *Biddle's* 1972 deployment, presented the awards.

Biddle loaded ammunition at Yorktown Naval Weapons Station in early June then loaded missiles in early July for LANTREDEX in the Western Atlantic-Caribbean OPAREA. While serving as task group electronic warfare commander and flagship at LANTREDEX, *Biddle* fired four missiles scoring two direct hits, had one missile failure, and one no-test. *Biddle* also re-qualified in Naval Gunfire Support during the exercise.

Next on *Biddle's* agenda was an INSURV Inspection scheduled from 30 July to 3 August. A Senior Board Member noted in his report of inspection that *Biddle* was exceptionally well prepared for the INSURV Inspection and commended the attitude and cooperation of *Biddle's* crew as "outstanding throughout." The inspection found *Biddle* "fit for further service."

On 15 November, Chief of Naval Operations Admiral Elmo Zumwalt received an original painting depicting the MiG engagement from the previous summer from Captain Carter and five members of the crew. The painting was slated to hang in the Naval Museum at the Washington Navy Yard. Following a combined Canadian and US Naval exercise CANUSEX 1-74 in late November, *Biddle* returned to Norfolk for leave and upkeep for the remainder of the year.

The remaining notable event for the year was an awards presentation during which *Biddle* received the Navy Unit Commendation and the Charleston, South Carolina, Chamber of Commerce Anti-Air Warfare Trophy. Vice Admiral D.C. Plate presented the Navy Unit Commendation "For exceptionally meritorious service from 4 May 1972 while engaged in combat operations against the enemy in North Vietnam." Rear Admiral R.S. Wentworth, COMCRUDESLANT, presented the AAW trophy because "During the fiscal year ending 30 June 1973, USS BIDDLE (DLG-34) was unsurpassed in Anti-Air Warfare Readiness in the Cruiser-Destroyer Force, U.S. Atlantic Fleet." The two awards were a fitting finale for a fantastic year.

1974

Just as she had in January 1973, *Biddle* began the New Year in a leave and upkeep status. From January through May, *Biddle* conducted two FAST cruises, participated in OPERATION SAFE PASSAGE in the Caribbean, conducted type training in the VACAPES OPAREA, and completed NGFS qualifications.

In June *Biddle* joined the U.S. Sixth Fleet in the Mediterranean. She completed turnover procedures with *Conyngham* (DDG-17) in Rota, Spain, and then departed on 26 June to assume duties during ASW operations as screen commander for TG 60.2. Upon conclusion of her ASW assignment, *Biddle* enjoyed five days liberty in Finale Ligure on the Italian Riviera. The Command History reported, "A warm reception was given by the townspeople. BIDDLE was able to anchor 2,000 yards from the beach in deep water and was one of the few U.S. ships to visit that city since World War II." *Biddle* then made a five day working visit in Valencia, Spain, where she debarked midshipmen on their summer cruise. Next, *Biddle* departed for San Remo, where, after anchoring off the beach, *Biddle* again received a warm greeting from the townspeople.

In spite of the great liberty in the sunny Mediterranean, not all *Biddle* sailors exhibited their best behavior. *Biddle* sonarman Bruce Reynolds recalled, "We had a bunch of snipes (engineering department personnel) jump overboard at our first stop in the Med—I think it was in San Remo. The sight was unbelievable. All you saw were plastic bags containing their civies floating off. They got slammed hard—restriction to the ship for the entire cruise."

Following a COMSIXTHFLT directive, *Biddle* got underway on 22 July for waters near Cyprus, which had been recently shocked by a coup. A month later, the U.S. Ambassador to Cyprus was assassinated and *Biddle*, along with Task Group members *Inchon* (LPH-12), *Little Rock* (CLG-4), *Santa Barbara* (AE-218), *Detroit* (AOE-4), *Richard L. Page* (DEG-5), *Blakely* (DE-1072), *Manley* (DD-940), *Wood* (DD-715), and *Barry* (DD-933), proceeded to Cyprus to help evacuate Americans living in Cyprus, if needed. The Task Group dissolved a few days later and *Biddle* proceeded to Naples, Italy, for a well deserved break after having been underway for 39 consecutive days.

On 5 August, while patrolling the waters near Crete, Captain Francis L. Carelli relieved Captain Edward W. Carter as *Biddle's* sixth commanding officer. Captain Carter had commanded *Biddle* for 26 months. A Massachusetts native, Captain Carelli graduated from the College of the Holy Cross in June 1950 and enlisted in the Navy in December 1950 where he served in *Salamonie* (AO-26). Captain Carelli was commissioned in 1953 then served in *Chemung* (AO-30), *Arequipa* (AF-31), *John A. Bole* (DD-755) and *Harry E. Yarnell* (DLG-17). He commanded *Skill* (MSG-471) and *Blakely* (DE-1072).

Biddle had quite a company when she arrived in Naples on 24 August—anchored with her in the outer harbor were *Forrestal* (CVA-59) and *Independence* (CV-62). *Dahlgren* (DLG-12), *Fiske* (DD-842), *Harold J. Ellison* (DD-864), and *William H. Wood* (DD-715) were anchored in the inner harbor. After ten days in a very crowded port, *Biddle* stood out for Gaeta, Italy, where she participated in a Sixth Fleet change of command ceremony on 5 September. Soon after the change of command ceremonies, *Biddle* and USS *Independence* departed for operations in the Eastern Mediterranean.

Occasionally, Navy combatant crews are called upon perform an unusual duty. That was the case on 8 September 1974 when *Biddle* received a report of a jet liner crash. The 1974 Command History explains: "On 8 September BIDDLE received a report of a TWA jetliner Flight No. 841 (Boeing 707) having crashed in the Ionian Sea off Kefallinia, Greece. BIDDLE proceeded to the area at flank speed arriving at approximately 2030 local time and began search and rescue operations for survivors, bodies, and debris. During the night, boat crews, with the aid of helicopters from Independence, recovered 12 bodies from the rough, shark infested waters. The search for survivors continued for two days without success."

Sonarman Bruce Reynolds remembers the event clearly: "I was a sonarman on board from December 1972 through August 1976. I recall the TWA encounter very well. The TWA thing was something else. I was in sonar. They turned that system off so I was rerouted over to help with the recovery. We used our hangar and the torpedo work shack to control the operation. I have some photos, but they don't come close to the horror of shark eaten bodies. Things like Gunners Mate shooting sharks without permission, grappling hooks, body parts all over the hanger, and we had only three body bags on board!"

Biddle departed the search area and headed west on 10 September to prepare for a firepower demonstration for the Secretary of the Navy, J. William Middendorf, on 14 September. The next day *Biddle* entered Augusta Bay, Sicily, for two days then was underway again to the Eastern Med. Chief of Naval Operations Admiral J. L. Holloway visited *Biddle* on 19 September.

Biddle, with *Dahlgren*, *Page*, and *Barry*, conducted torpedo and gunfire exercises on 20 September, with *Biddle* credited with "outstanding shooting" by COMDESRON FOUR. Following two days at training anchorage at Souda Bay, Crete, *Biddle* again joined *Dahlgren* and *Page* for missile exercises. Each ship fired a missile at an airborne target and a surface target. After anchoring at Souda Bay for the night, *Biddle* got underway for Civitavechia, Italy, to claim a boat that had been left behind for repairs. Inclement weather forced a delay, which "forced" the crew to take five days liberty in Rome.

At the conclusion of what must have been tough duty—five days in Rome—*Biddle* left to rendezvous with *Richard E. Kraus* (DD-849) to participate in OPERATION SILVERFOX. *Biddle's* 1974 Command History explains SILVERFOX as

> OPERATION SILVERFOX is the name given to periodic U.S. Naval ship transit into the Black Sea and associated fleet maneuvers. The purpose of the

visit is to exercise our right to operate in International Waters; exercise the provisions of the Montreux Convention, which governs passage through the straits; and to familiarize U.S. Navy crews with Black Sea environment. On 11 October, after five days of steaming in the Black Sea, investigating various contacts and being constantly investigated by Soviet Navy and Air Force units, BIDDLE departed the Black Sea. During the transit southward through the Aegean Sea, the ship received a directive to commence Bystander ops with the Soviet Fleet, south of Crete. Finding the Soviets on 12 October, BIDDLE maneuvered among various units obtaining close looks at the new KARA class cruiser, KASHIN class frigates, KOTLIN class destroyers and MIRKA class destroyer escorts.

OPERATION SILVERFOX, as well as the rest of the cruise, had some lighter moments, at least in some eyes. Sonarman Reynolds recalled "I remember hooking up an 8-track tape player to the Sonar and playing Allman Bros to the entire Black Sea basin underwater at 2000 amps and ¼ Million watts. We knew there were three Russian subs and six surface ships around. We just thought they wanted some entertainment. A very funny story, but I know the Captain hated it, was when we lost our helm. We were scheduled to leave port, the charts were out, the tugs were hooking up, and someone noticed that there was no helm! That's a great story. Did anyone find out who shot that hole in the missile bay ID badge box? Someone shot it with a .45. I was on that security guard force for a while. I remember things like a full party going on in after steering. All the bolts were secured on the hatch. I remember wives being locked in the torpedo hanger bay with their husbands for a bit of privacy."

With OPERATION SILVERFOX concluded on 13 October, *Biddle* steamed west, through the Straits of Messina to Naples, and then to Barcelona, Spain. On 15 October, she responded to a distress call from the British yacht *Khalidia*, off the west coast of Corsica. *Khalidia*, with 17 aboard, had lost her rudder in heavy seas and was floundering in violent swells. Even though *Biddle* had been directed to clear the area, she remained on the scene until the French destroyer *La Galissonnière* arrived. (God bless the French!)

After arriving in Barcelona, *Biddle* entered a standdown condition for two weeks. *Biddle* departed for Naples on 30 October and conducted a successful 20-knot economy run while enroute. An eight day tender availability alongside *Yosemite* (AD-19) in Naples followed. Refreshed after eight days of "tender" loving care, *Biddle* satisfactorily completed Basic Engineering Casualty Control Exercises (BECCE) and Basic Damage Control Exercises then participated in OPERATION POOPDECK, a simulated air attack on Spain by TG 60.1, consisting of USS *Independence*, USS *Page*, USS *Waccamaw*, USS *Sampson*, and USS *Vreeland*.

After detaching from the group for a port call to Genoa, Italy, *Biddle* rejoined the Task Group on 19 November for Western Med Operations. General Alexander Haig, Supreme Allied Commander, Europe, and Vice Admiral Turner, Commander, Sixth Fleet, toured the ship on 20 November. (I can only imagine how clean the ship was for *that* visit.) Following their departure, *Biddle* got down to the serious work of ASW operations with *Pargo* (SSN 650) the next day. *Biddle* then detached from TG 60.1 and proceeded to Palma de Mallorca, Spain, firing an ASROC missile and a torpedo at a telemetry buoy enroute. After a week in Palma, *Biddle* left for her last port-o-call, Rota, Spain, before heading home. With her turnover with *Tattnall* (DDG-19) and mission in the Mediterranean completed, *Biddle* stood out of Rota on 5 December and headed home. *Biddle* arrived in Norfolk on 14 December and was in standdown until the end of the year.

Biddle's first Med cruise spanned exactly six months—from 14 June to 14 December. Although combat was not involved as it was in her first three deployments, *Biddle* got a close look at some of her potential adversaries during OPERATION SILVER FOX and our Soviet counterparts got to listen to the Alllman Brothers band. There were somber moments dealing with the death and destruction from the TWA jet crash in the Ionian Sea, and light moments for some of the crew partying in the after steering room and "getting lucky" with their wives in the torpedo bay. Comparing itineraries and time in port, *Biddle's* first Med cruise had fewer demands than her previous deployments to the Gulf of Tonkin. But, that is how it works when you are in the United States Navy—you train hard, preparing for the worst but hoping for the best. You do what you are told to do, when to do it, and how to do it. But that's okay; everybody up the chain of command does the same thing.

1975

Biddle greeted 1975 as she had most previous years—in a leave and upkeep status. On 23 January, she completed offloading weapons at the Naval Weapons Station, Yorktown, in preparation for her upcoming complex overhaul, which was to be done by Norfolk Naval Shipyard. The contract was awarded to Bath Iron Works instead, so a request for homeport re-assignment was made and *Biddle* continued to prepare for the overhaul. The AN/SPS-40 radar antenna was removed on the same day a TEMPEST (compromising electronic emanations) inspection was conducted—28 January. Other inspections that would quickly follow were the Annual Supply Inspection on 29 January and a Comprehensive Readiness Inspection from 19 to 21 January. The dismantling process for Mount 54, Mount 32, and the starboard CHAFFOC launcher began on 28 January.

With all appropriate inspections passed and other preparations completed, *Biddle* got underway for Bath, Maine, on 15 April with 19 U.S. Naval Sea Cadets embarked. (Those cadets should be approaching retirement as I write this in 2004.) *Biddle* arrived at BIW on 18 April and remained there for the remainder of the year. The crew moved to NAS Brunswick, a few miles down the road, and administrative work was done aboard a barge moored ahead of the ship. Additionally, Bath Iron Works had purchased a local church and converted it to a messing facility for *Biddle's* crew. Meals were catered by NAS Brunswick.

On 30 June, as part of a broad reclassification that brought the US Navy's classification system more in line with the rest of the world, *Biddle* and all ships of the *Belknap* and *Leahy* Classes were designated a CG—Guided Missile Cruiser. The reclassification system also classified Attack Carriers (CVA/CVAN) as multi-mission carriers (CV/CVN), all WWII cruisers as CG, DL/DLG became CG cruisers, and ocean escorts (DE/DEG) became FF/FFGs.

In August *Biddle* was awarded an "E" for CIC Operations, Surface to Air Missile, and Engineering by the Commander Naval Surface Atlantic Fleet.

1976

Biddle's overhaul at Bath Iron Works was nearing completion in January 1976. NTDS improvements included the installation of an Extended Core Memory Unit, Refresher Memory Unit, Keyset Central Multiplexer, Control Formatting Unit, and Model 4.0 Operational Program. Combat Information Center received the AIMS Identification, Friend or Foe (IFF) MK XII system and the Missile Fire Control System was upgraded to Mk 76 Mod 6 Digital Fire Control System. The SPS-48 radar was upgraded to an AN/SPS-48A(V) model and the SPS-10F surface search radar was upgraded with IFF capability. A new 5-inch/54 caliber MK 42 Mod 10 gun mount was installed. Habitability improvements were made to messing areas as well as environmental improvements to meet environmental pollution control requirements. Other weapons systems were overhauled, as were many auxiliary and engineering types of equipment.

Biddle's Executive Officer from September 1975 to September 1977, Commander Gilbert H. McKelvey, came aboard *Biddle* during the latter half of the overhaul. His recollection of the overhaul is favorable for the crew, but not for Bath Iron Works.

I reported onboard *Biddle* in September 1975 while she was in a Complex Overhaul (COH) at Bath Iron Works (BIW) in Bath, Maine. The Commanding Officer was Captain Frank Carelli, now deceased.

Biddle at that time was the first commissioned ship to undergo overhaul at BIW, which created continuous problems throughout the COH. The Navy's expectations for proper administration and functions of a commissioned ship were not relieved, while the BIW workforce and management thought of *Biddle* as simply "Hull 1033", the original BIW designation when the ship was under construction, and believed they could do the overhaul without reference or concern for the ship's company responsibilities to the Navy.

The change in scheduled location from Norfolk Naval Shipyard to Bath Iron Works, Bath, Maine caused serious personal disruptions for the crewmembers and impacted negatively on retention and morale. The satisfactory completion of the COH under these circumstances is testimony to the true grit and professionalism of the crew.

The Maine winter had a severe impact on exterior work progress while schedule required timely completion disregarding this issue. The ship was icebound from time to time in the Kennebec River and periodically a tug would slam into the side of the ship to break up the ice pushing the ship away from the pier.

Everyone greeted the departure from BIW in the spring of 1976 with a high level of enthusiasm, especially the families who had been left behind in Norfolk. The end result was that the Navy received *Biddle* back into the fleet in first rate condition and readiness as proven by a superior performance in Refresher Training in Guantanamo Bay, Cuba, Fleet Exercises, and deployment performance in the Mediterranean.

On 23 January, *Biddle's* crew returned to the ship and the tremendous job of getting *Biddle* checked out and combat ready. The first major test event occurred on 9 February with the arrival of the System Integration Test (SIT) team from Fleet Combat Direction System Support Activity, Dam Neck, Virginia, who commenced the NTDS Model 3.3 Operational Program Functional Checkout (OPFCO). Their purpose, according to the 1976 Command History, was "to check out the integration of the NTDS/WDS (Weapons Direction System) Mk 11 Mod 0 Interface to ensure proper channelization, intersystem functions, functioning of the NTDS operational program and training the operating personnel in the use of the new program. This team was on board for five weeks completing the OPFCO when the ship departed the yards."

After conducting a FAST cruise on 24 February, *Biddle* got underway the next morning for three days of sea trials. The Command History reported, "During this underway period, air services were provided which flew two F-4B Phantoms against the ULQ-6 (electronic warfare system) in a Z-40_EW drill on 25 February and one B-52 in a low flight profile against the AN/SLQ-27 SHORTSTOP system. That day the ship completed a ninety-five per cent full power run which logged 238 rpms or 4 rpms over 32 knots for a four hour period; a successful sixty fathom anchor test drop and high speed maneuverability drills, which included several forty degree rudder orders at 32 knots. Each of the three days underway the ship exercised both the five-inch and three-inch gun batteries. She returned to Bath Iron Works on 27 February for an additional two-week period in order to correct outstanding overhaul discrepancies."

On 17 March, with the first phase of her complex overhaul complete, *Biddle* sailed south to Bayonne, New Jersey, for the dry dock phase. Interestingly, while draining the dock, strong winds dislodged several docking blocks, upon which the ship rests while sitting in dry-dock, requiring the dock to be reflooded and the badly behaved blocks realigned. *Biddle* was floated on 24 April and left the dry dock, resplendent in her new hull paint and fresh rubberized paint on her sonar dome.

OS2 Terry L. Bowles, who had reported aboard *Biddle* the previous summer, recalled that

> When I reported aboard *Biddle* in the summer of 1975, the ship was in Bath, Maine, for an overhaul. After we left Bath, we headed south for Bayonne, New Jersey, for more outer hull work. After a couple of months of enjoying Manhattan and the surrounding area, we were finally ending the ships overhaul. Our last task before we departed was to conduct shoreline wake tests on the banks of the rivers around lower Manhattan. The local government wanted to know what possible damage to the shorelines could be done by differing speeds up and down the rivers. This test was conducted for the upcoming Fourth of July celebration of our Nation's 200 birthday of independence. The celebration plan was to include tall ships from all around the world and numerous other ships of varying sizes cruising the rivers around Manhattan. After several passes up and down the rivers of Manhattan, we finally left for our homeport of Norfolk Virginia.

Biddle returned to Naval Weapons Station, Yorktown, on 26 and 27 April to load an inventory of ASROC, 3-inch, five-inch ammunition, and Standard missiles. The following day *Biddle* returned to Norfolk after a 54-week absence. *Biddle* would remain in port for one and a half months catching her breath before a succession of demanding exercises and tests would bring her to combat readiness.

Ships Qualification Trials began in earnest on 18 May when *Biddle* got underway for local operations in the VACAPES Op Area. Helicopter Certification Training Readiness Inspection quickly followed, as did TACAN (an electronic navigation aid for aircraft) and SONAR certification. On 2 June *Biddle* fired the 5-inch and 3-inch guns for training purposes in the VACAPES Op Area then set sail for Roosevelt Roads, Puerto Rico. *Biddle* fired five rounds from each gun on 7 June then three Standard missiles on 8 June. Only the second missile shot was a success—the first had a defective fuse and the last bird failed to ignite. Things were not going well that day—the Mk5 Mod 8 missile launcher also failed, delaying completion of the SQT missile tests until the launcher could be repaired

The Weapons Systems Accuracy Team (WSAT) team embarked and completed the inport phase of the test, which included firing a torpedo pierside at Roosevelt Roads. The SHORTSTOP system was tested at the Electronic Warfare range south of Puerto Rico and the island of Vieques on 14 June. *Biddle* then sailed for Fredericksted, St. Croix, and the WSAT range where a large part of the test was conducted. The ASROC test was postponed due to the CASREP missile launcher.

Refresher training at Guantanamo Bay, Cuba, began on 18 June soon after *Biddle's* arrival. She passed her ASW exam the first week then the Navigation and Low Visibility piloting, ASCM, BECCE, BDCCE, UNREP NGFS, Anti-Air Gunfire and Condition I Battle Problem. Repairs to the missile launcher were made on 1 July, enabling *Biddle* to reschedule the remainder of SQT and WSAT after refresher training. Refresher training continued after a three day break in Port au prince, Haiti, until completion three weeks later. The final hurdles of completing SQT and WSAT remained, however.

OS2 Bowles recalled that

> A short while later the *Biddle* left Norfolk heading for the Caribbean for Refresher Training at Guantanamo Bay Cuba. Every day at sea was long and filled with numerous training evolutions, and the much-needed Cinderella Liberty in Guantanamo Bay was too short lived. Finally, a much-needed break was headed our way with the 4th of July and the crew voted to spend the time off from training at Port-au-Prince Haiti.
>
> Arriving in Port-au-Prince we anchored out in the harbor, a first for me as a watch stander taking bearings on landmarks to ensure the *Biddle* was not drifting from its anchorage. Finally, my time came for me to take the motor whaleboat into port for liberty. I was amazed at the poverty and the vast visible presence of the police. After stepping off the motor whaleboat, I was suddenly over run by children begging for handouts. The police began to beat them off the pier with their nightsticks, until finally we could walk unencumbered off the pier.
>
> The city itself was impoverished, as were the people. We were told their per-capita annual income was a meager $80.00, and they preferred to trade for

goods rather than receive money. A carton of cigarettes sold for $2.00 in the ships store. Not being a cigarette smoker myself, however, I found gold in those smokes. In Port-au-Prince a pack of cigarettes could buy you a meal, a few packs for trinkets, and a carton for a hotel room for the night.

During our stay in Port-au-Prince, we observed our National Holiday, and learned of the numerous ships and boats in the rivers around Manhattan. The river wake tests we conducted was a success as the model correctly predicted the potential damage to the riverbanks. I felt pride in knowing the *Biddle* and her crew was a major contributor to the success of the biggest nautical celebration ever in Manhattan.

Then reality sunk in for me regarding the everyday life struggle of the Haitians. The United States, the greatest nation on the face of the earth, was celebrating the Fourth of July, a day of independence and the people of Haiti were in a struggle of their own to survive from one day to the next. Independence that day became to mean more to me than just the Fourth of July. It became a day of realization of how people from another nation are simply struggling to live and in desperate need of personal independence from poverty. The over whelming knowledge that you cannot help everyone around you set in. During the remainder of my stay in Port-au-Prince, I began to personally interact with the Haitians I met. I found them to be a fine people with similar dreams and goals much like my own. We spoke about the world's current events, and their genuine generosity became more apparent to me. I left Haiti a changed person forever with a fever to contribute to society, to make a difference in the lives of those around me and those I do not know.

Missile SQT requirements were met on 25 July when, off the southern coast of Puerto Rico, *Biddle* fired four missiles and all shots were evaluated as successful. The next day, off the northern coast of Puerto Rico, *Biddle* successfully completed her Missile SQT after firing the last missile at a surface target. NFGS requirements were met on 29 July at the Naval Gunfire Support range south of Vieques Island where *Biddle* fired 160 5-inch rounds during the day and well into the evening. I expect *Biddle's* gunners mates slept very soundly that night. WSAT was completed the next day at St. Croix and a very tired crew was soon on their way home.

Biddle arrived in Norfolk on 2 August. With only a month before her scheduled departure to northern Europe to participate in Exercise TEAMWORK, there was still much work to be done and training to endure. The Nuclear Weapons Training Group, Atlantic, conducted nuclear weapons training in preparation for Nuclear Weapons Acceptance Inspection (NWAI) later that month. In the meantime, *Biddle* welcomed aboard her seventh commanding officer, Captain Albert L. Henry, Jr. A 1956 Naval Academy graduate, Captain Henry's assignments included *Bremerton* (CA-130), *Gearing* (DD-710), and *W. C. Lawe*

(DD-763). He commanded *Seneca* (ATF-91), was *Ouellet's* (DE-1077) commissioning Commanding Officer, and Commander River Assault Squadron 15 in the Mekong Delta, Vietnam.

Biddle stood out of Norfolk on 3 September to participate in the NATO multinational exercise in Northern Europe, Exercise TEAMWORK. *Biddle* rendezvoused on 4 September with Atlantic Fleet units out of Mayport, Florida, and Charleston, South Carolina, to form Task Group 400. During the nine week cruise, *Biddle* operated independently, with Task Group 400 elements, and with units of the Federal German Navy in the Baltic Sea, Norwegian Sea, Norwegian fjords, and the Skaggerak. During that time *Biddle* was a permanent magnet for a host of Admirals and assorted dignitaries. Flags and pennants were broken and hauled down for Commodore R.K. Albright, Commander Destroyer Squadron 22; Vice Admiral J.J. Shanahan, Commander, Striking Fleet Atlantic; and Rear Admiral F.F. Palmer, Commander, Amphibious Group 2. *Biddle* and her crew enjoyed liberty in ports such as Scapa Flow, Scotland; Copenhagen, Denmark; Travemunde (Luebeck), Germany; Hamburg, Germany; Antwerp, Belgium; and Cherbourg, France. *Biddle* participated in several amphibious assaults. The first was an amphibious landing in Norwegian fjords, another on the Jutland coast of Denmark, and once each in the beer halls of Hamburg and Travemunde, Germany, and Tivoli Gardens in Copenhagen. The final exercise was a land assault on fine French restaurants in Cherbourg. Completely exhausted from multiple assaults that rivaled D-Day, *Biddle* departed Cherbourg on 29 October for Norfolk. She rendezvoused with USS *John F. Kennedy* (CV-67) and elements of Task Group 22.6 for the final push home.

With the exception of a brief underway period in late November for the Atlantic Fleet Operation Propulsion Plant Exam (OPPE), *Biddle* remained in port for the remainder of the year. NTDS Model 4.0 Operation Program, which gave *Biddle* increased ASW capabilities and a two-way link 4A interceptor control link capability with F-14 Tomcats, was delivered in late November as well.

1977

Biddle celebrated her 10th anniversary while underway from 17 January to 21 February with U.S., NATO, and South American Naval Forces units participating in a Caribbean Readiness Exercise (CARIBREX). *Biddle's* 1977 Command History stated that "Highlights were a missile exercise with COMCRUDESGRU TWO embarked as Chief Observer, exercise firings of a torpedo tube launched torpedo and an ASROC, and port visits in San Juan, Puerto Rico, and Frederickstead, Saint Croix." After passing an inspection by the Board of Inspection and

Survey in March, *Biddle* participated in a Competitive Training Unit Exercise (COMPTUEX 4-77) from 11 to 22 April. In June, prior to her next overseas deployment, her second Med cruise, *Biddle* passed numerous inspections including an Operation Propulsion Plant Examination, a Nuclear Technical Proficiency Inspection, and a Combat Systems Readiness Review.

Pronounced fit and ready, *Biddle* stood out from Pier 21, D and S Piers, Norfolk, on 11 July for a 22 week Mediterranean deployment as a unit of the Sixth Fleet. After an 11-day Atlantic crossing on "glassy seas," *Biddle* arrived at her first port, Tangier, Morocco, and relieved sister ship *Standley* (CG-32). An intriguing, hot, dry North African city, Tangier provided activities not normally available stateside—riding camels and visiting the Kasbah.

At the next port, *Biddle* was an eager, if not victorious participant, in the First Annual Motor Whaleboat Race at Golfo di Palma while anchored in the training harbor. Inexplicably, *Biddle's* entry came in second place.

Biddle's crew enjoyed liberty in Naples, Italy, and the surrounding area from 11 to 14 August. Taking advantage of the hot August weather, some *Biddle* sailors vacated the narrow streets and crazy drivers of Naples for the sandy beaches and bikinis at the Isle of Capri in the Bay of Naples. Good choice.

Biddle continued her travel backwards in time when she visited her third major port, Athens, Greece, from 27 August to 7 September. From Syntagma, a shipyard eight miles north of Athens, Biddlemen took tours to almost every part of Athens and to Delphi, 100 miles distant. The Acropolis, which is visible from anywhere in the city and older than most *Biddle* Senior Chiefs, was a favorite spot to visit and take pictures. Some *Biddle* sailors, not willing to give up their sea legs, took cruises to islands in the Saronic Gulf while, not surprisingly, some *Biddle* sailors chose to sample wine at a wine festival on an ancient pass leading into the city.

The second Italian port *Biddle* visited was the quiet town of Gaeta, located on the west coast approximately midway between the great cities of Rome and Naples. The grandeur and close proximity of Rome was irresistible—most Hard Chargers took advantage of both organized and unorganized tours to see the ancient city. Those Biddlemen who stayed in Gaeta were not disappointed with the small town atmosphere and outstanding Italian food, southern style. After leaving Gaeta, *Biddle* sailed for Naples to embark British Vice Admiral Roderick Macdonald, Commander Naval Forces South, for participation in NATO exercises including Exercise Display Determination.

Palma de Mallorca, situated off the coast of Spain in the Balearic Islands, was the port many *Biddle* wives chose to visit their husbands for a two week vacation.

Biddle sailors whose wives or girlfriends visited had numerous activities to choose from in the famous resort city—most of which they could write home about.

Biddle's third Italian port, La Spezia, is located at the top of the "boot," 65 kilometers north of the city of Pisa and its famous leaning tower. Not only did La Spezia offer the Italian Riviera and close proximity to Pisa, it also had Camp Darby, an Army post near Pisa with an "EM Club, an Officer's Club, a movie theater, a recreation center, hobby shop and, of course, an exchange," according to the '77 Med Cruise Book.

Biddle visited her last port, Toulon, France, twice—first on 15 November for one day, and again from 28 November to 5 December. Situated on the French Riviera, Toulon offered a unique snapshot of the French culture, cuisine, way of life, and an opportunity to snap up a few last minute Christmas presents.

With *Biddle's* mission complete, she anchored again at Tangier, Morocco, where she was relieved by *South Carolina* (CGN-37). The '77 Med Cruise book reported that "There was some confusion as to whether we would stay the night, but right after sunset, we were underway for Norfolk, Va! There was a wild roar as crewmembers lined the rails to gaze of into the sunset and think about home 11 days away." *Biddle* returned to Norfolk on 22 November and entered a post deployment standdown period.

1978

Sandwiched between commissioning and decommissioning are millions of hours of administration, paperwork, problem solving, maintenance, repair, inspections, overhauls, exercises, and training. For enlisted and officer alike, life aboard a U.S. Navy combatant is often routine and predictable, but periodically punctuated by a call to an exotic port, or a call to action. 1978 was a year that did not involve a call to action or an overhaul, but involved virtually everything else that could happen to a ship. It was a very busy year.

The new year found *Biddle* in a post deployment stand down mode until her eleventh birthday on 21 January. COMCRUSDESGRU EIGHT broke his flag on 30 January only to haul it down on 3 February, after an official call from the commanding officer of the Federal German ship *Luetjens*. Most of February was spent preparing for ASWEX 1-78, an experimental ASW exercise "designed to test and evaluate proposed tactics for protection of a Carrier Task Force," which was *Biddle's* primary mission. *Biddle* was underway for the Caribbean and ASWEX 1-78 on 24 February with HSL-34 Detachment 4 helicopter crew aboard and both COMCRUDESGRU TWO and COMSUBRON FOUR embarked. *Biddle's* 1978 Command History notes "During ASWEX 1-78 *Biddle* exercised her Sonar and ASW Weapons System often and well, holding contact on submarines for over one hour and conducting exercise torpedo attacks with installed launchers and with the LAMPS helicopter."

With ASWEX 1-78 completed and after a brief respite in Roosevelt Roads, *Biddle* participated with units from the Federal Republic of Germany, the Netherlands, Canada, the United Kingdom, and the United States in exercise SAFE PASS, which exercised NATO's ability to protect shipping routes in the Western Atlantic. *Biddle* arrived in Norfolk on 16 March, long enough to receive the usual flurry of congratulatory messages, and then got underway again, this time to provide services for operational readiness inspections for USS *John F. Kennedy* and USS *Forrestal*.

Composite Training Unit Exercise (COMPTUEX 2-78), designed to prepare a ship for overseas deployment, was next on *Biddle's* schedule. The 1978 Command History stated, "Although not immediately scheduled for a deployment, BIDDLE'S participation was needed in the exercise as a substitute for another cruiser which was unable to participate." Over and above her preparation for COMPTUEX 2-78, *Biddle* was also given a Technical Standardization Inspection/Nuclear Technical Proficiency Inspection "to evaluate all aspects of safety and security associated with the ship's special weapons capability." *Biddle* passed the inspection with a grade of excellent.

With preparations for COMPTUEX 2-78 complete and a successful Nuclear Proficiency Inspection under her belt, *Biddle* got underway on 10 April for three weeks of concentrated training at sea. Twelve U.S. Navy ships, one Coast Guard cutter, and two French destroyers joined *Biddle* in the exercise. *Biddle's* 1978 Command History reported "During the COMPTUEX, BIDDLE was able to utilize almost all aspects of her combat system suite, conducting successful torpedo attacks using LAMPS, ASROC, and deck launched torpedoes and firing Terrier Missiles at surface and air targets." *Biddle* enjoyed a few days liberty in Ft. Lauderdale, Florida, and then completed an Operational Readiness Evaluation (ORE) during transit to Norfolk.

Following a brief stand down, *Biddle* was underway again on 15 May to prepare for the upcoming Operational Propulsion Plant Examination (OPPE) and to conduct a family cruise to Yorktown, Virginia. The OPPE was "terminated before completion due to inadequate fire room performance," claimed the Command History. After an Administrative Inspection by COMCRUDESGRU EIGHT on 12 June, a formal personnel inspection on 14 June, and underway engineering casualty control training from 5 July to 11 July, *Biddle* passed her

OPPE inspection. The remainder of the month was spent in preparation for getting underway on 28 July for COMPTUEX 4-78.

With COMCRUDESGRU EIGHT and Staff embarked, *Biddle* got underway on 28 July for the Puerto Rico Operating Area with *Saratoga* (CV-60), *Valdez* (FF-1096), *John King* (DDG-3), and *Milwaukee* (AOR-2). The Mobile Sea Range (MSR) part, which "involved live firings of the HARPOON Cruise Missile in the Atlantic Fleet," according to the Command History, was completed, at which time *Biddle* departed for a two day port visit in Ft. Lauderdale. Next, *Biddle* sailed to Newport, Rhode Island, for a reception with direct descendants of Nicholas Biddle in association with the Seaport '76 Foundation.

Captain John N. Ryan, U.S. Navy, reported aboard as Prospective Commanding Officer on 21 August and assumed command as *Biddle's* eighth commanding officer on 25 August. A native of California, he was commissioned an Ensign on 14 August 1954. Captain Ryan served as Executive Officer of *Estero* (AKL-5), *Keenfish* (SS-393), *Argonaut* (SS-475), and *Standley* (CG-32). Captain Ryan commanded *Charles R. Ware* (DD-865)

A "Thank You" From HSL-34

The helicopter detachments that served aboard *Biddle* throughout her career were an essential part of *Biddle's* life. During *Biddle's* three deployments to the Gulf of Tonkin, they were used to rescue downed pilots and to bring mail and supplies from Yankee Station. They were also an ASW platform and a general utility transportation vehicle.

The pilots who landed them on *Biddle's* postage-sized landing area in any weather had nerves of steel and extraordinary flying skills. The remainder of the detachment that supported "Big Mother" or whatever the current, endearing, epithet happened to be, were dedicated and skilled professionals too—they were Hard Chargers! There was more than just a symbiotic relationship between *Biddle* and her helicopters. Over the many months that helo detachments served in *Biddle*, bonds were made and friendships were formed between the two crews. So, when *Biddle* arrived in Norfolk on 23 August and lost the services of HSL-34, the LAMPS Helicopter Detachment that had been aboard *Biddle* intermittently since December 1976, the crew of HSL-34, wrote an inspiring letter of appreciation to the crew of USS *Biddle*. The letter follows:

> As most of you already know, your LAMPS detachment from HSL 34 will be re-assigned to another ship in September. Since December 1976 when Detachment 4 joined the BIDDLE, it has enjoyed successful operations in

numerous exercises ad a long Med deployment. In recognition of these and other detachment's work our squadron has recently been awarded the Isabel Trophy for ASW excellence and the CNO Safety Award for safe and efficient operations.

We, the men of your LAMPS detachment, know full well that these awards and also our everyday operations would be impossible without the dedicated efforts of all Hard Chargers. Although our favorite announcement is "Flight Quarters, Flight Quarters for helo launch...", we know the sacrifices demanded of you to support our efforts.

Our appreciation goes to all hands but in particular: To <u>flight deck party members</u> who share the harsh elements, and the long and often unusual working hours, to the <u>HCO and phone talkers</u> who are a superb team, to the <u>crash boat party and fire suitmen</u> who we hold in high esteem as they stand ready to risk their lives to save ours, to the <u>ASAC'S and Operations Department</u> who direct and control us in our operational mission and help us return safely in all weather conditions, to the <u>Supply Department</u> for providing the steady stream of parts and equipment that keeps us 100% Op ready and for good food at very unusual hours. To the <u>Weapons Department</u> who supply our operational equipment of sonobouys, smoke markers, torpedoes and take care of our hangar while we're gone. To the <u>Engineers</u> who make all things possible as well as giving us power to start and good pure fuel to burn and to the <u>bridge team</u> for fair winds and steady deck from which to work.

Those members of the detachment who came aboard in '76 as well as those who have joined more recently pass their thanks for being accepted as true shipmates and wish you fair winds and following seas in all future operations.

Our aircraft, "Hard Charger 34", has been working a little too hard of late and has developed problems with its main transmission. She accumulated 100 hours in this last exercise with a total of 500 hours since January. This is 10% of the total of all Atlantic Fleet LAMPS (four entire squadrons), but even though she might disembark by crane at pierside we hope you feel she has earned your call sign, "Hard Charger".

Biddle departed for her third Mediterranean deployment on 3 October. Enroute, she conducted a missile exercise and gunshoot with *Saratoga* (CV-60) and other units of the transit group. *Biddle* relieved *Yarnell* (CG-17) in Lisbon, Portugal, on 14 October and assumed duties in the U.S. Sixth Fleet. *Biddle* arrived in La Spezia, Italy, on 24 October after operating with units of Task Group 60.2 for six days. Departing La Spezia on 27 October, *Biddle* again rendezvoused with *Saratoga* and Task Group 60.2 and proceeded to the Ionian Sea where *Biddle* and *Conyngham* (DDG-17) entered Phaleron Bay, Athens, Greece, on 4 November.

An interesting account in *Biddle's* Command History regarding the port visit is recalled: "On 9 November Brigadier General Nikolopoulos, Chief of the Athens Metropolitan Police Department, plus several other police officers, attended a memorable and touching luncheon in the Wardroom. Following an exchange of gifts, General Nikolopoulos made a memorable speech regarding the sense of security and friendship he and other Greek people felt when units of the Sixth Fleet are present in Greek waters. General Nikolopoulos' statement was given credence when, during daily playing of the U.S. National Anthem at morning colors, Greek fishermen fishing from small boats near BIDDLE would stop their work and rise to attention for the duration of the anthem."

Biddle departed Athens on 14 November and proceeded to Soudha Bay, Crete, to participate in a missile exercise and gun shoot. She returned to Athens on 20 November to embark the Commander Submarine Force Atlantic, Rear Admiral P. B. Tomb, and then proceeded through the Bosporous and Dardanelles (The Bosphorous channel connects the northern Marmora to the Black Sea while the Dardanelles is a channel connecting the north Aegean Sea with the south end of the Sea of Marmora) to visit the Socialist Republic of Romania. Escorted by a Romanian Naval vessel, *Biddle* arrived in Constanta on 22 November. *Biddle* was one of only four U.S. Navy ships to visit Romania in half a century. Soon, Rear Admiral Tomb, Captain Ryan, other *Biddle* officers, and the Defense Attaché Bucharest, made official calls to a long list of Romanian dignitaries. Following the official calls, the protocol party and 40 enlisted men laid a ceremonial wreath at Victory Monument in Constanta. There was a reception; there were tours and general sightseeing in the city as well as numerous luncheons, sport competition, and cocktails. *Biddle's* visit to the port city of Constanta in the Socialist Republic of Romania was a significant diplomatic event and spoke highly of *Biddle* and her crew.

On the *Biddle* web site at http://www.ussbiddle.org HTCM Richard Outland recalled an adventure that involved *Biddle* and elements of the Russian Navy in the Black Sea. That story is reprinted here.

> During a Med deployment in the 1970's—the usual visits to the usual ports—dullsville for an experienced crew. Shortly after the anchor was hoisted from yet another unnamed anchorage, the skipper came over the 1MC to tell us about a "special assignment."
>
> Because of our ability to operate in a stealthy mode, we had been selected to try a bold venture—we were to slip into the Black Sea and join up with a Russian task force "undetected."
>
> We played hide and seek games throughout the day and into the darkness of the night. A little past midnight the Russian task force was found. I don't know if it was by luck or if it was planned, but the Russians were in a long line taking on fuel from a support ship by the over the stern method. One could

only guess that the bridges and the CICs of the Russkie ships were busy keeping station and either did not notice or chose to ignore one additional ship among the others. This bold venture was about to become a little more bold.

The skipper had us fall into last place in the line of ships to be fueled. We were in the darkened ship mode and slowly made our way up to the support ship. As the last Russkie ship pulled away, we made our approach.

A Russian speaking crewman was on hand to handle the radio traffic. As expected, the support ship asked how much fuel we would need. "Just a token amount," was our reply. We continued making our approach, the yards between us and the support ship closing every second. I don't know about anyone else, but my heart was pounding and the ol' adrenaline was pumping.

When we were even with the support ship, the radio hailed us again—"What ship are you?"

"United States Battle Cruiser *Biddle*," we replied in perfect Russian.

The radio went silent—then all hell broke loose. Gongs, whistles, lights all seemed to go off at once on board the Russkie ships, as they scattered in every direction away from us.

We the changed course and came alongside the support ship. Our skipper and the Russian skipper exchanged pleasantries as we slowly slipped away into the darkness—unmolested, unfueled and pleased with ourselves.

Despite our victory over the Soviet Navy, it was not until we steamed past Izmir, Turkey, and headed for the open sea that I felt a little more comfy, and ready for an old familiar port. I'd had enough excitement for one week.

Biddle departed Constanta on 30 November to return to her normal duties. Four days of intense ASW exercises followed, and then *Biddle* enjoyed a five day visit in Kalamata, Greece. She left Kalamata on 7 December to join Task Group 60.2 for missile and gunnery exercise near Soudha Bay, Crete. On 15 December, *Biddle* joined *Conyngham* and *John King* in a transit to Naples, Italy, where *Biddle* rested until 2 January 1979.

One exciting incident that was not mentioned in the cruise book or the Command History can now be told. A very out of breath HTCM Richard Outland tells the story:

> *Biddle* deployed, inport Naples, Italy. Christmas time, Med moored to downtown pier, Cinderella liberty—crew returning from Blue Bird Club and CincSouth.
>
> Commotion at hand near foot of brow and on quarterdeck, crowd gathering, quarterdeck watch running back and forth. Closer observation shows circus wagons on pier being staged for loading on ferry, Hard Chargers full of Christmas cheer, one who opens door to lion cage—lion leaps out and heads for ship—up the brow and onto fantail/quarterdeck.

OOD EMC Randy Crider going out of his mind and pulls 45 caliber from messenger/Petty Officer of the Watch holster, chambers a round and with a shaky hand tries to point it at the lion which is now cavorting all over the fantail but only in a showmanship fashion—non-threatening.

OOD Crider calls the wardroom—CDO for instructions not covered in the standing orders. The POW now with a broom in his hand had spooked the lion which now had climbed the ladder to the flight deck, needless to say panic had set in; I slowly made my way past all of the ruckus and went to the CPO galley and got some of left over chicken parts and went back to the flight deck and by offering tasty chicken to the lion (which he ate in haste) finally I lured him back to his cage and bolted the door.

All of the armchair lion tamers in and around the quarterdeck said I was a nutcase. Somewhat true, I guess. Later as I reflected on the evening's events, I thought that just maybe I had just enough Christmas spirits in me to not be intimidated by a hungry Italian speaking lion.

1979

Biddle, after checking all spaces for circus animals, celebrated the new year by participating in SHAREM 30, "an ASW exercise conducted for the purpose of gathering data used in the research and development of ASW tactics," according to *Biddle's* 1979 Command History. *Conyngham, John King, Brumby,* and *McCloy* accompanied *Biddle* during the exercise. Enroute to a five day visit to the port of Bizerte, Tunisia, *Biddle* took part in PASSEX, in which Tunisian Naval ships and Air Force aircraft conducted a simulated attack on *Biddle*. Following the visit to Bizerte, *Biddle* shadowed the Soviet Navy's Kiev Task Group in the Eastern Mediterranean until 19 January when *Biddle* rejoined the *Saratoga* Task Group. From 22 January to 6 February, the crew enjoyed the mild temperatures and Spanish hospitality in Palma de Mallorca, located approximately 100 miles south of Barcelona, Spain.

February's activities began with participation in ASW Week from 6 to 10 February. During the exercise, *Biddle* not only located, tracked, and acted against submarines with her ASW weapons, she also "took advantage of local air assets provided by USS *Saratoga* (CV-60) for anti-air warfare freeplay, and also conducted test firings of ships guns," again according to *Biddle's* Command History. Following ASW Week, *Biddle* visited Spain's leading port city of Alicante for a week, then conducted communications, ASW, CIC, and Engineering exercises in the Western Mediterranean while simultaneously conducting logistic replenishment exercises. The ending of that series of exercises marked the preparation for the next exercise, National Week XXVI.

National Week XXVI simulated a conventional war between the theoretical Blue and Orange nations. The elaborate conflict required Blue nation's task force to simulate a combined amphibious landing in Capo Teulada, Sardinia, with *Biddle* securing control of the seas during the transit to the landing area. Three Turkish observers, a Turkish Air Force officer and two Turkish Naval Officers, went along for the ride. Captain Ryan and several other officers attended a post exercise debriefing aboard USS *Dwight D. Eisenhower* (CVN-69).

Biddle enjoyed a flurry of port visits in March—Barcelona from 6 to 13 March, Cadiz from 17 to 22 March, and Rota from 23 to 25 March. Sandwiched between Barcelona and Cadiz was *Biddle's* last exercise of the cruise, a series of AAW exercises with *Saratoga* (CV-60). While in Barcelona, *Biddle* took aboard a civilian contractor, Dennis O'Neill, to accomplish Ships Force Overhaul Management System (SFOMS) training. Mr. O'Neill was working for PERA [CRUDES] (Planning and Engineering for Repair and Alteration, Cruiser/Destroyer) at the time. His contribution to *Biddle's* story probably reflects what most civilians who came aboard *Biddle* feel about her.

> We rode the ship from Barcelona to Cadiz during which time [then] Lieutenant Commander Tom Marfiak, her Chief Engineer, and I became friends and are to this day.
>
> I was berthed with the Operations Officer and *Biddle* lived up to the *Belknap* Class' reputation of, "Cadillac of the Sea." A steady quartering swell from the Southeast gave her a motion that I found conducive to a good nights rest even though the two Department Head's staterooms were well forward and I tried to get as much aft as possible when riding a ship since that end is more likely to stay in contact with the ocean. At one point, however, we encountered the "100th Wave" and I still remember the feeling in the pit of my stomach.
>
> The bow rose and stopped as usual and I awaited the descent to the next trough when, suddenly, the bow continued rising! It seemed to go on forever and when it finally started back down I reached out with both hands to grab a frame member and hung on for dear life. My head said we were surely falling off the edge of the earth!
>
> When *Biddle* settled into the next trough I'm sure she took green water close to the bridge windows. She seemed to shudder from end to end and then settled back into her regular motion. That was the only episode of its kind in a 4-day transit but it's still quite clear in my memory.
>
> The other thing I remember about my visit to *Biddle* was the professionalism and courtesy, to a man, that I found in the ships company. SFOMS was considered to be another 'paper drill,' among so many requirements foisted upon ships in those days. *Biddle's* attitude seemed to be, "Well, if it's required,

let's figure out how to get it done." We got complete cooperation from every work center in loading their work package into the SFOMS data base.

During light-off in the After Engine Room in Barcelona a petty officer approached Mr. Marfiak and asked if he could extend on *Biddle* past the end of the upcoming overhaul. "Why do you want to do that?" Tom asked.

"Because I've seen our overhaul package and they're going to do quite a few upgrades to my main feed pumps and forced draft blowers and I'd like to see how they work afterwards. "Tom," I said, "Did he say 'my' feed pumps and blowers? I haven't heard that on a ship in at least 5 years!"

My involvement with SFOMS lasted three years; the second half with PERA [CV]. *Biddle* and *Waddell* (DDG-24) under Commander Brian Moynihan were the two high points of that time and *Biddle* was the highest.

USS *R. K. Turner* (CG-20) relieved *Biddle* at Rota and *Biddle* headed home. Arriving Norfolk on 5 April, *Biddle* entered a post deployment stand down until 30 April.

For the next three months *Biddle* entertained a variety of visitors. On 27 April, thirteen congressional staff members and officers from the Office of Legislative Affairs and CINCLANTFLT toured *Biddle* for a "naval orientation" tour. During May, June, and July, *Biddle* hosted U.S. Naval Academy and NROTC midshipmen, and on 11 May, *Biddle* was visited by a group of senior officers from ten countries that were sponsored by the U.S. Army War College. A week later, forty COMNAVSEASYSMCOM civilian employees visited *Biddle* to study her operation capabilities and habitability.

August's schedule included two exercises—SEABAT 3-79 from 6 August to 11 August and COMPUTEX 3-79 from 20 August to 31 August. SEABAT 3-79, a joint U.S. Navy and U.S. Air Force exercise, tested the ability to link NTDS with the USAF Electronic Warfare Platform. COMPUTEX involved 13 U.S. Navy Second Fleet ships, a carrier wing, four U.S. Air Force tactical fighter wings a tactical reconnaissance wing, a tactical air control wing, Air National Guard units, and Royal Navy units. The elaborate six-phase 12 day exercise, as reported in the COMPUTEX 3-79 press release, was designed "To improve overall unit readiness and to exercise the forces assigned in task group operations."

Regular Overhaul at Philadelphia

Biddle returned to Norfolk in late August to offload ammunition and prepare for a scheduled regular overhaul (ROH) at Philadelphia Naval Shipyard. Both of *Biddle's* 3-inch 50 caliber guns, the AN/SPG-55B missile radars, and portions of the SLQ-27 SHORTSTOP system were removed at Norfolk before departing for

Philadelphia on 24 September. The ROH officially began on 28 September and *Biddle* entered drydock on 22 October. The overhaul would install two Phalanx Close-In Weapons Systems (CIWS), the HARPOON missile system, AN/SPS-48C (ADT) Radar, Mk 76 Mod 8 GMFCS, and the computerized communications system NAVMACS.

Phalanx CIWS

Biddle would be the first CG to receive the Phalanx CIWS—the carriers *America*, *Enterprise*, and *Coral Sea* received the installation first. Developed by General Dynamics in the early seventies after a study showed that a radar-directed, high-rate-of-fire gun could be effective against close-in anti-ship missiles if the system employed a closed-loop spotting concept. The system's radar would detect the position of both the target and the projectile then adjusted the gun's aim accordingly. A test unit was built and underwent a successful ground test in 1970. Prototypes were installed on *King* (DDG-14) in 1973 and the decommissioned *Cunningham* in 1975. All missiles fired at *Cunningham* were destroyed. In 1976, the Phalanx was installed on the destroyer USS *Bigelow* (DD-942) for operational evaluation testing. Testing revealed that the Phalanx was four times more reliable than requirements and repair times were better than specified minimums. Phalanx was approved for production in 1978, deliveries began in 1979, and initial installations were made in 1980.

The gun's characteristics are impressive. The 12,500 pound 20 mm M-61A1 system could fire 3,000 rounds per minute of a ¼ pound depleted uranium 6-inch projectile at a muzzle velocity of 3,600 feet per second. Later models could fire at 4,500 rounds per minute and the system weighs 13,600 pounds. The gun's rate of train was 100 degrees per second and rate of elevation was 86 degree per second.

Harpoon

The Harpoon missile was designed to engage warships at a range of up to 60 nautical miles, allowing Standard and Terrier missiles, which were adapted for anti-ship use, to be used exclusively for AAW defense. The Harpoon boasts a sea-skimming cruise trajectory and mid-course active radar guidance capabilities. Before firing, target information is programmed into the harpoon. The booster section, which contains a solid fuel rocket motor and arming device, separates once sustained flight is achieved. The sustainer section, with a JP-10 burning jet engine, provides the thrust required to keep the missile airborne. Once airborne, the missile locates the target with its on-board radar and flies to the target without further operator control. The versatile, multi-service missile can be launched from submarines, aircraft (without the booster), or trucks. Given the missile's proven track record, budget restraints, continued improvement projects, and no successor on the horizon, we can expect the Harpoon to be around after 2015.

NAVMACS

Naval Modular Automated Communications System (NAVMACS) was, according to co-author and computer/communications specialist Dave Boslaugh, an "automated message preparation, routing, and distribution system aboard ship similar to the shore based Local Digital Message Exchange (LDMX). NAVMACS installations were modular like NTDS and could be tailored to large or small ships by using different amounts of the standard modular units. NAVMACS used AN/UYK-20 standard Navy minicomputers." *Biddle* was equipped with NAVMACS V2, which was designed for 15 different classes of ships from AOs to CGs.

AN/SPS-48 Radar

Biddle's air search capabilities were enhanced with the installation of the AN/SPS-48C radar with Automatic Detection and Tracking (ADT) features and a Moving Target Indicator (MTI) capability, giving *Biddle* multiple target detection and tracking capability. The 17 foot square, 4,500 pound antenna used changes in frequency to steer the beam in elevation, which provided the target's height. Elevation coverage was from zero to 45 degrees and targets could be detected up to a low angle range of 265 miles.

The Phoenix Rises From the Ashes

Tom Marfiak

Like a bride to a bridegroom, USS *Biddle* arrived at the Philadelphia Naval Shipyard in the late summer of 1979. The expectations were great. A welcome at Penn's Landing kicked off an effort to create a bond between the ship and the city. Unfortunately, once in the throes of the overhaul, that bond would undergo significant stress.

It did not take very long. The barracks for the crew were beyond belief! Windows were missing—not a good idea with winter coming on. The barracks barge allotted was far below Navy standards. Our first order of business was to turn the crew loose on improving their own living conditions. Even as their ship sat on the blocks of the dry dock, crew members worked day and night to create a living environment. The great ship had found a resting place, but at what cost?

Stripped of her ammunitions, white canvas and awnings, the ship sat astride the blocks like a patient waiting for the surgeon's care. She would have not long to wait.

Fairness requires that it be noted all ships encountered demanding industrial environments in those days. We had not yet learned to treat them as the thoroughbreds they are. Yet, these circumstances were especially arduous. The progressive malaise that had spread throughout the armed forces during the Carter era had reached even to the basic services required in a shipyard. Our dry dock, surrounded by four cranes, could muster only one working crane, far inadequate to the task of moving machinery off the ship. It reached the point where, on one day, I was forced to suspend all shipyard work, to the consternation of the shipyard commander, because the congestion below had come to such a state that even minimum efforts to assure the safety of the ship could not be assured.

Under the surgeon's scalpel, the ship sat, surrounded by the vast industrial sprawl of the yard, holes gapping in her superstructure, far from the sea. Today, improvements to weapons systems are frequently matters of installing new software, or changing computer drives. In this era, the installation of new systems required nothing less than the equivalent of open-heart surgery. Whether or not the patient would recover was simply a matter of the dedication of the crew and the hard work of myriad technicians and yard workers coming together as a team. Bit by bit, one rung at a time, The USS *Biddle* came to life. Within her superstructure, a new generation of combat systems had been installed. She was the newest and brightest. Her technicians were thrilled to have at their fingertips the best the United States could put to sea. Below decks, the pumps and boilers had been renewed. The rigors of thousands of miles at sea had been eliminated and she stood, once again, a gray hull ready for duty, with a crew of dedicated sailors to help her reach her maximum capability.

We can only imagine today the sacrifices that were made to bring each system on line, one after another. Finally the day came. The boilers came to life, and new steam coursed through systems that had for too long lain dormant, she would once again take to the sea. The Cold War had nearly a decade to run, and there was work to be done. USS *Biddle*, like her sister ships, would take to the seas again.

The Heart of the Ship

Tom Marfiak

What is the heart of the ship? For many, it is their work space, their computer system, and their weapons that give it the true cutting edge. For the engineers of the Cold War navy, it was and always will be their plant. Filling the ship from just aft of the forward missile magazines to just forward of the after gun mount, the steam plant provided the energy and power that gave life to the ship. First, there were the boilers, each as big as a small house, converting water to steam at great pressure to drive the steam turbines that turned the shafts that drove the ship. Two boilers drove each turbine set. Each turbine converted its great energy through massive reduction gears to drive the shaft spinning each propeller. In the center, the rudder provided, at speeds over seven knots, sufficient thrust to direct the hull in the desired direction. Then there were the turbine generators that provided power to give life to every electrically powered system throughout the ship. In addition, a host of auxiliary systems provided refrigeration, ice cubes, hot water and power to boat davits, guns and anchor windlass systems. No aspect of the ship's life was untouched.

Life for a steam ship started with a Zippo lighter. Once preparations for light off had been completed, and the watch stationed, a torch would be lighted in the fire room far below the combat systems. About four feet long, once flaming, it would be inserted into the boiler front, a valve would be opened, fuel introduced, and a flame ignite. From that first beginning, energy would begin to build, slowly at first, until steam pressure gauges began to reflect the incredible power of 1200 pounds per square inch of steam. At that pressure, an eight thousand ton cruiser could be propelled forward at over thirty knots. And at that pressure, the slightest leak, invisible to the naked eye, could kill a man outright. It was an unforgiving domain.

The men who drove these ships were from all ranks of America. They were talented and resourceful. They were a team, and they pulled together to keep the great ship, their ship, moving through all circumstances, from the sea, and from within. There were over a hundred men in the department—from skilled machinery repairmen who could make a part on a lathe within an evening, to boiler technicians who knew every nuance of the great beast they served. They were often the unsung heroes who made their ships the pride of the fleet.

Their job, their mission, was three fold. First, to provide propulsive power that enabled the ship to move with the battle group. Those needs could surge from moment to moment, but with a twist of the throttle in engineering control, usually the forward engine room, the ship would leap forward with the increased speed of its great screws. Many feet in diameter, cast of bronze, they were fixed in pitch, but not in revolutions. Between the two engine sets, they provided over eighty thousand horsepower to drive the hull through the great seas.

Next, they had the never ending and vital mission of providing electrical power to both ships systems and combat systems. The former required sixty cycle electricity, from the powerful ships service turbo generators, also powered by steam. They literally kept the lights burning, the galley on line, the bridge operating and the plant running. The combat systems required a power of a different sort, at 400 cycles per second. Without that power, the gyros ceased to function and the combat systems went dark. There were no denials or excuses. It was either there or not. You could fight or you could be a target.

Finally, there was water. Each boiler, and there were four if the plant was fully up and running, used a prodigious amount of water every day. Distilling plants, or evaporators, produced water for the plant and for the needs of the crew, over four hundred men. In addition, there had to be water to wash down the ship, clean the aircraft, do the laundry, and cook the food. Water was an important commodity for all steam ships. Each day, the commanding officer would receive a "Fuel and Water Report." If there were a problem with either, the Engineering Officer, or CHENG, for Chief Engineer, had better have an answer, and a plan.

One story will suffice to make this lesson whole. It will be, no doubt, felt by many who served in these great warships over the years. USS *Biddle* was westward bound, south through the Aegean, after a successful visit to the Black Sea and Romania in the year 1979. Homeric seas broke over us as we made our way steadily west through the darkening night. The bow threw spray high on either side. But below, everything was light and bright, the turbines spinning within their bright white casings. I awoke early in the morning, the phone ringing in my ear. The captain said, "We're losing the load. Something is wrong. You had better get down to Main Control."

For an Engineering Officer, there is no more dire circumstance than losing the load. It means that, in short, the lights are going out! There will be no electricity, no plant, no combat system no propulsion. Your ship, the ship for which you are responsible, will be dead in the water, wallowing like a dead whale. Under the circumstances, I was in the forward engine room in seconds, in time to see the steam gauges tumble south, while the all important gauge, indicating inches of vacuum, vital to the efficient transfer of energy, headed to zero.

In a few minutes it became clear what had happened. A casualty to a forward steam plant boiler, and there were two on the line, one forward and one aft, with the plant connected, led the engineering officer of the watch to authorize the cross connection of the plant so that the after boiler could provide steam to both sets of propulsion turbines. That would have been normally a routine operation, except in this instance, a key valve had not been completely shut. It might have been a communications error, or it might have been a case of sheer physical strength—the valves were not small, nor easily accessible. In any case, the order having been given to connect the two plants, the steam from the plant on line went quickly into the plant shutting down. The great gray hull came to a stop in the crashing seas of the Mediterranean.

I found myself in the after engine room, surrounded by steam from the plant as relief valves lifted and battle lanterns glowed. The skipper, Captain Ryan, asked me if we could get her going again and I assured him we could. He went back up the ladder whence he had come, and we began rebuilding the plant, and the steam pressure, by the book. The good news was, of course, that a steam plant does not give up all its energy at once. Provided the boiler valves are closed, as ours were, the pressure remains trapped within the boiler at a fairly high level and will remain there for some time. We still had nearly 1000 psi of steam pressure. What we needed was electricity.

These ships were built with a large diesel generator. Normally used for inport service where power from shore might not be available, they could also function as an emergency generator. That is exactly what we needed now! The first attempt to start the generator failed, so did the second and the third. We were down to our last shot of air pressure. It was do or die. I gathered the senior engineering chiefs around in the after engine room. Between them, they had over a hundred years of experience. "Go back there and start the generator", I said, "it's our last chance." A few minutes later, the diesel growled to life, only this time, it kept going, and growing in strength. Master Chief Greeley and his crew had come through. The solenoid valve that had been knocked out of alignment through the night's battle with the seas had been coaxed into compliance; we had a spark of life.

Two hours later, the plant was up and humming. Breakfast was being served in the galley and in the wardroom, the coffee was hot and stewards were making omelets. The seas outside the bridge windows revealed a streaking gray sea, but the wind had died and there was, in the promise of rising barometer, the promise of a better day to come.

Seakeeping

Tom Marfiak

The single and double ended cruisers of the Cold War shared a singular characteristic. They were great ships in heavy seas. Their bows were built in heavy sections, with massive bulwarks to defend against the ocean's best efforts. They could take a beating. Later, the AEGIS cruisers would bring the same ability to bear and the *Arleigh Burke* destroyers after them, in the same way. These capabilities are built in from the beginning, the product of the ship builder's art.

From the bridge, the bow extended in a graceful arc on either side. The windlasses and anchor chains extending to the bulwarks gave mute evidence of the need to keep the seas, even in shallow waters. The launcher raised its sloping house against the horizon. It was a purposeful presentation. There was no doubt about its ability to take the sea. At the front of the launcher assembly, great doors covered the launching rails, ready to extend their armament onto the launchers.

A quick study of the hull outline, even today, would reveal the genius of the design. Below the main deck, the hull swept away from the knife edge forward to fuller sections aft. Above the main deck, the bulwarks swept back on either side, extending aft to the central superstructure. The effect of this combination was to create a sea kindly hull that deflected the ocean outward as each wave was encountered in its turn. We never saw green water assault the bridge.

Within the bridge, consoles and helm controls were intermingled. During the day, the normal routine of the ship was maintained from the bridge. At night, it became a magic space, illuminated by the radar consoles. The watch went quietly about its business, the great ship lifting beneath. Over the years, countless sailors kept her on course, and never once did she meet the ground, or bring embarrassment to her commander. These were the sailors who met every challenge, in every port, and brought her home safely.

The underwater body of any hull is where the captain's attention often focuses. What are the clearances between screw tips and the bottom? How is the sonar dome going to handle the approach to the pier? For these cruisers, with their large hull mounted sonar domes well forward, just as for their AEGIS cruiser successors, a steep approach to the pier was not a good idea. We came in flat, and let the wind or tugs do the closing. In addition, the after body also played an important part in ship handling. Flat through the stern sections, she could turn swiftly, carving a swath at speed, with the pivot point just aft of the bridge. The art form was how to handle her at slow speeds. With two screws, and one giant barn door of a rudder, she handled well at speeds above seven or eight knots, where sufficient purchase could be generated. Below that speed regime, however, one was committed on the basis of the angle of approach and the wind and currents. A strong backing bell was never amiss.

Seakeeping has, however, many aspects. In the calm seas of the Caribbean in February, the challenge was not great. However, in 1977, returning from the Mediterranean with the USS *Saratoga* Battle Group, the extreme was encountered. Imagine seas as great as entire apartment blocks. Further, imagine that they may be so close together as to deny even the greatest ships the possibility of recovery between onslaughts. That was where USS *Biddle* found itself in the late fall as we progressed, ever so carefully, into a rapidly growing Atlantic storm.

Not long after passing the straits of Gibraltar, the seas began to build. In short order, we were enmeshed in a weather system that nearly brought us to our knees. Destroyers assembled about the carrier disappeared behind the rolling crests. Often, only their masts could be discerned beyond the crests of the following waves. Each moment, we would look to see if they would rise above the next sea. Each moment, our own bows would rise, streaming spray, to ready themselves for the next plunge.

A look at the carrier, so immense in close proximity, revealed the supremacy of the sea. White water cascaded down the side of the great ship, rising over the bows over seven stories above the sea. We would later learn she had lost thirteen life rafts and most of her starboard catwalks. And yet, we all pressed on toward home.

Flight operations were quite out of the question. Each aircraft was tied down with double chains. There would be time enough to get them ready to fly off before the carrier arrived in the region of Norfolk, Virginia, several days later.

Somewhere in this maelstrom of flying spray, I walked out onto the deck behind the bridge. Relatively sheltered there, it was a good place to smoke a pipe and gauge the seas. Looking up, I was startled to see the ECM mast, far above the bridge, swaying in opposite direction to the ship's movement. The weld holding it to its platform had broken, and the mast, with its sensitive antennae, promised to become a projectile, ready to plummet through the deck beneath. Only the most delicate ship driving and the luck of the engineers would keep it aloft through the remainder of the transit. That is how it would play out. We arrived in Norfolk, several days later with the mast still standing and the repairs would begin.

First the shipyard had to build scaffolding to extend to the upper mast platform. Then the delicate job of welding the mast to the deck could begin. But first, the deck had to be reinforced. A portion of the deck would be cut away, and a thicker plate welded in. Then the entire mast would be welded onto the new footing. Welding aluminum at that altitude above deck, in that cold, was not a casual exercise, nor was its inspection. As the engineer, it was my task to inspect the final weld. So, up the mast I went! Of course, every safety feature was available—harness, clamps, straps, the works. It was still a long way up! One click at a time, I mounted the mast. Along side a steady pier, I was thankful we were not still at sea. Finally, arrived at platform level, the weld could be inspected. It was bright and solid. I was prayerfully respectful for the workman who had climbed the same summit to make the repair. That was the way we did business—it would be done, silently, no matter what the sacrifice. Our nation depended on it.

There is so much more to keeping the sea than just the design of the hull. It is the heart of sailors who man it that give it life. It is the skill of the crew that keeps it going that makes it an operational ship, able to meet our country's needs, anywhere, anytime. This is one small story—there are so many others. USS *Biddle* was, and remains in our hearts, as one of those great ships that carried the presence of the United States to the far corners of the world, with grace and power and professionalism. We are proud, still, to have been a part of her.

[*The National Archives and Records Administration was unable to locate Biddle's Command Histories for 1980 and 1981. Reconstruction of Biddle's activities during those years was provided by Hard Chargers who were aboard Biddle. Lieutenant Mike Sasser, Biddle's CIC Officer, recalls some of the events from the early 80s.*]

Clash With Kadaffi

Mike Sasser

1980—1981

I believe we were in the shipyards all of 1980. I reported in March 1980 and the entire crew was living on those stupid barges. During the overhaul period, *Biddle* received upgrades to her weapons and electronics suites. The first production unit of the Vulcan Phalanx was installed, the Harpoon weapons system replaced the 3-inch guns and the famous SHORTSTOP electronic warfare suite was replaced by the "Slick 32" (SLQ-32 V3). We also added an 02 or 03 level between the macks. This was right above the wardroom where the 3-inch batteries used to be. We received the Classic Outboard equipment room which sat on top the Helo hanger. I believe Phalanx and Harpoon completed the visible upgrades. I also remember getting the new life boats. They were contained in a sealed fiberglass shell that was designed to open after sinking to a particular depth. I don't remember what that depth was, but I thought "Only the Navy would think of making a lifeboat sink before being able to use it."

Captain Hollis E. Robertson assumed command of *Biddle* in September of 1980. He enlisted in the Navy in 1951, entered the Naval Academy a year later and graduated from the Academy in 1956. He received a BS in Mechanical Engineering from the Naval Postgraduate School in Monterey, California and co-authored the Naval Engineer's Guide published by the Naval Institute in 1972. He served at sea in *Francis M. Robinson* (DE-220), *Franklin D. Roosevelt* (CVA-42), *Catamount* (LSD-17), *Columbus* (CG-12), *Wainright* (CG-28), and commanded *Charles S. Perry* (DD 697) and *Rich* (DD-820).

The overhaul was accomplished at the Philadelphia Naval Shipyards while our families remained in Norfolk. We worked long hard hours during the week so that those of us who did not have duty on the weekend could leave at noon on Friday and carpool the six hours back to Norfolk. For a while we even employed a beat up old school bus called the Blue Goose to ferry us back and forth, but the old bus succumbed to mechanical problems and quickly became economically unfeasible.

Gliding down the Delaware River during our shakedown cruise we were informed over the 1MC that 30% of the crew had never been to sea and 50% had not been to sea on *Biddle*. We were pretty green. I specifically remember OSCS Tomlinson trying to get his young CIC crew to report a contact to the bridge before we actually passed that contact's closest point of approach. Two hours into the trip he finally did it. He couldn't have been prouder if his wife had just presented him with a brand new son. After over a year of chipping and painting, it was clear that we all needed to be retrained for combat. Gitmo would provide just the services we needed.

There is an interesting story that goes along with the first shooting of the first production Phalanx. We were in the VACAPES after completing overhaul. The Navy didn't have any assets to give us to drag an airborne target, so we had to use civilians. The difference between civilians and Navy pilots is only a matter of days. They gave these civilians a Lear jet and a towed target and sent him to us. We told him what we wanted—for the target to be evaluated as a threat we wanted to have it come at *Biddle* on a collision course at about 50 feet off the deck. First of all the pilot had no intention of flying that low. Second of all he did not want to have his plane anywhere near the ship when we energized the fully auto, closed loop aircraft killing machine. He let out all his cable, which amounted to approximately one mile of cable. He started at about 1000 feet and steadily descended until the target was only a little too high.

He commenced his first run by flying directly over the fan tail. We switched on "R2D2" but by the time the target got there, Phalanx evaluated it a non-threat. We were only doing about 5 knots at the time. It took several attempts before the pilot gained enough confidence to fly directly over the missile launcher. This time the Phalanx jumped, tracked and fired for about two seconds. It scored a direct hit on the turn buckle holding the target to the cable. The second target was sawn in half. It still gives me goose bumps to think that the CIWS is on our side.

With the aid of the training received in Gitmo and at Vieques Island we were an extremely capable and confident force. We were ready to prove ourselves on our next deployment to the Mediterranean. This was scheduled to be a short deployment for us—we would leave in early August 1981, demonstrate our refusal to recognize Muammar Khaddafi's 200-mile territorial limits, tour the Black Sea, see a few ports and return to Norfolk in mid-October.

We were teamed with the *Nimitz* task force. Unfortunately we were not overly confident in the *Nimitz*. She was relatively easy to defeat in the war games we had with her in the Caribbean a few weeks earlier, and seemed to exhibit little pride in her seamanship. Scuttlebutt said that she had failed her ORI, but had to make the deployment anyway since there was no ship to replace her.

One of the ships in our task force had a mechanical failure that delayed our departure date for three days. Therefore the transit to the Med had to be made in six days instead of the usual nine. It wasn't until the third day of the transit that it finally dawned on the *Nimitz* staff that we were passing through time zones at a faster rate than the original plans had called for. Therefore we had to adjust the clocks every night for the rest of the transit. In fact, I believe that we had to adjust it two hours one night.

Nimitz arrived in the Mediterranean Sea, embarked the 6th Fleet battle staff and proceeded to confirm our impressions of her by losing every mock battle she was in. For the next few days we transited with *Nimitz* to the Gulf of Sidra where she was joined by the USS *Forrestal* task force. The *Forrestal* group was on its way out of the Med and played a supporting role over the next few days. The *Forrestal* was equipped with the older F-4 Phantoms while the *Nimitz* carried the F-14 Tomcats from VF-41, the "Black Aces.".

The Operations Officer, Lieutenant Commander Steve Pilnick, recognized the gravity of the situation and decided to brief the entire operations department on the potential ramifications of the upcoming operation. This briefing was so successful that Lieutenant Commander Pilnick was directed to brief a larger audience the next day. He began by comparing the United States government with the Soviet Union government. Even though our two nations were at odds and very antagonistic with each other, they were both very stable governments and each knew just how far he could push the other. Neither was going to do anything to jeopardize the delicate balance of power between them. He then said, "I said all that to say this. That is not the situation we have with Libya and its government. They have aircraft and pilots, very quiet submarines, and missile bearing patrol boats they don't mind sacrificing for their unstable leader." He simply reminded us to remain on our toes and do our jobs.

The missile exercise was scheduled for August 18th and 19th. The actual missile exercise required four ships. One ship launched the target drones and the other three ships would take turns shooting special missiles at the drone. These missiles were fitted with special telemetry packages in place of the warhead. The telemetry data would be captured by the firing ship and record data about the missile intercept. This would give detailed analysis of the performance of the entire Terrier missile system. The goal was not to hit the drone, but to determine if the drone would have been hit if an actual warshot version of the missile had been fired. That way the drone could be recovered and used again. Since we were one of the three missilex ships, we had two telemetry birds loaded and ready to fire at a moment's notice.

August 18th was a very frustrating day. From dawn the Libyans began flying fighter aircraft toward our positions. It was clear that they were looking for a carrier but they never did find her. The *Nimitz* launched E-2C Hawkeyes as early warning aircraft and to control the F-14s being launched. The orders for the F-14 pilots were to intercept the Libyan aircraft and maintain a firing position on them. The F-14s were not allowed to shoot unless they were fired upon. The Libyan fighter pilots had no intention of letting the F-14s remain in a firing position on them, so there was a lot of high G, air combat maneuvering going on amongst all the pilots. Add to this the inability of the Libyans to find their primary target, and it is easy to see how fuses can become very short.

The day was also frustrating for the missilex ships. The Libyans were continually fouling the missile range thereby preventing the shooting of any missiles. The only good news is that we were inside the Gulf of Sidra and demonstrating freedom of the seas. As night fell, the Libyan sorties quit and the missilex was suspended until daylight. However we all continued to read the latest intelligence reports in order to keep track of the other Libyan threats. Everything remained calm until daylight.

August 19th began pretty much as the day before. Just after daybreak, more Libyans were in the air along with the Hawkeyes and F-14s. The aircraft launched by *Nimitz* were all perfect. I remember one lost a backup radio just after leaving the cat and he was ordered to turn back. One of the F-14s was able to pick up radar contacts from its own radar at four times the expected range. The *Nimitz* made sure they had nothing but the best in the air.

As the CIC Officer I walked into Combat shortly after 0700. The OPS Officer had already assumed the duties as the Tactical Action Officer (TAO). I occupied the NTDS console as the Ships Weapons Coordinator (SWC). We were watching the screens and listening to the background noise chatter when we heard those chilling words for the first time. "Two fitters has (sic) fired at my leader." Then four seconds later came, "…this is 102, we've been fired on." The next several seconds were a blur. The TAO called the Captain then leaned over to me and said, "Well, I guess we should go to GQ." It is amazing what happens to your attitude when you've been briefed on the threat, lived through one tense day, and then hear the general quarters alarm go off without the "This is a drill" preamble. Immediately the telemetry missiles were struck below and warshots were in place and ready on the rails. We were on our toes and alert for all threats.

The entire transcript follows:

00:03	102	Going to [garbled] right now, I'll stay in[garbled]scan.
00:07	Bare Ace (Air Intercept Controller)	And 102 [garbled] 226 36
00:15	102	Twenty miles for 102. Twenty thousand feet.
00:19	Bare Ace	225 at 33 102.
00:24	Bare Ace	And what's your [garbled something about the contact]?
00:27	102	102's got one 214 16 miles out, that's all I've got.
00:31	102	He appears to be turning a little bit left giving us a left aspect. I'm in single target track.
00:38	102	14 miles 21,000.
00:44	Bare Ace	113 say your heading.
00:48	113	113s heading 070
00:54	102	10 miles
00:54	102	102. The bogeys got us on his nose now 8 miles.
01:03	102	We're at altitude, twenty thousand feet 6 miles.
01:06	Bare Ace	103, 113 your vector 100.
01:25	Bare Ace	103 state.
01:31	107	Two fitters has shot at my leader.
01:35	102	[garbled]…this is 102, we've been fire on.
01:46	Bare Ace	And 102.
01:50	Bare Ace	OK copy.
01:51	unknown	Did you copy that Bare Ace?
01:52	Bare Ace	Negative, what did one of them say?
01:54	102, 107	

02:03	unknown	Bare Ace, did you just copy 103?
02:05	Bare Ace	That's negative.
02:05	unknown	Because they said they've just been fired upon, that's what they transmitted.
02:15	Bare Ace	103 confirm you've been shot at, over.
02:18	unknown relay	[garbled]confirm you've been shot at.
02:21	102 amongst interference	Affirmative.[garbled] shot one of them down.
02:26	unknown relay	Did you shoot one of them down?
02:29	102	It was a clean target.
02:34	107	[garbled]Want me shoot my guy down?
02:35	102	That's affirm, shoot him…shoot him down.
02:45	Bare Ace	205, 223 vector inbound at this time.
02:49	223	223 inbound
02:53	107	Fox 2 kill from music. Fox 2 kill.
02:56	102	[name] did you get him?
02:58	107	Yes sir, I did kill him.[garbled several seconds]
03:05	107	Fox 2 kill. His chute is not deploying. He is falling free.
03:08	102	OK, roger that.
03:11	Bare Ace	106 Reset CAP 5. 106, 110 reset cap 5.
03:14	107	[garbled]123 DME on the 180. And my state ten two, ten two.
03:27	102	OK I'm nine five.
03:29	Nimitz	102 107, you are clear to defend yourself.
03:31	Bare Ace	102 107, you are clear to defend yourself. Pass from the ship.
03:35	102	And this is 102 107, ah two enemy kills.
03:40	Bare Ace	Say again.
03:41	102	Two enemy kills. Two MIG-23s killed.
03:45	unknown relay	Two MIG-23s. You copy Bare Ace?
03:48	Bare Ace	Roger.[garbled]

03:52	*107*	Mine was a Fitter, a Fitter.
03:59	*Bare Ace*	102 107 You copy? That's vector north.
04:41	*Bare Ace*	107, Bare Ace.
04:44	*102*	This is 102 go ahead.
04:47	*Bare Ace*	Were one or two hit?
04:55	*102*	102 and 107 are fine. We're both headed north. And there are two…
04:58	*Bare Ace*	Roger that. And confirm you've got two MIG-23 kills.
05:03	*102*	OK one was a Fitter and they're probably both Fitters. And there are two kills.
05:07	*unknown relay*	Bare Ace you copy? There are two kills. Either Fitters or Floggers.

The entire engagement from the Libyans pulling the trigger until pulling their rip cord took less than one and one-half minutes. Another one and one-half minutes later the *Nimitz* (presumably the sixth fleet battle staff) radioed that the two F-14 pilots were "Clear to defend yourself." The Libyans never had a chance. They took a bad shot by shooting head on with a heat seeking missile, they had much inferior aircraft, and they just happened to pick on the VF-41 Squadron Commander. The pilots I felt the most sorry for were the F-14 pilots ordered to cover the next Libyan flight coming out. They did not have permission to fire unless they were fired upon. As it happens, no more shots were fired. This remarkable incident was the first Navy air combat confrontation since the Vietnam War and the first for the F-14A Tomcat and *Biddle* was there! Again we went to bed with visions of intelligence reports dancing in our heads.

Next on the agenda was a trip to the Black Sea. We entered the Black Sea late in August 1981 after a port call in Istanbul. While in Istanbul we had invited an important leader in the Turkish government to visit the ship and have lunch with us. Shortly before he arrived someone realized that we were about to feed a Moslem man a meal with ham. The menu was quickly switched to spaghetti. Here is a hint. If you want to impress sailors wearing dress whites and about to go through the inspection of their lives, do NOT feed them spaghetti. I was assigned to the quarterdeck watch, so I just skipped lunch all together. Choker whites and spaghetti do not mix.

Repairing your ship is a way of life in the Navy. The *Biddle* was no different. In early October 1981 we pulled into Sardinia where we were able to moor next to a tender. We had several repairs to be attended to and used that time for a liberty call as well. It turned out to be a nice enough place though not very exciting until October 6th. That was the day Egyptian President Anwar Sadat was assassinated. We were immediately and indefinitely extended in the Med. Every ship was ordered to get underway. This was especially hard for us since some vital pieces of equipment lay in pieces in the bowels of the tender beside us. We had to wait two to three days to be back into operation. If memory serves me correctly, we fouled the anchor while we were hauling it in. We could not clear it, and since every ship in the Med was off the coast of Egypt (save one), we had no choice but to sever the chain and go…and go we did.

As hard and uncertain as the run-in with Khaddafi was, this was as bad or even worse. We already had our ticket punched and were anxious to go home, but now here we were headed the wrong direction with no relief in sight. Not only that but if the region ignited into war, who knows when we would see home again? At least in Libya, we held our destiny in our own hands. That was no longer the case. We had to sit still and allow the politicians to work their little games. History tells us that little, if anything important erupted at that time. The extension turned out to be a little over one month. We all made it home and life went on for everyone but President Sadat.

Biddle Middle Age

James Treadway

1982

Biddle celebrated her fifteenth birthday by getting underway on 21 January for COMPTUEX 2-82 in the Caribbean OPAREA. During the exercise she fired two SM-1 (ER) missiles then joined USS *Arkansas* as safety observer for *Arkansas'* shock tests in the Key West OPAREA. *Biddle* returned from her one month deployment on 21 February then offloaded ammunition on 1 March in preparation for an upcoming Selected Restrictive Availability (SRA) in Norfolk. Unfortunately, *Biddle* did not successfully pass her Operational Propulsion Plant Exam (OPPE) while operating in the VACAPES area from 10 to 12 March.

Biddle's SRA began 15 March at Metro Machine Corporation, Norfolk. During the SRA, training, a 3M inspection, Nuclear Weapons Assist Inspection (NWAI), and a major engineering repair were accomplished. Following Sea Trials from 1 to 2 May, *Biddle* loaded ammunition at Yorktown then got underway for Engineering Mobile Training Team Assist operations. Upon return to Norfolk, the vigorous pace continued with a Defense Nuclear Surety Inspection/Nuclear Technical Proficiency Inspection (DNSI/NTPI), OPPE Re-exam, Ordinance Systems Assist Team (ORDSAT), and pre Overseas Movement (POM) preparation through 28 May.

With COMDESRON TWENTY-TWO and staff embarked, *Biddle* got underway for another Mediterranean deployment on 8 June. During transit, *Biddle* and *Aylwin* conducted independent operations that probed the Soviet Strategic Ocean Surveillance System (SSOSS). *Biddle* anchored at Naples on 21 June for INCHOP support briefings aboard Independence.

The first item on *Biddle's* agenda was participation in the NATO exercise DAILY DOUBLE 82. Following the exercise, *Biddle* enjoyed a week of upkeep in Naples, and then departed on 9 July for underway operations in the Tyrrhenian Sea, Central Mediterranean, Eastern Med/PIRAZ, Ionian Sea, Aegean Sea, and Eastern Med Operations in support of USMC units in Lebanon.

Accompanied by *Estocin* (FFG-15), *Biddle* entered the Black Sea for a two day diplomatic visit to the port of Eregli, Turkey. Both ships continued their Black Sea operations until anchored at Istanbul on 5 August. The remainder of August found *Biddle* engaged as an escort for PLO refugees enroute from Beruit to Tunis, Tunisia, aboard the Cypriot merchant vessel Sol Phryne. Following completion of her escort duties, *Biddle* headed north to Gaeta, Italy, for two weeks of upkeep.

While in Gaeta, Captain Robertson was relieved by Captain Alvaro R. Gomez. Captain Gomez, a native of Hempstead, New York, had graduated from St. John's University and obtained a Master of Science from George Washington University. Commissioned in 1959, Captain Gomez served in *Saratoga* (CVA-60), *Eunice* (PCE-846), *Dahlgren* (DLG-12), *Pocono* (LCC-16), *Josephus Daniels* (DLG-27), *Damato* (DD-871), and *Richard L. Page* (FFG-5).

After departing Gaeta, *Biddle* conducted exercises with Italian Naval Units in the Adriatic Sea then made her second diplomatic port visit of the cruise at Rijeka, Yugoslavia. *Biddle* briefly joined NATO forces for Display Determination 82 in the Tyrrhenian Sea on 20 September before being diverted to Lebanon. The last week of September and all of October saw *Biddle* conducting numerous exercises over the Eastern and Central portions of the Mediterranean. *Biddle* participated in the SINKEX of the ex-USS *Lardner* then made a port visit to Athens, Greece, from 25 to 30 October. Next, *Biddle* transited to the western Mediterranean and the Gulf of Sidra to join *Nimitz* and her escorts for "Freedom of Navigation Ops." *Biddle* returned one last time to the eastern Med for turnover on 5 December then set a westerly course with USS *Independence* to antagonize Mr. Kadaffi once again, and then embark COMDESRON TWO at Rota, Spain.

The transit to Norfolk was demanding. *Biddle's* 1982 Command History stated that "Enroute CONUS, BIDDLE fired two successful missile shots using SM-1 (ER) missiles during an "Open Ocean MISSILE-EX." Numerous training evolutions covering every facet of shipboard life were conducted during transit operations. Before BIDDLE returned to Norfolk she successfully completed all competitive exercises in all warfare areas with the exception of one AAW gunshot and a Naval gunfire support exercise. BIDDLE returned to homeport (Norfolk) on 22 December, remaining there through 31 December."

YNC Michael Brodeur, who was aboard *Biddle* for the 82 Med deployment, fondly recalled many events of the cruise.

> I served on the *Biddle* from June 82 to June 84. We participated in the PLO evacuation but I don't recall a lot of details. We visited a lot of ports and I

took advantage of the tours that were available while in Naples, Rome, Bologna, and Florence as well as going to Hamburg, Munich (the Hoffbrauhaus), and the Dachau concentration camp.

I visited two of the three castles built by Ludwig the II, one of which is replicated in Disneyland. In Turkey (Istanbul) it was the Mosque and the bazaar shops, and a few CPO's sat high atop the roof of the Hilton hotel overlooking the Black Sea and *Biddle* at anchor. We walked the streets of Istanbul and enjoyed mingling with the Turkish people.

When we visited Yugoslavia, I took a tour of the National forest. At our lunch stop, which was a hotel, our chaplain was walking around and encountered a group of French tourists. Since I speak French he called me over to act as an interpreter because the 80 senior citizens from France had a message for America.

They told me that they were very grateful to the U.S. for coming to their aid during the war. The message went something like this: "Please tell your men that they look very sharp in their uniform. Also we want Americans to know that we will never forget what they did for us; we were prisoners in our own country and the Americans liberated us; for that we will forever be grateful. The anti American comments you hear from France come from a young generation that wasn't around during the war. If you ever visit France, come to the North where we are from and we will show you our appreciation."

I was surrounded a bus load of tourists from France and they all wanted to say something. They were so happy that they finally found someone who spoke their language and could receive and pass along their gratitude. I was very touched along with my shipmates who were there to hear me relay their message.

Another event that I call coincidence occurred on the *Biddle*. When I reported aboard in 1982, the Commanding Officer came to visit the Chief's Mess and I thought he looked familiar. After a short conversation we got back to 18 years earlier when Hollis Robertson, then an ensign, was the Communications Officer aboard the USS *Catamount* (LSD-17), our first ship. Now he was a Captain and the CO of the ship on which I was to retire in 1984. He was relieved by Captain Alvaro Gomez shortly after I reported aboard and was transferred to CINCLANTFLT in Norfolk. Since *Biddle* was in port in 1984, I asked Captain Robertson to preside at my retirement ceremony which he graciously agreed to do. How weird is it that our career path crossed 18 years apart and what are the odds?

1983

Biddle began 1983 in a leave and upkeep status that lasted until 16 January. For the remainder of January and all of February, *Biddle* prepared for her INSURV inspection scheduled for 14 to 18 March. Following the successful completion of INSURV, attention turned to preparing for underway operations with *Saratoga*

(CV-60) in the Caribbean OPAREA. *Biddle* got underway on 27 April for the operating area where she made a short refueling stop at Roosevelt Roads, Puerto Rico, and then qualified for Naval Gunfire Support at Vieques Island on 4 and 5 May. After a very short one day port call to St. Thomas on 6 May, *Biddle* operated with Saratoga for two weeks then returned to Norfolk on 19 May.

With only a week of preparation *Biddle* stood out of Norfolk on 26 May with COMDESRON 32 embarked for Exercise UNITED EFFORT/OCEAN SAFARI 83 and a North Atlantic deployment. The three week exercise with ships from the NATO nations of the United States, France, Great Britain, Portugal, and the Netherlands, concluded with a five day port call to Aarhus, Denmark, on the east coast of the Danish peninsula. Aurhus was settled many centuries ago by the Vikings, the original Hard Chargers! Now rested and relaxed, *Biddle* participated in BALTOP 83, an AAW exercise with air wings from West Germany, England, and Denmark. While underway off the coasts of the Soviet Union, East Germany, and Poland, *Biddle* sighted numerous Russian and WARSAW Pact vessels.

Biddle celebrated the 4th of July holiday and our nation's 207th birthday during a five day visit to the port of Kiel, Germany, where appreciative West Germans held a reception for *Biddle* crewmembers. Full of good will, German food, and beer, *Biddle* sailors got underway and immediately made her way for a three day visit to Leith, the port city of Edinburgh, Scotland. A *Biddle* press release stated that "Known to many as the Athens of the North, Scotland's capital city of Edinburgh boasts excellent sights, shopping, and entertainment. Special attention is taken to acquaint visitors with Scottish history and Edinburgh is filled with monuments, memorials, and museums. The city's most famous landmark is the spectacular Edinburgh Castle which overlooks the Gardens of Princess Street, and indeed the whole city."

"Crewmembers once again took advantage of offered tours. This time to the Scottish Highlands, the rugged mountainous are so well known for its lochs, castles and Highland music. The tours also included a trip to the city of Stirling and a stop at the Stirling Castle which dates back to the 16th century and was a favorite residence of Mary, Queen of Scots."

Biddle departed Leith on 12 July for her last NATO exercise, the Joint Maritime Course (JMC 832). Upon conclusion of the ten day exercise, *Biddle* returned to Leith for four days then departed for Norfolk on 27 July with kilts, Tartan and woolen sweaters safely stored, and many of the crew sporting a Scottish brogue.

Biddle's demanding pace continued for the remainder of the year. Only three weeks after returning from her North Atlantic deployment, *Biddle* was underway for an ASROC Quality Assurance Systems Test (QAST) in August, then a port call in New York City over the Labor Day weekend, and operations with USS *Jacksonville* (SSN-699) in the Narragansett OPAREA during September. In late September, *Biddle*, in competition with other Atlantic Fleet conventionally powered cruisers, learned that she had been awarded the Battle Efficiency award *and* the Arleigh Burke Fleet Trophy for the most improved unit in the Atlantic Fleet in Battle Readiness.

While underway in the VACAPES area from 3 to 5 October, *Biddle*, as reported in her Command History, "completed over 65% of the Selexes for the current competitive cycle (1984), with excellent to outstanding grades in all exercises." *Biddle* offloaded weapons at Yorktown from 11 to 13 October then commenced Selected Restricted Availability (SRA) at Norfolk Shipbuilding for the remainder of the year.

Biddle's 1983 Command History began with the statement, "The year 1983 was a year of superior achievement for USS *Biddle*." In support of the statement, three and a half pages of documentation followed, which is summarized below.

Biddle was awarded the following Department Excellence Awards:

Navigation and Deck Seamanship

Mobility (Propulsion) "RED E"

Damage Control "RED DC"

Electronic Warfare

Command Control and Communication "C"

Supply "BLUE E"

Anti Surface Warfare (ASUW)

Anti Submarine Warfare (ASW)

Anti Air Warfare (AAW)

Other highlights were:

All but two scores in all categories of SURFLANT Battle Efficiency were near 100.

All scores on her SMI were outstanding or excellent.

Completed all competitive exercises with an average grade of 96.38.

Completed Atlantic Fleet NGFS with an average grade of 82.25.

Completed OPPE, CMS, SMI, 3M, and NTPI inspections with high marks.

Awarded the Navy Expeditionary Medal for services while deployed to Sixth Fleet.

Selected as COMCRUDESGRU EIGHT nominee for the NEY award.

Biddle sailor nominated as COMCRUDESGRU EIGHT Sailor of the Year.

3M Inspection grade was highest CRUDES grade.

Nominated by COMCRUDESGRU EIGHT for SECNAV Energy Conservation Award.

Numerous accolades and commendations from various admirals for *Biddle's* superior performance in several areas.

The most prestigious awards were described on the last page:
As a result of the Battle Efficiency Competition, USS *Biddle* (CG-34) was awarded the Battle Efficiency "E" for conventional cruisers in the Atlantic Fleet. The Battle "E" symbolizes the peak of combat readiness and is a tribute to the hard charging crew of the world's finest cruiser.

Arleigh Burke Fleet Trophy

Background. During more than 38 years of active service in the United States Navy, Admiral Arleigh A. Burke, USN, distinguished himself in many ways. The name Arleigh Burke has come to symbolize the very element of sea power. He made vital contributions toward strengthening our Navy; these include the improvement of battle efficiency in war and peace, the development of new concepts and weapons systems and, on the human side, emphasis on naval leadership. It is fitting that the supreme dedication of this outstanding officer, to the Navy he served so well, be recognized by the establishment of a fleet award bearing his name, and that it pertains to battle efficiency.

In December 1983, USS *Biddle* (CG 34) was awarded the Arleigh Burke Fleet Trophy.

1984

Following completion of her Selected Restricted Availability, *Biddle* successfully completed required Sea Trials and then earned a grade of Outstanding on her Combat Systems Readiness Review (CSRR). On 7 February, with COMCRUDESGRU TWELVE embarked, *Biddle* participated in READINESS EXERCISE (READEX 1-84), which included firing a SM-1 (ER) missile, battle-group operations, gunfire support, anti-aircraft warfare, and anti-submarine warfare training. *Biddle* returned to homeport on 25 February and immediately began Preparations for Overseas Movement (POM).

Biddle departed Norfolk on 2 April and arrived with other units of the *Saratoga* Battle Group in Naples, Italy, on 14 April. *Biddle* departed Naples four days later to operate with amphibious units off the coast of Lebanon. While underway, *Biddle* received the 1983 Arleigh Burke Fleet Trophy from Vice Admiral Edward S. Briggs, Commander Naval Surface Force U.S. Atlantic Fleet.

Relieved of her duties off Lebanon, for which *Biddle* was awarded the Armed Forces Expeditionary Medal, *Biddle* proceeded to Toulon, France, for her first port visit in 40 days. After ten days of fine French food and wine, *Biddle* stood out for two days then anchored of Toulon for a change of command ceremony in which Captain Joseph T. Hock relieved Captain Alvaro R. Gomez as Commanding Officer.

Captain Hock, a native of New York City, enlisted in the Naval Reserve in August 1954. He graduated from St. John's University and was commissioned an Ensign in June 1959. His first assignment was in *Steinaker* (DDR-863) as head the Weapons Department. After earning a M.A. in history at the University of Rochester, Captain Hock joined the precommissioning crew of *Bradley* (DE-1041) as Weapons Officer, which was followed by an assignment as Officer-in-Charge of USS *A.T. Harris* (DE-447). After a year of study at the School of International Service, American University, he received orders to the Republic of Vietnam as Commander "Operation Searchturn." Captain Hock was Executive Officer of USS *Manley* (DD-940) and he commanded *Truett* (FF-1095).

With Vice Admiral E.H. Martin, Commander Sixth Fleet embarked, *Biddle* sailed for the Dardenelles and Bophorus Straits, arriving in Constanta, Romania, on June 25 for a four day visit. This was *Biddle's* fourth call to the Black Sea and her second to Constanta, Romania's major port and second largest city. July 4 found *Biddle* enjoying barbeque in the Black Sea, surrounded by the formidable Soviet Union and other East Bloc nations.

The months of July, August, and September were extremely busy for *Biddle*. Following her departure from the Black Sea, *Biddle* enjoyed two weeks in Marseille, France; operated with the *Saratoga* Battle Group in the Central Mediterranean; called on warm and sunny Valencia, Spain; anchored off St. Tropez, France, for eleven days; enjoyed tender availability in Marseilles for two weeks; visited the cities of Rijeka, Yugoslavia, and Naples, Italy; and participated in DISPLAY DETERMINATION 84. This exercise, which was held in the Ligurian, Tyrrhenian and Aegean Seas, "Involved the air, amphibious, land and naval forces of the Southern Region nations of NATO and was designed to enhance their effectiveness, readiness, coordination and interoperability," according to *Biddle's* 1984 Command History.

To conclude her deployment, *Biddle* disembarked SIXTH Fleet Staff at Gaeta, then spent three days at Gibraltar to turnover to inchopping forces. *Biddle* transited the Atlantic from 24 October to 2 November and remained in her homeport for the remainder of the year. During that time she benefited from a leave and upkeep status, participated in a Battleforce Inport Training (BFIT), as well as completing a Supply Management Inspection (SMI) and Shore Intermediate Maintenance Activities (SIMA).

1985

January commenced in a leave and upkeep status which was followed by an Intermediate Maintenance Availability, numerous short training periods in the Virginia Capes area, weapons transfer at Yorktown, Senior Officer Steam Machinery Refresher Course (SOSMRC), and Battle Force Inport Training (BFIT). During the period of 29 to 30 April, *Biddle* successfully completed her OPPE then immediately participated in Underway Exercise Solid Shield 85.

In June, *Biddle* began a multi-phase series of pre-deployment work-ups that would prepare her for another deployment in October to the Mediterranean. The work-ups included participation in COMPTUEX 3-85, NGFS qualifications, another IMAV, ammunition onload, READEX 3-85, and POM. Concurrent with the demanding work-up schedule, *Biddle* also underwent a Pre-overhaul Test and Inspection in preparation for her regular overhaul scheduled for the fourth quarter of 1986.

Biddle's exercises, inspections and qualifications eventually became history and she shoved off on 4 October with the *Coral Sea* Battle Group. *Biddle* participated in Exercise DISPLAY DETERMINATION 85 in the Aegean Sea then visited Naples and Trieste, Italy, before detaching from the Coral Sea Battle Group to join the *Saratoga* Battle Group in the Eastern Mediterranean. After transiting the

Suez Canal on 15 November, *Biddle* entered the Red Sea then steamed to her AAW Picket Station in the North Arabian Sea where she remained until 1 December. *Biddle* participated in Surface Warfare Training Week off the coast of the Republic of Oman, and then proceeded to the Indian Ocean for a five day visit to the port in Diego Garcia. *Biddle* then joined the *Saratoga* Battle Group in the Indian Ocean and Strait of Malacca for operations, which was followed by a Christmas holiday visit to Penang, Malaysia. *Biddle* stood out of Penang on 29 December and celebrated a new year while underway to Diego Garcia.

1986

Biddle returned to Diego Garcia on 4 January but departed on short notice the next day to rejoin the Sixth Fleet off the coast of Libya. Completing her first round of duty off the coast of Libya, *Biddle* visited Gaeta, Italy, for five days then returned to Libya for the second round. The third round of operations was preceded by a visit to Trieste, Italy, operations in the Central Mediterranean with the Coral Sea Battle Group, and a ten day port visit and upkeep period in Naples. Next, *Biddle* embarked COMDESRON 32 in Catania, Sicily, and then transited the Tyrhennian and Alboran basins for a call to Benidorm, Spain. *Biddle* operated twice more near Libya during the deployment, between 12 and 21 April and 26 April to 4 May, before departing Gibraltar, Spain, on 10 May, for the Atlantic transit to Norfolk.

On 15 June, Captain Benjamin E. Allen relieved Captain Hock and became *Biddle's* twelfth commanding officer. Captain Benjamin was born in Washington, North Carolina and graduated from the U.S. Naval Academy in 1961. He qualified as a Naval Aviator in November 1962 and flew from *Forrestal* (CV-59) with Carrier Air Wing Eight. Captain Allen transferred to the surface navy in September 1965 and served in *Boston* (CG-1) as Electronics Material Officer, Combat Information Officer, and Senior Air Intercept Controller. He also served in *Barry* (DD-933) and *Horne* (CG-30), Executive Officer of *Halsey* (CG-23), and Commanding Officer of *Waddell* (DDG-24).

After unloading weapons at Yorktown in late June, *Biddle* returned to Norfolk for final preparations for her scheduled eleven-month Regular Overhaul at Philadelphia Naval Shipyard (PNSY). *Biddle* arrived at PNSY on 15 July, changer her homeport to Philadelphia, and commenced her overhaul on 16 July.

A Grand Old Lady Gets NTU

James Treadway

Biddle was the first combatant to receive the New Threat Upgrade (NTU) in its production configuration. Initiated in 1975 and in full scale development in 1977, NTU was designed to substantially improve AAW capabilities of the older Terrier and Tarter ships with extensive sensor and weapon system upgrades. In company with NTU installation, the Naval Tactical Data System was massively upgraded and given the new name "Advanced Combat Direction System." Thirty one ships were to receive the upgrade.

NTU was designed to take advantage of the new Standard Missile—2 (SM-2) Block II surface-to-air missile, which provided increased range, speed and maneuverability over its predecessors. Terrier ships in the CG-16 and CG-26 classes received the extended range (ER) version that boasted a new rocket motor, booster, and "front-end" improvements. The published range of the Block II SM-2 (ER) was 65 to 100 nautical miles while modern Block IV extended range missiles have an incredible range of 100 to 200 nautical miles.

The major sensor improvement was the replacement of the ITT Gilfillan AN/SPS-48C with the "E" model. Except for the antenna, which weighed 1,700 pounds more, the SPS-48E equipment cabinets fit in the same space as its predecessor, simplifying installation. The SPS-48E also had far fewer components, 126,000 versus 280,000, which increased reliability while enhancing maintainability.

The radar contained critical circuit redundancies, corrosion protection, and a novel Built-In Test (BIT) capability that automatically performed routine system testing and remote testing. These features reduced both the mean-time-between-failures (MTBF) rate and manpower requirements. Only two maintenance technicians were required to keep the system fully operational. Performance enhancements included improved resistance to jamming and ECM, better detection of smaller targets and targets on the horizon, high-angle tracking, and it could accept and execute commands from external air defense or shipboard combat systems.

The other major sensor improvement was the replacement of the venerable AN/SPS-40 radar with the SPS-49(V)5 "2-D" radar. The SPS-49(V)5 has automatic target detection capability as well as anti-jamming features, and clutter suppression. The SPS-48E and SPS-49(V) operate on different frequencies and, understandably, have different ECM resistances.

Both air search radars acted as inputs to the Norden AN/SYS-2 integrated automatic target detection and tracking system. The computer-based AN/SYS-2 correlated tracks from both radars into a single, unduplicated, highly accurate track picture, and then supplied that information to the Combat Direction System (CDS).

Research on the Combat Direction System turned up little useful information so I turned to David Johnson for an explanation.

> NTDS and WDS MK 11 were together the primitive Combat Direction System, though not so characterized at first. During the update period when the Advanced Combat Direction System (ACDS) was developed for large-deck ships, NTDS lost its uniqueness and was assimilated into the ACDS. ACDS also provide weapons direction/control suitable for the few weapons then on carriers.
>
> The major redefinition for surface combatants was the UYK-7 suites on the new nuclear-powered Virginia class (DLGN-38 then CGN-38 class). The CDS was defined to include the NTDS variant referred to as the Command and Control Systems and the Weapons Direction/Control System. When AEGIS came along, still running UYK-7 computers, the CDS Mk 1 Mod 0 included the Command and Decision (C&D) Mk 1 Mod 0 and the Weapon Control System (WCS) Mk1 Mod 0. WCS ran in its own computer, as did the SPY-1 Radar program. All computers were integrated, of course.
>
> Today, however, the proliferation of embedded processors in almost every cabinet of every system makes the latest Combat Systems a total integration of functions with distributed processing and backup processors for self-management of casualty reconfigurations. Plus, some major weapon systems are still basically self-contained with embedded processors that support integration with the other ship systems.
>
> To add to the confusion, engine rooms and damage control facilities are computerized and on some ships allow the engineering watch to determine the state of Combat System systems. All this in the interest of reducing manning, increasing automation, and creating a more effective war-fighting ship with less requirements for man-machine interfaces (we called them operators.) So, definitions are tricky and don't always convey more that the tip of the iceberg, as it were.

Michael Daugherty describes the complex New Threat Upgrade installation:

The NTDS system as a whole was completely removed from the ship and replaced with new computer systems and display systems which were the basis for CDS. The AN/USQ-20 computer system, which was comprised of three Univac 642B computers, two Univac 1218 computers and one ECMU (External Core Memory Unit) were replaced with one AN/UYK-43 computer. I believe that the acronym for the new computer system was AN/SYQ-20. (You may have to verify that.)

There was actually a reserved space next to the AN/UYK-43 and the cabling already installed for a second AN/UYK-43 computer. The operating system was now loaded from a hard disk system with the RD-358 tape unit as the backup to the hard disk. This was a huge time saver with the ever expanding lines of code for the operating system for CDS.

The processing power of the AN/UYK-43 by itself far exceeded the AN/UYK-7 computer systems in production on many of the AEGIS platforms. This single computer allowed our CDS system to track over 500 discreet targets. This capability was a two edged sword, in that our Track Supervisor had to be careful when Link 11 was in NCS mode, as we could easily overload other NTDS systems. I remember that filters would be utilized to prevent track overload. The SYA-4 Display set was replaced with the UYQ-21.

The entire layout of CIC was changed to accommodate the new system. Numerous monitors hanging from the overhead in CIC and other tactical locations (total of 21 monitors I believe) displayed tactical information for the Commanding Officer and/or Tactical Affairs Officer. The bridge even had two monitors tied into CDS to give a more detailed picture of the surface picture to the OOD. Most of the new equipment had the BIT to provide for easy troubleshooting, however we did retain some of the older equipment such as the KCMX, DACs, teletypes for Link 14, that we would have to rely on our never forgotten troubleshooting techniques and use voltmeters along with o-scopes.

1987

Well into her overhaul on 1 January, *Biddle* undocked on 31 January but the crew did not return to the ship until 7 April. Following a Light-off Examination in late June, Dock Trials and a Fast Cruise in early July, and a pair of Sea Trials in mid-July and early August, *Biddle* returned to her original homeport of Norfolk on 5 August. During August *Biddle* entered an Intermediate Maintenance Availability then completed a Training Readiness Evaluation. Following loading weapons in early September, *Biddle* spent most of September and October in the VACAPES area testing the New Threat Upgrade and preparing for inspections and Refresher Training.

Biddle departed Norfolk on 28 October for six weeks of Refresher Training in Guantanamo Bay which she successfully completed on 12 December. She passed an Operational Propulsion Plant Examination on 15 December then returned to Norfolk on 18 December and began a holiday leave and upkeep period until the end of the year.

1988

The year began quietly for *Biddle* with half of the crew still enjoying the holidays with family and friends. By 13 January, an invigorated crew had completed preparations for a demanding series of underway test periods that would last until another Mediterranean deployment in August. The first series of tests were conducted exclusively in the VACAPES area. *Biddle*'s 1988 Command History stated that "Throughout the rest of January, February and March, BIDDLE would spend a week or two inport and a week or two underway in the local operating area testing radars, computers, computer programs, and missile systems as well as providing valuable training for both operator and maintenance personnel."

The intense training effort stepped up a notch on 1 April when *Biddle* departed Norfolk for a month of combat system tests and missile, gun, and ASW weapons exercises in the Puerto Rican Operating Area. Immediately upon arrival in the operating area, *Biddle* engaged multiple targets with the new long range SM-2 (ER) missile. Missile and combat systems tests continued for the next month with only two short periods in port.

Michael Daugherty was aboard *Biddle* during the tests and recalls some very interesting facts: "During the testing of the NTU capabilities in the Roosevelt Rhodes, Puerto Rico firing range, numerous civilian engineers and Navy personnel utilized sophisticated spectrum analyzers to monitor the jamming being performed by Air Force NKC-135 and Navy EA-6B aircraft. The 48-E and 49 radars were able to process and find holes in the jamming and locate aircraft flying in as simulated hostiles, which allowed CDS to process the targets and successfully engage. *Biddle* also performed a Remote Track Launch On Seach (RTLOS) test with the USS *Valley Forge*. *Valley Forge* tracked and processed the data, and *Biddle* in EMCON A, was in Receive Only mode on Link 11. We fired an SM-2 ER at a QF-4 target aircraft and destroyed the target at over 100 miles away. We actually had a target kill painted on the Link 11 Terminal set in the computer room."

Biddle returned to Norfolk on 9 May for a month of upkeep and to participate in an INSURV Inspection. The inspection was cancelled at the last moment from a lack of travel funds for the inspection team. Weapons were loaded at Yorktown on 7 June and *Biddle* began the transit to the Puerto Rican Operating

Area to join the USS *Kennedy* Battle Group for FLEETEX 2-88. This would be *Biddle's* first fleet exercise since her 1986 Mediterranean deployment. Things went well for *Biddle* during the exercise. Her 1988 Command History claimed that "The learning curve for the entire crew was very steep, but the crew performed extremely well and the NTU system performed flawlessly. *Biddle* and her crew were cited by Commander Second Fleet for their performance as the Battle Group Anti-Air Warfare Commander."

Before returning to Norfolk, *Biddle* participated in a three day exercise with the Marines off the coast of North Carolina. One day after arriving Norfolk, *Biddle* departed for deperming at a deperming facility near Norfolk, and then began a Pre-Overseas Movement (POM) leave and upkeep and Intermediate Maintenance Availability (IMAV) period. The Command History noted that

> ...numerous last minute details coupled with a Combat Systems Readiness Review (CSRR), an auxiliaries assist visit and some urgent repairs made POM a very demanding period for the entire crew.
> All hands breathed a collective sigh of relief as all lines were taken in at 0730 2 August and the ship steamed out of Norfolk enroute the Mediterranean. As the trans-Atlantic phase of the deployment began, the pace of underway operations quickly mounted. Again growing pains were experienced as everyone onboard became accustomed to the numerous operations going on around the clock as the battle group continued training enroute to the Sixth Fleet.
> The 10 day transit across the Atlantic ended with a late night, foggy transit of the Straits of Gibraltar. BIDDLE, as the second ship in the column, was forced to assume duties as the guide when USS JOHN RODGERS was forced to leave the column and maneuver to avoid another vessel.

Following a turnover west of the island of Corsica, *Biddle* served as the Force Anti-Air Warfare Commander in a National Week Exercise in the Central Mediterranean. After completing the exercise, *Biddle* visited the French port city of Toulon for ten days then began a two week maintenance period with USS *Yellowstone* in Naples.

Feeling rejuvenated, *Biddle* joined warships from Italy, Turkey, Great Britain, Spain and France in the major NATO exercise, Exercise Display Determination. NTU-equipped *Biddle* assumed AAW duties in the northern Aegean Sea while the remaining forces carried out an amphibious landing in the Turkish Straits. Enroute to Alexandria, Egypt, *Biddle's* crew and Captain Allen welcomed aboard *Biddle's* thirteenth commanding officer, Captain Grant Fulkerson, USN.

Captain Fulkerson, a 1964 U.S. Naval Academy graduate, was born in Baltimore, Maryland. Captain Fulkerson served in *Gridley* (DLG/CG-19) as Missile Ordnance Officer and *Beatty* (DD-756) as Weapons Officer. In Vietnam, Captain Fulkerson served a tour with the fleet command unit of the U.S. Military Advisory Group Vietnam as an advisor onboard Vietnamese river gun boats. He was awarded a Master of Science in personnel administration at the U.S. Naval Postgraduate School in Monterey, California, and was an instructor in naval weapons at the US Naval Academy. He also served in *Bainbridge* (DLGN/CGN-25) as Combat Systems Officer and in *Hull* (DD-945) as Executive Officer. Captain Fulkerson commanded the guided missile destroyer *Barney* (DDG-8).

Biddle arrived in Alexandria on 11 October, moored outboard of USS *John Rodgers* at the Egyptian Naval Shipyard, and began a two week maintenance period with USS *Yellowstone*. After two weeks of visiting a truly remarkable area of the world, *Biddle* transited the Eastern and Central Mediterranean to Villefranche, France, on the French Riviera, where *Biddle* was inport from 28 October to 4 November.

Biddle departed the mild, Central Mediterranean climate of Villefranche and steamed directly into the teeth of gale force winds and high seas. Still attached to the battle group after surviving the storm, *Biddle* anchored at Augusta Bay, Sicily, for Surface Warfare Training Week (SWTW). *Biddle's* Command History reported "These five days were filled with meetings, drills, competitive exercises and various other training evolutions. *Biddle* again demonstrated the tremendous capabilities of the NTU system by transmitting force track video to the entire battle group during an AAW training exercise."

On 11 November *Biddle* departed Augusta Bay with USS *John Rodgers* for the Black Sea. During four days of operation in the Black Sea, *Biddle* and *John Rodgers* operated with two Soviet destroyers. The Command History states the "Two Soviet *Krivak* destroyers remained in the company of the task unit throughout the four days in the Black Sea and provided all ships with numerous opportunities to practice the use of signals of the U.S.—Soviet Incident at Sea (INCSEA) Agreements. All four ships conducted all evolutions with extreme professionalism. During the southbound transit *Biddle* conducted a highly successful full power run and steamed in excess of 32 knots for over two hours."

After a four day transit and almost three weeks underway, *Biddle* anchored off the principality of Monaco, a few miles up the coast from Nice, France. Seven days later *Biddle* departed for the coast of Morocco in the Western Mediterranean to participate in Exercise African Eagle as Anti-air Warfare Commander. Following completion of the exercise, *Biddle* enjoyed a nine day break in Palma,

Spain, before departing for yet another exercise—Exercise Snake Pit. *Biddle's* 1988 Command History reports that "Immediately after leaving Palma the ship experienced gale conditions that cancelled the exercise. During the next two days enroute Naples the ship experienced winds in excess of 60 knots and seas in excess of 25 feet. BIDDLE remained inport Naples for the remainder of the year."

The Saga of Petty Officer Baskin Robbins

Soon after getting underway, most salty sailors begin to miss the simple things in life—like ice cream whenever you want it. That was the case when a young radioman, RM3 Sean Patrick, who apparently wasn't thinking right late one night, decided to raid the officer's wardroom for some Baskin Robbins ice cream. Sean offers his confession for all to hear…

> Anyone can appreciate a good ice cream cone, particularly when you are somewhere in the middle of the Atlantic Ocean and Baskin Robbins is nowhere to be found. It was a typical mid-watch in radio central on *Biddle*, traffic on the broadcasts was steady, and the ship was steaming silently through the night.
>
> Up in radio central the watch team was in no mood for "mid-rats" from the mess decks, we had an acquired taste for the finer things in life. That was when I decided it would be a good idea to get some ice cream from the wardroom pantry. We had done it in the past, and besides, who would miss a little ice cream taken from the wardroom mess?
>
> The passageway was dark as darken ship had been set at sunset. The path was a short one, out the door to radio central, turn left, and peek into the wardroom to ensure the coast was clear.
>
> The plan was to bolt straight through the wardroom into the mess and snag some fudge ripple ice cream, back through the wardroom, then back to radio central—five minutes at the most. I peeked through the small window, to ensure no one was up late—the coast was clear, the OP was a go. I sprinted 20 feet through the ward room, in one door, and out the other. I opened the door to ward room mess, grabbed the five gallon cardboard container of ice cream and about five spoons from the silverware drawer. The entire OP was no more than a couple of minutes. Everything was going as planned, but all that was about to change.
>
> Surely nobody had come into the wardroom in the two or three minutes that had passed since I came through—no need to check the little window again, right? WRONG! That was a mistake that would prove costly. Three steps into the wardroom I looked to my right and saw Lieutenant Mark Helstern, the CIC Officer, sitting on the couch reading some message traffic. I stopped dead in my tracks, speechless…what could I say? I'm standing before

him with a five gallon container of ice cream under one arm and five spoons in my other hand. I turned walked back to the wardroom mess, returned the captured ice cream, put the spoons back into the drawer and returned to the wardroom. Lieutenant Helstern smiled and said, "We'll talk in the morning". I returned to radio central dejected and scared to death. I announced to the rest of the watch section that I had gotten busted.

That had to have been the longest mid-watch ever—thoughts of how much trouble I was in danced in and out of my head. I had never gotten in trouble before. I always worked hard and I was an RM3 qualified in Surface Warfare (SW), one of only a handful of third classes with that qualification.

The next morning after quarters, Senior Chief Moore and my leading Petty Officer RM1 Wallbank called me into the back office. It was time for me to explain my actions. I stood before them and plead guilty. What could I say? I was caught red-handed and there was no getting out of this one.

The Communications Officer came in and I knew I was in for it. My clean record and the fact that I was well liked proved to be my saving grace. I thought for sure I was going to get written up and sent to and Executive Officer Investigation (XOI.)

Thankfully, the officers did not want to see a good sailor's record permanently marked for one small mistake. I was instructed to write a letter of apology to the wardroom, and it was pointed out that the officers paid for their food. That explained why officers always seemed to have better food—something that never had occurred to any of us prior to the OP that went bad.

The Communications Officer also assigned me several hours of "EMI" or scrub duty in the junior officers bunk room. Soon after, Lieutenant Bob Cooney and Lieutenant Larry Datko gave me the nickname, "Petty Officer Baskin Robbins," and they teased me and joked about that for some time. It was a funny story, one that I got teased about for some time.

My wife had not heard the story when it was recounted recently but she thought that was one of the funniest stories she had ever heard. Now she understands why I always make sure we have plenty of ice cream stored in our freezer.

1989

Biddle departed Naples on 3 January for a two day transit and an eight day port visit in Toulon, France. Her next assignment was to join the USS *Roosevelt* battle group in Exercise National Week 1-89. The Command History reported that "Participating with the USS ROOSEVELT battle group over the next three days was very challenging." No explanation was given defining the challenge. Following completion of her duties in Exercise National Week, *Biddle* and units of Med 3-88 began their 4,000-mile westerly transit home, arriving Norfolk on 1 February.

Biddle remained in Norfolk until 9 July except for a local three day underway training period, a two day transit to Boston to help Bostonians celebrate St. Patrick's Day, and off loading weapons at the Naval Weapons Station at Earle, New Jersey. A three and a half month Selected Restricted Availability (SRA) until 9 July at the Norfolk Naval Shipyard followed. Major repair items included habitability space renovations and major fuel oil tank repairs. Following the SRA, *Biddle* completed a two day FAST cruise, a dependants cruise to the Naval Weapons Station at Yorktown, a post-SRA shakedown and a training cruise in the VACAPES OPAREA.

Biddle began a two week training period with the Fleet Training Group at Guantanamo Bay when she stood out of Norfolk on 10 August. "Daily exercises including gun shoots, engineering casualty drills, seamanship evolutions and navigation exercises were routine," according to *Biddle's* Command History. After training was completed *Biddle* conducted Naval Gunfire Support Exercises on Vieques Island, refueled at Roosevelt Roads, visited St. Thomas for four days, and headed home. Enroute Norfolk *Biddle* was redirected to Onslow Bay, North Carolina, to participate in Special Operations Exercise (SOCEX) with Amphibious Squadron Two and Marine elements.

Biddle was underway again on 13 September to participate in VANDALEX, a missile firing exercise off Wallops Island, Virginia. Poor weather and frequent surface contacts resulted in cancellation of the exercise. During an inport period from 15 September to 15 October, *Biddle* completed a command inspection. On 16 October the ship got underway in the Virginia Capes Area for training and a Combat Systems Assessment. *Biddle* rounded out the month of October with an excursion to Annapolis, Maryland, to join the homecoming revelry at the U.S. Naval Academy. After returning to Norfolk on 31 October, *Biddle* spent only four days under way for the remainder of the year—all were related to an INSURV Inspection in November. December started well when *Biddle* was awarded the Meritorious Unit Commendation on 5 December for her Med 3-88 deployment. The remainder of the year was spent in am IMAV and leave/upkeep status.

1990

Biddle's leave and upkeep status continued until mid-January at which time the ship departed for the VACAPES Area to join the VANDALEX missile exercise. The 1990 Command History noted that "During the VANDALEX on 19 January, BIDDLE fired two missiles, an SM-1 and SM-2. The SM-1 succeeded in reaching and destroying its target drone first, despite being fired after an accompanying AEGIS cruiser's own VLS at the same target. The SM-2 missile did not reach its target drone before the drone was command detonated in flight. Telemetry data indicated, however, that the missile had positive lock on the drone despite its erratic movement." *Biddle's* performance in destroying the drone under the nose of the AEGIS cruiser is evidence that in many instances, NTU performed as well as AEGIS.

Biddle returned to Norfolk on 20 January for a Supply Assist, Safety Quick Look Inspection, and to load 5-inch ammunition from USS *Richard E. Bird* and USS *Kidd*. With preparations complete and Commander Cruiser Destroyer Group Eight embarked, *Biddle* got underway on 29 January for FLEETEX 1-90. After completing the initial segment of the exercise, *Biddle* departed the group and proceeded to the northern Puerto Rico Operational Area to fire two missiles. Again *Biddle* fired a SM-1 and SM-2 and both were direct hits. Before conducting ASW operations in the southern Puerto Rico Operational Area on 9 and 10 February, *Biddle* lobbed 5-inch projectiles toward Vieques Island to qualify for NGFS.

Following short visits to St. Thomas, Roosevelt Roads, and St. Martin, French West Indies, *Biddle* embarked a U.S. Coast Guard Law Enforcement Detachment (LEDET) and conducted Law Enforcement Operation (LEO) in the Caribbean until 15 March. During that time, *Biddle's* boarding team and LEDET officers boarded a private cabin cruiser suspected of transporting drugs. The vessel was not thoroughly searched due to rough seas, but was escorted to Roosevelt Roads the next day. Later, *Biddle* learned that 142 kilos of cocaine were found in a hidden compartment. *Biddle* boarded another boat that had been involved in a collision but no contraband was found. The disabled private vessel was towed by the Captain's gig to Curacoa, Venezuela with *Biddle* following. *Biddle's* Disbursing Officer and a Coast Guard officer settled with the boat's owners. USS *South Carolina* (CGN-37) relieved *Biddle* on 15 March. With her LEO tasks completed, *Biddle* got underway from Roosevelt Roads to make the three day transit to Norfolk.

Biddle remained in port in an upkeep status until 10 May while undergoing numerous qualifications and examinations. The Engineering Department passed an Operational Propulsion Plant Examination with an "outstanding" grade on 20 March. Phase I of and extensive Combat Systems Readiness Review (CSRR) began on 9 April and CSRR Phase II began on 23 May. The review concluded on 4 May with a grade of "outstanding." During April, *Biddle* served as host ship for the *Harry E. Yarnell* (CG-17) that was returning from deployment and the visiting West German guided missile destroyer FGS *Moelders*. Other events included a sonar dome rubber window radiograph inspection, a Food Management Assist visit, and dental availability with USS *Yellowstone*.

Biddle got underway on 8 May to load weapons at Yorktown then proceeded to the Puerto Rico Operating Area to join West German ships, including FGS *Moelders*, in a multi-national missile exercise. During the two-day exercise *Biddle* fired two SM-1 missiles. Following another visit to Roosevelt Roads and the conclusion of the exercise, *Biddle* found her way back to Norfolk on 19 May.

Biddle's full schedule prior to overseas deployment to the Mediterranean in August left little time for rest and relaxation except for a brief Pre-Overseas Movement period in late June. During the POM, a WRN-6 Global Positioning System (GPS) receiver was installed which enabled high precision navigation using satellites slaved to an atomic clock. The propellers were polished and the entire bottom of the hull was cleaned. *Biddle* underwent an Acoustic Readiness Visit in late May as well as an Industrial Hygiene Survey and a midshipman training period.

Biddle departed Norfolk on 6 June to join the Saratoga Battle Group for FLEETEX 3-90, her last exercise before overseas deployment. *Biddle* fired two SM-2 missiles and one SM-1. The ship's Command History noted that "Instrumental in correcting and refining the Battle Group's communication doctrine and procedures, BIDDLE commendably resolved this major area of complication, allowing the Battle Group to achieve a working communications plan by the end of FLEETEX 3-90. BIDDLE'S recommendations in the use of the communication spectrum would be used as guidance in the drafting of the Battle Group communications plan instituted once deployed." Bravo Zulu, *Biddle*!

After the wrapping up FLEETEX 3-90, *Biddle* steamed north to Onslow Bay, North Carolina, to participate in SOCEX and Outboard (an electronic direction finding system) Calibration. Upon returning to Norfolk on 26 June, a Pre-Overseas Movement leave and upkeep period began. Major evolutions conducted include the following: USS *Yellowstone* provided IMAV services, training for midshipmen continued, CIWS groom, LANTRAMID, and HSL 34 re-embarked.

Operation Desert Shield

When Iraq invaded Kuwait on 2 August 1990, the USS *Independence* Battle Group was near the island of Diego Garcia in the Indian Ocean and the USS *Dwight D. Eisenhower* Battle Group was in the Eastern Mediterranean. Both battle groups immediately made top speed to take positions in the Gulf of Oman and Red Sea, and to be ready to initiate combat operations on arrival. The USS

Saratoga Battle Group, including the battleship USS *Wisconsin* and USS *Biddle* departed East Coast ports on 7 August to join the action. A week later, as the *Saratoga* Battle Group transited the Straits of Gibraltar, the USS *John F. Kennedy* Battle Group sailed east in the wake of the *Saratoga* Battle Group. Within days after the invasion of Kuwait the United States Navy had clearly demonstrated unchallenged maritime superiority that presented a formidable deterrence to further aggression and provided protection for the imminent buildup of weapons, men, and equipment.

Biddle's 1990 Command History states "BIDDLE transited the Straits of Gibraltar on 16 August, and Suez Canal 22—23 August. Arriving in the Red Sea on 24 August, BIDDLE began Maritime Interdiction Force (MIF) operations in support of United Nations Resolution 661 barring the shipment of specific goods to or from Iraq. BIDDLE conducted its first Red Sea boarding on 29 August. On 31 August, BIDDLE became the first allied warship to board an Iraqi vessel (later released). This was BIDDLE'S third boarding."

In the middle of a tense situation on the far side of the world, *Biddle's* thirteenth change of command took place when Captain Louis F. Harlow relieved Captain Grant Fulkerson as *Biddle's* Commanding officer. Captain Harlow graduated at Fort Schuyler, New York, in 1968. He served in USS *Charles R. Ware* (DD-865) as Navigator and USS *Ainsworth* (FF-1090) as Chief Engineer. After receiving a Master's degree in Financial Management from the Naval Postgraduate School at Monterey, he served in USS *Vreeland* (FF-1086) as Executive Officer. Captain Harlow commanded USS *Caron* (DD-970).

On 12 September, only two days after Captain Harlow assumed command, *Biddle's* list of firsts continued. Her first divert and her seventh boarding, which was a freighter, occurred in the North Red Sea. Two more firsts occurred when she boarded her first vessel with a Soviet crew, and then on 17 September, *Biddle* boarded her first Soviet-flagged vessel.

On 18 September *Biddle* boarded her tenth vessel then steamed north through the Suez Canal to Izmir, Turkey, for a four day port visit. She was joined by USS *Philippine Sea* and USS *Saratoga* before shoving off for the NATO exercise Display Determination 1990. Display Determination involved naval, air and ground forces from the United States, Turkey, and Italy. Embarked NATO observers "All left highly impressed with the NTU cruiser's ability to defeat all air threats encountered during the two-week exercise," reported *Biddle's* 1990 Command History.

Following the conclusion of Display Determination, *Biddle* set sail for Alexandria, Egypt, arriving on 15 October. After a one week IMAV with USS *Yellow-*

stone (AD-41), *Biddle* departed Alexandria to resume her duties in the Red Sea. Concurrent with performing her interdiction duties, *Biddle* completed an engineering self-assessment from 7 to 11 November and a Combat Systems Assessment from 10 to 11 November. *Biddle* visited the Egyptian port city of Hurghada for three days beginning on 12 November then joined USS *South Carolina* on 16 November for a two-ship alongside address by the Chief of Naval Operations. Following the CNO's address, *Biddle* returned to the North Red Sea to continue boarding operations.

Biddle continued boarding operations until 4 December when, inexplicably, her rudder broke off the rudder post and sank. A replacement rudder was flown to the French Naval Shipyard at Toulon, France. Meanwhile, *Biddle* was towed to Port Suez, Egypt, by *Thomas C. Hart* (FF-1092) (Thanks, Tom!). Egyptian tugs towed *Biddle* through the Suez Canal to Port Said, where *Biddle* was met by USS *South Carolina*. *South Carolina* put her powerful nuclear propulsion system to good use until relieved by ocean tug USNS *Powhattan* (T-ATF 166) on 13 December. *Powhattan* completed the towing task after a week, arriving Toulon on 19 December.

Biddle's 1990 Command History summarized the remainder of the year: "BIDDLE took advantage of the Toulon inport period to proceed with a Restricted Availability carried out by the French. BIDDLE remained inport Toulon until 5 January 1991, with all hands taking the opportunity to visit the town and surrounding cities, including Marseilles, Monte Carlo, and Monaco, and even Paris, where two-day excursions were provided."

1991

With a new rudder firmly attached to the ship, *Biddle* departed Toulon on 6 January to continue GATEGUARD duty in the Northern Red Sea. She remained on duty in support of OPERATION DESERT SHIELD as Local Anti-Air Warfare Commander (LAAWC) until OPERATION DESERT STORM began on 17 January. According to *Biddle's* 1991 Command History, "The pinnacle of BIDDLE'S involvement in Maritime Interdiction occurred on February 26. BIDDLE boarded the Yugoslavian merchant Ledenice, uncovering chemicals used in SCUD missile warheads. The Saudi Arabian government authorized seizure of the vessel crediting BIDDLE with the only seizure during OPERATION DESERT SHIELD or DESERT STORM."

Credited with the first boarding of an Iraqi vessel, the first boarding of a Soviet-flagged vessel, the first diversion in the Red Sea, 36 total boardings, eight diversions, and one seizure, *Biddle* began the two week transit home on 14

March, confident that once again she had sailed in harm's way, met the challenge, and was returning home. *Biddle* arrived in Norfolk on 27 March "to a hero's welcome unseen since the end of World War II," according to *Biddle's* 1991 Command History.

From 28 March to 23 May *Biddle* remained in port to complete an ASW Fire Control Systems Material inspection, CMS inspection, and a Sonar Dome Rubber Window Radiographic Inspection. During the six week period from 23 May to 1 July, *Biddle* conducted COUNTER NARCOTIC OPERATIONS first in the mid-Atlantic and then off the coast of Columbia in the Caribbean Sea. Using her long-range air-search capabilities, *Biddle* tracked over 1600 contacts—40 were identified as possible drug transports which led to the arrest of twelve alleged drug runners and the seizure of 715 kilograms of cocaine.

Biddle returned to Norfolk where she remained until the end of the year except for off-loading then on-loading weapons in Yorktown, Virginia, and two short Sea Trials in December. After unloading weapons at Yorktown in preparation for a SRA, *Biddle* commenced a three month IMAV with USS *Yellowstone* from 2 September until 8 December. During the extensive maintenance period, *Biddle's* AN/SPS-48E waveguide and antenna were replaced, the Joint Operational Tactical System (JOT) II with two large screen displays were installed, 1A and 2A boilers were re-tubed, and numerous repairs were made to firerooms, machinery spaces, and the sewage Collection, Holding, and Transfer (CHT) system. The Command History also reported that *Biddle* had "a new look: an all-gray topside."

In addition to the SRA, *Biddle* successfully completed a Command Inspection, was awarded COMCRUDESGRU Eight's first Surface Warfare Excellence Award, and received an Aviation Certificate. During three days of Sea Trials in December, *Biddle* tested the results of her IMAV, then returned to port to enjoy a holiday stand-down for the remainder of the year.

1992

Biddle's holiday stand-down ended on 13 January when she got underway for Basic and Advanced FLEETEX 2-92. The five-week exercise consisted of qualification for employment of the SM-1(ER) and SM-2(ER) missiles, Harpoon Antiship missiles, Anti-Submarine Rocket (ASROC), and Mk 46 torpedoes; and Naval Gunfire Support Qualification at Viques Island. Sandwiched between the basic and advanced phases was a three day port visit to St. Thomas.

Upon return to Norfolk on 14 February, *Biddle* focused on the Operational Propulsion Plant Examination scheduled for 2 and 3 March. Unfortunately, *Bid-*

dle failed the Main Space Fire Drill but passed the second inspection on 22 and 23 March then passed a Combat Systems Assessment five days later. In April *Biddle* conducted an Intermediate Maintenance Availability with, you guessed it—USS *Yellowstone*.

Ensign Patrick Delaney reported aboard *Biddle* in early March, eager for his first assignment as *Biddle's* Gunnery Officer. Later he would be assume responsibilities as Gunnery/Missiles Officer, and finally as *Biddle's* last First Lieutenant. Young Mr. Delaney quickly found the atmosphere aboard *Biddle* to his liking. He explains:

> I walked onto *Biddle* on the morning of 1 April 1992 as a boot Ensign. *Biddle* was moored at the end of pier 10 in Norfolk. The crew had just started the pre-deployment standdown for Med 92-02. It also happened to be Captain Harlow's birthday. I walked onto the ship. Lieutenant (jg) Shawn Duffey found me after I walked out of the admin office and told me to quick change into civvies and that we were taking the Captain to lunch. After a good lunch at a reputable local establishment, the JO's took off for a long afternoon and night on the town. It was a great way to meet the wardroom and an introduction to a fun ship.
>
> Later during the pre-deployment standdown, Commander Cain, the new XO grabbed me at about 1600 and asked me to come to his stateroom to rehearse his introduction speech to the wardroom. In a little over 2 hours, he regurgitated 16 weeks of SWOS. Ironically, he never gave the speech to the wardroom. Some time after 1800 hours I saluted the ensign and when home.

Biddle departed Norfolk in May to join the Sixth Fleet in the Mediterranean for a six month deployment. Ensign Delaney remembers that "The morning of 6 May we left on Med 92-02. The first four days at sea were awful. We encountered sea storms and were taking rolls of up to 40 degrees. I was absolutely amazed how Mother Nature could undo in 30 minutes all the painting and preservation that the crew did in 30 days."

On 19 May *Biddle* took part in the international exercise DRAGON HAMMER with units from the Italian and Belgian navies. After departing the exercise, *Biddle* anchored at Naples, Italy, for a change of command ceremony in which Captain Larry Gionet relieved Captain Louis Harlow as commanding officer. Captain Gionet, *Biddle's* fifteenth and last commanding officer, graduated from Catawba College, Salisbury, NC in 1965 and received his commission at OCS, Newport, RI. He served in USS *Annapolis* (AGMR-1), USS *William H. Standley* (DLG-32) as Navigator and Administrative Officer, USS *Richard E. Kraus* (DD-849) as Operations Officer, USS *Donald B. Beary* (FF-1085) as Executive Officer, and USS *Yellowstone* (AD-41) as Executive Officer. Captain Gionet commanded USS *Green Bay* (PG-101) and USS *Samuel Elliot Morrision* (FFG-13). Captain Gionet also served as Navigation instructor, Company Officer, and an Administrative Officer, Office of the Commandant of Midshipmen at the U.S. Naval Academy, Annapolis, MD.

While in Naples, Ensign Delaney and a small group of junior officers met the Pope and participated in the change of command aboard *Biddle*. Ensign Delaney recalls both experiences with humor an insight:

> The first port visit was my favorite port in the entire world, Naples. The ship arranged a trip to Rome. We were encouraged to go in our whites. A group of the JO's, Eric Townsen, Matt Hurley, Hank Stevens, and myself attend a Papal audience. We got prime seats and got to shake the Pope's hand on two occasions. He wished us peace. He had the softest hands I'd ever felt…including my three kids.
>
> Naples was also the where we did the change of command when Captain Gionet relieved Captain Harlow. Captain Harlow was a great teacher for JO's and an even better motivator. I remember when we were doing honors for him on the quarter deck as he was departing; I was really hung over and hurting from the farewell the night before. I couldn't wait to go back to my rack. On his way through the honors line he shook all the officer's hands and said a few words to each. When he came to me, I don't remember what he said, but it was short. I then went back to my stateroom, changed into my khakis and went down to the hole and traced the main steam system.
>
> Captain Gionet was almost the perfect opposite of Captain Harlow. Where Captain Harlow was outwardly intense, passionate and allowed JO's to control the ship in tight spots under his tutelage, Captain Gionet had a quieter presence, didn't take unnecessary risks, and relied on his more senior JO's on his bridge. Both were great captains and leaders. I had the fortunate of having four different COs at sea. Each had very different leadership styles, but all of them were very good. To this day, they are among the best people I've worked with.

After weighing anchor at Naples, *Biddle* participated in the back-to-back exercises POOP DECK and DASIX-LAFAYETTE from 31 May to 11 June. *Biddle* followed the exercises with a port visit to Toulon, France, in conjunction with an IMAV with USS *Yellowstone*. During the eight day visit, many Hard Chargers participated in a very worthwhile community relation project. *Biddle's* 1992 Command History explains: "Additionally, BIDDLE conducted a community relations project for a local orphanage that served children of various ages, all with medical and/or psychological impairments. The BIDDLE volunteers repaired the heating system and several pieces of playground equipment, built a storage room and fire escape ladder, constructed a brick wall, cleared trees that doubled the available playground areas and painted several rooms. The project was a tremendous success, and follow-on visiting U.S. Navy ships continued the assistance."

Following the IMAV in Toulon, *Biddle* joined the exercise ELLIPSE BRAVO from 21 to 28 June. Designed to test our ability to rapidly assemble a Joint Task Force to conduct an emergency evacuation operation, ELLIPSE BRAVO consisted of a 22,000 strong Army, Air Force, Navy and Marine Corps Joint force, led by Commander, Sixth Fleet. The task force was completely assembled within 48 hours then moved to a command ship off shore while maintaining continuity of command.

Biddle's inspiring efforts to improve relations through the orphanage project were small compared to her next project. A world crisis had developed in the former Yugoslavia, now engulfed in civil war. Operation PROVIDE PROMISE, which was initiated by the United Nations, provided humanitarian relief to thousands of civilians in the form of food and supplies that was air-lifted by the military. *Biddle* was actively involved in PROVIDE PROMISE from 8 July to 2 August and again from 15 August to 16 September.

After a four day port visit to Thessaloniki in northern Greece, *Biddle* participated in the annual NATO exercise DISPLAY DETERMINATION. The ship displayed her "superior command and control capabilities while serving as the Anti-Air Warfare Commander for the opposing forces," according to *Biddle's* Command History.

Biddle's "superior command and control capabilities" during DISPLAY DETERMINATION and other exercises were evident to Mr. Delaney. He remembers "The next couple weeks involved changing port visits and during exercises with the French and Spanish Air Forces and Navies. As an avid follower of geopolitics and global affairs, I always wondered why Western Europe with a population of over 400 million needed the United States to defend it against the Soviet Union with a population of about 290 million. Well after a week of exercises with them, I knew the answer. They were militarily inept. We fooled them two days in a row with the same tactic by getting them to fly all their planes into a missile trap while our carrier planes him the air base that they took off from and left undefended."

Biddle's next port call was Piraeus (Athens), Greece. In addition to hosting a Columbus Day reception for the American Ambassador's wife and 245 guests during the three day visit, *Biddle* sailors organized a repair party for a local shelter sponsored by Mother Theresa.

While enjoying Athens, *Biddle's* next Operations Officer, Lieutenant Charles Landrum, and a detachment of *Biddle* enlisted men eager to report aboard, were trying to catch up to the ever active *Biddle*. Lieutenant Landrum describes the ordeal:

> I joined *Biddle* in October of 1992 while she was deployed to the Mediterranean. I had finished my course work on New Threat Upgrade and a class at Tactical Training Group Atlantic. In the course of preparing for my new assignment and to meet the ship, I made calls the operations branch of Commander, Cruiser Destroyer Group Eight (Rear Admiral Phillip Dur). I checked in with the *Biddle* detachment that I learned was formed at Group 8 and called the OMBUDSMAN and the Captain Gionet's wife to offer to mule mail over to the ship. In all instances everyone warmly greeted me and told me that they really liked my wife even though no one had yet met my wife. In fact, the OMBUDSMAN wondered why I had come back early. I later learned there was another Lieutenant Landrum onboard, John Landrum, the Missile Battery Officer. Two Lieutenant Landrums aboard was a source of confusion for the 10 months that we served together.
>
> I arrived via an Air Mobility Command charter flight at NAS Sigonella, Sicily, with a goal of getting to the ship and turning over with Lieutenant Commander Pelkofski so he could detach on or before return to homeport. When I arrived in theater, *Biddle* was in Athens and there were at least a dozen *Biddle* sailors in transient status waiting for transportation to the ship. They were living in the gym because the BEQ and the local hotels were full. The problem was that *Biddle* was only making three-day port calls and Air Services Coordination Mediterranean (ASCOMED) refused to take sailors to a port in advance of a ships arrival (in case the port call was cancelled) and on the last day of the port in case the ship left early. So that left a very narrow window to move personnel. These sailors (including the new NC1) were victims of this policy. So we didn't make it to Athens, but I vowed to board the ship in the next port, Trieste.
>
> I had a few days, so I worked the system and put in an airlift request to move the expanding *Biddle* det Sigonella to Trieste. The paper work went through and I had a C-9 reserved for the day of *Biddle's* arrival. With everything set in motion, I had time to sightsee in Sicily, during which I ran into a retired Army Colonel and his wife. The Colonel was the father of the Combat Systems Officer (CSO), Jose Vasquez!
>
> The night before the flight I dutifully checked in with the air terminal to verify the final arrangements, only to be told the flight was cancelled because we were not allowed to fly up in advance of the ship! I raised hell and they

called the Air Operations officer at home, who confirmed our special arrangement. We were set.

The next morning the *Biddle* Det and Colonel Vasquez and his wife boarded the C-9 for Trieste. At the air terminal for Trieste the plan nearly went awry. *Biddle* was not due in until the next day and the Italians were not going to let us off the plane since there were no representatives to pick us up. I wasn't in on the negotiations, but we were eventually allowed to deplane. That was when I realized that my plan was not as well thought out as I had hoped. As it turned out we were able to catch a ride with some postal clerks off of the LPH that was in port Trieste and the ship put us up for the night. The next morning the det was standing on the pier as *Biddle* Med Moored.

From Athens, *Biddle* steamed west to Trieste, Italy, for a six day port visit. *Biddle* hosted a reception for the Sixth Fleet Commander, Vice Admiral Thomas J. Lopez, and guests that included the American Ambassador to Italy. Lieutenant Landrum recalled that an uninvited guest took advantage of the situation:

> In Trieste *Biddle* was the host ship for a reception under a tent on the flight deck by the U.S. Ambassador. Attending were many Italian dignitaries including the mayor, the heads of the Carabinieri and Alpini military organizations, and many other uniforms with equally colorful hats. A ceremonial quarterdeck was set up on the fantail and the Ceremonial Officer and the side boys were kept very busy. A group of us commented on the particularly unattractive mustard and plaid suit of one of the guests.
>
> As the evening progressed and we enjoyed the alcohol served and the hors d'oevres, we noticed that the gentlemen was putting away more than his fair share of wine and food and that some went into his pockets. We inquired of our Italian liaison who this guy was. No one knew and a quick poll of the various Italian entourages soon led the liaison officer to deduce that the guy was homeless! Well we kindly escorted him off the ship, this time without honors! We figured that we had completed our community relations project for this port.

Lieutenant (jg) Patrick Delaney remembered that "We painted over rust *in the rain* in preparation for the reception. The JO's also made the local paper. We had a game of touch football in the city square. We had about 14 people playing and drew a curious crowd of locals. I estimate the crowd was 50-60 people watching Curtis Brown eat the rest of us for lunch. Curtis was the star half back at Annapolis a few years earlier."

Biddle departed Trieste and continued west to Rota, Spain, and then to Bermuda on 3 November. Many *Biddle* friends and family members flew to Bermuda to meet the ship and enjoy a three day end-of-employment "Tiger Cruise."

While embarked, "the guests received a rare glimpse of life at sea, culminating with a spectacular air demonstration presented by the aircraft carrier USS *Saratoga's* (CV 60) embarked air wing." *Biddle* returned to Norfolk on 6 November and immediately began a standdown until 6 December. After an IMAV from 24 November until 11 December, *Biddle's* crew enjoyed a Christmas party and holiday leave period until 6 January.

1993

Biddle's Command History for 1993 was not available from the Naval Historical Center. Several *Biddle* sailors helped to fill in the gap. Lieutenant Landrum describes the last few months of 1992 and 1993 until October:

> *Biddle* arrived home in late October and spent November and December of 1992 in post deployment and holiday stand down. We won the medium ship category for the Christmas decorations competition, possibly because we blared carols to all of the ships on the pier. In early January we sailed for the first of two six-week counter-drug operations (CD Ops). We returned mid-February for one week and returned a week later to the Caribbean and Eastern Pacific for March and part of April.
>
> We had the same detachment from HSL-34, the Green Checkers, for both pulses. We embarked a Navy Group Staff, a Coast Guard staff DESRON equivalent, a Coast Guard Law Enforcement Detachment, aerographers and extra Cryptological Technicians. In all there were nearly 500 people embarked, and space was at a premium. We also sailed with a seven meter rigid hull inflatable boat (RHIB), which we used for the Coast Guard boarding team. The boat was parked on a trailer on the port quarterdeck area and was lowered and raised by pneumatic chain hoist from a J-bar davit.
>
> The embarked staff for the first pulse was COMCRUSEDGRU Three, Rear Admiral Fitzgerald, out of San Diego (it was a first to have a West Coast group involved, previously the East coast staffs carried the load). During the second pulse the staff was COMCRUDESGRU 12 under Rear Admiral McDevitt.
>
> *Biddle* was primarily employed in an air surveillance role because of her powerful air search capability. We operated either in the western Caribbean or in the Eastern Pacific. It was very rough in the Western Caribbean and dead calm in the Pacific since the prevailing winds blew east to west and the mountains of Panama stopped the wind.
>
> Both times we transited the canal, so the ship made a total of four transits. The first time that we sailed through it was night and I was pretty disappointed not to be going during the day. As it turned out the temperature was much more agreeable and the canal well lit, it was like driving a highway.

Chief Engineer Dave Gilbert was spot promoted to Lieutenant Commander and we had the ceremony on the 04 level in a lock. His promotion meant that I was no longer the Senior Watch officer. We only made one daytime transit and that was more than enough, even during the winter months it was hot and humid.

As flagship, there was no break in the watch routine, so even inport we had four section watches to stand in combat. The four Tactical Affairs Officer (TAO) were myself, the CSO, Dave Gilbert, and Frank Holland, the Cryptological Officer. This rotation meant that the CIC watch teams had limited liberty in port.

Our one liberty port during the first drug ops, was Willemstad, Curacao, where we moored in the great canal opposite of the city. The wardroom went out for Rice Taffle (rice table), a Dutch Indonesian specialty. I remember that the junior officers in the wardroom went to the beach and forgot to put sun block on their feet. They all had bad sunburn and stood bridge watch in loosely laced tennis shoes. I nicknamed my Communications Officer, Tim Spollen, "Tim Swollen" after that. I used to go to Radio Central after lunch at sea since it was just forward of the wardroom on the starboard side. It was during this time that the radiomen taught me how to throw darts and we had some fiercely competitive matches.

One of the seriously sunburned junior officers was Patrick Delaney who offered the following defense: "In defense of Tim and me, we did apply a lot of factor 15, but we also applied a lot of beer for about 8 hours too many in the hot sun. As an American of Irish decent with a red headed son, I've been sun burnt many times, but never like that."

Lieutenant Landrum continues the narrative:

During the first drug ops pulse *Biddle* received commendation for two events. First we responded to a distress call in the southern Caribbean. A wooden coastal freighter carrying cement had the load shift and the ship capsized. At sunset Our HSL-32 SH-2G helo was able to locate and rescue three of the crew and recover the body of the fourth. The ship was gone. Even though we were off of the Guajira Peninsula of Columbia, the Coast Guard commodore recommended that we drop them off in Colon, Panama, since the Panamanian immigration was less bureaucratic than Colombia and the survivor would be able to go home soon.

We anchored in Colon and were met by a female LDO Boatswain from who arranged everything. The survivors were no problem but the corpse was. "Bob" as we named him because that's how we found him, was an issue of great concern and it took a lot of cajoling to get the Panamanians to take him. He had been taking up out limited freezer space.

> The boatswain was a Harley Davidson rider who was trying to stop smoking and she bummed a bunch of nicotine patches off the corpsman. She paid a call on us after that every time we were in Panama. *Biddle* was awarded the Coast Guard ribbon for this rescue.
>
> Our second commendation was for a drug bust that off the Guajira Peninsula near Colombia. We had intercepted the HF transmissions of a "go-fast" boat, the ops center ashore, and the mother ship. We were too late to stop the transfer from the mother ship to the boat but we caught up with the "go-fast". We engaged in an all night chase, with the "go-fast" having a speed advantage but we had the advantage of endurance and a helo. Green Checker stayed right on top the entire time. It was like a chase scene out of Miami Vice and we were even slaloming!
>
> By morning the boat had lost an engine and was low on fuel. They had dumped their cargo the night before, but upon boarding the LE Det gathered enough evidence to prove that drugs has been on board. One of the crew was stupid enough to announce his U.S. citizenship, thinking we would be lenient!

Lieutenant Delaney recalled "the morning when we were catching up, we were doing the slalom chase until his last engine died. We did a back full, and damn near ran him over. Lieutenants Matt Hurley and Ian Pollitt were on the bridge. By the time the boat was DIW, there was a CG, DD, 2 helos, and a P-3 surrounding this small boat. I also remember that our helo's video cassette recorder had a dead battery so they were unable to film any of the final chase.

Lieutenant Delaney cannot remember where the next story fits—either the first drug ops or the second, but tells it anyway: "On evening on the mid watch, we detected a small plan leaving Columbia flying about 100 feet off the water heading north through the Caribbean. We tracked on our own radar and sortied an F-15 out of Howard AFB in Panama to track it further north. The contact was then picked up by some radar on a rock in the middle of the Caribbean whose name I cannot remember. A P-3 out of Louisiana picked it up and tracked it until it crossed into Cuban airspace. North of Cuba, a Coast Guard P-3 picked it up. Off the coast of North Florida, the Coast Guard P-3, handed it off to a US Custom's plane. The Customs lost the target somewhere off Georgia. It was totally demoralizing. To make matters worse, we picked up the same guy (presumably) coming south two hours later and tracked him all the way back to Columbia."

Lieutenant Landrum continues:

> During our first deployment into the Pacific, Group 3 staff decided that the ship could safely make a run for the equator off Ecuador. We did and under

overcast skies 450 pollywogs (also called "Wogs"), myself included, were initiated by just 50 shellbacks. It was quite a production.

The day started with breakfast on the mess decks, which is exactly what it became. The CSO, Mike Pas, and I managed to escape and elude detection. We filled up green balloons that I had bought in Rodman Panama and put in shaved pieces of dye-mark. Joined by one of my OS1s we pelted the royal court unseen from atop the hangar. The OS1 was caught during our evasion attempts and the jig was up.

We joined the herd of "wogs" on the forecastle and kept wet with salt water—with no sun and a breeze it was chilly. The CSO and I were jumped ahead of the crowd due to our earlier hi-jinks and at least I had the pleasure of bring initiated twice. We crawled down the starboard side to the flight deck for the initiation stations. My SM1 Nash was the Royal Baby and I remember how sore he was the next week, having gotten sunburn and having 450 unshaved faces rub his belly!

The "wogs" had the last laugh! One of my OSCs to photographed me in the garbage trough, but made the mistake of wearing his khakis. I doused him with a liberal coating of slime, which earned me another crawl through the trough. My cannonball into the dunk tank got me extra credit as well. All in all it was good fun, but I had to wash my hair three times to get the lard out.

Operations in the Pacific were very pleasant. We operated at five knots, which gave the crew the opportunity to do a lot of fishing. I remember that the Gunner, CWO2 Ed Domick, had brought along $1000 dollars worth of deep-sea fishing gear and succeeded in catching nothing. Meanwhile sailors with the MWR fishing rods were pulling in fish all day. This became a joke ship wide and the when the EMO, CWO2 Carl Hoilman—the Gunner's roommate, when ever he had the bridge watch, would get on the 1MC and remind every one that we had it was the n th day that gunner hadn't caught a fish. When he finally did catch a fish, it was quite small, but nevertheless he paraded it all over the ship. We picked on Gunner a lot because he always brought a backpack full of snacks on watch in CIC. One day he was a bit late when we had the watch pierside in Rodman. We gave him grief for being late and having his ubiquitous backpack. After relieving the watch he handed everyone in CIC a small tub of ice cream that he had gotten at the mini-mart for 50 cents a piece. It was delicious ice cream and after that day we never picked on Gunner again!

Our second drug ops pulse started with a bust. We arrived off of Puerto Rico and the Coast Guard was looking for a semi-submersible that was approaching the coast. The vessel had eluded several cutters a frigate and a P-3 Orion. We put out HF direction finding gear to work and were able to steer a cutter onto the vessel. The boat began to jettison its cargo but it was too late and the crew and vessel were apprehended. Lieutenant Frank Holland let a crack team of CTs and EWs who interacted very effectively with CIC and were key to our success during this period.

During our second stint in the Pacific the engineer and I put our time to good use by getting the boats ready for our planned port visit to Cartagena, Colombia, over Easter. We ran two of the boats every day as we steamed at five knots and the boat crews got lots of training. Also, machinery operated every day runs better. Captain Gionet was very supportive and he enjoyed watching the boat bumper drills from his bridge wing chair.

In Cartagena we anchored out and the boats got quite a workout. While there we never suffered a boat casualty or incident. Rear Admiral McDevitt was elated and we had turned one of the gigs into a barge. He had been to Cartagena the year before on a nuke cruiser and none of the boats had worked the. The admiral was happy so Captain Gionet was happy.

The Admiral of the Colombian Atlantic Fleet had a big party in Cartagena for the wardroom at their officers club. One particular jewelry store in the resort area had an invitation to show their product lines. This invitation was extended to the crew and free beer and wine was served with lots or hors d'oevres and very attractive women in slinky black leotards modeled the jewelry. It was a tremendously popular marketing ploy. After the port visit, we learned that we had earned hazardous duty pay for our time in Cartagena (actually the cartels and the Colombian government declare a truce over Easter, the biggest holiday of the year). So we were reimbursed to the tune of $150!

Enroute to Cartagena was our second SAR in three months. We had launched Green Checker for a routine surface search and classification (SSC) so they could log hours before the port visit. Not long after lift off they flew over a sailboat the owner flung herself into the water. The rescue swimmer was dispatched and the woman was brought safely back to *Biddle*. As it turned out, the boat was adrift and she could not sail. She and her husband had sailed from their home in Martinique toward the canal. A day out a rogue wave hit the boat and washed her husband overboard. He had no lifejacket and the boat was under sail. She had no way to turn around and despairingly watched him drift out of sight. Seasick and distraught, she decided to force her rescue. We put a prize crew on the boat to bring it into Cartagena with us. The crew was led by Lieutenant Ian Pollit, who is an excellent sailor having grown up on sail boats. He was able to rig a spinnaker and followed us into Cartagena Harbor.

We had two memorable meals in the Wardroom during the two cruises. One was courtesy of Gunner who cooked for each officer a huge chimichanga, which we washed down with O'Douls. The second meal was Philly Cheese Steaks subs prepared by First Lieutenant Pat Delany. Hailing from New Jersey near Philadelphia, he naturally had relatives with a deli. Pat made a speed run before our second CD Ops pulse to pick up the authentic ingredients. He proved to be a great cook as well as a versatile First Lieutenant.

Commander Chris Cain was a nuclear qualified officer whose stateroom held a duplicate library of all of the Navy and ship's regulations and instructions. In fact, he had filed away every note he had taken in any navy school.

He used to slave away on FITREPs, EVALs and award citations, wanting the wording to be just right. None of the more junior officers, including the department heads, were up to the task. The CSO started a file of all of the hackneyed phrases that the XO used to insert into these write-ups. One day the CSO wrote up a brilliant eval that wove in all of the XO's pet phrases. Chris Cain shredded it with his red pen, denouncing his own pet phrases as poorly written. The CSO, rebutted the XO at 8'oclocks one night explaining that in an attempt to improve his writing, he had adopted and cataloged the XO's style. We were all in stitches and never heard anymore from the XO about our writing, he suffered in silence.

The Beginning of the End

It was during the second set of CD Ops that we learned *Biddle* would be decommissioned. *Biddle* was CASREP free and in excellent shape. Rear Admiral Dur thought so and fought to swap us with USS *Dale*, which was not yet on the list. *Dale* had a lot of engineering problems, but it would have meant that we pick up *Dale's* Standing Naval Force, Atlantic (STANAVFORLANT) deployment and it would have violated the crew's Personnel Tempo (PERSTEMPO) limit, a system to track individual deployment.

Captain Gionet and I tried many other times to keep *Biddle* operational, including sailing for WWII commemorations, but COMNAVSURFLANT had zeroed out our operating funds. I don't remember sailing to offload ammo—we may have done it pierside. Our last contribution to the nation came in May 1993. The Midwest was under the worst floodwater in 100 years and the rescue teams needed more lifejackets. One beautiful weekday afternoon a stake-bed truck pulled up alongside the ship and the crew emptied the holds of all of our kapok lifejackets. The truck went right to NAS Norfolk and the jackets were enroute the Midwest that night.

After that we started detailing the crew to new assignments and began emptying the ship and securing compartments. We were efficient and got it done a head of schedule. The Naval Historical Center took a portrait of the ship that hung in the wardroom. I got the builder's plate off the steering gear and the original dial phone from the signal bridge. I left a year after I arrived to join the staff of STANAVFORLANT and so I made that cruise on the *Dale* no less after all.

Lieutenant Delaney remembers another sad sign that the end was rapidly approaching: "The only other memorable event of the decommissioning period was when the NAVSEA gang came aboard and cut holes in the side of the superstructure to take out all the computers and consoles. They said they were going to be sent up to Philadelphia, stored for a year or two then fitted on a LHA."

In the spring of 1966, fresh out of Data Systems A and C schools, young DS3 Jim Treadway, a display tech, was *Biddle's* first data systems technician to report aboard. In the spring of 1990, fresh out of Data Systems A and C schools, young DS3 Jon Davidson, a display tech, was *Biddle's* last data systems technician to report aboard. Jon remembered that

> The crew started to dwindle during the summer and fall of 1993. The DS's in the shop had been given orders or gotten discharged and left one by one until I was the only one left. Towards the end, maybe September 1993, everyone was moved off the ship to a barracks near the air station. I lived off base so did not have to stay at the barracks, but had to stand watch there. The various departments set up offices in a nearby building while all the affairs were being closed out.
>
> While all this was going on the ship was starting to get stripped of what could be used elsewhere. I was a display tech and helped the contractors disconnect all of the equipment in the DS shop and up in CIC. They cut a hole in the side of the superstructure and pulled everything out with a crane, and loaded everything onto flatbed tractor trailers. It was a *very* strange and sad sight when the removal was complete—lots of empty space.
>
> There were decommissioning rehearsals that all of the crew that was going to be there at the end had to attend. There was an FCCS (last name Auman I believe) who was going to be the OOD during the decommissioning ceremony. I had stood watch with him numerous times before and he wanted me to be the POOW during the ceremony. I told him that I would be proud to do that. We practiced a few times and had the order of things down quite well.

Decommissioning

James Treadway

Leahy and *Belknap* Class cruisers, as well as most nuclear powered cruisers, had already reached, or were rapidly approaching, their 30-year service lives coincident with the diminished Soviet threat in the early 1990's. *Biddle* had received the New Threat Upgrade during her fourth major overhaul in 1986 and 1987, but her Mk 10 missile launcher and manual finning of missiles prior to launch was not fast enough to respond to the newest threat—saturation attacks from pop-up, low altitude cruise missiles. *Biddle's* tired and ancient steam power plant was maintenance and manning intensive and the population of *Ticonderoga* cruisers would soon reach sufficient numbers, 27, to protect all 11 carrier groups. All of these factors contributed to the obvious recourse—Cold War Cruisers were considered excess capacity and *Leahy* and *Belknap* cruisers were scheduled for decommissioning from 1993 to 1995.

The Navy's nuclear cruisers were not spared. *Long Beach*, worn out at 33, was decommissioned in 1994. *Truxtun* and *Bainbridge* were due for nuclear refueling and were decommissioned in September 1995 and September 1996, respectively. The relatively new *Virginia* Class, with rapid-fire Mk 26 launchers and large crews of 578 officers and enlisted but lacking NTU and helicopter landing space, were also coming due for nuclear refueling. The *Virginia* Class CGNs were eliminated between July 1993 and July 1998. Finally, the *California* Class CGNs, *California* and *South Carolina*, also burdened with large crews and high operating costs, were decommissioned by July 1999. In the six year period from 1993 to 1999, twenty seven Cold War cruisers were eliminated. Today, 27 *Ticonderoga* cruisers (CG 47—73) are on line. *Ticonderoga* herself is scheduled to be decommissioned in 2004.

At decommissioning, *Biddle's* characteristics—her weapons, radars, and combat system—had changed considerably since her early days. Her air and surface search radars had been significantly upgraded to new models, while her missile and fire control radars were upgraded to guide the new Standard missile to their target. The old Naval Tactical Data System had been upgraded to the Advanced

Combat Direction System (ACDS) making her more powerful and compatible with the AEGIS Combat System installed on newer ships. As a result of the constant changes, the old girl's displacement had swollen from 7,930 to 8,800 tons, an increase of almost 900 tons. Her powerplant accommodated the increased displacement and *Biddle* could easily serve many more years. *Biddle* was going out in style just as she came in—a powerful combatant, always ready for the next assignment.

The United States Navy, always looking forward, decommissioned *Biddle* on 30 November 1993 at D and S Piers, Norfolk, Virginia. The weather, which Captain Scott described as "Cold, windy, clear, sunny, and beautiful," was similar to the weather on her commissioning. Recalling the decommissioning events, *Biddle's* ninth commanding officer, Captain Hollis Robertson, wrote, "I vividly recall rounding the turn at the pier and my first glimpse of the ship revealed that the crew had cleverly 'grayed out' the hull numbers. It was like seeing them though a fog. I don't mind telling you it brought tears to my eyes and a lump in my throat! What a class act they were. I was so impressed with the squared away appearance of the ship I wrote as personal letter to Captain Gionet telling him how proud we all were, and what a great job of saying goodbye he had done. She went out like she came in; the competent and proud Hard Charger!"

Captain Albert Henry, *Biddle's* seventh commanding officer, told me "The decommissioning of *Biddle* was both a sad and a happy occasion for me. I was sad to see her sitting alongside the pier so lifeless—all the doors and hatches were already secured. It was a cold, windy day in November with tents on the pier for the reception after the decommissioning. It was so cold that I remember not lingering long at the reception. The happy part of the day was seeing old shipmates and swapping sea stories about our good memories sailing in *Biddle*. I was also very happy to get to meet all the former COs of *Biddle*."

When the ceremonies began, all 13 living *Biddle* commanding officers, many commissioning plankowners, the decommissioning crew, and numerous other crewmembers were present and accounted for. In spirit, all of the officers and all the men who served in *Biddle* were there, at attention, saluting one of the Navy's finest. Proud *Biddle*, now with a cold power plant, no rotating radars, and no missiles on the launcher, took a deep breath and tenaciously held her last crew to her bosom. Below the bridge wings, she proudly displayed her medals and achievements for all to see—three Meritorious Unit Commendations, two Navy Unit Commendations, a Navy Expeditionary Medal, and an Armed Forces Expeditionary Medal. Many in the decommissioning crew who were manning the rails must have sensed the solemnity of the moment, just as we did 27 years earlier on the bitterly cold morning of her commissioning. No doubt many of *Biddle's* past commanding officers, now seated in the audience in order of their commands, were reflecting over their commands, nodding in acknowledgement that "Yes, *Biddle* was my finest command."

The schedule of events included the standard items—a band played a medley of familiar Navy tunes, an invocation, speeches, and securing the watch. Prior to the ceremony, Captain Scott had thoughtfully made arrangements to raise the commissioning ensign, pennant, and jack, so that they would be the first and last to fly over *Biddle*. After the final watch had secured and the decommissioning ensign, pennant, and jack along with the Admiral's flag had been lowered, the officers, and men manning the rails silently filed down the gangplank for the last time. Captain Larry Gionet was the last to leave the ship. As Captain Gionet stepped on the pier, Captain Scott, in an unscripted moment, met Captain Gionet to unite *Biddle's* past and present with a salute, a handshake, and a "Well done!"

Soon, under cover of the pierside tent, the decommissioning cake was cut and enjoyed, and sailors did what sailors have done for centuries—recounted experiences while underway on the other side of the world, or at one of a hundred exotic foreign ports, or pierside at D and S piers. Backs were slapped, handshakes were strong and sincere. Knowing smiles and glances were exchanged while tears of silent respect were also evident. *Biddle's* bookends, her first and last commanding officers, met and compared notes. A few yards from the festivities, a proud ship that did her job as well as it could be done, stood fast to the pier, her name and exploits now history.

Captain Scott departed the ceremonies to attend to personal business, intending to return later for a few last goodbyes. Upon return, he found that all had left except for workmen who were dismantling the tent. *Biddle* had already been nudged from the pier into the channel and was being towed away to be stripped of her equipment and await her fate. Standing alone and at attention, Captain Scott watched as *Biddle* slowly disappeared. With one, last silent salute, *Biddle* faded from sight, but not from the hearts of Captain Scott and the thousands of Hard Chargers who served in the United States Navy's finest, USS *Biddle*!

[*After decommissioning, Biddle had one remaining cruise with Biddle sailors aboard. SKCS Dan Brunner was one of those sailors and remembers a "personal experience that I will never forget."*]

Biddle's Last Cruise

Dan Brunner

On a clear, cool, sunny day in late November 1993, *Biddle* made her final trip up the Elizabeth River from her berth at Norfolk Naval Station to Norfolk Naval Shipyard. In just a few months she had gone from a living, breathing, man of war to a lifeless, hollow shell. From the outside she looked as proud as ever. Her mooring lines taut, she looked like a racehorse just waiting to be released so she could pace briskly down Hampton Roads out past the Chesapeake light, and run loose—just like she did in 1992 when she chopped to the Med. The Commodore slowed down the "Classic Cruiser" because the top-heavy "Tico" class cruisers we were in company with could not take the pounding. Yeah, we slowed down but we were still the first ones to chop into the Med. Nope, those days were over.

When we walked aboard that morning for her dead-stick trip up the river the silence was spooky. No pumps, doors or hatches closing, the buzz of conversations, cursing sailors, smells from the galley or the 1MC sounding off with the daily routine. It was tomb like.

There were three of us left from the CPO Mess: SKCS Dan Brunner, BMC Jim Mills, and DCC Stan Gower. Three old goats to ride her up the river. Along with us were the First Lieutenant and a handful of deck seaman for line handlers. Not much to do except to watch the tugs come alongside and make sure the line handlers were in place. As the resident SK, I had the inevitable DD form 1149 that turned over a "*Belknap* Class Cruiser, CG-34, ex USS *Biddle*, 1 Each." After we got moving up the river the First Lieutenant wandered off while the deck seaman were clustered on the fo'c'sle and Chiefs Mills, Gower, and I found a couple of crates to park ourselves on, back on the fantail. We argued amongst ourselves a few minutes as to who would be the last man off. It was apparent to "Boats" Mills and myself that Gower really wanted the honor. So after putting up a suitable argument and trading the requisite insults we deferred to Chief Gower. He could be the last man off. That being settled we watched the First Lieutenant climb up the mast and walk around up there for a bit. "He wouldn't have done that a month ago," remarked "Boats" Mills. After a few minutes the First Lieutenant appeared on the flight deck. Chief Gower yells up to him "Hey Lieutenant! This is no longer a commissioned naval vessel, right?" The First Lieutenant looks down at us and says, "That's right Chief". He looked at us for a couple of seconds, shrugged his shoulders and wandered off. "Whatcha asked him that for Stan?" I asked. Chief Gower opens up his jacket and pulls out a bottle of Canadian Mist, reaches in one pocket and pulls out a can of coke, and pulls three Styrofoam cups out of his other pocket. "Well", he says, "I guess we can have one or two for the old girl." Feeling we were obliged not to insult Chief Gower's hospitality, we all shared several drinks. We did some reminiscing, told a few lies, talked some treason, and became quite cheerful. The First Lieutenant happened by once during our celebration and we cordially invited him to have one with us. He just shook his head and wandered off again.

At last we arrived at our new berth. We shooed everyone off and I can't remember in which order Boats Mills and I went off but Chief Gower went off last. The first Sand Crab I met on the pier I thrust the DD 1149 at him and said "Sign for her." He did, I gave him a copy and tucked the remaining copies in my jacket. I guess that officially put *Biddle* on the scrap heap.

We all had orders for new commands and more or less said "so long" and that was the end of it. I looked back at her a few times as we found our way back to the Norfolk Naval Base. Felt a little sad all day about the whole damn thing. You know, it was kind of like a wake and a funeral and we were the pallbearers.

All Hands Reunion

James Treadway

In March 2000, Bob Gerity e-mailed me after he found my name on the Locater page of Ken Ely's outstanding *Biddle* website. Soon thereafter I had e-mailed Captain Scott, Wes Boer, and several other *Biddle* plankowners who I had not seen in more than 30 years. In Captain Scott's reply to my e-mail, he wondered why there had been no attempt to organize an "All Hands Reunion." I realized that someone had to step forward and organize a reunion; otherwise it might not get done. It was time—*Biddle* had been decommissioned for more than seven years. I had no experience organizing a ship's reunion but I had organized three annual banquets for the Austin, Texas, Experimental Aircraft Association chapter. In my next e-mail to Captain Scott, I agreed to organize *Biddle's* first "All Hands Reunion" and the project was underway.

Several decisions were made early in the project that contributed to the success of the reunion. To promote the reunion to the widest possible audience, an informative web page was created that demonstrated that I was dedicated to making *Biddle's* first "All Hands Reunion" a success. Volunteers were solicited to help with the behind-the-scenes organizational details. Stepping forward were plankowners Captain Scott, David Johnson, Bob Gerity, Wes Boer, Ray Treadway, Ted Williams, my wife Holly, my cousin Karen Newsom, her husband Mike and others. Having an outstanding array of speakers and emcee at the banquet was a top priority and a significant attraction. With no public speaking skills myself, I was pleased (and relieved) when David Johnson agreed to be master of ceremonies. Finally, I chose the theme, "*Biddle* is a Proud Ship," which reflected my feelings towards the ship. I was confident it reflected the feelings of other Hard Chargers as well.

Within a few months the following speakers were on board: Captain Scott; Lieutenant Muse, and Rear Admiral Tom Marfiak, past *Biddle* Engineering Officer and CEO and publisher of the U.S. Naval Institute.

The sixteen months between the reunion's inception and culmination passed quickly. During that time I had secured an excellent banquet facility at the

Pinecrest Country Club in Longview; organized bus tours to the famous East Texas Oil Museum in Kilgore and the riverboat casinos in Shreveport, Louisiana; obtained block motel room reservations at several motels; ordered 200 *Biddle* caps and tote bags as souvenirs; obtained the services of a group panoramic photo photographer and a reunion book photographer; ordered George Bieda prints for sale and tokens of appreciation for the emcee and speakers; organized a golf tournament, buffet breakfast at a local restaurant, photo contest; and memorabilia display.

As the pre-banquet events unfolded on 14 July 2001, it was clear that the 16 months of planning and preparation were paying off. On several occasions I had opportunities to observe the unmistakable camaraderie that exists across multiple generations of *Biddle* crews. Plankowners traded sea stories with their counterparts in the decommissioning crew, senior officers and junior enlisted men recalled similar experiences from different times, and old buddies who had not seen each other for more than 30 years remembered what it was like way back then.

A few minutes before the banquet began with my opening remarks, I realized that the stricken *Biddle* was in the last phases of being dismantled. In a real sense then, the reunion had become a gathering of family and friends to pay our respects to a fine ship that would soon be no more. A short time later, as I looked out across the audience and saw 116 Hard Chargers and family, I realized that the effort put forth to organize the reunion was miniscule compared to the rewards.

Soon, master of ceremonies David Johnson relieved my watch. It was obvious that my old friend had prepared for the task in typical David Johnson fashion—his presentation was flawless. There was a toast, and then we remembered some Hard Chargers who had passed away. During the awards segment, Captain Henry's daughter Susan picked the winning lottery ticket for a handsome George Bieda *Biddle* print. Unbelievably, but appropriately, *Biddle* Webmaster Ken Ely's ticket was drawn. Then, it was my pleasure to present emcee Dave Johnson and each speaker with George Bieda *Biddle* prints. Also, awards were presented to winners of the photo and memorabilia contests and trophies were presented to the winning team in the golf tournament. Appropriately, Captain Scott's team had the best score. Captain Scott had a surprise of his own when he presented me a brass medallion of *Biddle's* crest from his personal collection. The "Sea Stories/ Open Mike" segment followed with several hilarious stories that weren't too embarrassing to tell.

David Johnson introduced the first speaker, *Biddle's* first commanding officer, Captain Maylon T. Scott. In spite of his claim of not being a good speaker, Captain Scott skillfully "spoke from the heart" about a ship that was his finest command and about a crew for which he will always have enormous respect. Next, the room became respectfully, almost deathly quiet, as Ralph Muse recalled the dramatic events in the Gulf of Tonkin of June 1972. To close the evening, Tom Marfiak expertly wove the themes of the two previous speakers together with a summary of *Biddle's* marvelous career and how the ship influenced our lives.

Another chapter in *Biddle's* life was closed as the reunion ended.

This Is the Captain Speaking

James Treadway

Captain Maylon T. Scott issued the following challenge to all Hard Chargers in his commissioning address:

> It is customary, fitting, and fundamental in the beginning of a new ship's life for the first Captain to establish a broad basic policy. One which will be instrumental in providing the crew with a solid foundation and positive direction throughout the ship's lifetime.
>
> Minutes ago *Biddle* was merely an inanimate object without life. Now she has LIFE, SPIRIT, PERSONALITY! Our SPIRIT, our PERSONALITY! We are BIDDLE.
>
> While we are in the Navy, regardless of the length of time—a year or thirty years—the Navy is our profession. We must strive to meet the high standards set by our profession.
>
> Thus, we who are BIDDLEMEN today, and those who will be in the future, I charge you—us—to the task of meeting the standards of our Navy, the task of being PROFESSIONAL Seamen.

Twenty seven years later, in Captain Larry Gionet's decommissioning memorandum to *Biddle* officers, Chief Petty Officers, and crew, he stated: "One common thread has endured throughout *Biddle's* years of service—she has always met all challenges in her typical hard-charging style and, more significantly her shipmates have striven for and attained through superior performance the excellence she is known for."

Captain Scott's challenge to all Biddlemen to meet "the standards of our Navy, the task of being PROFESSIONAL Seamen," was met in large measure because he did, in fact, establish a policy that provided "a solid foundation and positive direction throughout *Biddle's* lifetime." Succeeding commanding officers continued to build on that foundation. Thousands of officers and men who served in *Biddle*, whether they were aware of Captain Scott's challenge or not, responded to their own commanding officer's challenge, or to their own personal challenge, to excel. I can confirm that two years of technical training followed by four years of exposure to "meeting the standards of our Navy" while aboard *Biddle* contributed substantially to the person that I am today. Many of my fellow plankowners echo the same sentiments.

Most would agree that command of a ship at sea is a demanding task. But is it a difficult task? Later in this chapter, *Biddle's* ninth commanding officer, Captain Hollis Robertson, agrees with Fleet Admiral Chester Nimitz who claimed that command at sea is the easiest task in the world.

So, what are the qualities that compel some to seek command at sea—where, according to U.S. Navy Regulations, "the responsibility of the commanding officer for his or her command is absolute, "and that "the authority of the commanding officer is commensurate with his or her responsibility?"

The Chief of Naval Education Command Leadership School provides some clues. The school suggests that "To achieve success in command, the captain must work through those whom he or she leads; little can be accomplished alone, no matter how brilliant one's individual talents." Captains of industry would do well to follow the same advice. The school also recommends that commanding officers "must learn to become as one with his or her wardroom and crew; yet, at the same time, he or she must remain above and apart. This unique relationship has been the subject of study and story for centuries. It changes, yet is timeless." The tradition, responsibility, authority, and accountability of command at sea have no equal in the civilian world, and only a few in the U.S. Navy rise to meet the challenge. Those who accept the challenge then enjoy the prestige, privilege, and the awesome burden of command at sea. It would be difficult to improve upon Joseph Conrad's comments on the subject, unabashedly repeated here.

The Prestige, Privilege and the Burden of Command

Only a seaman realizes to what extent an entire ship reflects the personality and ability of one individual, her Commanding Officer. To a landsman this is not understandable, and sometimes it is even difficult for us to comprehend, but it is so.

A ship at sea is a distant world in herself and in consideration of the protracted and distant operations of the fleet units the Navy must place great power, responsibility and trust in the hands of those leaders chosen for command.

In each ship there is one man who, in the hour of emergency or peril at sea, can turn to no other man. There is one who alone is ultimately responsible for the safe navigation, engineering performance, accurate gun firing and morale of his ship. He is the Commanding Officer. He is the ship.

This is the most difficult and demanding assignment in the Navy. There is not an instant during his tour of duty as Commanding Officer that he can escape the grasp of command responsibility. His privileges in view of his obligations are most ludicrously small; nevertheless command is the spur which has given the Navy its great leaders.

It is a duty which most richly deserves the highest, time-honored title of the seafaring world—"CAPTAIN."

Captain Maylon T. Scott, USN

"This is the Captain speaking…I'll keep you informed." Now four decades later I know each and every Hard Charger that was on board *Biddle* at any time before my detachment on September 17, 1968, will never forget that message.

This was one of my ways to communicate with the crew—keep them always abreast of what was going on, what was planned, what could be expected and letting them know nothing was being kept from them. I would tell it like it was. This concept is "communications will make or break you." It is basic for any team, organization, company, and the like. The many periodic "Biddlegrams" to the crew's families kept them informed too, thus reinforcing the concept. This is one of my many memories. This reflection and other remembered vignettes follow.

One of my primary objectives was to develop *Biddle* as a professional combat team. At Bath in the building yard, great emphasis was given to cross training for the Pre-commissioning crew. Scheduled daily sessions brought the various diverse ratings together in separate classes. Engineering ratings would join CIC and Sonar type ratings to make each rate knowledgeable of what was required of each and how they affected one another and how they basically interacted—what their capabilities, problems, limitations, requirements were—how each could help ensure smooth efficient functioning of the other areas—in the end the ship itself. The cross training promoted mutual respect and understanding of the other ratings thus resulting in great comradeship and team play which in the end paid handsome dividends in developing the *Biddle* Hard Charger team.

Perhaps as the first for the US Navy, when general quarters was sounded, no one moved from their present operational position. Those not on watches augmented each area, such that the team on watch did not lose the big picture in a shift of personnel. Instead of mass transitions, off watch personnel quietly and calmly augmented those already on station to increase the overall readiness. Additionally, since the ship was generally in a condition of readiness, a system was devised such that the ship could go to a lesser degree than general quarters such as missile quarters, gun quarters, damage control quarters, or any combination thereof. This involved a great deal of training, but proved effective while in the combat zone.

Generally the OOD (officer of the deck) of a US Navy ship is the controlling officer on the bridge. However, in *Biddle*, the controlling officer was the combat control officer in CIC.

In 1967 in commissioning *Biddle*, I believe we established the first in the U.S. Navy in the "ship comes alive" concept. After reading my orders and accepting my command of *Biddle*, the executive officer was ordered to set the watch. He in turn ordered the officer of the deck to set the watch, who told the boatswain's mate to "Set the watch, watch one, first section on deck." At this time the band struck up the lively Washington Post March and all hands, who were out of sight, came forward and manned their stations on the double on the main, 01, 02, 03, 04, 05 and 06 decks. All antennae commenced rotating, two Terrier missiles were loaded on the launcher and elevated, the 3-inch and 5-inch guns rotated, the quarterdeck was set up, and the honor guard and sideboys were manned. At this time the executive officer reported, "Captain, the Watch is set" as the missiles on the launcher simulated a firing. The firing looked very much authentic by emitting smoke, which made the audience gasp at the realistic sight as if the missile actually did launch. At that moment there were contrails in the sky over Logan Airport indicating that an actual missile may have been fired. This added to the intensity of the audience's reaction.

Another major and memorable event was the Black Ship Festival in Shimoda, Japan. The US Ambassador to Japan, the Honorable U. Alexis Johnson, embarked in *Biddle* at Yokosuka Naval Station for the short cruise to Shimoda. The Black Ship Festival commemorates Commodore Matthew Calbraith Perry's opening of Japan. The commemoration involves major Japanese ceremonies, parades, dinners, and games. Dressed as Commodore Perry, I reenacted Commodore Perry's arrival to Japan by being rowed by eight oarsmen to shore in a long boat and was welcomed along with the Naval Station's band representing the Japanese equivalent. All this was covered by a major Japanese TV network and made the cover of the Japanese nationwide TV Guide. On return to Yokosuka Naval Station, in order to arrive before sunset, *Biddle* proceeded up Tokyo Bay with all four boilers on line at 37 ½ knots. Needless to say, the bearings changed rapidly but we arrived safely after approaching and crossing shipping. However, when turning into the Naval Station, it was necessary to go forward and back for 40 minutes to cool down the boilers before proceeding to the dock.

Another interesting speed run was going from Lisbon to Copenhagen up the English Channel at 27 knots in thick fog in order to anchor away from Copenhagen one day ahead of time to allow the crew a one day's rest. During this period a curious Russian cruiser circled us. Copenhagen and its Tivoli Gardens proved to be the number one liberty port of our Round-the-World Cruise. Unusual shore leave was granted: six section liberty instead of the usual three section; and civilian clothes were authorized ashore, which was not generally authorized for U.S. Navy overseas in 1968.

Part of shake down training included live missile firings. One particular firing included a live warhead. However, for this particular firing there was no telemetry available as was available for non-warhead missiles. Unfortunately, during the firing of the warhead missile, it malfunctioned and landed in a Puerto Rico rain forest, making a large crater in a deserted area, instead of landing in San Juan or some other populated area. Thereafter, telemetry was mandatory for all future warhead firings. Just as a side note, the *Biddle's* car in San Juan was the only one with snow tires.

The Commissioning plank owner officers of *Biddle's* wardroom were responsible for establishing her as the finest warship in the U.S. Navy. For almost four decades, to this date, they are still a close-knit group with the first 20 years of annual reunions and then every fifth year with the current 38th reunion planned for St. Louis, Missouri. This comradeship, which still exists to this day, personifies *Biddle*.

Perhaps the Hard Chargers during my tour will remember my following quotes:

"Don't fiddle with the *Biddle*!"
"You have the green light—GO!"
"Results count!"
"This is the Captain. I will keep you informed."

Captain Alfred R. Olsen, Jr., USN

I relieved Captain Maylon Scott a few days after the *Biddle* returned from her first deployment to WESTPAC. In the following months 60 percent of the crew who established "Hard Charger's" reputation for excellence were transferred. When we departed Norfolk for the Pacific in May 1969 only 140 were still aboard. But the spirit, standards, and professionalism that made the *Biddle* a great ship endured. The new Biddlemen bought into the Hard Charger concept.

When we cleared port, I told all hands that I would inform them as to what we were doing and where we going. Midway through our first tour of duty in the

Gulf of Tonkin, our subsequent upkeep period scheduled for Taiwan was changed to Subic Bay. No problem, I announced it on the 1MC. Several days later it was changed to Manila. I announced that. The embarked squadron commander then tried to get Taiwan reinstated. I announced that! That was disapproved. I announced that. Next the upkeep period was rescheduled to both Subic and Manila. I told the Exec, Commander Allen Smith, I felt like a yoyo and suggested he announce the next schedule change in the plan of the day. He replied, "Not to worry, Captain. I overheard two mess cooks talking. One said, "The next time the Captain gets on the 1MC he's going to say that due to the difficulty of scheduling the period 3-13 August, the period 3-13 August has been canceled." If the crew could laugh about it, I figured I could continue to make the announcements and did.

Our first tour was a success. We connected with the tactical data system before we were on station. Five weeks later, we almost didn't get relieved when the *Long Beach* couldn't get on-line. The Under Secretary of the Navy, John Warner, now the senior senator from Virginia, visited during our second tour in the Gulf and presented the *Biddle* the Meritorious Unit Commendation earned during her first deployment. He was so impressed that he toured the entire ship and stayed an hour longer than scheduled.

When we left station for upkeep in Yokosuka, Japan, the typhoon season was underway. The stretch of Pacific Ocean between the Gulf and Yoko is called typhoon alley. To ensure our safe passage, we were authorized to make that 2600 mile voyage at 27 knots, the equivalent of crossing the Atlantic in four days! Well done to our engineers!

Another tour in the Gulf and a couple assignments at Yankee Station and we headed for home arriving just before Christmas 1969. In April *Biddle* was awarded a second Meritorious Unit Commendation, this time for outstanding performance during our second deployment to Vietnam. She became the only surface ship in the Atlantic Fleet and one of a handful of ships in the entire U.S. Navy to have received this award twice. This was an achievement to which every man contributed and in which every man shared.

At the change of command ceremony in June 1970, I chose my words carefully when I said that the officers and men of the *Biddle* were the finest ship's company with whom I had ever served. I added, "I have been reassured in this time of turmoil when most of the news about American youth seems to be bad, our society has continued to produce young men who are intelligent, responsible and levelheaded—who receive little publicity—who are intent on building, not tearing down. I know this to be a fact because they have been my shipmates in the USS *Biddle*." I stand by those words.

Rear Admiral Edward W. Carter, III, USN

It is so unfortunate that media stories about the Navy have obscured some fundamental facts that ought never to be forgotten. Today's sailor in the United States Navy is as fine a man as, if indeed not better than his forebears. To insinuate or allege otherwise is a powerful injustice to the thousands upon thousands of Americans who served our nation well and faithfully in its fleets.

A modern man-of-war, of which *Biddle* is one, is more complex and sophisticated than could have been imagined possible just a few short years ago. Men who sail these ships are still mariners; they still endure long and repeated separations from friends and loved ones; they still know and cope with the unleashed furies of the sea from the equatorial typhoon to the arctic gales; all this and more.

Today's sailor is also an electronics expert, a computer wizard, a nuclear propulsion genius, a guided missile technician. He is smarter and better trained than his predecessor; he has to be. He asks more questions and expects better answers, for he needs these in order to do his duty to the best of his ability. And this he wants to do. He still has pride in his ship and his role in his ship.

Three times in the past six years I have sailed into combat with him into a war that his press and television tell him is not supported by his countrymen. For two years I have stood beside him under attack and attacking, and have watched him stand to this station as staunchly as has any man in the almost 200 year history of our Navy, and when the attacks were over, have seen him work over his gear to the point of exhaustion to be ready for the attack.

Don't misunderstand me, today's sailor is no angel, but then sailors never were. He is a salty philosopher of sorts, but sailors have always been. He is a product of his time in America. He is what we make him; and, in the main, we have made him well. I am proud of him, proud to serve with him and proud to command him. He is the United States Navy.

Action at Red Crown, Surface Warfare Magazine, January 1979

Captain Albert L. Henry, USN

Biddle saw no combat action during my tour as "Hard Charger #7." Our primary goal during this period of the Cold War in 1976 to 1978 was that of Ambassador, building good will for the United States, while at the same time to be combat ready. During TEAMWORK '76 we were flagship for Commander Second Fleet for port visits to Copenhagen, Denmark; Hamburg, Germany; and Antwerp, Belgium. Vice Admiral Jack Shanahan, COMSECONDFLT, sent the following message to *Biddle* at the completion of TEAMWORK '76: "I want to express my appreciation to the officers and men of USS *Biddle*, the 'sometimes' flagship of COMSECONDFLT during recent NATO operations and port visits. *Biddle* performed admirably in supporting me and in hosting and entertaining foreign dignitaries while in port. I received many laudatory comments from the guests about the appearance of the ship and crew. From my observations, the *Biddle* is a first class ship with a proud and professional crew. Keep Charging! Shanahan."

Several short periods at sea followed our return to Norfolk in November, 1976, always with a flag officer embarked....each of whom complimented the ship and crew for hospitality and outstanding performance at sea. In March 1977, to December 1977, we spent many hours preparing for an inspection by the main board of Inspection and Survey, INSURV for short. Rear Admiral John D. Bulkely, the President of INSURV, spent several days with us at sea and in port giving a most thorough inspection. In a message back to Washington, D.C., he said in part, "*Biddle* is the final ship in INSURV's CG-26 class baseline study. Her engineering material condition and performance far exceed that seen by the board for some time, for all classes of ships inspected. It is a pleasure to see a solid engineering plant which is ready for prompt, sustained reliable operations and can so perform." This was a most rigorous inspection and the entire ship's company had worked hard preparing for it. This "can do" attitude was ever present during my tour....we never missed a commitment and took several for other CGs who were not able to get underway because of engineering difficulties.

During the Mediterranean cruise from 11 July 1977 to 22 December 1977, we participated in several 6th Fleet operations but the highlight of the cruise for me was the period from 24 September through 8 October when we were privileged to be flagship for Vice Admiral Sir Roderick Macdonald, Royal Navy, COMNAVSOUTH afloat. (A NATO command based in Naples, Italy.) This at sea period was for NATO exercise DISPLAY DETERMINATION in the Eastern Mediterranean and the Aegean Seas. Not only was this a fine example of cooperation in the Mediterranean, but also very important for *Biddle* to have been chosen to be Flagship for the British Admiral in charge of the operation. *Biddle* was named for Captain Nicholas Biddle who started his career at the Royal Navy where he served in the Artic as a fellow midshipman with Horatio Nelson. There is a truly common heritage between our Navy and the Royal Navy and we are proud that Nicholas Biddle, a hero of our Revolutionary War, and Lord Horatio Nelson who both died in battles were shipmates in their early careers. Vice

Admiral Macdonald and his staff were most gracious guests, teaching us many sea chanties, limericks, and customs of the Royal Navy. At the end of DISPLAY DETERMINATION Vice Admiral Macdonald sent the following message to COM SIXTH FLEET: "USS *Biddle* has given outstanding service as my flagship throughout DISPLAY DETERMINATION. Courtesy, Helpfulness, and efficient service are the hallmarks of this ship. Nothing has been too much trouble. No one could have been more welcome. I have been proud to fly my flag in her. I am most grateful to the United States for this unique privilege given to a NATO flag officer of the Royal Navy with his NATO Staff."

I have chosen only three episodes of my time in *Biddle* to show *Biddle's* reputation in the fleet....not due to my leadership but due primarily to the leadership of Captain Maylon Scott and the commissioning crew of *Biddle* in establishing the first reputation of *Biddle* in the fleet as a "can do" HARD CHARGER. Once that reputation is established, particularly if it is a good reputation, it is easy to follow suit and continue. I also want to express my appreciation for each member of the crew while I was aboard for their teamwork, their hard work, and sacrifices made to keep *Biddle's* performance at sea and ashore superb. We received many kudos for the operation of our missile and weapons systems, our engineering reliability, our abilities in communications and NTDS capabilities, and our superior cuisine for the many luncheons for dignitaries while deployed, and our seamanlike, shipshape appearance. All of these are due to teamwork of people; none of these systems function without people manning and operating them. As I look back on the twenty-five years that have elapsed since I left *Biddle*, my fondest memories are of my shipmates, whose wisdom, sincerity, loyalty, patriotism, and courage, and hard work made her the fine ship that she was. I also remember the humor of several occasions and a ship's company where morale was always high, no matter what the circumstances.\

Captain Hollis E. Robertson, USN

Command of *Biddle* was the highlight of my 34-year career in the Navy. It was my third command at sea and in some ways the easiest job I ever had. In other ways it was the most difficult. I couldn't agree more with Admiral Chester Nimitz's quote, *"Commanding a ship is the simplest task in the world, even if at times it seems complicated. A captain has only to pick good courses of action and stick to them no matter what. If he is good and generally makes good decisions, his crew will cover for him if he fails occasionally. If he is bad, this fact will soon be known, and he must be removed with the speed of light."*

I have always placed great value in the article that follows. Although it was written over fifty years ago it still has the solid ring of truth. Read it and think about it and you will see what I mean.

Hobson's Choice

One night past some thirty thousand tons of ships went hurtling at each other through the darkness. When they met, two thousand tons of ship and a hundred and seventy-six men lay at the bottom of the sea in a far off place.

Scenario:

> On 26 April 1952, the aircraft carrier USS *Wasp* and the destroyer-minesweeper USS *Hobson* were engaged in night maneuvers 700 miles off the Azores. The USS Hobson was acting as plane guard for the carrier. Just before midnight, the USS *Hobson* initiated maneuvers to change her position according to a prearranged plan. The plan's purpose was to permit the *Wasp* to head into the wind and thus recover aircraft she had sent aloft. In executing the maneuver, the Hobson ran across the bow of the carrier and was split in two. The 1,630-ton craft sank within four minutes of impact, with the loss of 176 members of her crew of 237—including the CO.
>
> The court of inquiry identified as the "sole cause" of the accident the maneuvering of the *Hobson* and the order by the *Hobson's* CO to execute "left rudder," putting his ship on a collision course with the fast-moving carrier. Some testimony brought out in the inquiry suggested that the CO had devised his turning plan under the stimulus of a recent order to the naval force that had encouraged "expeditious" handling of ships, even at the risk of mistakes.
>
> A seaman gave an account of the last words uttered by the CO after his ship collided with the carrier. "I said, 'What happened, Captain?' He turned to me and said, 'Somebody didn't change course.'"
>
> The court found that the *Hobson's* CO had committed a "grave error of judgment" in handling his ship and absolved all other officers in the incident.

Now comes the cruel business of accountability. Those who were there, those who are left from who were there, must answer how it happened and whose was the error that made it happen.

It is a cruel business because it was no wish of destruction that killed this ship and its hundred and seventy-six men; the accountability lies with good men who erred in judgment under stress so great that it is almost its own excuse. Cruel because no matter how deep the probe, it cannot change the dead, because it cannot probe deeper than remorse.

And it seems more cruel still, because all around us in other places we see the plea accepted that what is done is done beyond discussion, and that for good men in their human errors there should be afterward no accountability.

We are told it is all to no avail to revise so late the courses that led to the crash of Pearl Harbor; to debate the courses set at Yalta and Potsdam; to inquire how it is that one war won leaves us only with wreckage, and with two worlds still hurtling at each other through the darkness. To inquire into these things now, we are reminded, will not change the dead in Scholfield Barracks or on Heartbreak Ridge, nor will it change the dying that will come from the wrong courses.

We are told too how slanderous it is to probe into the doings of a captain now dead who cannot answer for himself, to hold him responsible for what he did when he was old and tired and when he did what he did under terrible stresses and from the best of intentions. How useless to debate the wrong courses of his successor, caught in a storm not of his own devising. How futile to talk of what is past when the pressing question is how to keep from sinking.

Everywhere else we are told how inhuman it is to submit men to the ordeal of answering for themselves. To haul them before committees and badger them with questions as to where they were and what they were doing while the ship or state careered from one course to another.

This probing into the sea seems more merciless because almost everywhere else we have abandoned accountability. What is done is done and why torture men with asking them afterwards, why?

Whom do we hold answerable for the sufferance of dishonesty in government, for the reckless waste of public monies, for the incompetence that wrecks the currency, for the blunders that killed and still kill many times a hundred and seventy-six men in Korea? We can bring to bar the dishonest men, yes. But we are told men should no longer be held accountable for what they do as well as for what they intend. To err is not only human; it absolves responsibility.

Everywhere, that is, except on the sea. On the sea there is a tradition older even than the traditions of the country itself and wiser in its age than this new custom. It is the tradition that with responsibility goes authority and with them both goes accountability.

This accountability is not for the intentions but for the deed. The Captain of a ship, like the captain of a state, is given honor and privileges and trust beyond other men. But let him set the wrong course, let him touch ground, let him bring disaster to his ship or to his men, and he must answer for what he has done. No matter what, he cannot escape.

No one knows yet what happened on the sea after that crash in the night. But nine men left the bridge of the sinking ship and went into the darkness. Eight men came back to tell what happened there. The ninth, whatever happened, will not answer now because he has already answered for his accountability.

It is cruel, this accountability of good and well-intentioned men. But the choice is that or an end to responsibility and finally, as the cruel sea has taught, an end to the confidence and trust in the men who lead, for men will not long trust leaders who feel themselves beyond accountability for what they do.

And when men lose confidence and trust in those who lead, order disintegrates into chaos and purposeful ships into uncontrollable derelicts.

The enormous burden of this responsibility and accountability for the lives and careers of other men and often, the outcome of great issues, is the genesis of the liberty, which distinguishes the orders to officers commanding ships of the United States Navy. (The Wall Street Journal © 1952)

Commanding Officers
USS Biddle (DLG/CG 34)

Name: **Dates:**

Captain Maylon T. Scott, USN Jan 67 to Sep 68

Captain Alfred R. Olsen, USN Sep 68 to May 70

Captain Louis J. Collister, USN May 70 to Jun 71

Captain William O. McDaniel, USN Jun 71 to Jul 72

Captain Edward W. Carter III, USN ** Jul 72 to Aug 74

Captain Francis L. Carelli, USN Aug 74 to Aug 76

Captain Albert L. Henry, USN Aug 76 to Aug 78

Captain John N. Ryan, USN Aug 78 to Sep 80

Captain Hollis E. Robertson, USN Sep 80 to Sep 82

Captain Alvaro R. Gomez, USN* Sep 82 to Jun 84

Captain Joseph T. Hock, USN Jun 84 to Jun 86

Captain Benjamin E. Allen, Jr., USN Jun 86 to Oct 88

Captain Grant D. Fulkerson, USN Oct 88 to Sep 90

Captain Louis F. Harlow, Jr., USN Sep 90 to May 92

Captain Laurence J. Gionet, Jr., USN May 92 to Nov 93

*—Attained rank of Rear Admiral (Lower Half)

**—Attained rank of Rear Admiral (Upper Half)

HULL THIRTY-FOUR

It was home to us, no less, no more,
    a large gray ship, Hull Thirty-Four.

She's sailed into battle on distant shore,
    it was our home, Hull Thirty-Four.

We sailed her proudly across the sea
    to protect the land we call free.

Ask yourself too, why we do the things we do.
    It's to protect our homeland and people like you.

The price of freedom is not easy, they say,
    so that's why we're here on any given day.

Then why were we there, I ask you once more,
    the men who sailed on Hull Thirty-Four?

We will soon sail again to some distant shore,
    the men with their courage on ships like Hull Thirty-Four.

What do you owe the men who blocked harm's door?
    The men of courage who sailed on Hull Thirty-Four.

Nothing is asked for doing their parts,
    just keep them in mind and locked in your hearts.

This is all that is asked, no less, no more,
    The men whose home was Hull Thirty-Four.

    HTCM Richard Outland, US Navy, Retired

HULL THIRTY-FOUR II

A new world order, men no longer speak of war
    a chance for peace on very shore.

Word has it, up on Capital Hill
    budgets are tough, no money in the till.

A list came out to cut expenses afloat and shore
    included in that list was Hull Thirty-Four.

Many felt sadness, some felt dismay—
    this gallant gray lady is to go away.

Men destined to sail the sea no more
    as the crew of Hull Thirty-Four.

What is to become of the men who helped block harm's door
    on that gallant gray lady, Hull Thirty-Four?

The men will be transferred on a given day,
    the gallant gray lady towed away.

The men to serve again and give their best,
    that gallant gray lady, a well deserved rest.

    HTCM Richard Outland, US Navy, Retired

Nicholas Biddle
1750—1778

I fear nothing but what I ought to fear. I am much more afraid of doing a foolish action than of loosing my life. I aim for a character of conduct, as well as courage, and hope never to throw away a vessel and crew merely to convince the world I have courage. No one has dared to impeach it yet. If any should, I will not leave them a moment of doubt.

—Nicholas Biddle to his brother, Charles, 16 June 1776

Credit for graphic: George Bieda

Biddle Characteristics
(Decommissioning brochure)

Displacement	8,800 tons
Length	547 feet
Beam	55 feet
Max Speed	32 knots
Power Plant	4—1200 psi boilers; 2 geared turbines, 2 shafts; 85,000 shaft horsepower 1—500 KW Fairbanks-Morse Diesel Generator 1—750 KW Solar Gas Turbine Generator
Aircraft	1—SH-2F LAMPS Mk 1 Helicopter
Armament	Standard Missiles SM-2 (ER) 8—Harpoon (from two quad launchers) 2—20mm Vulcan Phalanx CIWS 6—MK 46 torpedoes (from 2 triple tube mounts) 1—5-inch/54 caliber MK 42 gun
Radar	AN/SPS-48E 3D Air Search Radar AN/SPS-49(V)5 Long Range Air Search Radar AN/SPS-67 Long Range Surface Search Radar AN/SPS-64 Short Range Surface Search Radar
Sonar	SQS-26BX bow mounted
Fire Control	1 Mk 14 weapon direction system 1 Mk 68 GFCS with SPG-53F radar 2 AN/SPG-55B radar.
Complement	485 enlisted, 30 officers

Table of Acronyms and Abbreviations

A

AA Anti-Aircraft
AAW Anti-Air Warfare
AAWC Anti-Air Warfare Commander
ACD Automatic Clutter Detection
ACDS Advanced Combat Direction System
ACM Anti-ship Cruise Missile
ADT Automatic Detection and Tracking
AEW Airborne Early Warning
AFB Air Force Base
AFWR Atlantic Fleet Weapons Range
AMD Advanced Micro Devices
AP Armor Piercing
ARRS Aerospace Rescue and Recovery Service
ASAC Airborne Surveillance and Control
ASCM Anti-ship Cruise Missile
ASMD Anti-Ship Missile Defense
ASROC Anti-Submarine Rocket
ASUW Anti-Surface Warfare
ASW Anti-Submarine Warfare
ASWEX Anti-Submarine Warfare Exercise
AW Alpha Whisky (Task Force 77 at Yankee Station)

B

BARCAP Barrier Combat Air Patrol
BFIT Battle Force Inport Training
BIT Built-In Test
BIW Bath Iron Works
BECCE Basic Engineering Casualty Control Exercises

BOQ Bachelor Officers Quarters
BT Builder's Trials. Beam-rider Tail, Boiler Technician
BUORD Bureau of Ordnance
BUSHIPS Bureau of Ships
BVP Beacon Video Processor
BW Beamrider, Wing

C

CAP Combat Air Patrol
CASREP Casualty Repair
CBT Continuous Boat Track
CDS Combat Direction System, Comprehensive Display System
CEC Cooperative Engagement Capability
CHAFFROC Chaff Rocket
CHENG Engineering Officer
CIC Combat Information Center
CICO CIC Officer
CINCLANTFLT Commander in Chief Atlantic Fleet
CINCPAC Commander in Chief Pacific
CINCPACFLT Commander in Chief Pacific Fleet
CINCPACAF Commander in Chief Pacific
CIWS Close-In Weapons System
CMS Control Systems Material
COMCRUDESLANT Commander, Cruiser-Destroyer Force, US Atlantic Fleet
COMDESRON Commander Destroyer Squadron
COMSIXTHFLT Commander Sixth Fleet
COMSUBRON Commander Submarine Squadron
CONUS Continental United States
CNO Chief of Naval Operations
COH Complex Overhaul
COMNAVFORV Commander Naval Forces Vietnam
COMNAVSOUTH Commander, Allied Naval Forces Southern Europe
CPA Central Pulse Amplifier
CPO Chief Petty Officer
CRB Change Review Board
CRT Cathode Ray Tube
CRUDESLANT Cruiser Destroyer Atlantic (Fleet)
CSAR Combat Search And Rescue

CSMTC Combat System Maintenance Training Center
CSRR Combat Systems Readiness Review
CSSQT Combat System System Qualification Test
CTF Carrier Task Force
CWO Chief Warrant Officer

D

DASH Drone Anti-Submarine Helicopter
DATAR Digital Automated Tracking and Resolving System
DC Damage Control
DCA Damage Control Assistant
DDSOT Daily Digital Systems Operability Tests
DLOS Disturbed Line Of Sight
DNSI/NTPI Defense Nuclear Surety Inspection/Nuclear Technical Proficiency Inspection
DS Data System (Technician)
DSDS Dynamic Synchro Data Source
DSOT Daily Systems Operability Tests
DMZ Demilitarized Zone

E

ECC Electronic Casualty Control
ECM Electronic Counter Measures
EDS Electronic Data System
ELINT Electronic Intelligence
EM Electricians Mate
ENIAC Electronic Numerical Integrator and Computer
ER Extended Range
ERA Engineering Research Associates
ESM/ASMD Electronic Support Measure/Anti-Ship Missile Defense
ET Electronics Technician
EW Electronic Warfare (Technician)

F

FCP Field Change Proposal
FOIA Freedom of Information Act
FROG Free Rocket Over Ground

FRUIT False Replies Uncorrelated In Time
FT Fire Control Technician

G

GFCS Gun Fire Control System
GITMO Guantanamo Bay, Cuba
GOT Gulf of Tonkin
GQ General Quarters
GPS Global Positioning System

H

HCO Helicopter Operations
HMAS Her Majesty's Australian Ship
HMS Her Majesty's Ship
HT Homing, Tail

I

IDAC Interconnecting Digital to Analog Converter
IFF/SIF Identification Friend Foe/Selective Identification Feature
IMAV Intermediate Maintenance Availability
INCSEA U.S. Soviet Incident at Sea
INSURV Inspection and Survey

L

LAAWC Local Anti-Air Warfare Commander
LAMPS Light Airborne Multipurpose System
LDMX Local Digital Message Exchange
LEDET Law Enforcement Detachment
LEO Law Enforcement Operation
LSO Landing Signal Officer

M

MACS Marine Air Control Squadron
MDS Minimum Discernible Signal
MFCS Missile Fire Control System
MIF Maritime Interdiction Force
MM Machinists Mate

MRI Material Readiness Inspection
MTB Motorized Torpedo Boat
MTBF Mean Time Between Failure
MTDS Marine Tactical Data System
MTI Moving Target Indicator
MTU Magnetic Tape Unit

N

NARA National Archives and Records Administration
NAS Naval Air Station
NATO North Atlantic Treaty Organization
NAVMACS Naval Modular Automated Communications System
NAVSEA Naval Sea Systems Command
NAVSHIPS Naval Ship Systems Command
NAVSECNORDIV Naval Ship Engineering Center, Norfolk Division
NCS Net Control Ship
NELC Naval Electronics Laboratory Center
NGFS Naval Gunfire Support
NRL Naval Research Laboratory
NSA National Security Agency
NSAR North Search and Rescue
NTDS Naval Tactical Data System
NTU New Threat Upgrade
NVA North Vietnamese Army
NWAI Nuclear Weapons Acceptance Inspection

O

OOD Officer Of the Deck
OPAREA Operating Area
OPFCO Operational Program Functional Checkout
OPNAV Office of the Chief of Naval Operations
OPPE Operation Propulsion Plant Exam
OPTEVFOR Operational Test and Evaluation Force
ORDALT Ordnance Alteration
ORDSAT Ordinance Systems Assist Team
ORE Operational Readiness Evaluation
ORI Operational Readiness Inspection

P

PAT Preliminary Acceptance Trials
PCO Prospective Commanding Officer
PD Point Detonating
PERT Program Evaluation and Review Technique
PIRAZ Positive Identification Radar Advisory Zone
PMS Planned Maintenance System
PNSY Philadelphia Naval Shipyard
PLO Palestine Liberation Organization
PMS Planned Maintenance System
POD Plan Of the Day
POFA Programmed Operational Functional Appraisals
POM Preparations for Overseas Movement
POW Petty Officer of the Watch, Prisoner of War
PPI Planned Position Indicator
PU Participating Unit
PRC Peoples Republic of China
PSA Post Shakedown Availability

Q

QAST Quality Assurance Systems Test

R

RAC Radar Azimuth Converter
RAF Royal Air Force
RCN Royal Canadian Navy
RD Radarman
RM Radionam
RESCAP Rescue Combat Air Patrol
RF Radio Frequency
ROH Regular Overhaul
RTC Real Time Clock
RSDS Radar Signal Distribution Switchboard

S

SAGE Semi-Automatic Ground Environment
SAR Search and Rescue

SCAT System Calibration and Alignment Tests
SEALORDS Southeast Asia Lake, Ocean, River and Delta
SHP Shaft Horse Power
SIMA Shore Intermediate Maintenance Activities
SINKEX Sink Exercise
SIT System Integration Test
SM Standard Missile
SMI Supply Management Inspection
SONAR Sound Navigation and Ranging
SORT Ship's Operational Readiness Tests
SOSMRC Senior Officer Steam Machinery Refresher Course
SQAT Ship Qualification Assist Team
SQT Ship Qualification Trial
SRA Selected Restricted Availability
SSAR South Search and Rescue
SSORT Ship Systems Operational Readiness Tests
SSOSS Soviet Strategic Ocean Surveillance System
SUPPRAD Supplemental Radio
SWC Ship's Weapons Coordinator
SWTW Surface Warfare Training Week (SWTW

T

TACAN TACtical Air Navigation
TAO Tactical Action Officer
TDS Tactical Data System
TG Task Group
TBMD Theater Ballistic Missile Defense
TSAM Training Surface to Air Missile
TYCOM Type Command

U

UNREP Underway Replenishment
USAF United States Air Force
USMC United States Marine Corp
USN United States Navy

V

VACAPES OPAREA Virginia Capes Operating Area
VERTREP Vertical Replenishment
VLS Vertical Launching System

W

WCP Weapon Control Panel
WDS Weapons Direction System
WESTPAC Western Pacific
WSAT Weapons Systems Accuracy Team, Weapons System Alignment Tests

X

XOI Executive Officer Investigation

Works Cited

Bailey, Dennis M., AEGIS Guided Missile Cruiser. Motorbooks International Publishers & Wholesalers, Osceola, WI, 1991.

Bailey, Donald C. Interview with D. L. Boslaugh. 22 Oct. 1994.

Boslaugh, David L. When Computers Went to Sea—The Digitization of the United States Navy. Los Alamitos, CA: IEEE Computer Society Press, 1999.

Boyne, Walter J. Messerschmitt Me 262. Smithsonian Institution Press, Washington, D.C., 1980.

Bryant, William C., LT, USNR, and Hermane, Heith I., LT, USNR,."History of Naval Fighter Direction". C.I.C. Magazine, April, May, and June 1946. Declassified 3 May 1972, June issue.

Bureau of Ships, NTDS Project Office. Unsigned point paper on the development of Weapons Direction System Mark 11. Dated 1967.

Bureau of Ships. Technical Development Plan for the Naval Tactical Data System (NTDS)—SS 191. 1 Apr. 1964.

Foreman, CAPT Robert P. Interview with D. L. Boslaugh. 8 Sept. 1994.

Friedman, Norman. The Naval Institute Guide to World Naval Weapons Systems 1991/92. Naval Institute Press, Annapolis, MD, 1991.

Gebhart, Louis A. Evolution of Naval Radio-Electronics and Contributions of the Naval Research Laboratory, NRL Report 7600. Naval Research Laboratory, Washington, D.C. Jan 1967.

Gibbs, Jay and Scotto, Michael F. "Question 23/86." Warship International, No.3, 1987.

Graf, R. W. Case Study of the Development of the Naval Tactical Data System. National Academy of Sciences, Committee on the Utilization of Scientific and Engineering Manpower, Jan. 29, 1964.

Hanson, Victor Davis. "Our Islands in the Storm—Carriers as the new phalanxes," National Review Online. 13 December 2002.

Hickey, John. "Now Hear This! Brass in Blast On Lowly Tug." Boston Sunday Advertiser. 22 Jan. 1967.

Howse, Derek. Radar at Sea—The Royal Navy in World War 2, Naval Institute Press, Annapolis, MD, 1993.

King, RADM Randolph W., USN and Palmer, LCDR Prescott, USN, eds. Naval Engineering and American Seapower. Nautical and Aviation Publishing Company of America, Baltimore, MD.

Langley, William. "BIW Women Employees Help Deliver Missile Frigate Biddle To Navy." Portland Press Herald 12 Jan. 1967: A1+

Laning, Captain Clifford. Letter to D. L. Boslaugh. 21 Jan. 1995.

Lundstrom, David E. A Few Good Men From Univac, The MIT Press, Cambridge, MA, and London, 1998.

Mahinske, CAPT Edmund B. Letter to D. L. Boslaugh. 19 July 1944.

McNally, CDR Irvin L. Interview with D. L. Boslaugh. 20 April 1993.

Navy Department, Office of the Chief of Naval Operations, Naval History Division. Dictionary of American Naval Fighting Ships—Volume III. United States Government Printing Office, Washington, D.C., 1968.

Nichols, John B. and Tillman, Barrett. On Yankee Station: The Naval Air Action over Vietnam. Annapolis, Maryland. Naval Institute Press. 1987.

Sanders, Michael S. The Yard: Building a Destroyer at the Bath Iron Works. HarperCollins, New York, NY. 1999.

Smith, P. and Lancaster M. "Collision at Sea," Vietnam. August 2001.

Swallow, CAPT Chandler E. Letter to D. L. Boslaugh. 16 Nov. 1994.

Swenson, Annette M. Interview with D. L. Boslaugh. 17 April 1993.

Swenson, CAPT Erick N., Stoutenburgh, CAPT Joseph S., and Mahinske, CAPT Edmund B. Draft of NTDS—A Page in Naval History, dated 29 Sep. 1987.

Swenson, CAPT Erick N., Stoutenburgh CAPT Joseph S., and Mahinske, CAPT Edmund B. "NTDS—A Page in Naval History," Naval Engineer's Journal, Vol. 100, No. 3, May 1988.

Svendsen, CAPT Edward C. Interview with D. L. Boslaugh. 3 Feb. 1995.

Vardalas, John N. Moving Up The Learning Curve: The Digital Electronic Revolution in Canada, 1945-70, Thesis submitted to the School of Graduate Studies and Research in partial fulfillment of the requirements for the Ph.D. degree in History, University of Ottawa, 1966.

Watson, Thomas j., Jr. and Peter. Peter, Father Son and Co.—My Life at IBM and Beyond. Bantam Books, New York, 1990.

"5-in/54 Mk 42." Guns:Gunners United in Naval Service. Vol. 10, Spring/Summer 2001. 44.

Contributors

James Treadway

Many shipmates, family members, friends, and others provided the encouragement, advice, and material required to write this book. I met most shipmates almost 40 years ago as we prepared to commission *Biddle* then sail her around the world. Others I met recently over the Internet while conducting research and soliciting material. All deserve credit for contributing their stories, their skills as proofreaders, and for providing support and advice.

Those who made literary contributions deserve special recognition—I would not have attempted to write this book without their first hand accounts. Like smoke on brisket, their accounts surround the meat and give it full flavor. All gave *Biddle* their full effort more than a generation ago and some more recently; now they have taken the time and effort to tell their stories in their own words.

Dr. Timothy L. Francis, Historian at the Naval Warfare Division, Naval Historical Center, and Barry L. Zerbey at the National Archives and Records Administration provided research support, for which I am thankful.

Two men who made enormous contributions well beyond their first hand accounts and who would be happy to not receive any recognition at all, are two *Biddle* plankowners and friends, Captain Maylon T. Scott and Data System Chief David R. Johnson.

Captain Scott's contagious "Can do" attitude provided the initial spark to start this book. Next, he contributed much of his personal *Biddle* library, which includes irreplaceable photos, official messages, Biddlegrams, press releases, letters, and personal notes. Finally, Captain Scott's quiet, behind the scenes support, encouragement and advice kept me going when I questioned my ability to complete the project.

David R. Johnson, who was my boss aboard *Biddle* and has been my friend for almost 40 years, is a remarkable man. His mastery of the technical details, specifications, and requirements of complex, integrated combat systems such the Naval Tactical Data System found on *Biddle*, is phenomenal. When confronted with an important task, he always gives 110 percent. As an example, I asked him for a paragraph or two that would describe how our group of data systems technicians aboard *Biddle* contributed to the ongoing success of the Naval Tactical Data System. He responded with a complete chapter, "When Computers Went to Sea", one of the centerpieces of this book. Bravo Zulu, Chief Johnson and Captain Scott!

The Authors

The authors, a civilian and two retired senior naval officers, blend divergent yet complimentary viewpoints to tell the story of the USS *Biddle*. Our common interest was to chronicle the remarkable achievements of a single ship and the class of ships she represented. While my contribution to the Navy was only a six year enlistment, my esteemed co-authors were senior career Navy officers whose contributions were significant and long lasting. Both were in unique positions to recognize *Biddle's* distinctive role in the Navy as a "Cold War Cruiser" and write about her place in naval history. Rear Admiral Marfiak, who served in destroyers, cruisers, and aboard *Kitty Hawk*, admitted, "Long gray hulls were my life and love. USS *Biddle* was special amongst them. Aboard her, in the midst of the Cold War, I became a leader of men." Captain David L. Boslaugh, a Navy engineering duty officer for most of his 30-year career, worked behind the scenes on the design, installation, and maintenance of complex electronic systems that were, and still are, the heart of security, communications, and weapons systems that protect our great fleets. The commitment to excellence of these two gentlemen, their encouragement, their skill as authors, their knowledge of naval matters, and their devotion toward the effort to complete this book, explain why the United States Navy is the finest organization in the world and why we enjoy freedom in this country. I salute these two fine officers and extend a sincere, "Thank you and well done!"

James A. Treadway

Though not a career Navy man, I served proudly for six years—four of those years as a data systems technician aboard *Biddle* when she was a newly commissioned ship. I first saw her raw and unfinished, helped to commission her, then sailed her for tens of thousands of miles across the world's oceans. I lived in an enlisted man's world between reveille and taps—long hours on duty, doing my job, mail call, inspections, standing watches, training, chow on the mess decks, and liberty call in exotic places. The most important results of the experience were that I gained a life-long respect for both the people I worked with and for people in foreign lands, and that my technical training and four years practical experience aboard *Biddle* launched my civilian career while providing much needed maturity, purpose, and direction.

The training and experience prepared me for positions in the high tech industry with companies such as Digital Equipment Corporation, Texas Instruments and Advanced Micro Devices (AMD). Eventually I earned a Bachelor of Liberal Studies (summa cum laude) in Computer Science from St. Edward's University in Austin, Texas. While employed at AMD I was fortunate to work with the team of engineers that designed the K5, K6, and Athlon superscalar microprocessors. I am listed as inventor on three U.S. patents as a result of my work at AMD. Currently I am an instructor at Texas State Technical College in Marshall, Texas, where I attempt to impart as much knowledge as I can about programming languages to my students before I forget it.

Rear Admiral Thomas F. Marfiak U.S. Navy (Retired)

Rear Admiral Thomas F. Marfiak graduated from the United States Naval Academy in 1966. Selected for Flag rank in January 1992, he served in positions of increasing responsibility in the Navy and in the Joint arena until his retirement in July 1999.

His final assignment at sea was in command of the USS *Kitty Hawk* Aircraft Carrier Battle Group, consisting of nine ships, more than ninety aircraft, and seven thousand sailors. During that tour he was personally responsible for the training of the battle group for subsequent combat operations in the Arabian Gulf. As senior battle group commander, he was also instrumental in the formation of other carrier groups as they headed for operational duties in the Pacific and Gulf regions. Previously, Rear Admiral Marfiak commanded the USS *Bunker Hill* (CG-52) during Operation Desert Shield/Desert Storm, leading four carriers and allied air forces during the first conflict with Iraq. Rear Admiral Marfiak commanded the USS *Doyle* (FFG-39) through several deployments to the Mediterranean, Black Sea, and Caribbean. His early operational assignments included serving as Executive Officer of USS *Conyngham* (DDG-17), Engineering Officer/TAO on USS *Biddle* (CG-34) and extensive service in Vietnam aboard USS *Camp* (DER-251) and in the Mediterranean aboard USS *Brumby* (DE-1044).

Ashore, Rear Admiral Marfiak was selected as an Olmsted Scholar and educated at the Institute of Political Studies, Paris, France before continuing his studies at the Fletcher School of Law and Diplomacy, Tufts University. Several tours in the Pentagon included duty as an Action Officer in the Office of Strategic Studies (OP-603), as the Special Assistant to the Secretary and Deputy Secretary of Defense and as the Deputy Director and then Acting Director of the

CNO's Long Range Planning Group (Op-OOK). Following his selection for Flag rank, he became the Director of Surface Navy Plans and Programs. After his battle group command, he served as Director of Plans and Policy for U.S. Central Command, Tampa, Florida, with principal responsibility for the development of plans and programs to implement US policy in southwest and central Asia. In his final active duty assignment, he served as the Commandant of the National War College at NDU, Ft. McNair, Washington, DC.

Upon leaving active service, Rear Admiral Marfiak became the Chief Executive Officer/Publisher of our nation's foremost military and scholarly organization, the U.S. Naval Institute, Annapolis, MD. Now an independent consultant specializing in national security issues, acquisition, and the planning, programming and budget process, Rear Admiral Marfiak serves as an advisor to defense companies involved with our most significant development efforts.

A nationally recognized spokesman, Rear Admiral Marfiak is an articulate, dynamic and far-seeing member of the national security team. Recognized for his leadership and insight, he is sought after as a leader of critical efforts affecting us all.

Captain David L. Boslaugh, U.S. Navy (Retired)

Except for destroyer duty and a tour in a naval shipyard, Dave Boslaugh spent most of his 30-year Navy career in research and development and project management assignments as a naval engineering duty officer. These included duty as a flight test engineer where he worked with sister ships of the X-1 research airplane and on the X-15 research plane. Other assignments included five years in the Naval Tactical Data System Project Office, command of the Naval Security Engineering Facility in charge of Navy cryptographic and cryptologic equipment engineering, director of telecommunications R&D in the Naval Electronic Systems Command, assistant project manager of the Navy Command, Control, and Communications Project Office, and director of the Navy Embedded Computer Program Office. He also authored the book, *When Computers Went to Sea—The Digitization of the United States Navy*.

Contributors

Captain Albert Henry, U.S. Navy (Retired), was *Biddle's* seventh commanding officer from August 1976 to August 1978. He is a Georgia native and a 1956 graduate of the US Naval Academy. During his Navy career, Al also commanded USS *Seneca* (ATF-91), USS *Ouellet* (DE-077), and River Assault Squadron 15 in Vietnam. Military decorations include the Legion of Merit and the Bronze Star

Medal, 2 awards each. After retiring from the Navy in 1978, Al returned to Georgia where he taught high school math and was a guidance counselor for 18 years. As a teacher, he was listed in Who's Who Among America's Teachers. Al currently enjoys volunteer tutoring at two schools, is a Lay Speaker in The United Methodist Church, and is active with the Interfaith Assistance Ministry in Hendersonville, North Carolina.

Captain Fred Howe, U.S. Navy (Retired), *Biddle's* Commissioning Weapons Officer, retired from active service in 1981 after service in several different types of surface ships including minesweepers, cruisers and five different destroyers, culminating in command of *Coontz* (DLG-9). He was subsequently employed by several private firms and spent 15 years working in support of the Royal Saudi Naval Forces Attaché in Washington D.C. prior to retirement to Fredericksburg, Virginia in 2001.

Biddle plankowner **David R. Johnson** served as an Electronics Technician on a minesweeper and auxiliary tanker on the way to *Biddle* via a plankowner tour at the Combat System Maintenance Training Center, Mare Island. After staff duty at the Naval Tactical Data Systems NTDS school that included conversion to DS, he was promoted to DSC and invited by Lieutenant Bob Gerity to be his System chief on new-construction *Biddle* at Bath. Following the *Biddle* tour, Johnson left the Navy and worked for Navy contractors in various projects as a computer programmer, system engineer, and precommissioning crew trainer. Retired from a small combat system engineering company of which he was one of seven founding owners, Dave now lives in Virginia Beach.

Plankowner **DSC Rodney J. Merrill, U.S. Navy (Retired)** may be the only person who served aboard *Biddle* three separate times. Rodney retired from the Navy as a Data Systems Chief in 1985. During his last seven years in the navy he worked at MOTU-7 (Japan) and MOTU-13 (Philippines). Currently he is working for Science Applications International Corporation (SAIC) integrating and testing the Joint Tactical Terminal (JTT) onboard US Naval ships.

Lieutenant Commander Ralph B. Muse, U.S. Navy (Retired) was *Biddle's* CIC Officer during the MiG attack on July 19, 1972. Muse joined the Navy Reserves while in high school, reaching the rate of Second Class Sonarman before graduating from Christian Brothers University in Memphis, TN in 1968. Commissioned in 1969, he was Project Officer for the NMCSSC supporting the Joint Chiefs of Staff in the Pentagon. In 1970 he was given orders to the USS *Biddle* (DLG-34) as NTDS Officer. In 1972 Lieutenant Muse was augmented to regular Navy and given the additional duties as CIC Officer. Lieutenant Muse left the *Biddle* and the Navy in 1973. He is a senior level executive with extensive technology management experience, expertise in general management, manufacturing, and multinational sales/marketing, and operations. He has an extensive background in wireless data, networking, systems, electronics, energy, and consulting, with industry leaders. Mr. Muse founded Muse Consulting in 1993 to provide interim management, turnaround management, and consulting services to high tech and manufacturing companies throughout North America. Muse holds a BS in Electrical Engineering from the Christian Brothers University, and a MS in Operations Management from the University of Arkansas.

Captain Alfred R. Olsen U.S. Navy (Retired), *Biddle's* second commanding officer, is a native of Atlantic City, New Jersey, and graduated from the Naval Academy in 1944. He is a graduate of the Armed Forces Staff College, the Industrial College of the Armed Forces and the postgraduate course of the U. S. Naval Intelligence School, and holds an MSBA degree from George Washington University.

A true Cruiser-Destroyerman, Captain Olsen served in the cruisers *Biloxi* and *Providence* and the destroyer *Allen M. Sumner*. He commanded the LST *Ouachita County*, destroyer escort *Lester*, destroyer *John Paul Jones* and destroyer tender *Sierra*. *Biddle* was his fifth command at sea. Other assignments include duty on the staffs of the Commander in Chief Atlantic Fleet and Commander Destroyer Force Atlantic Fleet, in the Office of the Chief of Naval Operations, and as Chief of Staff to Commander Cruiser-Destroyer Flotilla FOUR.

Following the *Biddle*, Captain Olsen served four years in the office of the Deputy CNO for Surface Warfare in the Pentagon. Retiring from the Navy in 1974, he worked for the Raytheon Company for 12 years in support of NTDS project office in the Naval Sea Systems Command. In 1985 Captain Olsen helped to found the Surface Navy Association and served as national treasurer for seven years. In 1997 he was elected to a two year tour as president of the Washington Chapter of the Circumnavigators Club. Captain Olsen continues to be active in a variety of Navy and volunteer organizations.

Captain Hollis E. Robertson U.S. Navy (Retired), *Biddle's* ninth commanding officer, enlisted in the Navy in 1951, entered the United States Naval Academy in 1952 from which he graduated in June 1956. Captain Robertson also graduated from the Naval Postgraduate School with a Bachelor of Science degree in Mechanical Engineering. As a ship's engineering sub-specialist, he co-authored the Naval Engineer's Guide published by the U.S. Naval Institute. At sea he served in *Francis M. Robinson* (DE-220), *Franklin D. Roosevelt* (CVA-42), *Catamount* (LSD-17), *Columbus* (CG-12), *Wainwright* (CG-28) and commanded *Charles S. Sperry* (DD-697), *Rich* (DD-820) and *Biddle* (CG-34).

After completing his tour as the *Biddle's* CIC Officer in December 1981, **Mike Sasser** left the Navy to return to civilian life. He took his Purdue engineering degree and security clearance and found an engineering position with ITT Aerospace/Communications Division in Fort Wayne, Indiana. He is now an experienced digital electronics design engineer working on various communications and satellite programs for military and commercial use. Mr. Sasser's oldest son is in the Air Force flying air crew on AWACS.

Captain Maylon T. Scott, US Navy (Retired) is a June 1943 graduate of the US Naval Academy, class of 1944. He began his long destroyer career aboard USS *Hull* (DD-350) in the raid of Wake Island in October 1943, the invasion of the Marianas in June-August 1944, and operations off the Philippines in December 1944.

In January 1945, Captain Scott, then a Lieutenant (j.g.) was assigned to the USS *Orleck* (DD-886) as Gunnery Officer from her commissioning until December 1946. After shakedown training, *Orleck* headed for China and Japan early in 1946 for duties in connection with post-war occupation operations. After the war, as a lieutenant, Captain Scott was Executive Officer of USS *Begor* (APD-127), Damage Control Officer and First Lieutenant of USS *Curtis* (AV-4) carrying atomic bombs to Eniwetok 1948, Executive Officer of USS *Marsh* (DE-699) and an instructor of Marine Engineering at the U.S. Naval Academy.

A two year overseas tour followed as Aide and Flag Secretary to Chief of Naval Group, Joint American Mission for the Aid of Turkey. On 5 February 1955, as Lieutenant Commander, he took command of USS *Otterstetter* (DER-244).

In November 1956, he joined the staff of Commander Destroyer Force US Atlantic Fleet, as Assistant Readiness and Training Officer. As a Commander, from July 1959 through 1961, he was Commanding Officer of the destroyer leader USS *Mitscher* (DL-2) which made its first deployment with the Sixth Fleet in the Mediterranean Sea. Subsequently, he served in Washington, D.C. in the Plans and Policy Division of the Chief of Naval Personnel until July 1963.

In June 1964, Captain Scott graduated from the Naval War College, Newport, Rhode Island. and from George Washington University with a Master's Degree in International Relations. From July 1964 until August 1965, he was Commander Destroyer Division TWENTY-TWO and conducted extensive operations in the Mediterranean and Western Atlantic.

In August 1965, he was assigned Chief of Staff, Commander Cruiser-Destroyer Flotilla TWO and Commander Task Group CHARLIE, whose primary responsibility was the development and advancement of Anti-Submarine Warfare.

He was the Commissioning Commanding Officer of USS *Biddle* (DLG-34) on 21 January 1967. In 1968 *Biddle* received the Secretary of the Navy's Meritorious Unit Commendation for combat operations in South-East Asia and then completed a Round the World Cruise. For these combat operations, he was awarded the Bronze Star Medal with combat "V."

As Director of Enlisted Personnel U.S. Navy, Bureau of Naval Personnel, from October 1968 to July 1971, he was awarded the Legion of Merit. He was Chief Naval Group MAAG, Norway from August 1971 until September 1972 when he was assigned as Special Advisor to Commander Cruiser Destroyer Force U.S. Atlantic Fleet.

He retired 1 February 1973 in Newport, Rhode Island. He was Development Director for a successful environmental organization, "Save The Bay" (Narragansett). In 1974, he was Director then Chief Executive Officer of "Seaport '76 Foundation Ltd." building the reproduction of the first authorized ship of the Continental Navy sloop "Providence," John Paul Jones' first command, now sailing up and down the coasts and into the Great Lakes.

Married in 1946 to Betty Wilson Chambliss, daughter of Colonel and Mrs. Turner M. Chambliss, they have a son, two daughters, and six grandchildren.

978-0-595-67313-1
0-595-67313-9

Printed in the United Kingdom by
Lightning Source UK Ltd., Milton Keynes
141251UK00002B/28/A